MEDITERRANEAN

The Ultimate Cookbook

13-Digit ISBN: 978-1-64643-288-2
10-Digit ISBN: 1-64643-288-6

This book may be ordered by mail from the publisher. Please include $5.99 for postage and handling.
Please support your local bookseller first!

Books published by Cider Mill Press Book Publishers are available at special discounts for bulk purchases in the United States by corporations, institutions, and other organizations. For more information, please contact the publisher.

Cider Mill Press Book Publishers
"Where good books are ready for press"
PO Box 454
12 Spring Street
Kennebunkport, Maine 04046
Visit us online
cidermillpress.com

Typography: Adobe Garamond, Brandon Grotesque, Lastra, Sackers English Script
Front cover image: Mediterranean Grilled Chicken Salad, see page 447
Front endpaper image: Modern Hummus, see page 31
Back endpaper image: Grilled Romaine & Sweet Potato, see page 441

Printed in China

1 2 3 4 5 6 7 8 9 0

First Edition

MEDITERRANEAN

The Ultimate Cookbook

DEREK BISSONNETTE

CIDER MILL PRESS

BOOK
PUBLISHERS
KENNEBUNKPORT, MAINE

CONTENTS

Introduction   9

Appetizers   29

Entrees   125

Soups & Stews   301

Salads & Sides   377

Breads   531

Desserts   605

Beverages   679

Sauces, Seasonings & Condiments   743

Index   813

INTRODUCTION

By Kimberly Zerkel

*M*ention Mediterranean culture in passing, and bright, produce-driven dishes laden with garlic and olive oil frequently come to mind. Dieticians and chefs will laud the health benefits of recipes involving sun-ripened tomatoes from Italy or Spain, feta and olives from Greece, or bundles of French herbes de Provence. But this picture of Mediterranean cooking, though accurate, is incomplete. The cuisine so many now associate with a healthy, active lifestyle, and the Southern European imagery it evokes, is merely one iteration of Mediterranean gastronomy. Like the fishermen who have made their living in the Mediterranean Sea for millennia, we must cast a wider net. Mediterranean cooking comes from a much larger geographical area and much more diverse cultural backgrounds than what popular culture often credits.

The countries that make up the Mediterranean basin are Albania, Algeria, Bosnia and Herzegovina, Croatia, Cyprus, Egypt, France, Greece, Israel, Italy, Lebanon, Libya, Malta, Monaco, Montenegro, Morocco, Slovenia, Spain, Syria, Tunisia, and Turkey. Though each of these countries technically comes under the same Mediterranean umbrella, there is sometimes more that divides them than unites them. Their differences are often so pronounced that some historians and food writers disagree on a united Mediterranean cuisine really existing at all.

For centuries, these countries saw themselves as neighbors, but not cousins. After all, what did Bosnian cevapi—grilled meat, raw onions, and pita bread—have to do with French ratatouille? What similarities, if any, are there between the filling Egyptian ful medames, made of mashed fava beans, and a light Greek salad with pungent olives and feta? When traveling from one Mediterranean country to the next, the differences between the cultures and customs seem more pronounced than their similarities.

Distance was required. It took interest

from the English-speaking world to tie an oblong bow around these varying countries and unify them under a common theme. British food writer Elizabeth David coined the term "Mediterranean cooking" in her 1950s cookbook *A Book of Mediterranean Food*. According to David, what binds Mediterranean countries together is the shared bounty of the sea, as well as the olive trees that grow on their every shore. And from a midcentury British kitchen that likely relied heavily on tinned food, and had since the end of World War II, the cornucopia of fresh fruits and vegetables from this region must have loomed large in the imagination.

From this perspective, Mediterranean cooking can be defined by what it is not. It is not the canned, packaged, or processed foods that gained popularity in the United States and Great Britain during the twentieth century. It is not centered around beef, cheese from cow's milk, or butter. It does not rely on potatoes, like Northern and Eastern Europe, or rice, like Asia and sub-Saharan Africa, or corn, like the Americas.

How, then, can you define Mediterranean cooking? National dishes and cooking methods vary. Therefore, it all comes down to key ingredients. Mediterranean cooking is an exploration of how each country utilizes these ingredients to perfection. Like variations on a common theme, each culture has taken the produce, fats, grains, proteins, and spices available to them and created recipes that are now known the world over for their vibrant color and flavor.

Before exploring each of those variations, it is vital to understand the basics. There are actually only three ingredients that act as pillars for all Mediterranean food: wheat, olives, and grapes. This holy trinity is vital to the region for their by-products.

Mediterranean cooking is all about bread, olive oil, and wine. And from these three key ingredients was born a culinary tradition that today is celebrated the world over.

WHEAT

Many who seek out Mediterranean recipes for their health benefits also tend to restrict their intake of (or abstain entirely from) carbohydrates and gluten. For this trendy bunch, Mediterranean cuisine is rooted in healthy proteins, such as fish and seafood, as well as vegetables. But one of the three pillars of the Mediterranean diet isn't grilled octopus, raw garlic, or fire-roasted bell peppers.

It's bread. Bread in the form of loaves and pitas, made from the wheat that grows all around the region. When that wheat isn't being used for bread, then it's eaten as farro, rolled up as pasta, made into couscous, or consumed as

bulgur wheat. Feel free to ignore all of the diet gurus—those living in Mediterranean countries eat an unapologetic amount of carbs.

Although it is easy to find rice and potatoes in most Mediterranean countries today, bread was a mainstay for thousands of years. Wheat was first cultivated around 9,600 BCE in the southern Levant—what we now refer to as Syria, Lebanon, Jordan, Israel, and a large portion of Turkey—almost all of which touches the Mediterranean Sea. Under the Roman Empire, North Africa was considered the breadbasket of the world, the ancient equivalent to modern-day Kansas and Iowa.

Wheat appears in various forms across the Mediterranean region today. There are various flatbreads, such as the Egyptian aish baladi, Algerian kesra, and Lebanese za'atar man'ouche, not to mention the well-known Greek pita and

its Turkish relative, pide. Then there are heartier loaves, from the French baguette and fougasse to Italian ciabatta and Croatian pinca, also known as Easter bread.

Bread has been an essential part of each country's diet for centuries now. Most of the population, rich and poor, start out their day with one form of bread or grains, plus coffee or tea. The poorest populations have relied on bread as their main source of calorie intake since its inception; meat and even some fruits and vegetables were, and are, simply too expensive for most. Pasta, couscous, farro, and bulgur wheat recipes also developed out of wheat's accessibility and affordability, and are now staples in a Mediterranean diet.

Bread's importance goes beyond daily meals. Bread is an important symbol in the three major religions that originate from this area. In Islam, bread is a gift from God that sustains life. In Judaism, bread plays an important role in most holidays and weekly traditions. And in Christianity, bread symbolizes Christ's body and is consumed during religious ceremonies.

OLIVES

There is perhaps no silhouette more iconic in this region than that of the dark, sturdy, twisted olive tree. And although these trees now grow around the world, particularly in Australia and on the West Coast of the United States, they are most at home along the Mediterranean coastline, their place of origin. Fossil evidence shows that olive trees may have been growing in modern-day Italy anywhere from 20 to 40 million years ago. But olives were not cultivated until roughly 7,000 years ago in the eastern Mediterranean region. Their edible form appeared in 3150 BCE; they have become an essential part of the Mediterranean diet ever since.

The fruit that olive trees bear is hard and bitter, but made edible (and delicious) through a curing and fermentation process. Although the end result—marinated olives—is enjoyed in many Mediterranean countries, this preparation is not what makes the olive so essential. Most harvested olives, about 90 percent, are used to make olive oil, the main ingredient and source of fat in the vast majority of Mediterranean cooking. In Greece alone, each person is estimated to consume 12 liters of olive oil per year, with Spain and Italy not far behind.

Olive oil is used as a dressing on salads, a dip for flatbreads, and a fat to cook all food in. Its rich, pungent flavor is nuanced from batch to batch; some prefer a mild, delicate oil, while others go for one that is bright and fruity. Many varieties of olive oil can be sharp and spicy, making them the perfect condiments to drizzle over crudités or a soft cheese. Like bread, this essential ingredient is plant based. It is also historically more affordable than other fats, like butter or lard, that come from animals. In countries like France, the use of olive oil over butter creates a clear cultural distinction between its northern regions and its southern coastline.

Beyond cooking, olive oil has also been used in the Mediterranean region for spiritual purposes. In Christian and Judaic storytelling, olive oil has produced miracles or been used to anoint kings. For Muslims, olive oil is essential to good health. Outside of religion, the symbol of an olive branch is now associated worldwide with peace. But for believers and nonbelievers, a good bottle of olive oil is simply a staple that should always be present in the home.

GRAPES

Although it would be perfectly normal to find the citizens of this region snacking on a fresh bunch of grapes or adding raisins to their bread, this regional ingredient is not renowned for eating purposes. Grapes are essential to the Mediterranean coast because they can be turned into wine. And although wine is made on nearly every continent in the world today, one of its first homes was the Mediterranean basin.

The journey from the first drops of wine

to today's Provençal rosé or robust Chianti was a long one. The first domesticated grapes in this area appeared between 7000 and 4000 BCE. Wine began to be made in Georgia and Persia around 6000 BCE, followed by Greece and Crete a thousand years later. It wasn't until the last millennium BCE that wine appeared in Spain, then Italy, then France. The drink became so popular that a cult worshipping the Greek god Dionysus (and his Roman counterpart, Bacchus) was formed. Wine was also readily consumed throughout the Middle Ages. It became a part of Roman Catholic ceremony, and was given to every member of families who could afford it, including children, as a cleaner alternative to water.

Today, wine is still considered a staple in this region, but with a few caveats. The popularity of wine is no longer confined to this geographical location. Countries like the United States, China, Australia, New Zealand, and South Africa are major wine producers. The United States is the top consumer of wine in the world. Beer and other spirits have also grown in popularity in the Mediterranean region, meaning younger generations don't necessarily have the same knowledge or cultural appreciation of wine that their parents or grandparents did. And North African and Middle Eastern countries in this region whose official religion is Islam usually abstain from alcohol altogether, although beer and wine are available to visitors.

But the importance of wine in the Mediterranean can never be overlooked. France, Italy, and Spain are not only top consumers of wine, but are recognized as some of the most skilled winemakers in the world. Lebanon and Greece, among others, also produce beautiful vintages that are an essential part of any dinner spread.

From the rock and soil around the Mediterranean basin to the hot sun that ripens grapes to perfection, the conditions and sense of terroir here are ideal for wine making. This is why vintages from this region are considered some of the finest ever made and will continue to be a key ingredient in all Mediterranean cuisine.

OTHER KEY INGREDIENTS & DISHES

PRODUCE

If bread, olive oil, and wine are the staples of Mediterranean cuisine, the plethora of fresh fruits and vegetables available there is what gives this style of eating its colorful reputation. The climate of the region is not only ideal for ripening grapes and olives, but also some of the most succulent produce in the world. One only needs to remember the ingredients of ratatouille—the onions, garlic, eggplants, zucchini, and tomatoes in this recipe are found in dishes on both sides of the Mediterranean, although nightshade fruits and vegetables like tomatoes and bell peppers grow more readily in Southern Europe.

Other common vegetables in the Mediterranean diet include artichokes, cucumbers, fennel, potatoes, scallions, and spinach, to name

a few. Many of these ingredients can be eaten raw in a variety of fresh salads, or cooked to perfection and served hot or cold, depending on the season.

The region is also known for its array of delicious fruits. Citrus is vital to this area. Corsican clementines or Sicilian oranges are delicacies that can stand on their own or enhance the flavor of a number of desserts. Lemons are used in both savory and sweet recipes; they are preserved in Morocco and added to sauces and stews. They are squeezed over grilled fish in the

South of France and over potatoes in Greece. Their juice is mixed with sugar and frozen to create refreshing Italian granita. The lemon's bright acidity is part of the Mediterranean's unmistakable flavor profile.

Regional fruits also include other citrus such as grapefruit and nectarines, as well as dates, figs, and pomegranates, just to name a few. Fruits are eaten raw or cooked throughout the day, consumed in jams or spreads for breakfast, or baked into pastries or cake for afternoon tea and dessert.

HERBS & SPICES
A natural assortment of herbs grows in this region, including basil, bay leaf, chervil, chives, cilantro, dill, fennel, fenugreek, lavender, marjoram, mint, oregano, parsley, rosemary, saffron, sage, tarragon, and thyme. A dried mixture of many of these herbs is commonly referred to as herbes de Provence, a blend that is most often used in Southern French cooking, but that features a flavor profile similar to what is found in much of Mediterranean cuisine. And across the Levant, za'atar—a dried-herb mixture that uses many of the same herbs, along with sumac and sesame seeds—is used to flavor countless dishes. Like wheat, olives, and other produce, these herbs grow well in this part of the world, due to its warm, sun-drenched climate.

The origin of spices in the Mediterranean basin has more to do with history than with

botany. The spice trade, which forged a path through the region, introduced ingredients like cinnamon, cardamom, black pepper, nutmeg, star anise, clove, and turmeric to the cuisine. Originating in Asia, these spices were precious trading goods in the Levant, North Africa, Greece, and Southern Europe from ancient times through the Middle Ages. Today, you can find a combination of these flavors in North African and Middle Eastern cooking, as well as in Southern European baked goods and desserts.

Star anise especially has had an influence on this region. It flavors spirits found all around the Mediterranean basin. The Greek have ouzo, the Italians sambuco, the French pastis and absinthe, the Middle East region arak, the Balkan region raki, and the Spanish anisado. Anise-flavored liquor is often enjoyed cold during warm weather, accompanied by water. It's considered both refreshing and good for digestion.

CHEESE

Although olive oil is considered the staple fat of all Mediterranean cooking, cheese and other dairy products are also available. For centuries, many cheeses in the area came from sheep's milk, because sheep were easier to raise than cows in most of the basin. Thus, quintessential Mediterranean cheeses like feta were born. But there are numerous sheep's milk cheeses in the region. Middle Eastern halloumi—a "squeaky" cheese with a pleasantly rubbery texture that's perfect for grilling—as well as Italian pecorino and French Roquefort, are sheep's milk cheeses that are now well-known around the world.

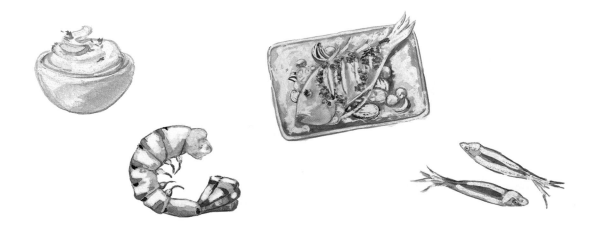

Goat cheese is widely used in many Mediterranean countries, as is cheese made from cow's milk, although historically, cow's milk has always been less available. Labneh is one of the few examples of a cow's milk yogurt, used throughout the Levant and parts of Northern Africa. It is a staple of Israeli breakfast, one of the few times in a day when Israelis consume dairy. Parmigiano Reggiano is made from cow's milk as well, as is modern-day ricotta, which was historically made from any variety of milk. These cheeses can be eaten on their own with bread, but are often added to sauces or dishes to impart richness in both flavor and texture.

PROTEINS

One of the main factors that differentiates Mediterranean cooking from cuisines farther north is the heavy presence of fish and seafood, as opposed to livestock raised on the land. Hearty fish like sea bream and bass can be roasted or steamed whole, swordfish and tuna are grilled, and small fish like anchovies and sardines add flavor to salads, tapas, and sauces. Prawns, squid, and octopuses cooked in a variety of ways are also found on many menus throughout the region.

But meat is not completely absent from the Mediterranean diet. Lamb is the most common red meat available; a leg or rack of lamb is crusted with an array of herbs and spices before being roasted, or cuts of lamb can be stewed alongside vegetables, then served with bread or couscous. Goat, pork, and poultry are also consumed, as is beef, which has grown not only in popularity of late, but in availability.

Availability—and affordability—are key. The Mediterranean diet being more closely associated with produce and fish over meat was not only related to climate, but also to the fact that for centuries, red meat and cream from cows were too expensive for the vast majority of the population. This trend has slowly changed over time, and beef can now be found throughout the basin, although it is still not considered a staple by any means.

REGIONS

Although the countries around the Mediterranean basin often share dishes containing key ingredients, their way of executing these dishes is entirely different. For this part of the world, there are regions within regions and cultures within cultures. Oftentimes, recipes and cooking styles can even vary within a single country. It would be nearly impossible to document every last variation of certain dishes from country to country, let alone from village to village. But an overview of the different corners of the basin and their various styles of cuisine provides a useful guide.

SOUTHERN EUROPE

Food from Italy, France, and Spain is often cited in the Western world as being quintessentially Mediterranean. But it's important to remember that only food from certain parts of these countries fits the profile.

For Italy, Mediterranean cooking means food from coastal and southern cities, as well as the islands of Sicily and Sardinia. Dishes from the mountainous north of Italy—which are heavy with butter, cream, and beef—are excluded from receiving the Mediterranean label. Italian Mediterranean cuisine is rich with tomatoes, which are served in salads, as sauces, or as the base for many other dishes. Though Italy has many varieties of bread, it is best known for its pasta, as well as the Neapolitan favorite: pizza. Italians also enjoy a diet full of fruits and vegetables, as well as a variety of fish and seafood.

When it comes to France, only the southern coastline can be considered Mediterranean. Like its Italian cousin, the northern part of the country relies more heavily on the land and on animal-based products. The use of olive oil instead of butter sharply divides the south from the north. Mediterranean French cooking is full of fresh fish, seafood, and produce. Vegetable stews or sides, like ratatouille or pistou, are common, as are dishes created with tomatoes and seafood, like the deliciously filling bouil-labaisse. Fougasse is a typical flatbread found in the South of France that can be served plain, stuffed with olives, or covered in herbs. Another popular bread-based dish is pissaldière, a distant relative of pizza that is served covered in onions and anchovies.

Lastly, there is the southern coast of Spain, which encompasses Valencia, Catalonia, and the Balearic Islands. Southern Spain is known for its paella, a dish that consists of short-grain rice cooked in olive oil, then seasoned with saffron. Many variations of paella exist. Some insist that the original version contains rabbit meat, but most of the world knows paella as a combination of seafood and pork. Other versions include chicken, artichokes, peppers, and string or lima beans. Ingredients from the Mediterranean region that are available in abundance, such as fish and nightshade fruits and vegetables, are served as tapas in southern Spain. Tortilla Española, a potato-and-egg frittata served cold, adds earthy balance to a usually seafood-rich spread.

Portugal is part of the Mediterranean basin, but its coastline faces the Atlantic Ocean, not the Mediterranean Sea. Most of Portugal's diet, therefore, is reliant on the fish and seafood from the Atlantic. But Portuguese cuisine shares similarities with Mediterranean cooking; like its Southern European neighbors, it relies on bread, wine, and olive oil as dietary staples.

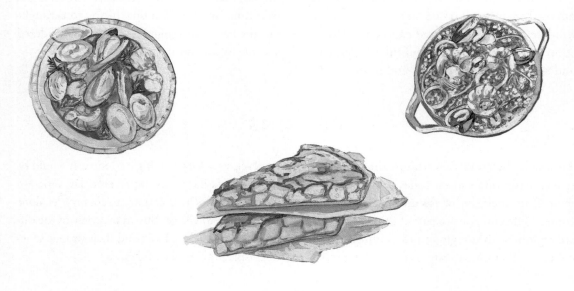

GREECE

Greek cuisine stands apart from that of the rest of Southern Europe, although it still relies heavily on vegetables, olive oil, bread, fish, and wine. And although Greek cooking also involves meat—notably lamb, chicken, rabbit, and pork—many of its traditional meals are vegetarian or even vegan. Look for fresh salads filled with olives and feta, or warm dishes that involve eggplants and zucchini. Enjoy flatbreads and yogurt, and be sure to finish off each recipe with a healthy dose of chopped herbs and a squeeze of lemon juice to achieve the quintessential Greek flavor profile.

The culinary history in Greece dates all the way back to the ancient world. Lentil soups, feta cheese, dried sausage, honey-based desserts, and wine were all featured in the meals eaten in the Hellenistic, Roman, and Byzantine periods. Pita bread has likely been a staple for thousands of years. This is also a region where avgotaraho, what we commonly refer to as bottarga, probably first appeared. Avgotaraho is a delicacy that is made of roe (fish eggs) that has been pressed,

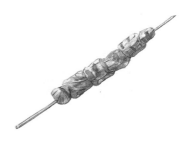

salted, and dried into a small brick, then shaved to add a salty, briny flavor to any dish. Variations of this exist all around the Mediterranean; bottarga is one of the most expensive ingredients you can buy in specialty shops throughout Southern Europe.

Other classics of Greek cooking include stifado, a meat stew with onions; spanakopita, a savory pastry filled with spinach and cheese; and souvlaki, skewered and grilled meat eaten with pita, a dish that is considered fast food in Greece. Some of the recipes we associate the most with Greek cuisine actually come from outside influences. The bright and creamy tzatziki dip and the rich and filling moussaka are most likely of Arabic, Persian, or Turkish origin, but are staples of Greek cuisine today.

THE FORMER OTTOMAN EMPIRE

What was once referred to as the Ottoman Empire is now Turkey, and includes certain parts of the Balkans, Cyprus, and Greece. Ottoman cuisine is roughly related to Greek cuisine and is actually the birthplace of moussaka. One of the most popular foods in this region is a savory pastry called börek. Börek is made of flaky phyllo pastry and is commonly filled with meat and onions, but cheese and spinach are also very popular fillings. Other meat-based dishes, like kebabs, are well-known and popular throughout the area. But most dishes are based on vegetables and bread, with the addition of rice.

This region, similar to nearby Middle Eastern countries, is also known for its mezze spreads, consisting of small dishes and sauces served both hot and cold and often accompanied by bread. For dessert, each country is renowned for its variation of sticky, honey-drenched sweets, like baklava, that are made from phyllo dough, dried fruits such as dates, and a variety of nuts. And a description of Ottoman cuisine would not be complete without mentioning dolmas, a series of stuffed dishes also eaten either hot or cold. Most associate dolma with stuffed cabbage or grape leaves, but many variations of this recipe exist.

EGYPT

Egyptian cuisine stands apart from the Maghrebi cuisine to the west and the Levantine cuisine to the east. This is mainly to do with ancient Egyptian culture flourishing on its own and then influencing those regions around it. Take, for example, falafel. Israel's national dish has its origins in Egypt. These small, fried, chickpea-based patties or balls are part of a larger culinary history that relies heavily on beans, pulses, and legumes. A common dish for any working-class Egyptian citizen from ancient times until now would be a bean stew and bread. Hummus or ful medames—hummus's fava-bean cousin—are also regularly enjoyed throughout the country today.

The Egyptians are also historically credited with helping to create more "luxurious" ingredients, such as cheese and beer. The latter, which would have been a thicker, mealier drink than the lagers and ales we think of today, was a staple that many historians believe contributed to the building of Egyptian civilization. Workers who helped build the pyramids were given daily rations of beer, not only to quench their thirst but to provide them with the calories and nutrition needed to fulfill their task. Beer is still considered the most popular alcoholic drink in Egypt, although the majority of its Muslim population abstains.

Another popular Egyptian dish is dukkah, a dip made from herbs, spices, and ground hazelnuts. This aromatic and savory condiment is usually enjoyed with flatbread, though it has recently started to make appearances in a number of dishes, thanks to the creativity of contemporary chefs. There is also koshari, a filling mixture of rice, lentils, and pasta that is considered one of Egypt's national dishes.

NORTH AFRICA

A large portion of North Africa's cultural heritage is referred to as Maghrebi. Maghrebi cooking describes the food found in Algeria, Libya, Morocco, and Tunisia. The staple of this cuisine is couscous, semolina that has been rolled into tiny grains, steamed, and then

served in heaping mounds. Couscous is often accompanied by a stew. The stew can be vegetarian, but most versions are based around lamb or another meat. Couscous and stew is an ancient meal that has been served in the Maghreb for centuries and is now popular in many Mediterranean countries, such as Israel, Italy, and France.

One version of the stew that accompanies couscous is called tagine, which gets its name from the triangular clay pot it is cooked in. Tagine is typically made up of meat and vegetables, and then flavored with dried raisins or dried apricots, other staples in this region's diet, along with preserved lemons. Maghrebi cuisine is also known for cooking with spices, such as cumin, coriander, cinnamon, cloves, and paprika. Heat and complexity are also added to dishes with the popular ras el hanout (a combination of the aforementioned spices, as well as chilies and saffron), and fire-hot harissa, a chili paste.

THE LEVANT

The Levant refers to the countries of Lebanon, Israel, Jordan, and Syria, or Middle Eastern countries to the east of Egypt. The name Levant comes from the French verb "to rise," and refers to these countries being in the east, where the sun rises.

Levantine cuisine shares similar flavor profiles with North African, Egyptian, and Ottoman cooking. Like the latter, the Levant is known for mezze—a spread of small dishes and dips, served hot or cold, accompanied by bread. And, like Egypt, many bean- and legume-based recipes are popular there. Ful medames, made from crushed fava beans seasoned with olive oil and cumin, is popular throughout the Levant, as is hummus. Two dishes that are renowned from this region are tabbouleh and baba ghanoush. The first is a refreshing cold salad often served as mezze, made from bulgur wheat and a healthy serving of parsley and mint; it's mixed together with tomato and onion, and seasoned with lemon juice and olive oil. Tabbouleh is so popular that it can be found ready-made in grocery stores around the Mediterranean (and now in much of the United States). Baba ghanoush is a smoky dip referred to in many languages as "eggplant caviar." It is a puree of eggplant and olive oil, often enriched with onion, tomato, cumin, parsley, lemon, and lots of garlic.

HEALTH BENEFITS

Make the mistake of searching online for "Mediterranean diet" instead of "Mediterranean food," and you will soon be bombarded with ads and websites promoting weight loss. This is because the foods eaten around the Mediterranean basin are more than delicious—they're also wonderfully healthy and nutritionally balanced, and can promote weight loss. Health gurus advocating for the Mediterranean diet praise its variety of produce-focused recipes. The amount of fruit and vegetables consumed contributes to high dietary fiber intake, which is excellent for health and maintained weight loss. They applaud a lifestyle that allows for regular, yet moderate, wine drinking. They also recognize that olive oil is a potential dietary factor for reducing chronic disease and mortality. By using olive oil over butter or other fats, Mediterranean cooking is low in saturated fats and high in monounsaturated fats, which lowers the risk

of cardiovascular diseases. Other health benefits include a lower risk of cancer and diabetes.

But many North American adaptations of the Mediterranean diet get one particular element wrong: bread. In an effort to keep up with the low-carb or gluten-free frenzy that has emerged over the past few decades, diet experts have pushed out a staple that has fed countries around the Mediterranean Sea for more than a thousand years. Make no mistake: a true Mediterranean diet includes bread, pasta, and other forms of wheat. Most Mediterranean people would consider replacing these vital ingredients with more meat as absurd.

The real benefit of the Mediterranean diet doesn't come from one single ingredient, but rather through a rule that dictates every facet of the region's lifestyle: enjoy everything, but in moderation.

GLOBAL REACH

The bread, olive oil, and wine that were once localized staples for those living around the Mediterranean are now essential ingredients worldwide. In some cases, other countries and continents now outperform the Mediterranean in producing these key supplies. The Midwestern United States is now one of the world's breadbaskets. The state of California is also a major supplier of grains, not to mention olive oil and wine.

Beyond just ingredients, many of the staple dishes from this region can also be found around the world. Pasta is just as much a part of an American's life today as it is an Italian's. Feta, olives, and hummus can surely be found in refrigerators across the globe. And even reci-

pes that were once considered rare delicacies, like ratatouille, baba ghanoush, tabbouleh, or dolma, are familiar treats that can be found on many a restaurant menu or in many home kitchens.

The influence goes both ways, however. A region that once ate a balanced, almost entirely plant-based diet is now following the traditionally Western trends of consuming more beef, more fast food, and less fresh fruits and vegetables. So, in choosing to celebrate each of these recipes, and preserve their method and memory, you are helping to keep alive a way of life that has added color, flavor, and spice to this beautiful region of the world for thousands upon thousands of years.

APPETIZERS

When the food of the Mediterranean is mentioned, many find their mind turning to preparations featured in this chapter—hummus, baba ghanoush, stuffed grape leaves, falafel, and spanakopita, to name a few. As with so many of our immediate associations today, this one is due in part to the global marketplace making these dishes available throughout the world. But it is also because these small, delicious bites are perfect expressions of the region's culinary philosophy—amplifying the very best aspects of a single ingredient, and remaining straightforward while also supplying dynamic flavors.

SALATA MECHOUIA

YIELD: 6 SERVINGS / ACTIVE TIME: 1 HOUR AND 15 MINUTES / TOTAL TIME: 3 HOURS AND 15 MINUTES

The smoky char of the grilled vegetables pairs perfectly with a burst of garlicky flavor. Enjoy alongside good bread.

1. Preheat the oven to 375°F. Use a knife to poke a small slit in the jalapeño.

2. Place the tomatoes, bell peppers, jalapeño, and garlic on an aluminum foil–lined baking sheet. Place it in the oven and roast until the vegetables are well browned and just tender, about 30 minutes for the garlic and 1 hour for the peppers and tomatoes.

3. Remove the vegetables from the oven. Place the garlic cloves on a plate and let them cool. Place the other roasted vegetables in a large bowl and cover it with plastic wrap. Let them rest for about 15 minutes.

4. Peel the garlic cloves and set them aside. Remove the charred skins from the other vegetables, place them in a colander, and let them drain.

5. Using a fork, mash the roasted garlic.

6. Transfer the drained vegetables to a cutting board. Remove the seeds from the bell peppers and the jalapeño. Finely chop all of the vegetables and place them in a mixing bowl. Add the mashed garlic, salt, pepper, lemon juice, and olive oil and stir well until combined.

7. Enjoy immediately with the Pita Bread.

INGREDIENTS:

1	JALAPEÑO CHILE PEPPER
6	LARGE PLUM TOMATOES
3	GREEN BELL PEPPERS
2	GARLIC CLOVES, UNPEELED
1	TEASPOON KOSHER SALT
¼	TEASPOON BLACK PEPPER
¼	CUP FRESH LEMON JUICE
3	TABLESPOONS EXTRA-VIRGIN OLIVE OIL
	PITA BREAD (SEE PAGE 532), FOR SERVING

MODERN HUMMUS

YIELD: 20 SERVINGS / **ACTIVE TIME:** 1 HOUR / **TOTAL TIME:** 24 HOURS

While stories of origin might differ, hummus is a beloved staple throughout the Mediterranean region. This recipe shows how simple this classic dish is to make—and how the flavor of this homemade dip and spread far outshines anything from the store.

1. Place the chickpeas, baking soda, and water in a large saucepan, stir, and cover. Let the chickpeas soak overnight at room temperature.

2. Drain the chickpeas and rinse them. Place them in a large saucepan, add the stock, and bring to a steady simmer. Cook until the chickpeas are quite tender, about 1 hour.

3. In a blender or food processor, combine all of the remaining ingredients and puree until achieving a perfectly smooth, creamy sauce; the ice water is the key to getting the correct consistency.

4. Add the warm, drained chickpeas to the tahini mixture and blend until the hummus is perfectly smooth and not at all grainy, occasionally stopping to scrape down the sides of the bowl. This blending process may take 3 minutes; remain patient and keep going until the mixture is ultracreamy and fluffy, adding water as necessary to make the hummus move.

5. Taste, adjust the seasoning as necessary, and enjoy.

INGREDIENTS:

2	LBS. DRIED CHICKPEAS
1	TABLESPOON BAKING SODA
12	CUPS ROOM-TEMPERATURE WATER
12	CUPS VEGETABLE STOCK (SEE PAGE 371)
1	CUP TAHINI PASTE
2	TABLESPOONS ZA'ATAR (SEE PAGE 766)
2	TABLESPOONS SUMAC
2	TABLESPOONS CUMIN
2	TABLESPOONS KOSHER SALT
2	TABLESPOONS BLACK PEPPER
2	GARLIC CLOVES, GRATED
½	BUNCH OF FRESH CILANTRO, ROUGHLY CHOPPED
1	CUP EXTRA-VIRGIN OLIVE OIL
1	CUP SESAME OIL
1	CUP ICE WATER
½	CUP FRESH LEMON JUICE

Modern Hummus, see page 31

SWEET POTATO BÖREK

YIELD: 24 SERVINGS / ACTIVE TIME: 45 MINUTES / TOTAL TIME: 2 HOURS

This savory pastry is known throughout Eastern Europe and the Mediterranean. If you're looking to tweak the flavor slightly, try substituting nigella seeds for the poppy seeds.

1. Place the sweet potato in a small saucepan and cover it with water. Bring to a boil, reduce the heat, and simmer until the sweet potato is very tender, 15 to 20 minutes. Drain and let the sweet potato cool.

2. Place the olive oil in a large skillet and warm it over medium heat. Add the onions and cook, stirring occasionally, until they have softened, about 5 minutes. Add the garlic and ginger and cook for 1 minute. Add the white wine and cook until it has evaporated, about 8 minutes. Remove the pan from heat and let the mixture cool.

3. Preheat the oven to 400°F. In a food processor, combine the sweet potato, onion mixture, 6 of the eggs, the salt, and pepper and blitz until smooth.

4. Place the Fontina, yogurt, heavy cream, mint, and lemon zest in a bowl and stir to combine. Place the milk and the remaining egg in a separate bowl and whisk until combined.

5. In a deep 13 x 9–inch baking pan, spread ¾ cup of the sweet potato puree evenly over the bottom. Place 5 sheets of phyllo on top and press down gently on them. Brush the top sheet of phyllo with the egg wash.

6. Repeat with the puree, phyllo, and egg wash and then sprinkle half of the cheese mixture over the phyllo. Top with another 5-sheet layer of phyllo and press down gently on it.

7. Repeat Steps 5 and 6.

8. Brush the top sheet of phyllo with the egg wash. Sprinkle the poppy seeds over the börek and place it in the oven. Bake until the top is puffy and golden brown, about 45 minutes.

9. Remove the börek from the oven and let it cool slightly before cutting and enjoying.

INGREDIENTS:

1	SWEET POTATO, PEELED AND CUBED
1	TABLESPOON EXTRA-VIRGIN OLIVE OIL
1½	CUPS CHOPPED ONIONS
4	GARLIC CLOVES, MINCED
1	TEASPOON GRATED FRESH GINGER
1	CUP WHITE WINE
7	EGGS
1	TEASPOON KOSHER SALT
½	TEASPOON BLACK PEPPER
¾	LB. FONTINA CHEESE, GRATED
1	CUP FULL-FAT GREEK YOGURT
⅓	CUP HEAVY CREAM
½	CUP CHOPPED FRESH MINT
	ZEST OF 1 LEMON
½	CUP MILK
1	LB. FROZEN PHYLLO DOUGH, THAWED
2	TEASPOONS POPPY SEEDS

TARAMASALATA

YIELD: 4 SERVINGS / ACTIVE TIME: 15 MINUTES / TOTAL TIME: 45 MINUTES

A traditional Greek dip that accommodates a surprising number of accompaniments.

1. Place the panko and water in a mixing bowl. Let the panko soak for 5 minutes.

2. Place the soaked panko, roe, onion, and lemon juice in a food processor and blitz until smooth.

3. With the food processor running, slowly drizzle in the olive oil until it has all been incorporated and the mixture is smooth. If the taramasalata is thinner than you'd like, incorporate more panko. If it is too thick, incorporate a little more olive oil.

4. Season the dip with salt and pepper, garnish with parsley, and serve with the olives, cucumber, artichokes, pitas, and lemon wedges.

INGREDIENTS:

10   OZ. PANKO, PLUS MORE AS NEEDED

½   CUP WATER

10   OZ. TARAMA CARP ROE

½   RED ONION, CHOPPED

JUICE OF ½ LEMON

½   CUP EXTRA-VIRGIN OLIVE OIL, PLUS MORE AS NEEDED

SALT AND PEPPER, TO TASTE

FRESH PARSLEY, CHOPPED, FOR GARNISH

½   CUP KALAMATA OLIVES, PITS REMOVED, FOR SERVING

½   CUCUMBER, PEELED AND SLICED, FOR SERVING

1   CUP MARINATED ARTICHOKES (SEE PAGE 86), FOR SERVING

PITA BREAD (SEE PAGE 532), FOR SERVING

LEMON WEDGES, FOR SERVING

BEET CHIPS WITH SPICY HONEY MAYONNAISE

YIELD: 8 SERVINGS / ACTIVE TIME: 30 MINUTES / TOTAL TIME: 1 HOUR

Sprinkled with a little salt, these crunchy chips are delicious on their own. But take them to the next decadent level when paired with a sweet and spicy pareve mayonnaise.

1. Place the canola oil in a Dutch oven and warm it to 375°F. Line a baking sheet with paper towels and set a cooling rack in it.

2. Cut the root end from the beets and use a mandoline to cut the beets into ⅛-inch-thick slices.

3. Working in batches to avoid crowding the pot, gently slip the beets into the hot oil and fry until they are browned and stop bubbling and sizzling, 3 to 4 minutes. Remove the chips with a slotted spoon, season them with salt and pepper, and let them cool—they will crisp up as they do.

4. When all of the beets have been fried, serve the chips with the spicy mayo.

INGREDIENTS:

4   CUPS CANOLA OIL

3   BEETS, RINSED WELL AND DRIED

SALT AND PEPPER, TO TASTE

SPICY HONEY MAYONNAISE (SEE PAGE 779), FOR SERVING

BABA GHANOUSH

YIELD: 12 SERVINGS / **ACTIVE TIME:** 15 MINUTES / **TOTAL TIME:** 1 HOUR AND 15 MINUTES

Though recipes may vary, and this or that can be added to please any palate, there are some basic rules for preparing this eggplant dish. Like hummus, this spread can be enhanced with various seasonings.

1. Preheat the oven to 400°F. Place the eggplants on a baking sheet, cut side up, and roast until they have collapsed, about 50 minutes. Remove the eggplants from the oven and let them cool for 10 minutes.

2. Scoop the flesh of the eggplants into a food processor and discard the skins. Add the garlic, lemon juice, salt, and tahini and blitz until the mixture is smooth and creamy, about 1 minute. Taste and add more lemon juice and salt as necessary.

3. Transfer the mixture to a bowl, top with the pomegranate seeds, parsley, and olive oil, and serve with Pita Bread.

INGREDIENTS:

2	LARGE EGGPLANTS, HALVED
4	GARLIC CLOVES, SMASHED
4	TEASPOONS FRESH LEMON JUICE, PLUS MORE TO TASTE
1½	TEASPOONS KOSHER SALT, PLUS MORE TO TASTE
½	CUP TAHINI PASTE
¼	CUP POMEGRANATE SEEDS
2	TEASPOONS FINELY CHOPPED FRESH PARSLEY
¼	CUP EXTRA-VIRGIN OLIVE OIL
	PITA BREAD (SEE PAGE 532), FOR SERVING

Baba Ghanoush, see page 39

KEFTES DE ESPINACA

YIELD: 12 SERVINGS / **ACTIVE TIME:** 15 MINUTES / **TOTAL TIME:** 30 MINUTES

A delicious vegetarian take on the decidedly meaty kefte concept.

1. Place the tablespoon of avocado oil in a large skillet and warm it over medium heat. Add the onion and cook, stirring frequently, until it starts to soften, about 5 minutes.

2. Add the garlic and cook until fragrant, about 1 minute. Add half of the spinach, cover the pan, and cook until the spinach has wilted. Add the remaining spinach, cover the pan again, and cook until all of the spinach has wilted.

3. Transfer the mixture to a fine-mesh strainer and gently press down on the mixture to remove excess moisture. Transfer the mixture to a cutting board and roughly chop it.

4. Place the mixture in a mixing bowl. Add the remaining ingredients and stir until thoroughly combined. Form ¼-cup portions of the mixture into patties and place them on a parchment-lined baking sheet.

5. Place the remaining avocado oil in the skillet and warm it to 365°F. Working in batches to avoid crowding the pan, slip the patties into the hot oil and fry until brown on both sides, about 8 minutes. Transfer the keftes to a paper towel–lined plate to drain before serving.

INGREDIENTS:

½ CUP PLUS 1 TABLESPOON AVOCADO OIL

1 ONION, MINCED

½ TEASPOON GRATED GARLIC

10 OZ. FRESH SPINACH

1 LARGE EGG

1 CUP MASHED POTATOES

½ CUP BREAD CRUMBS

1 TEASPOON KOSHER SALT

¼ TEASPOON BLACK PEPPER

PINCH OF CAYENNE PEPPER

LAVASH CRACKERS WITH RED PEPPER FETA & RICOTTA AND SPICED HONEY

YIELD: 4 SERVINGS / ACTIVE TIME: 45 MINUTES / TOTAL TIME: 2 HOURS AND 30 MINUTES

A great appetizer for a summer cocktail party.

1. Place the flours, ½ teaspoon of the salt, 2 tablespoons of the olive oil, the yeast, and water in the work bowl of a mixer fitted with the dough hook and work the mixture on low until it comes together as a dough. Increase the speed to medium and work the dough until it no longer sticks to the side of the work bowl, about 10 minutes.

2. Cover the bowl with a linen towel and let the dough rise in a naturally warm space until it has doubled in size, about 1 hour.

3. Line two baking sheets with parchment paper. Dust a work surface with all-purpose flour. Divide the dough into two pieces, place one piece on the work surface, and roll it out into a rectangle that is about ⅛ inch thick. Place the rolled-out dough on one of the baking sheets and repeat with the other ball of dough. Don't be overly concerned with the shape of the dough, a rustic look is what we are looking for in these crackers.

4. Brush the pieces of dough with the remaining olive oil. Sprinkle the remaining salt over them.

5. Place the Za'atar, sesame seeds, and poppy seeds in a bowl and stir to combine. Sprinkle the mixture over the dough and press down gently to help the mixture adhere. Place the dough in a naturally warm spot and let it rest for 30 minutes.

6. Preheat the oven to 425°F. Place the baking sheets in the oven and bake until the crackers are a deep golden brown, about 15 minutes. Remove the crackers from the oven and let them cool.

7. Break the crackers into pieces and serve alongside the Spiced Honey and Red Pepper Feta & Ricotta.

RED PEPPER FETA & RICOTTA

1. Place all of the ingredients, except for the garnishes, in a food processor and blitz until pureed.

2. Garnish with Za'atar, chives, sesame seeds, and additional olive oil and enjoy.

INGREDIENTS:

½	CUP SEMOLINA FLOUR
6	TABLESPOONS WHOLE WHEAT FLOUR
½	CUP PLUS 2 TABLESPOONS ALL-PURPOSE FLOUR, PLUS MORE AS NEEDED
1	TEASPOON FINE SEA SALT
3	TABLESPOONS EXTRA-VIRGIN OLIVE OIL
1	TEASPOON INSTANT YEAST
½	CUP WARM WATER (105°F)
1	TABLESPOON ZA'ATAR (SEE PAGE 766)
1	TABLESPOON SESAME SEEDS, TOASTED
1	TABLESPOON POPPY SEEDS
	SPICED HONEY (SEE PAGE 761)
	RED PEPPER FETA & RICOTTA (SEE RECIPE)

RED PEPPER FETA & RICOTTA

4	OZ. FETA CHEESE
2	OZ. RICOTTA CHEESE
1	CUP CHOPPED ROASTED RED PEPPERS
¼	CUP EXTRA-VIRGIN OLIVE OIL, PLUS MORE FOR GARNISH
1	TABLESPOON FRESH LEMON JUICE
	ZA'ATAR (SEE PAGE 766), FOR GARNISH
	FRESH CHIVES, CHOPPED, FOR GARNISH
	SESAME SEEDS, TOASTED, FOR GARNISH

EGGPLANT & CHORIZO BOUREKAS

YIELD: 6 SERVINGS / ACTIVE TIME: 30 MINUTES / TOTAL TIME: 1 HOUR

With savory chorizo and fried eggplant, these will be richer than the bourekas on the opposite page—enough that they could easily serve as the evening meal.

1. Place ¼ cup of the avocado oil in a large skillet and warm it over medium-high heat. Season the eggplant with the salt and pepper and place the eggplant in the hot oil. Cook, tossing the eggplant until it has absorbed all of the oil, and then reduce the heat and gently fry the eggplant until it is soft and the oil has been released back into the pan. Using a slotted spoon, transfer the eggplant to a paper towel–lined plate.

2. Add the onion to the pan and cook, stirring occasionally, until it starts to brown, about 10 minutes. Add the garlic and cumin and cook, stirring frequently, until fragrant, about 1 minute. Transfer the mixture to a bowl, add the eggplant, and stir to combine.

3. Add the chorizo to the pan and fry until it has browned and is starting to crisp up, about 10 minutes. Transfer it to a paper towel–lined plate to drain and then stir the chorizo into the eggplant-and-onion mixture. Stir the parsley into the mixture, season it with salt and pepper, and let it cool.

4. Place the remaining avocado oil in a large skillet and warm it to 350°F. Fill a bowl with water and place it beside your work surface.

5. Cut the puff pastry into six 5-inch squares. Divide the filling among the squares, placing it in the center. Make wells in the center of the filling and crack an egg into each one. Dip your fingers in the water and moisten the edges of the squares, then fold in half vertically to form triangles. Pinch the edges to seal the pockets.

6. Gently slip the bourekas into the hot oil, working in batches to avoid crowding the pan. Spoon the hot oil over the bourekas and fry until golden brown on the bottom, about 30 seconds. Turn them over, cook until golden brown on this side, and then transfer to a paper towel–lined plate to drain.

INGREDIENTS:

1½	CUPS AVOCADO OIL
1	EGGPLANT, CUBED
1	TEASPOON KOSHER SALT
1	TEASPOON BLACK PEPPER
1	LARGE ONION, SLICED THIN
2	GARLIC CLOVES, MINCED
1	TEASPOON CUMIN SEEDS
7	OZ. CHORIZO, FINELY DICED
1	HANDFUL OF FRESH PARSLEY, CHOPPED
½	(1 LB.) PACKAGE OF FROZEN PUFF PASTRY, THAWED
6	EGGS

BOUREKAS

YIELD: 12 SERVINGS / **ACTIVE TIME:** 1 HOUR / **TOTAL TIME:** 1 HOUR AND 50 MINUTES

The potato-and-cheese filling is simple enough to make, which is good news, considering that these savory bites will be requested again and again.

1. Place the potatoes in a stockpot and cover them by 1 inch with cold water. Bring to a boil over medium-high heat and cook until the potatoes are fork-tender, 20 to 25 minutes. Drain the potatoes, place them in a bowl, and mash them. Let them cool.

2. Place the olive oil in a large skillet and warm it over medium-high heat. Add the onion and cook, stirring occasionally, until it is starting to brown, about 7 minutes. Add the garlic and cook, stirring frequently, until fragrant, about 1 minute. Remove the pan from heat and set it aside.

3. Place the nutmeg and cheeses in a bowl and stir until combined.

4. Add the onion mixture and the cheese mixture to the mashed potatoes and stir until well combined. Season the mixture with salt and pepper and set it aside.

5. In a bowl, beat one of the eggs. While stirring the cool potato mixture, slowly incorporate the beaten egg.

6. Preheat the oven to 375°F and line a large baking sheet with parchment paper. Fill a bowl with water and place it beside your work surface.

7. Cut the puff pastry into 5-inch squares. Place a heaping tablespoon of filling in the center of each square. Dip your fingers in the water and moisten the edges of the squares, then fold in half vertically to form triangles. Pinch the edges to seal the pockets.

8. Beat the second egg and brush it over the tops of the bourekas. Sprinkle the sesame seeds on top.

9. Place the bourekas in the oven and bake until puffy and golden brown, about 30 minutes.

10. Remove from the oven and let the bourekas cool slightly before enjoying.

INGREDIENTS:

- 3   YUKON GOLD POTATOES, PEELED AND CUT INTO 1-INCH CUBES
- 2   TABLESPOONS EXTRA-VIRGIN OLIVE OIL
- 1   SMALL ONION, CHOPPED
- 1   GARLIC CLOVE, MINCED
- ⅛   TEASPOON FRESHLY GRATED NUTMEG
- 1   CUP RICOTTA CHEESE
- 1   CUP GRATED KASHKAVAL CHEESE
-     SALT AND PEPPER, TO TASTE
- 2   LARGE EGGS
- ½   (1 LB.) PACKAGE OF FROZEN PUFF PASTRY, THAWED
-     SESAME SEEDS, TOASTED, FOR TOPPING

Bourekas, see page 47

HANDRAJO

YIELD: 16 SERVINGS / **ACTIVE TIME:** 1 HOUR / **TOTAL TIME:** 1 HOUR AND 45 MINUTES

Washing the eggplants after peeling them is key here, as it prevents them from soaking up too much oil.

1. Place the oils in a large skillet and warm over high heat. Add the eggplants to the pan in an even layer, season with ½ teaspoon of the salt, and cook, undisturbed, until the eggplants start to brown, about 5 minutes.

2. Add the garlic and onions and stir to combine. Cover the pan with a lid, reduce the heat to medium, and cook until the vegetables are soft, about 10 minutes. Remove the lid and cook for 5 more minutes, until all of the liquid has evaporated.

3. Stir in the tomatoes, sugar, paprika, pepper, and the remaining salt and cook until the flavors have melded, 5 to 7 minutes. As the mixture cooks, break up any large chunks with a wooden spoon.

4. Remove the pan from heat, discard the garlic clove, and let the mixture cool completely.

5. Preheat the oven to 425°F and position a rack in the middle. Line a baking sheet with parchment paper. Spread the sheets of puff pastry on a clean work surface and cut each sheet in half lengthwise; you should end up with four 10 x 7–inch rectangles.

6. Divide the filling among the pieces of puff pastry, spreading it on one half of their length and leaving about 1 inch of pastry uncovered at the edge. Fold the other half of the dough over the filling, bringing the edges of the rectangles together. Using a fork, press down along each edge of the rectangles to seal the pastry together. Carefully transfer each pastry to the prepared baking sheet and brush them with the beaten egg.

7. Place in the oven and bake the handrajo until they are golden brown and crispy, 20 to 25 minutes.

8. Remove from the oven, cut the handrajo diagonally, and serve with the Labneh.

INGREDIENTS:

- ¼ CUP SUNFLOWER OIL
- 2 TABLESPOONS EXTRA-VIRGIN OLIVE OIL
- 2 MEDIUM EGGPLANTS, PEELED, WASHED, AND CUT INTO ½-INCH CUBES
- 1 TEASPOON KOSHER SALT, PLUS MORE TO TASTE
- 1 GARLIC CLOVE
- 2 ONIONS, FINELY DICED
- 3 TOMATOES, HALVED, PEELED, AND GRATED
- 1½ TEASPOONS SUGAR
- ½ TEASPOON SWEET PAPRIKA
- ½ TEASPOON BLACK PEPPER
- 2 (28 OZ.) PACKAGES OF PUFF PASTRY, THAWED (PREFERABLY BUTTER BASED)
- 1 EGG, BEATEN

    LABNEH (SEE PAGE 67), FOR SERVING

TIROPITAKIA

YIELD: 6 SERVINGS / ACTIVE TIME: 45 MINUTES / TOTAL TIME: 1 HOUR AND 15 MINUTES

Kefalotyri is a hard cheese with a sharp, salty flavor that brings to mind a souped-up Gruyère.

1. Place the feta in a mixing bowl and break it up with a fork. Add the kefalotyri, parsley, eggs, and pepper and stir to combine. Set the mixture aside.

2. Place one sheet of the phyllo dough on a large sheet of parchment paper. Gently brush the sheet with some of the melted butter, place another sheet on top, and brush this with more of the butter. Cut the phyllo dough into 2-inch-wide strips, place 1 teaspoon of the filling at the end of the strip closest to you, and fold one corner over to make a triangle. Fold the strip up until the filling is completely covered. Repeat with the remaining sheets of phyllo dough and filling.

3. Preheat the oven to 350°F and coat a baking sheet with some of the melted butter. Place the pastries on the baking sheet and bake until golden brown, about 15 minutes. Remove the tiropitakia from the oven and let them cool briefly before serving.

INGREDIENTS:

½   LB. FETA CHEESE

1   CUP GRATED KEFALOTYRI CHEESE

¼   CUP FINELY CHOPPED FRESH PARSLEY

2   EGGS, BEATEN

    BLACK PEPPER, TO TASTE

1   (1 LB.) PACKAGE OF FROZEN PHYLLO DOUGH, THAWED

1   CUP UNSALTED BUTTER, MELTED

STUFFED GRAPE LEAVES

YIELD: 4 SERVINGS / **ACTIVE TIME:** 30 MINUTES / **TOTAL TIME:** 1 HOUR AND 30 MINUTES

You will also see these referred to as dolmas, which refers to the family of stuffed dishes that are popular in the region.

1. Remove the grape leaves from the jar and rinse off all of the brine. Pick out 16 of the largest leaves and lay them on a baking sheet. Cover them with plastic wrap and set them aside.

2. Place half of the olive oil in a medium saucepan and warm it over medium heat. Add the red onion and cook, stirring occasionally, until it has softened, about 5 minutes.

3. Add the rice and cook, stirring frequently, for 2 minutes. Add 1½ cups water and bring it to a boil. Reduce the heat to low, cover the pan, and simmer for about 15 minutes.

4. Remove the pan from heat, fluff the rice with a fork, and let it cool.

5. Add the raisins, mint, dill, lemon zest, and cinnamon to the rice and fold to combine. Season the mixture with salt and pepper and form it into 16 balls.

6. Lay down a grape leaf and remove the stem. Fold in the edges of the leaf. Place a ball of the rice mixture at the bottom of the leaf, fold the bottom of the leaf over the filling, and then roll the leaf up tightly. Place the stuffed grape leaf on a baking sheet, seam side down, and repeat with the remaining grape leaves and rice mixture.

7. Place the remaining olive oil in a large saucepan and warm it over medium-high heat. Add the stuffed grape leaves to the pan, seam side down, and cook for 1 minute.

8. Reduce the heat to the lowest setting and carefully add 1½ cups water to the pan. Cover the pan and cook for 30 minutes, adding more water if the pan starts to look dry. You should finish with very little water in the pan.

9. Drizzle more olive oil over the grape leaves, garnish with additional mint, and serve with the slices of lemon.

INGREDIENTS:

1   (1 LB.) JAR OF GRAPE LEAVES

¼   CUP EXTRA-VIRGIN OLIVE OIL, PLUS MORE TO TASTE

1   RED ONION, CHOPPED

1   CUP LONG-GRAIN RICE, RINSED WELL

¼   CUP RAISINS, FINELY CHOPPED

¼   CUP CHOPPED FRESH MINT, PLUS MORE FOR GARNISH

¼   CUP CHOPPED FRESH DILL

    ZEST OF 1 LEMON

    PINCH OF CINNAMON

    SALT AND PEPPER, TO TASTE

1   LEMON, SLICED, FOR SERVING

TZATZIKI

YIELD: 2 CUPS / **ACTIVE TIME:** 5 MINUTES / **TOTAL TIME:** 1 HOUR AND 5 MINUTES

You can also puree this popular dip and serve it as a chilled soup.

1. Place the yogurt, cucumber, garlic, and lemon juice in a mixing bowl and stir to combine. Taste and season with salt and pepper. Stir in the dill.

2. Place in the refrigerator and chill for 1 hour before serving.

INGREDIENTS:

- 1 CUP PLAIN FULL-FAT YOGURT
- ¾ CUP SEEDED AND MINCED CUCUMBER
- 1 GARLIC CLOVE, MINCED
- JUICE FROM 1 LEMON WEDGE
- SALT AND WHITE PEPPER, TO TASTE
- FRESH DILL, FINELY CHOPPED, TO TASTE

FALAFEL

YIELD: 4 SERVINGS / **ACTIVE TIME:** 30 MINUTES / **TOTAL TIME:** 2 HOURS

Now known as Israel's national dish, these fried chickpea balls likely originated in Egypt.

1. Line a baking sheet with parchment paper. Place all of the ingredients, except for the canola oil, in a food processor and blitz until pureed.

2. Scoop ¼-cup portions of the puree onto the baking sheet and place it in the refrigerator for 1 hour.

3. Add canola oil to a Dutch oven until it is 2 inches deep and warm it to 320°F over medium heat.

4. Working in batches, add the falafel to the oil and fry, turning occasionally, until they are golden brown, about 6 minutes. Transfer the cooked falafel to a paper towel–lined plate to drain.

5. When all of the falafel have been cooked, serve with the hummus and Tahini Sauce.

INGREDIENTS:

1	(14 OZ.) CAN OF CHICKPEAS, DRAINED AND RINSED
½	RED ONION, CHOPPED
1	CUP FRESH PARSLEY, CHOPPED
1	CUP FRESH CILANTRO, CHOPPED
3	BUNCHES OF SCALLIONS, TRIMMED AND CHOPPED
1	JALAPEÑO CHILE PEPPER, STEM AND SEEDS REMOVED, CHOPPED
3	GARLIC CLOVES
1	TEASPOON CUMIN
1	TEASPOON KOSHER SALT, PLUS MORE TO TASTE
½	TEASPOON CARDAMOM
¼	TEASPOON BLACK PEPPER
2	TABLESPOONS CHICKPEA FLOUR
½	TEASPOON BAKING SODA
	CANOLA OIL, AS NEEDED
	MODERN HUMMUS (SEE PAGE 31), FOR SERVING
	TAHINI SAUCE (SEE PAGE 767), FOR SERVING

Falafel, see page 57

ARANCINI

YIELD: 8 SERVINGS / ACTIVE TIME: 30 MINUTES / TOTAL TIME: 1 HOUR AND 30 MINUTES

Yet another Sicilian specialty that has found fans the world over.

1. Bring the stock to a simmer in a large saucepan and remove the pan from heat.

2. In a skillet, melt the butter over high heat. Once the butter is foaming, add the rice and onion and cook until the rice has a toasty fragrance, about 4 minutes.

3. Deglaze the skillet with the white wine and cook until the wine has almost completely been absorbed. Then, reduce the heat to medium-high and begin adding the stock ¼ cup at a time, stirring until it has been incorporated. Continue adding the stock until the rice is al dente.

4. Turn off the heat, stir in the cheese, and season the risotto with salt and pepper. Pour it onto a baking sheet and let the risotto cool completely.

5. Add the oil to a Dutch oven until it is 2 inches deep and warm over medium heat until it reaches 350°F. When the rice mixture is cool, form it into golf ball–sized spheres. Dredge them in the eggs and then the panko until coated all over. Place the balls in the oil and fry until warmed through and golden brown. Transfer the arancini to a paper towel–lined plate to drain and cool slightly before enjoying.

INGREDIENTS:

5	CUPS CHICKEN STOCK (SEE PAGE 368)
8	TABLESPOONS UNSALTED BUTTER
2	CUPS ARBORIO RICE
1	SMALL WHITE ONION, GRATED
1	CUP WHITE WINE
4	OZ. FONTINA CHEESE, GRATED
	SALT AND PEPPER, TO TASTE
	CANOLA OIL, AS NEEDED
6	LARGE EGGS, BEATEN
5	CUPS PANKO

2. Place the couscous and the seasonings in a mixing bowl and stir until well combined. Add the boiling water to the couscous and cover the bowl with plastic wrap. After 10 minutes, use a fork to fluff the couscous.

3. Add ½ cup of feta to the couscous and stir to incorporate it.

4. Add canola oil to a Dutch oven until it is about 4 inches deep and warm it to 350°F.

5. Using your hands, form 1-oz. portions of the couscous into balls. Press into each ball with your thumb and make a depression. Fill this with some of the remaining feta and then close the ball over it.

6. Working in batches of four to avoid crowding the pan, gently slip the balls into the hot oil and fry until golden brown, about 4 minutes. Transfer the fried arancini to a paper towel–lined plate to drain and cool and enjoy once all of them have been cooked.

2	CUPS COUSCOUS
1	TABLESPOON PAPRIKA
1	TABLESPOON GARLIC POWDER
2	TEASPOONS KOSHER SALT
1	TEASPOON CUMIN
1	CUP CRUMBLED FETA CHEESE
	CANOLA OIL, AS NEEDED

Couscous Arancini, see page 61

PECAN MUHAMMARA

Muhammara traditionally features walnuts, but the sweetness of pecans is a good fit for the fruity character of the Aleppo pepper.

1. Warm a cast-iron skillet over medium-high heat. Place the peppers in the pan and cook until they are charred all over, turning them as needed.

2. Place the peppers in a bowl, cover it with plastic wrap, and let them steam for 15 minutes.

3. Remove the stems, skins, and seed pods from the peppers and place the peppers in a blender.

4. Add the pecans, salt, Aleppo pepper, olive oil, lemon juice, and molasses and puree until smooth.

5. Add the bread crumbs and fold to incorporate them. Sprinkle the parsley on top and enjoy.

INGREDIENTS:

2	RED BELL PEPPERS
¼	CUP PECANS
1	TEASPOON KOSHER SALT
1	TEASPOON ALEPPO PEPPER
½	CUP EXTRA-VIRGIN OLIVE OIL
	JUICE OF 1 LEMON
1	TABLESPOON POMEGRANATE MOLASSES
¼	CUP BREAD CRUMBS
1	TABLESPOON CHOPPED FRESH PARSLEY

LABNEH

YIELD: 8 SERVINGS / **ACTIVE TIME:** 10 MINUTES / **TOTAL TIME:** 2 DAYS

The easiest recipe for homemade cheese, and one of the very best recipes for anything, anywhere.

1. Place the yogurt in a large bowl and season it with the salt; the salt helps pull out excess whey, giving you a creamier, thicker labneh.

2. Place a fine-mesh strainer on top of a medium-sized bowl. Line the strainer with cheesecloth or a linen towel, letting a few inches hang over the side of the strainer. Spoon the seasoned yogurt into the cheesecloth and gently wrap the sides over the top of the yogurt, protecting it from being exposed to air in the refrigerator.

3. Store everything in the refrigerator for 24 to 48 hours, discarding the whey halfway through if the bowl beneath the strainer becomes too full.

4. Remove the labneh from the cheesecloth and store it in an airtight container.

5. To serve, drizzle the olive oil over the labneh and sprinkle the Za'atar on top.

INGREDIENTS:

4   CUPS PLAIN GREEK YOGURT

½   TEASPOON KOSHER SALT

1   TABLESPOON EXTRA-VIRGIN OLIVE OIL

2   TEASPOONS ZA'ATAR (SEE PAGE 766)

Caponata, see page 70

CAPONATA

YIELD: 6 SERVINGS / **ACTIVE TIME:** 1 HOUR / **TOTAL TIME:** 2 HOURS

Because eggplant absorbs flavors like a sponge, it's particularly good in a dish as varied as this.

1. Preheat the oven to 425°F. Place the eggplant on a baking sheet, place it in the oven, and roast until it has collapsed and is starting to char, about 25 minutes. Remove from the oven and let the eggplant cool. When cool enough to handle, roughly chop the eggplant.

2. Place 1 tablespoon of the olive oil in a large skillet and warm it over medium heat. Add the onion and celery and cook, stirring, until the onion starts to soften, about 5 minutes. Stir in the garlic, cook for 1 minute, and then add the peppers. Season with salt and cook, stirring frequently, until the peppers are tender, about 8 minutes.

3. Add the remaining olive oil and the eggplant and cook, stirring occasionally, until the eggplant begins to fall apart and the other vegetables are tender. Stir in the tomatoes and the pinch of sugar, season the mixture with salt, and cook, stirring frequently, until the tomatoes start to collapse and smell fragrant, about 7 minutes.

4. Stir in the capers, olives, remaining sugar, and vinegar. Reduce the heat to medium-low and cook, stirring often, until the mixture is quite thick, sweet, and fragrant, 20 to 30 minutes. Taste, season with salt and pepper, and remove the pan from heat.

5. Let the caponata cool to room temperature before serving. If time allows, chill in the refrigerator overnight and let it return to room temperature before serving.

INGREDIENTS:

1	LARGE EGGPLANT (ABOUT 1½ LBS.)
2	TABLESPOONS EXTRA-VIRGIN OLIVE OIL
1	ONION, CHOPPED
2	CELERY STALKS, PEELED AND CHOPPED
3	LARGE GARLIC CLOVES, MINCED
	BELL PEPPERS, STEMS AND SEEDS REMOVED, CHOPPED
	SALT AND PEPPER, TO TASTE
1	LB. RIPE ROMA TOMATOES, PEELED, SEEDS REMOVED, AND FINELY CHOPPED; OR 1 (14 OZ.) CAN OF CRUSHED TOMATOES, WITH THEIR LIQUID
2	TABLESPOONS PLUS 1 PINCH SUGAR
3	TABLESPOONS (HEAPING) CAPERS, RINSED AND DRAINED
3	TABLESPOONS CHOPPED GREEN OLIVES
3	TABLESPOONS RED WINE VINEGAR

EGGPLANT RINGS

YIELD: 4 SERVINGS / **ACTIVE TIME:** 40 MINUTES / **TOTAL TIME:** 1 HOUR

The almost-custardy texture of eggplant cries out for the crunch supplied by a fried breading.

1. Cut the centers out of the slices of eggplant, creating rings that have about an inch of eggplant left inside.

2. Place the eggs, flour, and panko in separate bowls. Add the salt and pepper to the bowl of panko and stir to combine. Dredge an eggplant ring in the flour, then the eggs, followed by the panko, repeating until all of the rings are coated. Place the coated rings on a baking sheet.

3. Add canola oil to a cast-iron skillet until it is about 1 inch deep and warm to 375°F over medium-high heat. Working in batches to avoid crowding the pan, gently lay the eggplant rings in the oil and fry until browned and crispy all over, about 4 minutes, turning as necessary. Place the cooked rings on a paper towel–lined plate to drain.

4. Place the zhug and ketchup in a small bowl, stir to combine, and serve alongside the eggplant rings.

INGREDIENTS:

1	LARGE EGGPLANT, TRIMMED AND SLICED
2	EGGS, BEATEN
1	CUP ALL-PURPOSE FLOUR
1	CUP PANKO
1	TABLESPOON KOSHER SALT
1	TABLESPOON BLACK PEPPER
	CANOLA OIL, AS NEEDED
¼	CUP RED ZHUG (SEE PAGE 748)
¼	CUP KETCHUP

Sicilian Bar Nuts, see page 74

SICILIAN BAR NUTS

YIELD: 4 SERVINGS / **ACTIVE TIME:** 10 MINUTES / **TOTAL TIME:** 20 MINUTES

Double the batch and store the leftovers in an airtight container so that you'll have something special ready to go when a friend drops by unexpectedly.

1. Preheat the oven to 350°F. Place the nuts on a baking sheet, place them in the oven, and toast until fragrant, about 12 minutes. Remove from the oven and transfer the nuts to a mixing bowl.

2. Add the melted butter and toss until the nuts are evenly coated. Add the remaining ingredients, toss to coat, and serve.

INGREDIENTS:

¾   CUP WALNUTS

¾   CUP CASHEWS

¾   CUP PECAN HALVES

2   TABLESPOONS UNSALTED BUTTER, MELTED

2   TABLESPOONS CHOPPED FRESH ROSEMARY

1   TEASPOON CAYENNE PEPPER

1   TABLESPOON BROWN SUGAR

1   TABLESPOON FLAKY SEA SALT

ROASTED & STUFFED SARDINES

YIELD: 2 SERVINGS / **ACTIVE TIME:** 20 MINUTES / **TOTAL TIME:** 45 MINUTES

When dressing sardines, keep in mind that the bones are edible, and full of helpful nutrients.

1. Clean the sardines: make an incision in the belly of each one from head to tail. Remove the guts and carefully snap the spines at the neck and tail. This will leave the sardines intact enough to hold their shape when roasted. Rinse the sardines and set them aside.

2. Place 2 tablespoons of the olive oil in a medium skillet and warm it over medium-high heat. Add the onion, celery, salt, paprika, cumin, and garlic and cook, stirring frequently, until the onions are translucent, about 3 minutes.

3. Add the water and simmer for 3 or 4 minutes. Add the parsley and bread and cook, stirring frequently, allowing the bread to absorb the liquids and brown a bit. After 5 minutes, remove the pan from heat.

4. Preheat the oven to 450°F.

5. Place the sardines in a cast-iron skillet, keeping them nestled against each other so hold their shape better. Fill the sardines' bellies with the stuffing, drizzle the remaining olive oil over them, and place the pan in the oven.

6. Roast the stuffed sardines until they reach an internal temperature of 145°F, 15 to 20 minutes.

7. Remove the sardines from the oven and serve with the Tahini Sauce.

INGREDIENTS:

5	WHOLE, FRESH SARDINES
3	TABLESPOONS EXTRA-VIRGIN OLIVE OIL
½	WHITE ONION, CHOPPED
¼	CUP CHOPPED CELERY
1	TEASPOON KOSHER SALT
1	TABLESPOON PAPRIKA
	PINCH OF CUMIN
2	GARLIC CLOVES, MINCED
2	TABLESPOONS WATER
¼	CUP CHOPPED FRESH PARSLEY
1	CUP DAY-OLD BREAD PIECES
	TAHINI SAUCE (SEE PAGE 767), FOR SERVING

Roasted & Stuffed Sardines, see page 75

CHICKEN LIVER MOUSSE

YIELD: 6 SERVINGS / **ACTIVE TIME:** 30 MINUTES / **TOTAL TIME:** 3 HOURS AND 30 MINUTES

Adding a bit of air and the complexity of balsamic rejuvenates a traditional pâté.

1. Place the butter in a large skillet and melt it over medium-high heat. When the butter begins to foam, add the liver, onion, salt, and pepper, and cook, stirring frequently, until the liver is no longer pink, about 8 minutes.

2. Transfer the mixture to a food processor and puree. With the food processor running, slowly add the balsamic vinegar. When all of the vinegar has been incorporated, slowly add the cream and puree until smooth.

3. Transfer the mixture to a container, place it in the refrigerator, and chill, uncovered, for 1 hour.

4. Cover the mousse and refrigerate for another 2 hours, or until the mousse is set.

5. Serve with crackers or grilled bread.

INGREDIENTS:

1	TABLESPOON UNSALTED BUTTER
½	LB. CHICKEN LIVER, CHOPPED
2	TABLESPOONS CHOPPED WHITE ONION
1	TEASPOON KOSHER SALT
1	TEASPOON BLACK PEPPER
2	TABLESPOONS BALSAMIC VINEGAR
3	OZ. HEAVY CREAM

SPANAKOPITA

YIELD: 8 SERVINGS / **ACTIVE TIME:** 1 HOUR / **TOTAL TIME:** 1 HOUR AND 30 MINUTES

This dish has opened the door to Greek cuisine for many people, and, as you'll see, it remains a gracious host.

1. Prepare an ice bath. Fill a large saucepan three-quarters of the way with water and bring it to a boil. Add the spinach and boil for 2 minutes, making sure it is all submerged. Drain the spinach, place it in the ice bath, and let it cool.

2. Place the spinach in a linen towel and wring the towel to remove as much water from the spinach as possible. Chop the spinach, place it in a bowl, and add the feta, yogurt, scallions, egg, mint, garlic, lemon zest, lemon juice, nutmeg, and cayenne. Stir to combine, season the mixture with salt and pepper, and set the filling aside.

3. Preheat the oven to 425°F. Line a baking sheet with parchment paper. Place a piece of parchment paper on a work surface, place a sheet of phyllo on it, and brush with some of the butter. Lay another sheet of phyllo on top, gently press down, and brush it with butter. Sprinkle a thin layer of the Pecorino over the second sheet. Repeat so that you have another layer of Pecorino sandwiched between two 2-sheet layers of phyllo. Make sure you keep any phyllo that you are not working with covered so that it does not dry out.

4. Working from the top of the rectangle, find the center point and cut down, as though you were cutting an open book in half. Cut these halves in two, so that you have four strips. Place 2 tablespoons of the filling on the bottom of each strip and shape the filling into a triangle.

5. Maintaining the triangle shape of the filling, roll the strips up into triangles, as if you were folding a flag. Crimp the pastries to seal and place the spanakopita on the baking sheet, seam side down.

6. Repeat Steps 3, 4, and 5, giving you eight spanakopita. Sprinkle the sesame seeds over each spanakopita, place them in the oven, and bake until golden brown, about 20 minutes.

7. Remove the spanakopita from the oven, sprinkle the dill over them, and enjoy.

INGREDIENTS:

- ½ LB. BABY SPINACH, STEMS REMOVED
- 1 CUP CRUMBLED FETA CHEESE
- 6 TABLESPOONS FULL-FAT GREEK YOGURT
- 2 SCALLIONS, TRIMMED AND CHOPPED
- 1 EGG, BEATEN
- 2 TABLESPOONS CHOPPED FRESH MINT
- 2 GARLIC CLOVES, MINCED
- ZEST AND JUICE OF ½ LEMON
- ½ TEASPOON FRESHLY GRATED NUTMEG
- PINCH OF CAYENNE PEPPER
- SALT AND PEPPER, TO TASTE
- ½ LB. FROZEN PHYLLO DOUGH, THAWED
- 6 TABLESPOONS UNSALTED BUTTER, MELTED
- 1 CUP FRESHLY GRATED PECORINO ROMANO CHEESE
- 1 TABLESPOON SESAME SEEDS
- 1 TABLESPOON CHOPPED FRESH DILL

GRILLED CANTALOUPE

YIELD: 4 SERVINGS / **ACTIVE TIME**: 20 MINUTES / **TOTAL TIME**: 20 MINUTES

Grilling cantaloupe completely changes its texture and adds a slightly bitter, charred element to its inherent sweetness. Married with creamy mozzarella and tangy balsamic, this is a very simple yet wonderfully complex dish.

1. Prepare a gas or charcoal grill for high heat (about 500°F). Remove the rind from the cantaloupe, halve it, remove the seeds, and then cut the cantaloupe into ½-inch-thick slices.

2. Place the cantaloupe in a mixing bowl, add the oil, and toss to coat.

3. Place the cantaloupe on the grill and cook until lightly charred on both sides and warmed through.

4. To serve, pile the warm cantaloupe, top with the mozzarella, and drizzle the Balsamic Glaze over the top. Garnish with parsley and enjoy.

INGREDIENTS:

1 CANTALOUPE

1 TABLESPOON EXTRA-VIRGIN OLIVE OIL

4 OZ. FRESH MOZZARELLA CHEESE, TORN

1 TABLESPOON BALSAMIC GLAZE (SEE PAGE 759)

FRESH PARSLEY, CHOPPED, FOR GARNISH

CHICKPEA POUTINE

YIELD: 4 SERVINGS / **ACTIVE TIME:** 45 MINUTES / **TOTAL TIME:** 2 HOURS

You don't need the short rib or brisket to make this preparation delicious, but one of them is necessary to make it memorable.

1. Place the flour, salt, garlic powder, parsley, and cumin in a mixing bowl and stir to combine. Add the boiling water and beat until the batter is smooth. Pour the batter into a small baking dish (small enough that the batter is about 1 inch deep), cover with plastic wrap, and refrigerate for 1 hour.

2. Turn the mixture out onto a cutting board and cut it into wide strips.

3. Add canola oil to a Dutch oven until it is about 3 inches deep and warm it to 350°F over medium heat. Add the chickpea fries and turn them as they cook until they are crispy and golden brown, 3 to 4 minutes. Place on a paper towel–lined plate to drain.

4. Place the short rib in a small saucepan, add about ½ cup of water, and bring it to a simmer. Cook until the liquid has reduced by half.

5. Arrange the fries on a platter and spoon the gravy from the short rib over them. Top with the short rib, sprinkle the feta over the fries, and serve.

INGREDIENTS:

1	CUP CHICKPEA FLOUR
2	TEASPOONS KOSHER SALT
1	TEASPOON GARLIC POWDER
2	TABLESPOONS DRIED PARSLEY
	PINCH OF CUMIN
2	CUPS BOILING WATER
	CANOLA OIL, AS NEEDED
½	LB. LEFTOVER SHORT RIB OR BRISKET
½	CUP CRUMBLED FETA CHEESE

Chickpea Poutine, see page 83

MARINATED ARTICHOKES

YIELD: 4 SERVINGS / **ACTIVE TIME:** 30 MINUTES / **TOTAL TIME:** 1 HOUR

A dish that will help you understand why people go through all the trouble of getting artichokes prepped.

1. Place the olive oil and the artichokes in a medium saucepan. The artichokes need to be completely covered by the oil, as any contact with the air will make them turn brown. Add more oil to cover the artichokes, if necessary.

2. Add the remaining ingredients, except for the basil, and bring the mixture to a simmer over medium heat. Reduce the heat to the lowest setting and cook the artichokes until they are tender, about 30 minutes.

3. Remove the pan from heat and let the artichokes cool. Remove them from the oil, garnish with basil, and enjoy.

INGREDIENTS:

2   CUPS EXTRA-VIRGIN OLIVE OIL, PLUS MORE AS NEEDED

4–8   GLOBE ARTICHOKES, PEELED AND QUARTERED

     JUICE OF 1 LEMON

6   GARLIC CLOVES

¼   TEASPOON RED PEPPER FLAKES

2   SPRIGS OF FRESH THYME

1   SHALLOT, SLICED THIN

     FRESH BASIL, CHOPPED, FOR GARNISH

Fried Feta, see page 90

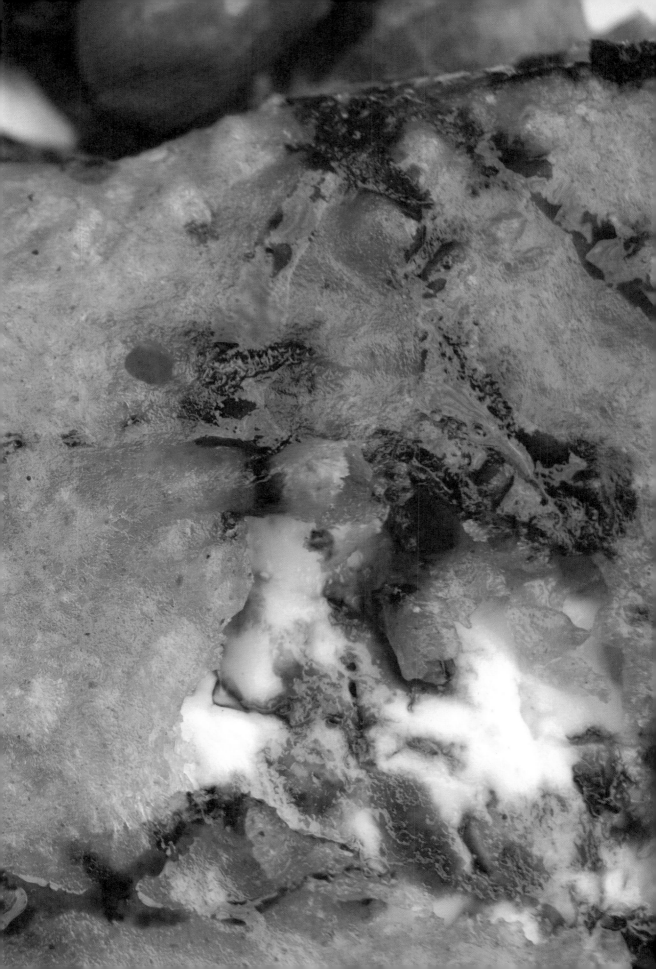

FRIED FETA

YIELD: 2 SERVINGS / **ACTIVE TIME:** 25 MINUTES / **TOTAL TIME:** 25 MINUTES

A bit of time in a hot bath amplifies feta's creamy character.

1. Place the flour, salt, baking powder, and water in a small bowl and whisk until the mixture is smooth.

2. Add canola oil to a small saucepan until it is about 1 inch deep and warm it over medium-high heat.

3. Carefully dip the block of feta in the batter until it is completely coated.

4. Submerge half of the feta in the canola oil for 5 seconds, then release it so that it floats. Fry for 1½ minutes on each side, while keeping a close eye on the feta; if the batter doesn't seal, the feta will ooze, out and this won't work. Once the feta has browned, remove from the oil and set it on a cooling rack.

5. Place the olive oil in a medium skillet and warm it over high heat. Add the tomatoes and cook until they start to blister, 2 to 3 minutes. Add the lettuce leaves and brown them for about 1 minute. Remove the pan from heat.

6. To serve, place the lettuce in a shallow bowl, scatter the tomatoes on top, and nestle the fried block of feta on top. Drizzle the Balsamic Glaze over the cheese and enjoy.

INGREDIENTS:

1	CUP ALL-PURPOSE FLOUR
1	TEASPOON KOSHER SALT
1	TEASPOON BAKING POWDER
1	CUP WATER
	CANOLA OIL, AS NEEDED
1	BLOCK OF FETA CHEESE (½-INCH THICK)
1	TEASPOON EXTRA-VIRGIN OLIVE OIL
1	CUP GRAPE TOMATOES
	LEAVES FROM ½ HEAD OF ROMAINE LETTUCE
1	TABLESPOON BALSAMIC GLAZE (SEE PAGE 759)

STUFFED AVOCADOS

YIELD: 2 SERVINGS / **ACTIVE TIME**: 45 MINUTES / **TOTAL TIME**: 1 HOUR AND 30 MINUTES

Topping the mashed avocado mixture with a seafood salad is another solid option here.

1. Preheat the oven to 450°F. In a bowl, combine the squash with 1 tablespoon of the olive oil, the salt, and pepper. Transfer the squash to a baking sheet, place it in the oven, and roast until lightly browned and soft enough to mash, 15 to 20 minutes. Remove from the oven and set the squash aside.

2. Halve the avocados and remove their seeds. Using a spoon, remove the avocado flesh and place it in a bowl. Add the feta and roasted squash and mash the mixture until it is smooth and well combined.

3. Fill the avocado skins with the mixture and lightly brush the top of each one with the remaining oil. Place them on a baking sheet and place them in the oven.

4. Roast in the oven until the tops of the avocados are browned, 10 to 15 minutes. Remove from the oven, drizzle the aioli over the top, and enjoy.

INGREDIENTS:

1	CUP FINELY DICED BUTTERNUT SQUASH
2	TABLESPOONS EXTRA-VIRGIN OLIVE OIL
1	TEASPOON KOSHER SALT
1	TEASPOON BLACK PEPPER
2	RIPE AVOCADOS
½	CUP CRUMBLED FETA CHEESE
2	TABLESPOONS SMOKED EGG AIOLI (SEE PAGE 770)

Stuffed Avocados, see page 91

MUSSELS ESCABECHE

YIELD: 2 TO 4 SERVINGS / **ACTIVE TIME:** 30 MINUTES / **TOTAL TIME:** 1 HOUR

Reducing the acidic cooking liquid before adding the mussels back to it makes for a gentler, more subtle interpretation of this classic preparation.

1. Place the olive oil in a medium saucepan and warm it over medium heat. Add the chopped shallot and cook, stirring frequently, until it starts to soften, about 2 minutes.

2. Add the garlic and cook for 1 minute. Add the white wine and cook until the alcohol has been cooked off, about 2 minutes.

3. Add the water, lemon zest, lemon juice, thyme, and mustard and bring the mixture to a boil. Add the mussels and cover the pan. Cook until the majority of the mussels have opened, about 5 minutes. Discard any mussels that do not open.

4. Using a slotted spoon, remove the mussels from the liquid and place them in a bowl.

5. Boil the remaining liquid until about ¼ cup remains.

6. When mussels are cool enough to handle, remove the meat from the shells. Discard the shells and place the mussels in a bowl.

7. Strain the reduction into a clean pan and bring to a simmer. Add the shallot rings and cook for 1 minute. Stir in the paprika and parsley and season with salt and pepper.

8. Remove the pan from heat and let it cool. Fold in the mussels and enjoy.

INGREDIENTS:

1	TABLESPOON EXTRA-VIRGIN OLIVE OIL
2	SHALLOTS, 1 CHOPPED; 1 SLICED INTO RINGS
2	GARLIC CLOVES, MINCED
½	CUP WHITE WINE
½	CUP WATER
	ZEST AND JUICE OF 1 LEMON
2	SPRIGS OF FRESH THYME
1	TEASPOON DIJON MUSTARD
2	LBS. MUSSELS, SCRUBBED AND DEBEARDED
1	TEASPOON PAPRIKA
2	TABLESPOONS CHOPPED FRESH PARSLEY
	SALT AND PEPPER, TO TASTE

SCALLOP CEVICHE

YIELD: 2 SERVINGS / **ACTIVE TIME:** 15 MINUTES / **TOTAL TIME:** 30 MINUTES

This ceviche is crisp and fresh, with a flavor that bounces around the Mediterranean, from the Greek Isles to Israel.

1. In a mixing bowl, combine the honey, pomegranate molasses, lime juice, and white vinegar. Add the salt, shallot, scallions, mint, and jalapeño to the bowl, mix well, and let the mixture rest for 15 minutes.

2. Using a sharp knife, cut the scallops into ⅛-inch-thick slices. Add the scallops to the marinade and gently stir to coat. In a minute or two, the scallops will cure and turn fully white. Enjoy immediately.

INGREDIENTS:

1	TEASPOON HONEY
½	TEASPOON POMEGRANATE MOLASSES
	JUICE OF 1 LIME
	SPLASH OF WHITE VINEGAR
	PINCH OF KOSHER SALT
½	SHALLOT, DICED
1	TABLESPOON SLICED SCALLIONS
2	FRESH MINT LEAVES, CHOPPED
1	TEASPOON CHOPPED JALAPEÑO CHILE PEPPER
6	LARGE SEA SCALLOPS, RINSED, FEET REMOVED

Scallop Ceviche, see page 95

TURMERIC & GINGER SHRIMP COCKTAIL

YIELD: 6 SERVINGS / ACTIVE TIME: 30 MINUTES / TOTAL TIME: 2 HOURS AND 30 MINUTES

The bright, slightly citrusy flavor of fresh turmeric provides the clean, refreshing taste you want from a shrimp cocktail.

1. Peel the shrimp, leaving only the tails, and devein them. Set them aside.

2. Place the remainder of the ingredients in a mixing bowl, stir until well combined, and then add the peeled shrimp. Cover the bowl with plastic wrap and chill in the refrigerator for at least 2, and no more than 6 hours.

3. Warm a large skillet over medium-high heat. Working in batches to avoid crowding the pan, add the shrimp and the marinating liquid to the pan and cook until the shrimp have turned pink, 2 to 3 minutes. Remove the cooked shrimp from the pan and let them cool.

4. Serve at room temperature or chilled.

INGREDIENTS:

1½	LBS. SHRIMP
1	TABLESPOON GRATED FRESH GINGER
2	GARLIC CLOVES, MINCED
1	TABLESPOON GRATED FRESH TURMERIC
2	TABLESPOONS CHOPPED SCALLIONS
1	SHALLOT, MINCED
	JUICE OF 1 LIME
	JUICE OF 1 SCALLION
1	TABLESPOON KOSHER SALT
1	TEASPOON HONEY
1	TABLESPOON EXTRA-VIRGIN OLIVE OIL

TUNA KIBBEH NAYEH

YIELD: 2 SERVINGS / **ACTIVE TIME**: 30 MINUTES / **TOTAL TIME**: 45 MINUTES

This can be enjoyed on its own, with lettuce leaves, pita chips, tortilla chips, or over buttery, flaky phyllo that has been crisped up in a skillet.

1. Place the bulgur wheat in a small saucepan, cover it with water, and cook over medium heat until tender, 15 to 20 minutes. Drain and run under cold water until the bulgur has cooled.

2. Using a sharp knife, cut the tuna into slices and then dice it into ¼-inch cubes.

3. Place the fresh herbs, lime and lemon juices, salt, and pepper in a mixing bowl and stir until well combined. Stir in the tuna, making sure to cover it with the liquid as much as possible. Let the mixture sit for 5 minutes.

4. Stir in the bulgur wheat, red onion, and the aioli.

5. Cut the avocado into ¼-inch cubes and gently fold these into the mixture, taking care to mash them up as little as possible. Serve immediately, with any or all of the accompaniments suggested above.

INGREDIENTS:

1   CUP BULGUR WHEAT

½   LB. SUSHI-GRADE TUNA

2   FRESH BASIL LEAVES, CHIFFONADE

2   FRESH MINT LEAVES, CHIFFONADE

    JUICE OF 1 LIME

    JUICE OF 1 LEMON

1   TEASPOON KOSHER SALT

    PINCH OF BLACK PEPPER

¼   CUP RED ONION, FINELY DICED

2   TABLESPOONS SMOKED EGG AIOLI (SEE PAGE 770)

    FLESH FROM 1 AVOCADO

Tuna Kibbeh Nayeh, see page 99

CRUSHED AVOCADO

YIELD: 6 SERVINGS / ACTIVE TIME: 10 MINUTES / TOTAL TIME: 10 MINUTES

The zip of the Za'atar guarantees that no one will confuse this for guacamole.

1. Place all of the ingredients in a bowl and gently stir until combined. You want the texture to be chunky, as this provides the best mouthfeel.

INGREDIENTS:

2   CUPS AVOCADO

½   CUP FRESH LEMON JUICE

1   TABLESPOON KOSHER SALT

1   TEASPOON BLACK PEPPER

2   TABLESPOONS ZA'ATAR
     (SEE PAGE 766)

½   CUP CHOPPED FRESH
     CILANTRO

¼   CUP EXTRA-VIRGIN OLIVE
     OIL

FIRE-ROASTED OYSTERS

YIELD: 4 SERVINGS / ACTIVE TIME: 20 MINUTES / TOTAL TIME: 40 MINUTES

A charcoal grill is always better than gas, particularly so with this preparation, as the oysters become even lovelier with a touch of smoke.

1. Prepare a charcoal or gas grill for medium-high heat (about 450°F). Rinse and shuck the oysters, making sure to separate them from the shell at the tendon.

2. Put a small dollop of butter, a pinch of garlic, and a pinch of Parmesan into each oyster's shell.

3. Place the oysters on the grill and cover it. Cook until the butter and cheese turn golden brown, about 2 minutes.

4. Garnish with the parsley and enjoy.

INGREDIENTS:

20	FRESH OYSTERS
3	TABLESPOONS UNSALTED BUTTER
½	CUP MINCED FRESH GARLIC
½	CUP FRESHLY GRATED PARMESAN CHEESE
¼	CUP CHOPPED FRESH PARSLEY, FOR GARNISH

Fire-Roasted Oysters, see page 103

SWEET POTATO & TAHINI DIP
WITH SPICED HONEY

YIELD: 1 CUP / ACTIVE TIME: 15 MINUTES / TOTAL TIME: 1 HOUR

The recommended amount of chile powder here is the bare minimum—go with as much as you can bear, as all the sweetness here cries out for spice.

1. Preheat the oven to 400°F and coat a baking sheet with olive oil. Place the sweet potato, cut side down, and the onion on the baking sheet. Place the garlic in a small piece of aluminum foil, sprinkle a few drops of oil on them, wrap them up, and place on the baking sheet.

2. Place the baking sheet in the oven and roast for approximately 20 minutes, then remove the garlic. Roast the sweet potato and onion until the sweet potato is very tender, another 10 minutes or so. Remove from the oven and let cool.

3. Scoop the sweet potato's flesh into a food processor. Add the roasted onion, garlic, tahini, lemon juice, and salt. Pulse until the mixture is a smooth paste. Taste and adjust the seasoning as necessary.

4. Place the honey in a very small pot and warm it over low heat. Add the ancho chile powder, remove the pan from heat, and let it sit for a few minutes.

5. Place the puree in a shallow bowl and make a well in the center. Pour some of spiced honey in the well, garnish with the chopped pistachios, and enjoy.

INGREDIENTS:

	EXTRA-VIRGIN OLIVE OIL, AS NEEDED
1	SWEET POTATO, HALVED
1	YELLOW ONION, QUARTERED
2	LARGE GARLIC CLOVES
¼	CUP TAHINI PASTE
1	TEASPOON FRESH LEMON JUICE
½	TEASPOON KOSHER SALT
2	TABLESPOONS HONEY
½	TEASPOON ANCHO CHILE POWDER
1	TABLESPOON MINCED PISTACHIOS, FOR GARNISH

SWORDFISH CRUDO

YIELD: 2 SERVINGS / **ACTIVE TIME:** 15 MINUTES / **TOTAL TIME:** 30 MINUTES

The meaty, mild flavor of swordfish makes this a good dish to serve at a summer dinner party where you're unsure of everyone's stance on seafood.

1. Chill a plate in the refrigerator for 10 minutes.

2. Slice the swordfish thin against the grain and arrange the slices on the chilled plate, making sure they do not overlap.

3. Season the fish generously with salt, then sprinkle the pepper and lemon juice over it. Drizzle the olive oil over the top and sprinkle the scallions over the fish.

4. Arrange the jalapeño and tomato on the side of the plate and chill in the refrigerator until ready to serve.

INGREDIENTS:

4   OZ. SUSHI-GRADE SWORDFISH

     SALT, TO TASTE

1   TEASPOON BLACK PEPPER

     JUICE OF ½ LEMON

1   TABLESPOON EXTRA-VIRGIN OLIVE OIL

1   TABLESPOON SLICED SCALLIONS

4   SLICES OF JALAPEÑO CHILE PEPPER

3   SLICES OF TOMATO

Swordfish Crudo, see page 107

CHEESY POOFS

YIELD: 4 SERVINGS / ACTIVE TIME: 15 MINUTES / TOTAL TIME: 45 MINUTES

The cheese, creamy potatoes, and fried goodness are more than enough to make this a treasured preparation—the bit of smoke in the potato puree makes it a transcendent one.

1. Add canola oil to a Dutch oven until it is 3 inches deep and warm to 350°F over medium heat.

2. Place the potato puree and egg in a mixing bowl. Add the flour and baking powder and stir until the mixture is smooth.

3. Add the cheeses one at a time and fold to incorporate.

4. Form tablespoons of the mixture into balls and gently slip them into the oil. Turn the balls as they cook until they are golden brown. Remove and drain on a paper towel–lined plate before enjoying.

INGREDIENTS:

CANOLA OIL, AS NEEDED

2 CUPS SMOKED POTATO PUREE (SEE PAGE 396)

1 EGG

½ CUP ALL-PURPOSE FLOUR

½ TEASPOON BAKING POWDER

¼ CUP FRESHLY GRATED ASIAGO CHEESE

¼ CUP FRESHLY GRATED PARMESAN CHEESE

⅓ CUP SHREDDED MOZZARELLA CHEESE

FRIED EGGPLANT WITH GARLIC & RAS EL HANOUT

YIELD: 4 SERVINGS / **ACTIVE TIME:** 30 MINUTES / **TOTAL TIME:** 1 HOUR

A perfect example of decadent simplicity. Fried eggplant is enhanced with pungent garlic and earthy cumin to create this favorite. This is also good when made on a charcoal grill.

1. Sprinkle both sides of the eggplant with the salt, place the slices on a baking sheet in a single layer, and let them rest for 30 minutes.

2. Add avocado oil to a Dutch oven until it is 1 inch deep and warm it over high heat. Pat the eggplant dry with paper towels.

3. When the oil is sizzling, gently slip about five eggplant slices into the pan and fry until golden brown on both sides, 7 to 10 minutes, turning as needed. Transfer the fried eggplant to a paper towel–lined baking sheet and then repeat with the remaining slices.

4. Arrange the fried eggplant on a large platter, sprinkle the garlic and Ras el Hanout on top, drizzle the salsa verde over it, and enjoy.

INGREDIENTS:

1	MEDIUM EGGPLANT, CUT INTO ½-INCH-THICK SLICES
½	TEASPOON KOSHER SALT
	AVOCADO OIL, AS NEEDED
4	GARLIC CLOVES, MINCED
1	TEASPOON GROUND RAS EL HANOUT (SEE PAGE 747)
2	TABLESPOONS GRILLED SERRANO SALSA VERDE (SEE PAGE 798)

FRIED EGGPLANT WITH MINT VINAIGRETTE

YIELD: 4 SERVINGS / ACTIVE TIME: 15 MINUTES / TOTAL TIME: 45 MINUTES

Any heaviness from the richness of fried eggplant is offset by the light and refreshing mint vinaigrette.

1. Sprinkle both sides of the eggplants with the tablespoon of salt, place the slices on a baking sheet in a single layer, and let them rest for 30 minutes.

2. Add avocado oil to a Dutch oven until it is 1 inch deep and warm it over high heat. Pat the eggplants dry with paper towels.

3. When the oil is sizzling, gently slip about five eggplant slices into the pan and fry until golden brown on both sides, 7 to 10 minutes, turning as needed. Transfer the fried eggplant to a paper towel–lined baking sheet and then repeat with the remaining slices.

4. In a bowl, combine the pomegranate molasses, olive oil, mint, Ras el Hanout, remaining salt, and the pepper.

5. Arrange the fried eggplants on a large platter, drizzle the vinaigrette over them, sprinkle the pomegranate seeds on top, and enjoy.

INGREDIENTS:

- 2   MEDIUM EGGPLANTS, SLICED INTO ¼-INCH-THICK PIECES
- 1   TABLESPOON PLUS 1 TEASPOON KOSHER SALT
-     AVOCADO OIL, AS NEEDED
- 2   TABLESPOONS POMEGRANATE MOLASSES
- ⅓   CUP EXTRA-VIRGIN OLIVE OIL
- 1   CUP CHOPPED FRESH MINT LEAVES
- 1   TEASPOON RAS EL HANOUT (SEE PAGE 747)
- ¼   TEASPOON BLACK PEPPER
- 1   TABLESPOON POMEGRANATE SEEDS, FOR GARNISH

GOAT CHEESE, OLIVE & FENNEL
PHYLLO TRIANGLES

YIELD: 16 SERVINGS / **ACTIVE TIME:** 30 MINUTES / **TOTAL TIME:** 1 HOUR AND 30 MINUTES

Incorporating some Pernod into the filling ensures that the anise-flavor is at its best.

1. Place the olive oil in a medium saucepan and warm it over medium heat. Add the fennel and cook, stirring occasionally, until it has softened and is starting to brown, about 8 minutes.

2. Add the garlic and cook, stirring continually, until fragrant, about 1 minute. Add the white wine, Pernod, and raisins and cook until the liquid has evaporated, about 5 minutes. Remove the pan from heat and let it cool for 5 minutes.

3. Place the olives, goat cheese, chives, lemon zest, and lemon juice in a mixing bowl and stir to combine. Add the fennel mixture, fold to combine, and season the mixture with salt and pepper. Set the filling aside.

4. Preheat the oven to 425°F. Line a baking sheet with parchment paper. Place a piece of parchment paper on a work surface. Lay one sheet of phyllo on the parchment and brush it with some of the butter. Lay another sheet of phyllo on top and gently press down. Brush the phyllo with butter and then cut the rectangle into 2-inch-wide strips. Make sure to cover the rest of the phyllo dough so that it does not dry out.

5. Place 2 teaspoons of the filling at the bottom of each strip and shape the filling into a triangle. Taking care to maintain that triangle shape, roll up the strip, as if you were folding a flag. Crimp the folded-up pastries to seal them and place them, seam side down, on the baking sheet.

6. Repeat Steps 4 and 5 until you have 16 filled pastries.

7. Sprinkle the sesame seeds over the pastries, place them in the oven, and bake until golden brown, about 10 minutes.

8. Remove from the oven and let the pastries cool before serving.

INGREDIENTS:

1	TABLESPOON EXTRA-VIRGIN OLIVE OIL
½	FENNEL BULB, TRIMMED, CORED, AND CHOPPED
2	GARLIC CLOVES, MINCED
6	TABLESPOONS WHITE WINE
1	TABLESPOON PERNOD
1	TABLESPOON MINCED RAISINS
6	GREEN OLIVES, PITS REMOVED, MINCED
1	CUP CRUMBLED GOAT CHEESE
1	TABLESPOON FINELY CHOPPED FRESH CHIVES
1	TEASPOON LEMON ZEST
1	TEASPOON LEMON JUICE
	SALT AND PEPPER, TO TASTE
½	LB. FROZEN PHYLLO DOUGH, THAWED
6	TABLESPOONS UNSALTED BUTTER, MELTED
1	TABLESPOON BLACK SESAME SEEDS

POMEGRANATE-GLAZED FIGS & CHEESE

YIELD: 4 SERVINGS / ACTIVE TIME: 35 MINUTES / TOTAL TIME: 1 HOUR

A combination of simple, mouthwatering ingredients. This dish balances the creamy richness of the cheese and the candy sweetness of the figs with a tart pomegranate glaze.

1. Place the pomegranate juice, fennel seeds, peppercorns, bay leaf, and salt in a small saucepan and simmer the mixture over medium-high heat until it has been reduced to ⅓ cup.

2. Strain and let the glaze cool completely.

3. In a bowl, combine the cheeses. Add 1 tablespoon of the glaze and season the mixture with salt and the pepper. Place the mixture in a pastry bag that has been fitted with a plain ½-inch tip and set it aside.

4. Preheat the broiler on the oven. Cut the figs in half from tip to stem and place them in a heatproof dish, cut side up. Brush the cut sides with some of the glaze and dust with the caster sugar.

5. Pipe a ½-inch-wide and 6-inch-long strip of the cheese mixture on four plates.

6. Place the figs under the broiler until glazed and just warmed through, about 5 minutes.

7. To serve, arrange six fig halves on top of each strip of cheese, garnish with pomegranate seeds, and drizzle any remaining glaze over the top.

INGREDIENTS:

2 CUPS POMEGRANATE JUICE

1 TEASPOON FENNEL SEEDS

1 TEASPOON BLACK PEPPERCORNS

1 BAY LEAF

PINCH OF KOSHER SALT, PLUS MORE TO TASTE

½ CUP RICOTTA CHEESE

½ CUP MASCARPONE CHEESE

⅛ TEASPOON FRESHLY GROUND BLACK PEPPER

12 FRESH FIGS

1 TEASPOON CASTER SUGAR (SUPERFINE)

POMEGRANATE SEEDS, FOR GARNISH

FRIED ARTICHOKES

YIELD: 8 SERVINGS / ACTIVE TIME: 1 HOUR AND 15 MINUTES / TOTAL TIME: 2 HOURS

A preparation that accentuates the nutty flavor of artichokes like no other.

1. Prepare an ice bath in a large bowl. Squeeze two lemons into the ice bath, stir, and then throw the spent lemon halves into the ice bath. This lemon water will keep the artichokes fresh and green until you're ready to fry them. Keep a couple of fresh lemon halves on hand as you prep.

2. Rinse the artichokes under cold water. Pat them dry with a linen towel or paper towels. Using kitchen shears, remove the thorny tips from the leaves. For each artichoke, remove the bitter, fibrous end of the stem with a knife, leaving about 1½ inches of stem attached to each artichoke.

3. Using a serrated knife, peel the outer skin from the remaining stem. As the stem is more bitter than the rest of the artichoke, removing the skin tempers the bitterness. Rub the peeled stem with fresh lemon to keep it from browning.

4. Peel off 5 or 6 layers of external leaves from each artichoke, snapping off the leaves and setting them aside, until you reach inner leaves that are fresh looking and white at their base.

5. Using a serrated knife or sharp chef's knife, slice each artichoke horizontally, about ¾ inch above the base (aka the heart), and remove the pointy top of the artichoke, leaving a flat crown of leaves at the base of the artichoke while exposing the purple inner leaves.

6. Slice the artichokes in half lengthwise, splitting the stem and heart to reveal the fuzzy choke.

7. Scoop out the white spines and purple leaves from each artichoke half with a melon baller, leaving two hollowed-out halves of the heart with a small crown of flat leaves.

8. Rub the artichokes with lemon and place them in the ice bath.

9. Remove the artichoke halves from the lemon water. Pour the ice bath and spent lemon halves into a large saucepan. You will need about 1½ inches of water to steam the artichokes, so add more water if needed.

INGREDIENTS:

5   LEMONS, HALVED

4   LARGE ARTICHOKES

AVOCADO OIL, AS NEEDED

SALT AND PEPPER, TO TASTE

Continued . . .

10. Place a steaming tray inside the pan and bring the water to a boil. Place the cleaned artichoke halves in the steaming tray and cover the pan. Reduce the heat to medium and steam the artichokes until the thickest part of the stem is just tender, 15 to 20 minutes. You want the artichokes to still be a bit firm—they should only be partially cooked.

11. Place the steamed artichokes on a paper towel–lined plate and let them dry completely.

12. Add avocado oil to a cast-iron skillet until it is 1 inch deep and warm it to 325°F. Season the artichokes with salt and pepper, making sure to season between the layers of leaves as well.

13. Gently slip the artichokes into the hot oil and fry them until the leaves are crispy and golden brown, about 15 minutes, turning the artichokes as needed.

14. Remove the artichokes from the oil, transfer to a paper towel–lined plate, and let them drain before serving.

MARINATED OLIVES

YIELD: 8 SERVINGS / ACTIVE TIME: 20 MINUTES / TOTAL TIME: 3 HOURS

The recipe for marinating is just the beginning. Once you feel comfortable with the process, you can begin adding an assortment of different herbs and spices to make it all your own.

1. Rinse any dark olives under cold water so their juices don't discolor the other olives. Place all of the olives in a colander and drain them. Transfer the olives to a wide-mouthed jar and set them aside.

2. Warm a dry skillet over medium-high heat. Add the coriander and fennel seeds and toast until very fragrant, about 2 minutes, stirring occasionally. Add the olive oil and vinegar and cook for 1 minute.

3. Remove the pan from heat and add all of the remaining ingredients. Stir to combine and let the mixture cool completely.

4. Pour the marinade over the olives, cover, and shake the jar so that the olives are evenly coated.

5. Chill the olives in the refrigerator for 2 hours before serving. If preparing the olives a few days ahead of time, shake the jar daily to redistribute the seasonings.

INGREDIENTS:

- 1½ LBS. ASSORTED OLIVES
- 2 TEASPOONS LIGHTLY CRACKED CORIANDER SEEDS
- 1 TEASPOON LIGHTLY CRACKED FENNEL SEEDS
- ¾ CUP EXTRA-VIRGIN OLIVE OIL
- 2 TABLESPOONS RED WINE VINEGAR
- 4 GARLIC CLOVES, SLICED THIN
- 1½ TEASPOONS CHOPPED FRESH ROSEMARY
- 1½ TEASPOONS FRESH THYME
- 4 BAY LEAVES, TORN
- 1 SMALL DRIED RED CHILE PEPPER, STEM AND SEEDS REMOVED, CHOPPED
- 2 STRIPS OF LEMON ZEST

SWEET POTATO & TAHINI DIP WITH ZA'ATAR

YIELD: 8 SERVINGS / **ACTIVE TIME:** 15 MINUTES / **TOTAL TIME:** 1 HOUR AND 15 MINUTES

The base of this dip is so simple—but the homemade Za'atar really helps the flavors stand out.

1. Preheat the oven to 400°F. Place the sesame seeds in a dry skillet and toast them over low heat until fragrant, about 3 minutes, shaking the pan as necessary.

2. Transfer the toasted sesame seeds to a bowl, add the thyme, sumac, and salt, and stir to combine. Set the mixture aside.

3. Pierce the sweet potatoes all over with a fork and wrap them in foil. Place the sweet potatoes on a baking sheet and roast until fork-tender, about 1 hour. Remove from the oven, remove from the foil, and let the sweet potatoes cool completely.

4. Peel the sweet potatoes and place them in a food processor, along with the tahini, water, lemon juice, lime zest, hot sauce, pepper, and 2 tablespoons of the sesame seed mixture. Puree until smooth.

5. Taste, adjust the seasoning as necessary, and transfer the dip to a serving bowl. Drizzle the olive oil on top, sprinkle the remaining sesame seed mixture and Za'atar over it, and enjoy.

INGREDIENTS:

1 TABLESPOON BLACK SESAME SEEDS

1 TABLESPOON FRESH THYME

1 TABLESPOON SUMAC

¼ TEASPOON KOSHER SALT, PLUS MORE TO TASTE

1 LB. SWEET POTATOES

2 TABLESPOONS TAHINI PASTE

2 TABLESPOONS WATER

1 TABLESPOON FRESH LEMON JUICE

1 TEASPOON LIME ZEST

3 DASHES OF TABASCO

BLACK PEPPER, TO TASTE

1 TEASPOON EXTRA-VIRGIN OLIVE OIL

1 TABLESPOON ZA'ATAR (SEE PAGE 766)

ENTREES

In the Mediterranean region, a main course satisfies without overwhelming, manages to comfort without also being so rich that the rest of the evening is unpleasant. This increasingly rare approach is indebted to the incredible bounty that Mother Nature has made available in the area, a bit of good fortune that organically leads to a diet that is far more balanced than it would be in other areas of the world, featuring copious amounts of vegetables, seafood as much if not more than the poultry that is ubiquitous on dinner tables in the Americas, and little, if any, beef.

However, these inclinations are not exclusive. Whatever one has a hankering for, whatever a particular situation calls for, whatever you have in the refrigerator that needs to be utilized, you are sure to find a solution here.

EASY PAELLA

YIELD: 4 TO 6 SERVINGS / ACTIVE TIME: 30 MINUTES / TOTAL TIME: 1 HOUR AND 30 MINUTES

Making paella the traditional way is demanding, as much a sacred ritual as it is a meal. This method is much easier, and just as delicious.

1. Preheat the oven to 350°F. Place the olive oil in a Dutch oven and warm it over medium-high heat. Add the chicken and cook until browned all over, about 6 minutes, stirring as necessary. Remove the chicken thighs with a slotted spoon and place them in a bowl.

2. Add the chorizo to the pot and cook, stirring occasionally, until it is browned all over, about 6 minutes, breaking it up with a wooden spoon. Transfer the chorizo to the bowl with the chicken.

3. Add the onion to the pot and cook, stirring occasionally, until it has softened, about 5 minutes. Add the pepper and cook, stirring occasionally, for 3 minutes.

4. Add the garlic and cook, stirring frequently, for 1 minute. Stir in the tomatoes and cook until the mixture thickens slightly, about 3 minutes. Add the rice and cook for 2 minutes.

5. Stir in the stock, wine, saffron, paprika, and bay leaves and bring the mixture to a boil, stirring frequently. Return the chicken and chorizo to the pot, season the mixture with salt and pepper, cover the pot, and place it in the oven.

6. Bake until all the liquid has evaporated, about 15 minutes, stirring occasionally.

7. Remove the pot from the oven and place the mussels and shrimp on top of the rice. Make sure to put the mussels in the rice so that their hinges are facing down. Cover the pot and return it to the oven. Bake until the shrimp are cooked through and the majority of the mussels have opened, about 10 minutes.

8. Remove the paella from the oven, discard the bay leaves and any mussels that did not open, and garnish with parsley. Serve with lemon wedges and enjoy.

INGREDIENTS:

2	TABLESPOONS EXTRA-VIRGIN OLIVE OIL
1½	LBS. BONELESS, SKINLESS CHICKEN THIGHS, CHOPPED INTO 1-INCH CUBES
9	OZ. GROUND CHORIZO
1	ONION, CHOPPED
1	RED BELL PEPPER, STEM AND SEEDS REMOVED, CHOPPED
6	GARLIC CLOVES, MINCED
1	(14 OZ.) CAN OF DICED TOMATOES, DRAINED
2	CUPS BOMBA RICE
4	CUPS CHICKEN STOCK (SEE PAGE 368)
⅓	CUP WHITE WINE
½	TEASPOON SAFFRON
1	TEASPOON PAPRIKA
2	BAY LEAVES
	SALT AND PEPPER, TO TASTE
16	MUSSELS, SCRUBBED AND DEBEARDED
1	LB. JUMBO SHRIMP, SHELLS REMOVED, DEVEINED
¾	CUP FROZEN PEAS
	FRESH PARSLEY, CHOPPED, FOR GARNISH
	LEMON WEDGES, FOR SERVING

RATATOUILLE WITH POACHED EGGS

YIELD: 6 SERVINGS / **ACTIVE TIME:** 30 MINUTES / **TOTAL TIME:** 1 HOUR

If you are someone who loves nothing more than spending a summer day in the garden, this simple, beautiful dish allows you to make the most of your labors.

1. Place the olive oil in a Dutch oven and warm it over medium heat. Add the onion and cook, stirring occasionally, until it has softened, about 5 minutes. Add the garlic and tomato paste and cook, stirring continually, for 1 minute.

2. Add the bell peppers and cook, stirring occasionally, until they have softened, about 5 minutes.

3. Add the zucchini, water, and herbes de Provence, cover the pot, and cook for 10 minutes. Remove the cover and cook until the liquid has reduced, about 5 minutes.

4. Season the ratatouille with salt and pepper. Using the back of a wooden spoon, make six wells in the ratatouille. Gently crack an egg into each well, reduce the heat so that the ratatouille simmers, and cover the pot. Cook until the egg whites are set, 6 to 8 minutes.

5. Spoon the ratatouille and poached eggs into bowls, garnish each portion with basil and Parmesan, and enjoy.

INGREDIENTS:

¼ CUP EXTRA-VIRGIN OLIVE OIL

1 CUP CHOPPED ONION

4 GARLIC CLOVES, MINCED

2 TABLESPOONS TOMATO PASTE

1 CUP CHOPPED RED BELL PEPPER

1 CUP CHOPPED YELLOW BELL PEPPER

1 CUP CHOPPED ZUCCHINI

½ CUP WATER

2 TABLESPOONS HERBES DE PROVENCE

SALT AND PEPPER, TO TASTE

6 EGGS

¼ CUP FRESH BASIL, FOR GARNISH

½ CUP SHAVED PARMESAN CHEESE, FOR GARNISH

CHICKEN B'STILLA

YIELD: 4 TO 6 SERVINGS / ACTIVE TIME: 1 HOUR / TOTAL TIME: 2 HOURS AND 30 MINUTES

Morocco's take on chicken pot pie is sure to become your favorite spin on the comforting classic.

1. Place 1 tablespoon of the olive oil in a medium saucepan and warm it over medium heat. Add the onions and salt and cook, stirring occasionally, until the onions start to soften, about 5 minutes.

2. Add the garlic, ginger, turmeric, and paprika and cook, stirring continually, until fragrant, about 1 minute. Add the water and bring the mixture to a boil.

3. Reduce the heat so that mixture simmers and add the chicken. Cook until the chicken can be shredded, about 15 minutes. Remove the chicken, shred it, and let it cool.

4. Reduce the heat to low, add the eggs in a slow drizzle, and cook until they are just set, 2 to 3 minutes.

5. Remove the pan from heat, fold in the shredded chicken, cilantro, and parsley, and let the mixture cool.

6. Preheat the oven to 375°F. Place the almonds, 1½ tablespoons of the confectioners' sugar, and half of the cinnamon in a bowl and stir until combined.

7. Brush a medium cast-iron skillet with some of the remaining olive oil. Lay one sheet of the phyllo in the pan, letting it hang over the sides, and brush it with olive oil. Lay another sheet on top, 2 inches to the right of where you laid the first one. Brush it with olive oil and repeat with eight more sheets of phyllo. Make sure to keep any sheets of phyllo that you are not working with covered so that they do not dry out.

8. Spread the almond mixture over the layer of phyllo. Pour the egg mixture on top of the nuts and use a rubber spatula to spread it into an even layer.

9. Place a piece of parchment paper on a work surface. Place a sheet of phyllo in the center of the parchment and brush it with olive oil. Repeat with three more sheets of phyllo dough. After brushing the top sheet with olive oil, fold the stack of phyllo like a book.

10. Lay this stack of phyllo on top of the egg mixture and fold any overhanging phyllo over the top. Combine the remaining confectioners' sugar and cinnamon and sprinkle this mixture over the phyllo.

11. Place the pan in the oven and bake until the b'stilla is crispy and golden brown, about 40 minutes. Remove the b'stilla from the oven and let it cool briefly before serving.

INGREDIENTS:

- ¼ CUP EXTRA-VIRGIN OLIVE OIL
- 1 CUP CHOPPED ONIONS
- ½ TEASPOON KOSHER SALT
- 1 GARLIC CLOVE, MINCED
- 2 TEASPOONS GRATED FRESH GINGER
- ¼ TEASPOON TURMERIC
- ½ TEASPOON PAPRIKA
- 2 CUPS WATER
- 1 LB. BONELESS, SKINLESS CHICKEN THIGHS, CUT INTO ½-INCH-WIDE STRIPS
- 4 EGGS, BEATEN
- 2 TABLESPOONS CHOPPED FRESH CILANTRO
- 2 TABLESPOONS CHOPPED FRESH PARSLEY
- ¾ CUP SLIVERED ALMONDS, TOASTED
- 2 TABLESPOONS CONFECTIONERS' SUGAR
- 2 TEASPOONS CINNAMON
- ½ LB. FROZEN PHYLLO DOUGH, THAWED

BRAISED PORK WITH GREEK SALAD & SKORDALIA

YIELD: 6 SERVINGS / **ACTIVE TIME:** 45 MINUTES / **TOTAL TIME:** 2 HOURS

As the olive flavor comes through well in this dish, I would recommend going without them in the salad, unless you're an absolute olive fanatic.

1. Preheat the oven to 300°F. Place 1 tablespoon of the olive oil in a Dutch oven and warm it over medium heat. Season the pork with salt and pepper. Working in batches to avoid crowding the pot, add the pork and cook until it is browned all over, about 8 minutes, turning it as necessary. Transfer the browned pork to a paper towel–lined plate to drain.

2. Add the remaining olive oil and the onions to the pot and cook, stirring occasionally, until they have softened, about 5 minutes. Add the celery and carrot and cook, stirring occasionally, for 3 minutes.

3. Add the thyme and garlic and cook, stirring continually, for 1 minute. Add the white wine and cook until the alcohol has been cooked off, about 3 minutes. Add the tomatoes, olives, stock, bay leaf, and oregano, return the pork to the pot, and bring the mixture to a simmer.

4. Cover the Dutch oven and place it in the oven. Braise the pork until it is extremely tender and almost falling apart, about 2 hours.

5. Remove the pork from the oven and serve it alongside the Skordalia and Greek Salad.

SKORDALIA

1. Bring water to a boil in a medium saucepan. Add the potatoes, reduce the heat, and simmer the potatoes until they are fork-tender, 15 to 20 minutes. Drain the potatoes and let them cool until they have stopped steaming.

2. Place the garlic, vinegar, bread, and water in a mixing bowl, stir to combine, and let the mixture sit for 5 minutes.

3. Using a fork, mash the bread mixture until it is smooth. Use a potato ricer or a fork to mash the potatoes, add them to the bowl, and stir until the mixture is smooth.

4. Stir in the olive oil and the yogurt, season the sauce with salt and pepper, and use as desired.

INGREDIENTS:

2	TABLESPOONS EXTRA-VIRGIN OLIVE OIL
2	LBS. BONELESS PORK SHOULDER, CUT INTO 1-INCH CUBES
	SALT AND PEPPER, TO TASTE
2	ONIONS, CHOPPED
1	CELERY STALK, CHOPPED
1	CARROT, PEELED AND CUT INTO THIN HALF-MOONS
1	TEASPOON FRESH THYME
2	GARLIC CLOVES, MINCED
¾	CUP WHITE WINE
1	(14 OZ.) CAN OF DICED TOMATOES, DRAINED
½	CUP KALAMATA OLIVES, PITS REMOVED
4	CUPS CHICKEN STOCK (SEE PAGE 368)
1	BAY LEAF
1	TABLESPOON DRIED OREGANO
	SKORDALIA (SEE RECIPE), FOR SERVING
	GREEK SALAD (SEE PAGE 451), FOR SERVING

SKORDALIA

2	CUPS PEELED AND CHOPPED YELLOW POTATOES (½-INCH CUBES)
4	GARLIC CLOVES, GRATED OR MASHED
2	TABLESPOONS RED WINE VINEGAR
1	CUP DAY-OLD BREAD PIECES
½	CUP WARM WATER (105°F)
2	TABLESPOONS EXTRA-VIRGIN OLIVE OIL
3	TABLESPOONS FULL-FAT GREEK YOGURT
	SALT AND PEPPER, TO TASTE

STUFFED MACKEREL

YIELD: 2 SERVINGS / ACTIVE TIME: 30 MINUTES / TOTAL TIME: 1 HOUR AND 15 MINUTES

Consider preparing this on the grill, as mackerel is a relatively oily fish that will soak up a good deal of the smoke.

1. Preheat the oven to 450°F. Place 1 tablespoon of the olive oil in a large skillet and warm it over medium-high heat. Add the onion and peppers and cook, stirring occasionally, until they are browned, about 8 minutes.

2. Add the garlic and thyme and cook, stirring constantly, for 1 minute. Remove the pan from heat and fold in the olives, lemon zest, lemon juice, parsley, and panko. Season the stuffing with salt and pepper and set it aside.

3. Coat a baking sheet with the remaining olive oil. Place the mackerel on the baking sheet and season the insides of the fish with salt and pepper. Fill the fish with the stuffing and then use kitchen twine to tie the fish closed.

4. Sprinkle salt and pepper over the fish, place them in the oven, and roast until they are cooked through (internal temperature of about 135°F), about 10 minutes.

5. Remove the fish from the oven, cut off the kitchen twine, and serve with the Braised Green Beans.

INGREDIENTS:

2	TABLESPOONS EXTRA-VIRGIN OLIVE OIL
½	RED ONION, CHOPPED
½	RED BELL PEPPER, CHOPPED
½	GREEN BELL PEPPER, CHOPPED
2	GARLIC CLOVES, MINCED
1	TEASPOON FRESH THYME
¼	CUP CHOPPED GREEN OLIVES
	ZEST AND JUICE OF 1 LEMON
1	TABLESPOON CHOPPED FRESH PARSLEY
¼	CUP PANKO, TOASTED
	SALT AND PEPPER, TO TASTE
2	(10 OZ.) MACKEREL, GUTTED, CLEANED, AND BUTTERFLIED
	BRAISED GREEN BEANS (SEE PAGE 496), FOR SERVING

'NDUJA SHAKSHUKA

YIELD: 6 SERVINGS / **ACTIVE TIME**: 25 MINUTES / **TOTAL TIME**: 40 MINUTES

'Nduja is a spicy, spreadable sausage from Calabria that adds deep flavors and warmth to any dish it appears in.

1. In a food processor, combine olive oil and garlic and blitz until pureed.

2. Place the puree in a large, deep skillet and warm it over medium-high heat. After about 2 minutes, add the onions and cook, stirring occasionally, until they are translucent, about 3 minutes.

3. Add the 'nduja and cook, stirring occasionally, until it starts to brown, about 2 minutes. Stir in the tomatoes, salt, pepper, cumin, paprika, and chile, cover the pan, and let the mixture simmer for 15 minutes, stirring only if it seems like the bottom may be burning. If the tomatoes don't produce enough liquid to keep the bottom from burning, add water in ¼-cup increments.

4. Reduce the heat to medium and let the mixture simmer until the flavor has developed to your liking.

5. Sprinkle the goat cheese over the shakshuka. Make six indentations in the sauce and crack an egg into each one. Cover the pan and cook until the egg whites are set, 3 to 4 minutes.

6. Sprinkle the parsley over the top and enjoy.

INGREDIENTS:

½	CUP EXTRA-VIRGIN OLIVE OIL
8	GARLIC CLOVES
2	YELLOW ONIONS
6	OZ. 'NDUJA
6	TOMATOES, EACH CUT INTO 8 WEDGES
1	TABLESPOON KOSHER SALT
1	TEASPOON BLACK PEPPER
2	TEASPOONS CUMIN
1	TABLESPOON PAPRIKA
1	CHILE PEPPER, STEM AND SEEDS REMOVED, DICED
4	OZ. GOAT CHEESE, CRUMBLED
6	LARGE EGGS
1	BUNCH OF FRESH PARSLEY, CHOPPED, FOR TOPPING

RISI E BISI

YIELD: 4 SERVINGS / **ACTIVE TIME:** 30 MINUTES / **TOTAL TIME:** 2 HOURS AND 30 MINUTES

This rice dish can easily be made into a risotto or a soup, based on the amount of broth you want to use.

1. Place the olive oil in a large saucepan and warm it over medium-high heat. Add the prosciutto and cook, stirring frequently, until it is golden brown and crispy, about 5 minutes. Using a slotted spoon, transfer the prosciutto to a paper towel–lined plate and let it drain.

2. Add the shallots to the saucepan and cook, stirring occasionally, until they start to soften, about 3 minutes.

3. Add the garlic and rice and cook, stirring frequently, for 2 minutes.

4. Add the white wine and cook, stirring frequently, until the rice has absorbed the wine.

5. While stirring continually, add the broth ¼ cup at a time, waiting until each addition has been fully absorbed before adding more. Add broth until the rice is tender, about 15 minutes.

6. Add the peas and cook, stirring frequently, until warmed through, 4 to 5 minutes.

7. Stir in the Parmesan and lemon juice. Season the dish with salt and pepper, garnish with the crispy prosciutto and parsley, and enjoy.

PEA BROTH

1. Place the olive oil in a medium saucepan and warm it over medium-high heat. Add the pancetta and cook, stirring frequently, until it is golden brown, about 5 minutes.

2. Add the onion and cook, stirring occasionally, until it starts to soften, about 5 minutes. Add the garlic and cook, stirring continually, for 1 minute.

3. Add the remaining ingredients and bring the broth to a boil. Reduce the heat and simmer the broth for 30 minutes.

4. Strain the broth through a fine-mesh sieve and use as desired.

INGREDIENTS:

2	TABLESPOONS EXTRA-VIRGIN OLIVE OIL
6	OZ. THINLY SLICED PROSCIUTTO, CUT INTO ¼-INCH-WIDE STRIPS
2	SHALLOTS, MINCED
1	GARLIC CLOVES, MINCED
1	CUP ARBORIO RICE
½	CUP WHITE WINE
	PEA BROTH (SEE RECIPE), AS NEEDED
1	LB. FROZEN PEAS
1	CUP FRESHLY GRATED PARMESAN CHEESE
	JUICE OF ½ LEMON
	SALT AND PEPPER, TO TASTE
	FRESH PARSLEY, CHOPPED, FOR GARNISH

PEA BROTH

1	TABLESPOON EXTRA-VIRGIN OLIVE OIL
4	OZ. PANCETTA, CHOPPED
1	ONION, CHOPPED
2	GARLIC CLOVES, MINCED
1	CUP FROZEN PEAS
6	CUPS WATER
1	TEASPOON KOSHER SALT

LAMB SHANKS WITH POMEGRANATE SAUCE

YIELD: 4 SERVINGS / ACTIVE TIME: 30 MINUTES / TOTAL TIME: 2 HOURS AND 30 MINUTES

As if lamb wasn't already succulent enough, the extra layer of fat around each shank adds even more richness when cooked. The pomegranate packs a tart punch, making this recipe layered and sophisticated.

1. Preheat the oven to 350°F. Season the lamb shanks with salt and pepper.

2. Place the avocado oil in a Dutch oven and warm it over medium-high heat. Add the lamb shanks and cook until they are browned on all sides, taking care to stand them on their edges and brown those sides as well.

3. Remove the lamb shanks from the pot and set them aside. Add the onion and garlic, reduce the heat to medium, and cook, stirring frequently, until the onion has softened slightly, about 5 minutes. Add the spices, tomato paste, wine, and stock and cook, stirring continuously, for 5 minutes.

4. Return the lamb shanks to the pot, cover it, and place it in the oven. Roast the lamb shanks for 2 hours, checking them every 30 minutes, and turning them over in the sauce each time you check them.

5. When the lamb is nearly done cooking, about 1½ hours, stir in the pomegranate juice. Cook for another 30 minutes longer, until the meat on the shanks is very tender, to the point of nearly falling off the bone.

6. The sauce will be thick and concentrated; if desired, thin it with a little water. Spoon the sauce over the lamb shanks and serve with rice or couscous.

INGREDIENTS:

4	LAMB SHANKS (ABOUT 1 LB. EACH)
	SALT AND PEPPER, TO TASTE
2	TABLESPOONS AVOCADO OIL
1	LARGE ONION, SLICED
6	GARLIC CLOVES, SMASHED
1	TEASPOON CINNAMON
1	TEASPOON CORIANDER
½	TEASPOON GROUND GINGER
1	TEASPOON CUMIN
24	JUNIPER BERRIES
2	TABLESPOONS TOMATO PASTE
1	CUP SWEET RED WINE
2	CUPS BEEF STOCK (SEE PAGE 369)
1	CUP POMEGRANATE JUICE
	RICE OR COUSCOUS, FOR SERVING

KUKU SABZI

YIELD: 4 SERVINGS / ACTIVE TIME: 15 MINUTES / TOTAL TIME: 25 MINUTES

Many variations of this dish exist, but filling it with as many chopped herbs as possible gives it an undeniably unique flavor.

1. In a large bowl, whisk the eggs until smooth. Add the remaining ingredients, except for the oil, and whisk until incorporated.

2. Place the avocado oil in a 10-inch nonstick skillet and warm it over medium-low heat. Pour the egg mixture into the pan and let it cook for 1 to 2 minutes. Reduce the heat to low, cover the pan, and cook until the frittata begins to set and the bottom is lightly golden brown, 7 to 8 minutes. Flip the frittata using a spatula (or slide it onto a plate and invert it back into the pan) and cook until set, 2 to 3 minutes more.

3. Transfer the frittata to a platter, slice, and enjoy.

INGREDIENTS:

4	EGGS
1	TEASPOON CUMIN
1	TEASPOON BLACK PEPPER
1	TEASPOON KOSHER SALT
5	SCALLIONS, TRIMMED AND SLICED THIN
1	CUP CHOPPED FRESH PARSLEY
1	CUP CHOPPED FRESH CILANTRO
1	CUP CHOPPED FRESH DILL
2	TABLESPOONS AVOCADO OIL

Kuku Sabzi, see page 141

CHICKEN IN WALNUT SAUCE
WITH VEGETABLE KEBABS

YIELD: 4 SERVINGS / ACTIVE TIME: 30 MINUTES / TOTAL TIME: 1 HOUR AND 15 MINUTES

This sweet and nutty sauce is a natural for poultry.

1. Place the olive oil in a Dutch oven and warm it over medium-high heat. Season the chicken with salt and pepper, add it to the pot, and cook, stirring occasionally, until it has browned, about 6 minutes.

2. Reduce the heat to medium, add the onion, and cook, stirring occasionally, until it has softened, about 5 minutes. Add the garlic and cook, stirring continually, for 1 minute. Add the white wine and cook until the alcohol has been cooked off, about 3 minutes, scraping up any browned bits from the bottom of the pan.

3. Add the stock, paprika, and cayenne and bring the mixture to a boil. Cover the pot, reduce the heat, and simmer until the chicken is very tender, 10 to 15 minutes.

4. Remove the pan from heat and strain the braising liquid into a bowl. Place the chicken on a cutting board and shred it with a fork.

5. Place the braising liquid, bread, and walnuts in a food processor and puree until the sauce is smooth and thick, adding stock as needed to get the desired consistency.

6. Place the sauce in the Dutch oven, add the chicken breast, and cook until warmed through. Garnish the dish with the chives and serve with the pita and Vegetable Kebabs.

INGREDIENTS:

2 TABLESPOONS EXTRA-VIRGIN OLIVE OIL

1½ LBS. BONELESS, SKINLESS CHICKEN BREASTS, POUNDED THIN AND CUT INTO 1-INCH CUBES

SALT AND PEPPER, TO TASTE

1 ONION, CHOPPED

3 GARLIC CLOVES, MINCED

½ CUP WHITE WINE

4 CUPS CHICKEN STOCK (SEE PAGE 368), PLUS MORE AS NEEDED

1 TABLESPOON PAPRIKA

¼ TEASPOON CAYENNE PEPPER

1 CUP DAY-OLD BREAD PIECES

2 CUPS WALNUTS, TOASTED

FRESH CHIVES, CHOPPED, FOR GARNISH

2 PIECES OF PITA BREAD (SEE PAGE 532), CUT INTO TRIANGLES, FOR SERVING

VEGETABLE KEBABS (SEE PAGE 455), FOR SERVING

MOROCCAN CORNISH HENS
WITH PINE NUT COUSCOUS

YIELD: 8 SERVINGS / ACTIVE TIME: 25 MINUTES / TOTAL TIME: 2 HOURS AND 40 MINUTES

The Cornish hens are massaged with a blend of spices that gives it that distinctive Moroccan flavor. The pine nuts in the couscous add an irresistible texture and richness. If you'd rather, swap in two whole chickens for the Cornish hens.

1. Preheat the oven to 350°F. Prepare the couscous according to the instructions on the package.

2. Place the pine nuts on a rimmed baking sheet, place them in the oven, and toast until golden brown, 8 to 10 minutes. Remove from the oven and set them aside.

3. When the couscous is ready, reserve ½ cup and combine it with 2 tablespoons of the avocado oil. Add the pine nuts to the remaining couscous and fold to incorporate. Season the mixture with salt and set it aside.

4. Place the remaining avocado oil in a large skillet and warm it over medium-high heat. Add the onions and cook, stirring occasionally, until translucent, about 3 minutes. Add the ginger, garlic, mint, cilantro, cumin, paprika, honey, tomatoes, red pepper flakes, and oregano and simmer, stirring occasionally, until the liquid from the tomatoes has reduced slightly.

5. Season the Cornish hens with the pepper and stuff them with the pine nut-and-couscous mixture, making sure to pack it quite firmly. Place the stuffed Cornish hens in large baking dishes.

6. Cover the hens with the warm onion-and-herb sauce and sprinkle the reserved couscous over the top. Cover the baking dishes with aluminum foil, place the Cornish hens in the oven, and roast for 1½ hours.

7. Remove the foil from the baking dishes and roast the Cornish hens until they are cooked through and the couscous on top is crispy, about 45 minutes, basting them on occasion.

8. Remove the Cornish hens from the oven and let them rest for 5 to 10 minutes before serving.

INGREDIENTS:

2	CUPS COUSCOUS
4	OZ. PINE NUTS
3	TABLESPOONS AVOCADO OIL
	SALT, TO TASTE
2	ONIONS, HALVED AND SLICED
1	TEASPOON FRESHLY GRATED GINGER
4	GARLIC CLOVES, CRUSHED
1	TABLESPOON CHOPPED FRESH MINT
1	TABLESPOON CHOPPED FRESH CILANTRO
1	TEASPOON CUMIN
1	TEASPOON PAPRIKA
1	TABLESPOON HONEY
1	(14 OZ.) CAN OF DICED TOMATOES, WITH THEIR LIQUID
1	TEASPOON RED PEPPER FLAKES
1	TEASPOON DRIED OREGANO
8	CORNISH HENS
1	TEASPOON BLACK PEPPER

LEG OF LAMB WITH GARLIC & ROSEMARY

YIELD: 8 SERVINGS / **ACTIVE TIME:** 30 MINUTES / **TOTAL TIME:** 2 HOURS AND 30 MINUTES

A classic recipe to recreate, and pass on through the generations.

1. Coat a roasting pan with olive oil and set it aside. Trim any fatty areas on the leg of lamb so that the fat is within approximately ¼ inch of the meat, keeping in mind that it is better to leave too much fat than too little. Pat the lamb dry and score the remaining fat with a sharp paring knife, making sure not to cut into the flesh.

2. Using a mortar and pestle, grind the garlic and salt into a paste. Add the rosemary, Ras el Hanout, sumac, berbere seasoning, and pepper and stir to combine.

3. Place the lamb in the roasting pan and rub the paste all over it. Let the lamb marinate at room temperature for 30 minutes.

4. Preheat the oven to 350°F and position a rack in the middle.

5. Place the lamb in the oven and roast until an instant-read thermometer inserted about 2 inches into the thickest part of the meat registers 130°F, about 1½ hours.

6. Remove the lamb from the oven, transfer it to a cutting board, and let it rest for 15 to 25 minutes (the internal temperature will rise to about 135°F, perfect for medium-rare).

7. Place the wine or stock in the roasting pan and place it over high heat, scraping up any browned bits from the bottom of the pan. Season the pan sauce with salt and pepper and serve it beside the lamb.

INGREDIENTS:

	EXTRA-VIRGIN OLIVE OIL, AS NEEDED
7	LB. SEMIBONELESS LEG OF LAMB
4	GARLIC CLOVES
1	TABLESPOON KOSHER SALT, PLUS MORE TO TASTE
2	TABLESPOONS CHOPPED FRESH ROSEMARY
2	TABLESPOONS RAS EL HANOUT (SEE PAGE 747)
2	TABLESPOONS SUMAC
2	TABLESPOONS BERBERE SEASONING
½	TEASPOON BLACK PEPPER, PLUS MORE TO TASTE
¼	CUP DRY RED WINE OR BEEF STOCK (SEE PAGE 369)

Leg of Lamb with Garlic & Rosemary, see page 147

FISH & CRISPY RICE CAKE
WITH SAFFRON CRUST

YIELD: 6 SERVINGS / **ACTIVE TIME:** 1 HOUR / **TOTAL TIME:** 25 HOURS

This classical fish preparation defines Moroccan cuisine. Vibrant reds, yellows, and greens are matched with an equally colorful, spicy aroma, and are offset by delicate textures.

1. To begin preparations for the fish, place the Paprika Oil in a large skillet and add the garlic, cilantro stems, bell peppers, and chiles. Place the fish on top and then add the preserved lemons. Pour the Saffron Water over the fish and rub it into the fish. Season with salt and pepper, cover the pan, and refrigerate overnight.

2. To begin preparations for the rice cake, bring 4 cups of water to a boil in a large saucepan. Stir in the rice and 1 teaspoon of salt, reduce the heat to medium-low, cover the pan, and cook for about 9 minutes; you don't want the rice to be fully cooked. Spoon the rice into a fine-mesh sieve placed over a bowl and let it sit until all of the liquid has drained.

3. Place the avocado oil in a large skillet and warm it over medium-high heat. Use a wooden spoon to stir the saffron and paprika into the oil. When the oil starts to sizzle, carefully spoon in the rice, pressing it into the bottom of the pan to form a cake. Reduce the heat to medium, place a few paper towels over the rice, and cover the pan. Cook until the rice cake is nicely browned and crispy, 15 to 20 minutes. Using a spatula, lift the cake occasionally to make sure the rice isn't burning. When the cake is ready, uncover the pan and let the rice cake cool for a few minutes.

4. Remove the paper towels. Carefully invert a large plate over the top of the pan, invert the plate and pan together, and then lift the pan away. Serve right away. The rice cake can also be made up to 1 hour ahead of time and left at room temperature, while covered. Reheat in a 300°F oven before serving.

5. To resume preparations for the fish, remove the pan from the refrigerator, place it over medium-high heat, and cook, covered, for 10 minutes. Reduce the heat to low, sprinkle the cilantro leaves over the fish, and cook, uncovered, until the dish looks bright and bubbly, about 10 minutes. Serve immediately.

INGREDIENTS:

FOR THE FISH

¼	CUP PAPRIKA OIL (SEE PAGE 792)
4	GARLIC CLOVES, QUARTERED
1	BUNCH OF CILANTRO, STEMS RESERVED AND LEFT WHOLE, LEAVES CHOPPED, PLUS MORE FOR GARNISH
2	BELL PEPPERS, SEEDS AND STEMS REMOVED, FINELY DICED
3	DRIED RED CHILE PEPPERS
6	(6 OZ.) GROUPER OR TILAPIA FILLETS
1–2	PRESERVED LEMONS, CUT INTO SMALL PIECES
3	TABLESPOONS SAFFRON WATER (SEE RECIPE)
1	TEASPOON KOSHER SALT
1	TEASPOON BLACK PEPPER

FOR THE RICE CAKE

2	CUPS BASMATI RICE, RINSED WELL AND DRAINED
	SALT, TO TASTE
3	TABLESPOONS AVOCADO OIL
4	SAFFRON THREADS, CRUSHED
1	TEASPOON (HEAPING) SWEET PAPRIKA

SAFFRON WATER

1. Preheat the oven to 425°F. Place the saffron on a small piece of aluminum foil and fold it over to ensure that the saffron is secure inside. Toast in the oven for no more than 1 minute.

2. Remove from the oven and use your fingers to crumble the saffron into tiny pieces. Place the saffron in a small glass jar, pour in the boiling water, and shake until well blended. Set aside and strain before using.

INGREDIENTS:

SAFFRON WATER

1 TABLESPOON SAFFRON

1 CUP BOILING WATER

Mahshi Laban, see page 154

MAHSHI LABAN

YIELD: 6 SERVINGS / **ACTIVE TIME:** 1 HOUR AND 30 MINUTES / **TOTAL TIME:** 2 HOURS AND 30 MINUTES

Stuffed zucchini is effortlessly rich and luxurious on its own. But add in a creamy, yogurt-based sauce and this dish becomes next-level decadent.

1. Bring water to a boil in a small saucepan and add 1 teaspoon of the salt and the rice. Cook the rice for 5 minutes and drain; the rice will only be partially cooked. Transfer the rice to a large mixing bowl and set it aside.

2. Trim about ½ inch from each end of the zucchini. Partially peel the zucchini with a striped pattern and then cut them in half crosswise. Using a zucchini or apple corer, carefully hollow out the inside of the zucchini, leaving a wall that is about ¼ inch thick around the edge. Set the hollowed-out zucchini aside and reserve the pulp for another preparation.

3. Add the chickpeas, half of the butter cubes, 1 teaspoon of salt, and pepper to the rice and stir until well combined, making sure the butter is evenly distributed.

4. Preheat the oven to 350°F.

5. Using your hands, fill each piece of zucchini three-quarters of the way with the rice mixture. Once each zucchini is filled, place them side-by-side in one layer in the bottom of a large Dutch oven. Sprinkle the remaining salt over the zucchini.

6. Distribute the remaining butter over the stuffed zucchini and then fill in any empty gaps with the remaining rice mixture. Place a small plate or saucepan lid (the lid should be small enough to fit) over the stuffed zucchini to weigh them down. Cover the pot with its own lid, place it over low heat, and cook for about 10 minutes, until the zucchini release some water.

7. In a bowl, combine the water with the juice of the lemon. Remove the lid of the Dutch oven and add the mixture to the pot until the water reaches the level of the small plate or saucepan lid that is weighing down the zucchini. Place the lid back on the Dutch oven and transfer the pot to the oven. Cook for 1 hour or until the liquid is absorbed.

8. Remove the Dutch oven's lid and the small plate or saucepan lid. Set the oven to broil, or 500°F, and cook until the tops of the zucchini are golden brown.

9. Remove from the oven and enjoy with Labneh and cucumbers.

INGREDIENTS:

2½ TEASPOONS KOSHER SALT, DIVIDED

1 CUP BASMATI RICE, RINSED AND DRAINED

9 ZUCCHINI

¾ CUP CANNED CHICKPEAS, RINSED AND DRAINED

½ CUP SALTED BUTTER, SOFTENED AND CUT INTO ½-INCH CUBES, DIVIDED

¼ TEASPOON BLACK PEPPER

2 CUPS WATER

1 LARGE LEMON

LABNEH (SEE PAGE 67), FOR SERVING

CUCUMBERS, SLICED, FOR SERVING

WHITEFISH POACHED IN PEPPER SAUCE

YIELD: 6 SERVINGS / ACTIVE TIME: 15 MINUTES / TOTAL TIME: 30 MINUTES

This recipe is versatile and can be made with any type of whitefish, as well as salmon. Take the spice factor to a new level by adding some harissa sauce (see page 791) or more chili powder.

1. Cut the fish into 2 x 5–inch pieces and let them rest at room temperature.

2. Place the avocado oil in a large skillet and warm it over medium-low heat. Add the garlic and onions and cook, stirring occasionally, for 5 minutes. Add the peppers and cook for another 4 minutes.

3. Stir in the paprika, salt, black pepper, and chili powder. Add the water, raise the heat to medium-high, and bring to a boil.

4. Reduce the heat to low, place the fish slices on top of the vegetables, cover the pan, and cook for 5 minutes.

5. Use a fork to place some of the peppers and onions on top of the fish. Cover the pan and cook for another 5 minutes, or until the fish can easily be flaked with a fork. Taste the sauce and season as necessary.

6. Sprinkle the cilantro over the dish and enjoy.

INGREDIENTS:

2   LBS. WHITEFISH (SUCH AS TILAPIA, HALIBUT, OR FLOUNDER)

3   TABLESPOONS AVOCADO OIL

2   GARLIC CLOVES, SLICED THIN

2   MEDIUM ONIONS, HALVED AND SLICED THIN

1   RED BELL PEPPER, STEM AND SEEDS REMOVED, SLICED THIN

1   ORANGE BELL PEPPER, STEM AND SEEDS REMOVED, SLICED THIN

1   YELLOW BELL PEPPER, STEM AND SEEDS REMOVED, SLICED THIN

¼   TEASPOON PAPRIKA

¾   TEASPOON SEA SALT

    BLACK PEPPER, TO TASTE

½   TEASPOON CHILI POWDER

1½ CUPS WATER

⅔   CUP CHOPPED FRESH CILANTRO

Pomegranate & Honey–Glazed Chicken, see page 158

POMEGRANATE & HONEY–GLAZED CHICKEN

YIELD: 4 SERVINGS / ACTIVE TIME: 20 MINUTES / TOTAL TIME: 1 HOUR AND 20 MINUTES

This sweet and tangy sauce is so tasty you'll want to try it on everything. To really get this dish to sing, be sure not to crowd the pan when browning the chicken, because you want the skin to crisp up before the sauce hits it.

1. Place 2 tablespoons of the avocado oil in a large skillet and warm it over medium-high heat. Add the onion and cook, stirring occasionally, until it is soft and translucent, about 3 minutes.

2. Add the garlic and cook, stirring frequently, until fragrant, about 1 minute. Stir in the pomegranate molasses, pomegranate juice, honey, stock, and seasonings and bring the mixture to a boil. Lower the heat and simmer the sauce until it has reduced by half and thickened slightly, about 20 minutes. Taste the sauce and adjust the seasoning as necessary. Transfer the sauce to a bowl and set it aside.

3. Rinse the chicken pieces, pat them dry, and season with salt and pepper.

4. Place the remaining avocado oil in the pan. Add the chicken pieces, skin side down, and cook until browned. Turn the chicken over, pour the sauce into the pan, reduce the heat, and cover the pan. Cook the chicken until cooked through and tender, 35 to 40 minutes.

5. Transfer the cooked chicken to a platter, garnish with parsley and pomegranate seeds, and enjoy.

INGREDIENTS:

¼   CUP AVOCADO OIL

1   LARGE ONION, CHOPPED

3   GARLIC CLOVES, MINCED

½   CUP POMEGRANATE MOLASSES

½   CUP SWEETENED POMEGRANATE JUICE

½   CUP HONEY

2   CUPS VEGETABLE OR CHICKEN STOCK (SEE PAGE 371 OR 368)

1   TEASPOON CUMIN

½   TEASPOON GROUND GINGER

⅛   TEASPOON ALLSPICE

½   TEASPOON TURMERIC

4   LBS. BONE-IN, SKIN-ON CHICKEN PIECES

   SALT AND PEPPER, TO TASTE

   FRESH PARSLEY, CHOPPED, FOR GARNISH

   POMEGRANATE SEEDS, FOR GARNISH

LAMB BELLY HASH

YIELD: 6 SERVINGS / ACTIVE TIME: 1 HOUR / TOTAL TIME: 12 HOURS

Lamb belly is a delicious and fatty cut, beautiful braised or smoked. Use it in any preparation that calls for pork belly, or in this delightful hash.

1. Preheat the oven to 250°F. Season the lamb belly with the salt and pepper and place it in a roasting pan. Add water to the pan until it is 2 inches deep, cover the pan with aluminum foil, and place it in the oven. Braise the lamb belly for 8 hours.

2. If using a smoker, preheat the smoker to 250°F.

3. Place the applewood chips in a smoker or cast-iron skillet. If using the skillet, place the pan over high heat. When the wood chips start to smoke, place the skillet in a deep roasting pan. Set the potatoes in the roasting pan (not in the skillet) and cover the roasting pan with aluminum foil. Place the roasting pan in the oven. Smoke the potatoes for 2 hours.

4. Bring water to a boil in a medium saucepan.

5. Remove the smoked potatoes from the smoker or oven, place them in the boiling water, and boil until fork-tender, about 30 minutes. Drain and let the potatoes cool.

6. Remove the lamb from the oven and let it rest.

7. Place the truffle oil in a large cast-iron skillet and warm it over high heat. Add the garlic and cook, stirring continuously, until fragrant, about 1 minute.

8. Add the potatoes and mash them so that they break apart. Add the lamb, trying to add as little of the excess fat from the pan as possible. Break up the potatoes and the lamb as they crisp up in the pan, stirring occasionally so that everything is evenly distributed.

9. Reduce the heat to medium and cook until the hash is crispy on both sides, 5 to 7 minutes. Serve immediately.

INGREDIENTS:

2	LBS. LAMB BELLY
1	TEASPOON KOSHER SALT
2	TEASPOONS BLACK PEPPER
	APPLEWOOD CHIPS, AS NEEDED
2	POTATOES, UNPEELED
2	TABLESPOONS TRUFFLE OIL
3	GARLIC CLOVES, MINCED

CHICKEN TAGINE WITH
WARM COUSCOUS SALAD

YIELD: 6 SERVINGS / **ACTIVE TIME:** 25 MINUTES / **TOTAL TIME:** 40 MINUTES

Should you find that the flavor of this tagine is not quite hitting the mark, try incorporating a little bit of saffron and/or turmeric.

1. Place the olive oil in a Dutch oven and warm it over medium-high heat. Season the chicken with salt and pepper, add it to the pot, and cook, stirring occasionally, until it has browned, about 6 minutes. Remove the chicken from the pot and set it aside.

2. Reduce the heat to medium, add the onion, and cook, stirring occasionally, until it has softened, about 5 minutes. Add the garlic, ginger, lemon zest, paprika, cumin, cayenne, coriander, and cinnamon and cook, stirring continually, for 1 minute.

3. Add the white wine and cook until the alcohol has been cooked off, about 3 minutes, scraping up any browned bits from the bottom of the pot.

4. Add the stock, carrot, honey, and apricots and bring the mixture to a simmer. Nestle the chicken into the mixture and cook until it is cooked through (internal temperature of 165°F), about 10 minutes.

5. Add the chickpeas, cover the pot, and cook until they are heated through, about 5 minutes.

6. Garnish the tagine with mint and serve it over the couscous salad.

INGREDIENTS:

2	TABLESPOONS EXTRA-VIRGIN OLIVE OIL
8	BONE-IN, SKIN-ON CHICKEN DRUMSTICKS OR THIGHS
	SALT AND PEPPER, TO TASTE
1	ONION, MINCED
4	GARLIC CLOVES, MINCED
1	TEASPOON GRATED FRESH GINGER
	ZEST OF 1 LEMON
1	TEASPOON PAPRIKA
½	TEASPOON CUMIN
⅛	TEASPOON CAYENNE PEPPER
½	TEASPOON CORIANDER
¼	TEASPOON CINNAMON
½	CUP WHITE WINE
2	CUPS CHICKEN STOCK (SEE PAGE 368)
1	CARROT, PEELED AND CUT INTO THIN HALF-MOONS
1	TABLESPOON HONEY
¾	CUP HALVED DRIED APRICOTS
1	(14 OZ.) CAN OF CHICKPEAS, DRAINED AND RINSED
	FRESH MINT, CHOPPED, FOR GARNISH
	WARM COUSCOUS SALAD (SEE PAGE 503), FOR SERVING

HONEY-GLAZED TUNA WITH ROMESCO
& WARM ASPARAGUS SALAD

YIELD: 2 TO 4 SERVINGS / ACTIVE TIME: 30 MINUTES / TOTAL TIME: 1 HOUR AND 30 MINUTES

Make sure you do not overcook the tuna—if it gets past a certain point, you're better off saving your money and just opening up a couple of cans.

1. Place the honey and 3 tablespoons of the olive oil in a mixing bowl and whisk to combine. Add the tuna, season it with salt and pepper, and place the bowl in the refrigerator. Let the tuna marinate for 1 hour, flipping it over every 15 minutes.

2. While the tuna is marinating, place 1 tablespoon of olive oil in a large skillet and warm it over medium heat. Add the garlic and tomatoes and cook, stirring continually, until the tomatoes start to collapse, about 3 minutes. Transfer the mixture to a bowl and set it aside.

3. Place the remaining olive oil in the skillet and warm it over medium heat. Add the asparagus in a single layer, cover the pan, and cook until the asparagus is bright green, about 5 minutes. Uncover the pan and cook until the asparagus is well browned on one side, about 5 minutes.

4. Add the asparagus to the garlic and tomatoes and season the mixture with salt and pepper. Add the olives, toss to combine, top the dish with the basil and Parmesan, and set it aside.

5. Warm a medium skillet over high heat. Add the marinade and then place the tuna in the center of the pan. Reduce the heat to medium and cook the tuna until browned on each side, about 1 minute per side.

6. Remove the tuna from the pan and let it rest for 2 minutes before slicing it and serving alongside the asparagus salad and Romesco Sauce.

INGREDIENTS:

1 TABLESPOON HONEY

5 TABLESPOONS EXTRA-VIRGIN OLIVE OIL

1 LB. TUNA FILLET

SALT AND PEPPER, TO TASTE

2 GARLIC CLOVES, MINCED

10 OZ. CHERRY TOMATOES, HALVED

1 LB. ASPARAGUS, TRIMMED

½ CUP KALAMATA OLIVES, PITS REMOVED, CHOPPED

2 TABLESPOONS CHOPPED FRESH BASIL

¼ CUP FRESHLY GRATED PARMESAN CHEESE

ROMESCO SAUCE (SEE PAGE 782), FOR SERVING

Olive Oil–Poached Fluke, see page 166

OLIVE OIL–POACHED FLUKE

YIELD: 2 SERVINGS / **ACTIVE TIME:** 15 MINUTES / **TOTAL TIME:** 2 HOURS AND 15 MINUTES

Fluke carries a fresh taste that you want to be very delicate with, meaning it is perfect for cooking sous vide.

1. Place the fluke and 1 cup of the olive oil in a vacuum bag and vacuum seal it. Cook it sous vide at 145°F for 1 hour.

2. Remove the fluke from the water bath, place it in the refrigerator, and chill for 1 hour.

3. Slice the fish into 1-inch-thick pieces and arrange them on chilled serving plates. Season with the salt and pepper, drizzle the remaining olive oil around the plate, and squeeze the lemon over the pieces of fluke. Garnish with parsley and enjoy.

INGREDIENTS:

½   LB. FLUKE FILLET

1¼   CUPS EXTRA-VIRGIN OLIVE OIL

1   TEASPOON KOSHER SALT

    PINCH OF BLACK PEPPER

½   LEMON

    FRESH PARSLEY, FOR GARNISH

ROASTED GRAPES & SAUSAGE

YIELD: 4 SERVINGS / ACTIVE TIME: 10 MINUTES / TOTAL TIME: 45 MINUTES

This simple oven-roasted preparation contrasts salty and spicy sausage against the almost-excessive sweetness of grapes. Cooking them together adds complexity without adding work.

1. Preheat the oven to 500°F. Cut the sausage into ¼-inch-thick slices, place them in a baking dish, and add the grapes. Toss to evenly distribute.

2. Place the baking dish in the oven and cook until the sausage is well browned and cooked through, 15 to 20 minutes.

3. Remove from the oven and transfer the mixture to a serving platter.

4. Sprinkle the mozzarella over the sausage and grapes, drizzle the Balsamic Glaze over the top, and enjoy.

INGREDIENTS:

½   LB. SAUSAGE (HUNGARIAN OR SPICY ITALIAN RECOMMENDED)

1   BUNCH OF MUSCAT GRAPES

3   OZ. FRESH MOZZARELLA CHEESE, TORN

2   TABLESPOONS BALSAMIC GLAZE (SEE PAGE 759)

Roasted Grapes & Sausage, see page 167

MARINATED LAMB HEART

YIELD: 2 SERVINGS / **ACTIVE TIME**: 30 MINUTES / **TOTAL TIME**: 4 HOURS AND 30 MINUTES

This dish is born out of a desire not to waste food. But aside from that, lamb heart is tasty and tender—it eats very much like filet mignon. Pair with a creamy starch, such as polenta or mashed potatoes, for an easy yet memorable dinner.

1. Place all of the ingredients, except the lamb heart, in a bowl and stir until well combined.

2. Place the lamb heart on a cutting board and use a sharp knife to remove any connective tissue—it is white with a honeycomb-like texture—from the outside of the lamb heart. Place the lamb heart in the marinade and chill in the refrigerator for 2 to 4 hours.

3. Warm a large cast-iron skillet over high heat. Place the lamb heart in the skillet and cook until the lamb heart is seared on both sides and cooked to medium-rare, about 2 minutes per side. Remove from the skillet and let the lamb heart rest for a few minutes. Cut it into ½-inch-thick slices and enjoy.

INGREDIENTS:

½	CUP WHITE VINEGAR
2	TABLESPOONS EXTRA-VIRGIN OLIVE OIL
¼	CUP CHOPPED FRESH PARSLEY
1	TEASPOON CORIANDER
½	WHITE ONION, MINCED
3	FRESH MINT LEAVES, CHOPPED
3	FRESH BASIL LEAVES, CHOPPED
2	GARLIC CLOVES, MINCED
2	TEASPOONS KOSHER SALT
6–8	OZ. LAMB HEART

SHAKSHUKA

YIELD: 4 SERVINGS / **ACTIVE TIME:** 30 MINUTES / **TOTAL TIME:** 1 HOUR

A North African classic that is breakfast for dinner at its best.

1. Place the olive oil in a large cast-iron skillet and warm it over medium heat. Add the onion and cook, stirring occasionally, until it has softened, about 5 minutes. Add the bell peppers and cook, stirring occasionally, until they have softened, about 5 minutes.

2. Add the garlic, coriander, paprika, cumin, turmeric, red pepper flakes, and tomato paste and cook, stirring continually, for 1 minute. Add the tomatoes and bring the mixture to a boil. Reduce the heat, cover the pan, and simmer for 15 minutes.

3. Remove the cover and cook until the shakshuka has reduced slightly, about 5 minutes.

4. Season the shakshuka with salt and pepper. Using the back of a wooden spoon, make six wells in the mixture. Crack an egg into each well and sprinkle the feta over the shakshuka.

5. Reduce the heat to a simmer, cover the pan, and cook until the egg whites are set, 6 to 8 minutes.

6. Remove the pan from heat, garnish with parsley and mint, and enjoy.

INGREDIENTS:

2	TABLESPOONS EXTRA-VIRGIN OLIVE OIL
1	ONION, CHOPPED
2	GREEN BELL PEPPERS, STEMS AND SEEDS REMOVED, CHOPPED
2	GARLIC CLOVES, MINCED
1	TEASPOON CORIANDER
1	TEASPOON SWEET PAPRIKA
½	TEASPOON CUMIN
1	TEASPOON TURMERIC
	PINCH OF RED PEPPER FLAKES
2	TABLESPOONS TOMATO PASTE
5	RIPE TOMATOES, CHOPPED
	SALT AND PEPPER, TO TASTE
6	EGGS
1	CUP CRUMBLED FETA CHEESE
¼	CUP CHOPPED FRESH PARSLEY, FOR GARNISH
¼	CUP CHOPPED FRESH MINT, FOR GARNISH

BACON & EGGS JACHNUN

YIELD: 8 SERVINGS / ACTIVE TIME: 45 MINUTES / TOTAL TIME: 12 HOURS

The eggs traditionally cooked alongside jachnun are called huevos haminados, or "slow-cooked eggs." They brown and caramelize in their shell. Once you master the technique, you'll find this to be a rewarding and fun breakfast!

1. Preheat the oven to 210°F. In the work bowl of a stand mixer fitted with the dough hook, combine the flour, water, and baking powder. Knead until the mixture comes together as a smooth, springy ball of dough, about 5 minutes. Cover the bowl with a linen towel and let the dough rest for 10 minutes.

2. Divide the dough into eight pieces and form them into even-sized balls. Place them on a flour-dusted work surface and roll them into rectangles, and as thin as possible. Be gentle so that the dough doesn't rip. If you're struggling to roll the balls of dough out, coat each one in butter before rolling. This is messy, but it makes the process easier.

3. Brush the butter over the top of the dough. Place two strips of bacon on each piece of dough, leaving about an inch between the pieces of bacon.

4. Fold in the sides of the wide edge of dough 1 inch. Fold in the narrow sides 2 inches, and then fold the dough closed over itself so that it is crescent shaped.

5. Place the pieces of dough tightly against each other in a circular baking pan. They must be packed tightly so they hold their shape as they cook.

6. Place the eggs on top of the dough. Cover the pan with foil and put it in the oven. Bake for 8 to 10 hours.

7. Remove from the oven and serve, allotting one piece of dough and one egg for each portion.

INGREDIENTS:

3¼	CUPS ALL-PURPOSE FLOUR, PLUS MORE AS NEEDED
1½	CUPS WATER
1	TEASPOON BAKING POWDER
½	CUP UNSALTED BUTTER, MELTED
16	STRIPS OF BACON
8	EGGS, LEFT WHOLE

TOASTED PASTA WITH CRAB

YIELD: 4 SERVINGS / ACTIVE TIME: 15 MINUTES / TOTAL TIME: 45 MINUTES

Giving the pasta a deep toasting lends this dish an authentic Spanish flavor.

1. Preheat the oven to 425°F. Place 1 tablespoon of the olive oil and the pasta in a large cast-iron skillet and toast the pasta over medium-high heat until it is browned, about 8 minutes. Transfer the pasta to a bowl.

2. Wipe out the skillet, add the remaining olive oil, and warm it over medium heat. Add the onion and cook, stirring occasionally, until it has softened, about 5 minutes. Add the garlic and cook, stirring continually, for 1 minute.

3. Add the wine and cook until the alcohol has been cooked off, 2 to 3 minutes. Add the stock, bay leaf, tomatoes, and paprika and bring the mixture to a boil. Reduce the heat, add the pasta, and simmer until the pasta is tender, about 10 minutes.

4. Season the dish with salt and pepper, add the crab, place the pan in the oven, and bake until the pasta is crispy, about 5 minutes.

5. Remove the pan from the oven, garnish the dish with the parsley, and enjoy.

INGREDIENTS:

¼ CUP EXTRA-VIRGIN OLIVE OIL

½ LB. ANGEL HAIR PASTA, BROKEN INTO 2-INCH PIECES

1 ONION, CHOPPED

3 GARLIC CLOVES, MINCED

¼ CUP WHITE WINE

4 CUPS CHICKEN STOCK (SEE PAGE 368)

1 BAY LEAF

1 (14 OZ.) CAN OF DICED TOMATOES, DRAINED

1 TEASPOON PAPRIKA

SALT AND PEPPER, TO TASTE

1 LB. LUMP CRABMEAT

FRESH PARSLEY, CHOPPED, FOR GARNISH

CRAB ROULADE

YIELD: 10 SERVINGS / ACTIVE TIME: 25 MINUTES / TOTAL TIME: 40 MINUTES

As far as seafood dishes go, this is as elegant a preparation as you'll find.

1. Place the crab, shallots, mayonnaise, crème fraîche, and chives in a mixing bowl, season the mixture with salt and pepper, and stir until well combined.

2. Place a piece of plastic wrap on a damp work surface. Place one-tenth of the crab salad on the plastic wrap and roll it up tightly into a cylinder, twisting the ends. Repeat until you have 10 cylinders of the crab salad. Place them in the refrigerator and chill for 15 minutes.

3. Remove the crab salad from the refrigerator and wrap each portion with the slices from half of an avocado.

4. Garnish the roulade with the Passionfruit Emulsion, chile, sesame seeds, microgreens, and additional chives and enjoy.

PASSION FRUIT EMULSION

1. Place the shallot and passionfruit puree in a blender and puree on medium until smooth.

2. Reduce the speed to low and slowly drizzle in the canola oil until it has emulsified.

INGREDIENTS:

1   LB. LUMP CRABMEAT

¼   CUP MINCED SHALLOTS

¼   CUP MAYONNAISE

¼   CUP CRÈME FRAÎCHE

¼   CUP CHOPPED FRESH CHIVES, PLUS MORE FOR GARNISH

SALT AND PEPPER, TO TASTE

5   AVOCADOS, HALVED, PITS REMOVED, SLICED THIN

PASSION FRUIT EMULSION (SEE RECIPE), FOR GARNISH

1   FRESNO CHILE PEPPER, SLICED THIN, FOR GARNISH

¼   CUP SESAME SEEDS, TOASTED, FOR GARNISH

½   CUP MICROGREENS, FOR GARNISH

PASSION FRUIT EMULSION

1   SHALLOT, CHOPPED

1   CUP PASSION FRUIT PUREE

1   CUP CANOLA OIL

BRAISED HALIBUT WITH CRISPY POLENTA CAKES

YIELD: 4 SERVINGS / ACTIVE TIME: 30 MINUTES / TOTAL TIME: 1 HOUR AND 30 MINUTES

This dish will work with any whitefish, but sweet and succulent halibut stands as the very best option.

1. Place the olive oil in a Dutch oven and warm it over medium-high heat. Pat the halibut dry with a paper towel and season it with salt and pepper. Place the halibut in the pan and sear it until the bottom is golden brown, about 5 minutes.

2. Gently lift the halibut and remove it from the pan. Transfer it to a plate and set it aside.

3. Add the leek and cook, stirring occasionally, until it starts to brown, about 10 minutes.

4. Stir in the Dijon and white wine and bring to a simmer. Return the halibut to the pan, seared side facing up. Cover the pot and cook until the halibut is cooked through (internal temperature 140°F), about 8 minutes.

5. Remove the halibut from the pot and set it aside. Place the Dutch oven over high heat and cook until the sauce has thickened, about 2 minutes. Transfer to a serving dish, place the halibut on top, and garnish with parsley. Serve with the Crispy Polenta Cakes and lemon wedges and enjoy.

INGREDIENTS:

3	TABLESPOONS EXTRA-VIRGIN OLIVE OIL
1½	LBS. CENTER-CUT HALIBUT FILLETS
	SALT AND PEPPER, TO TASTE
1	LEEK, TRIMMED, HALVED, RINSED WELL, AND SLICED THIN
2	TEASPOONS DIJON MUSTARD
½	CUP WHITE WINE
	FRESH PARSLEY, CHOPPED, FOR GARNISH
	CRISPY POLENTA CAKES (SEE RECIPE), FOR SERVING
	LEMON WEDGES, FOR SERVING

CRISPY POLENTA CAKES

2	TABLESPOONS EXTRA-VIRGIN OLIVE OIL
1	SHALLOT, MINCED
1	TEASPOON FRESH THYME
2	CUPS MILK
⅔	CUP POLENTA
1	CUP FRESHLY GRATED PARMESAN CHEESE
	SALT AND PEPPER, TO TASTE

CRISPY POLENTA CAKES

1. Line a square 8-inch baking dish with plastic wrap. Place 1 tablespoon of the olive oil in a small saucepan and warm it over medium heat. Add the shallot and cook, stirring frequently, until it softens, about 3 minutes.

2. Add the thyme and cook, stirring continually, for 1 minute. Add the milk and bring to a boil. Add the polenta and cook, stirring frequently, until the mixture looks like scrambled eggs, about 10 minutes. Remove the pan from heat, add the Parmesan, and fold to incorporate.

3. Season the polenta with salt and pepper and transfer it to the baking dish, pressing down to ensure it is in an even layer. Place the polenta in the refrigerator and chill until it is firm, about 30 minutes.

4. Remove the polenta from the refrigerator and cut it into round or square cakes. Place the remaining olive oil in a large skillet and warm it over medium-high heat. Add the cakes to the pan and cook until they are golden brown on both sides, about 6 minutes. Transfer to a paper towel–lined plate to drain before serving.

DUCK BREAST WELLINGTON

YIELD: 2 SERVINGS / **ACTIVE TIME:** 20 MINUTES / **TOTAL TIME:** 45 MINUTES

The crispy skin and zesty feta make for an explosive flavor combo.

1. Warm a cast-iron skillet over medium-high heat.

2. Using a sharp knife, score the skin of the duck breast in a cross-hatch pattern, taking care not to cut into the breast meat.

3. Reduce the heat to medium and place the duck breast in the pan, skin side down. Use your hand to move the duck around the pan—this will prevent it from sticking as the fat renders. Cook until the skin begins to brown and duck fat starts to pool, 5 to 7 minutes. Remove the duck breast from the pan.

4. Preheat the oven to 375°F.

5. Place the square of puff pastry on a flour-dusted work surface and roll it out until it is about ⅛ inch thick. Place the duck breast, skin side up, in the center of the square and spread the feta over the skin. Fold the dough over the duck breast and gently press down to seal.

6. Coat a baking sheet with butter, place the puff pastry on the pan, and place it in the oven.

7. Bake until the pastry is golden brown and the duck breast is cooked through, 15 to 20 minutes. Remove from the pan and enjoy, making sure to serve the pastry with the skin of the duck breast facing down.

INGREDIENTS:

1   SKIN-ON DUCK BREAST

     5-INCH SQUARE OF PUFF PASTRY

     ALL-PURPOSE FLOUR, AS NEEDED

1   TABLESPOON WHIPPED FETA WITH ZA'ATAR (SEE PAGE 771)

     UNSALTED BUTTER, AS NEEDED

SUMAC & LIME MAHIMAHI

YIELD: 2 SERVINGS / **ACTIVE TIME:** 25 MINUTES / **TOTAL TIME:** 3 HOURS

Mahimahi is such a tender fish that it partners with a marinade very well.

1. In a small bowl, whisk together the lime juice, sumac, honey, salt, and garlic. Add the mahimahi and stir until the fillets are coated. Chill in the refrigerator for 2 hours.

2. Place the olive oil in a large skillet and warm it over medium heat. Add the mahimahi to the pan and cook until it is browned on both sides and flakes easily at the touch of a fork, 8 to 10 minutes.

3. Remove the mahimahi from the pan and serve over couscous.

INGREDIENTS:

	JUICE OF 2 LIMES
1	TABLESPOON SUMAC
1	TEASPOON HONEY
1	TEASPOON KOSHER SALT
1	GARLIC CLOVE, MINCED
2	(6 OZ.) MAHIMAHI FILLETS
1	TABLESPOON EXTRA-VIRGIN OLIVE OIL
	COUSCOUS, FOR SERVING

Sumac & Lime Mahimahi, see page 183

ROASTED EGGPLANT PITA

YIELD: 6 SERVINGS / **ACTIVE TIME:** 30 MINUTES / **TOTAL TIME:** 1 HOUR AND 30 MINUTES

Take these to-go, or make them part of a spread and let people build their own.

1. Place 2 tablespoons of the olive oil in a large saucepan and warm it over medium heat. Add the eggplant and cook, stirring occasionally, until it has browned and softened, about 10 minutes. Add the garlic and cook, stirring continually, for 1 minute.

2. Season the mixture with salt and pepper and remove the pan from heat. Let the mixture cool.

3. Place the tomatoes, pickles, onion, scallion, artichokes, parsley, Za'atar, and remaining olive oil in a bowl and stir to combine. Refrigerate the mixture for at least 30 minutes.

4. Build your desired sandwich from the tomato-and-artichoke mixture and any or all of the remaining ingredients.

SOUS VIDE EGGS

1. Fill a container with warm water and set the temperature on a sous vide machine to 146.5°F.

2. Once that temperature has been reached, gently slip the eggs into the water bath. Sous vide for 1 hour before using—the eggs can continue cooking at this temperature until they are needed.

INGREDIENTS:

¼ CUP EXTRA-VIRGIN OLIVE OIL

1 EGGPLANT, TRIMMED, SEEDS REMOVED, CHOPPED INTO ½-INCH CUBES

2 GARLIC CLOVES, MINCED

SALT AND PEPPER, TO TASTE

1 CUP CHERRY TOMATOES, HALVED

3 PICKLE SPEARS, SLICED THIN

⅓ CUP CHOPPED RED ONION

1 SCALLION, TRIMMED AND SLICED THIN

¼ CUP MARINATED ARTICHOKES (SEE PAGE 86), QUARTERED

1 TABLESPOON CHOPPED FRESH PARSLEY

1 TEASPOON ZA'ATAR (SEE PAGE 766)

6 PIECES OF PITA BREAD (SEE PAGE 532)

1 CUP MODERN HUMMUS (SEE PAGE 31)

6 SOUS VIDE EGGS (SEE RECIPE)

½ CUP TAHINI & YOGURT SAUCE (SEE PAGE 796)

½ CUP GREEN ZHUG (SEE PAGE 749)

SOUS VIDE EGGS

6 EGGS

CRISPY LEMON & CHICKPEA CAKES

YIELD: 4 SERVINGS / **ACTIVE TIME:** 15 MINUTES / **TOTAL TIME:** 45 MINUTES

Panfrying the chickpea patties amplifies their nutty taste, and supplies the cakes with a contrasting texture that is much needed.

1. Place 1 tablespoon of the olive oil in a medium saucepan and warm it over medium heat. Add the leek and cook, stirring occasionally, until it has softened, about 5 minutes. Add the garlic and cook, stirring continually, for 1 minute.

2. Remove the pan from heat, stir in the toasted pine nuts, and set the mixture aside.

3. Place the chickpeas in a food processor and pulse until they are minced. Add them to the leek mixture, fold in the egg, lemon juice, lemon zest, mustard, and panko, and season the mixture with salt and pepper.

4. Place the flour in a shallow bowl. Working with wet hands, form the chickpea mixture into eight patties. Dredge the patties in the flour until coated and gently brush off any excess.

5. Place the remaining olive oil in a skillet and warm it over medium heat. Working in batches, place the patties in the skillet and cook until crispy and golden brown on each side, 8 to 10 minutes.

6. Place the Crushed Avocado in a bowl, add the tomato, cayenne, and cumin, and stir to combine. Serve alongside the cakes, with lemon wedges as well.

INGREDIENTS:

3   TABLESPOONS EXTRA-VIRGIN OLIVE OIL

1   LEEK, TRIMMED, HALVED, RINSED WELL, AND SLICED THIN

2   GARLIC CLOVES, MINCED

½   CUP PINE NUTS, TOASTED

1   (14 OZ.) CAN OF CHICKPEAS, DRAINED AND RINSED

1   EGG

1   TABLESPOON FRESH LEMON JUICE

    ZEST OF 1 LEMON

1   TABLESPOON DIJON MUSTARD

¼   CUP PANKO

    SALT AND PEPPER, TO TASTE

¼   CUP ALL-PURPOSE FLOUR

    CRUSHED AVOCADO (SEE PAGE 102)

1   TOMATO, SEEDS REMOVED, CHOPPED

¼   TEASPOON CAYENNE PEPPER

½   TEASPOON CUMIN

    LEMON WEDGES, FOR SERVING

Smoked Pork Belly in Pickled Applesauce, see page 192

SMOKED PORK BELLY IN PICKLED APPLESAUCE

YIELD: 2 SERVINGS / ACTIVE TIME: 30 MINUTES / TOTAL TIME: 11 HOURS

Traditionally, pork belly is smoked for a short time and then braised. By smoking the belly all the way through, the flavors become richer, and the texture is more in line with the beloved crispy edges of a well-prepared brisket.

1. Preheat your smoker to 225°F, using the applewood chips.

2. In a small bowl, combine the shawarma seasoning and brown sugar. Rub the mixture all over the pork belly and place it on a rack in the smoker, fat side up. Smoke until the pork belly is crispy and tender, about 10 hours.

3. Remove the pork belly from the smoker and let it rest for 30 minutes.

4. Divide the Pickled Applesauce between the serving plates. Slice the pork belly, arrange the slices on top of the applesauce, and enjoy.

INGREDIENTS:

- APPLEWOOD CHIPS, AS NEEDED
- ½ CUP SHAWARMA SEASONING BLEND
- 1 TABLESPOON BROWN SUGAR
- 6 OZ. CENTER-CUT PORK BELLY
- ½ CUP PICKLED APPLESAUCE (SEE PAGE 799)

ALBONDIGAS

YIELD: 4 SERVINGS / ACTIVE TIME: 25 MINUTES / TOTAL TIME: 40 MINUTES

In every cuisine, meatballs embody comfort and express the seasonings and flavors dear to that region. Albondigas are the Spanish entry into this tradition.

1. Preheat the oven to 400°F.

2. In a large mixing bowl, combine all of the ingredients, except for the olive oil and sauce. Working with wet hands, divide the mixture into eight equal portions (about 2 oz. each) and form them into balls. Shape the balls so that they are oblong instead of round.

3. Place the oil in a large cast-iron skillet and warm it over medium-high heat. Add the meatballs and cook, turning as necessary, until they are browned all over.

4. Add the sauce to the pan and place it in the oven.

5. Bake until the meatballs are cooked through, 10 to 15 minutes.

6. Remove from the oven and enjoy.

INGREDIENTS:

1	LB. GROUND BEEF
½	CUP CHOPPED FRESH PARSLEY
4	GARLIC CLOVES, MINCED
2	TEASPOONS KOSHER SALT
1	TABLESPOON PAPRIKA
1	TEASPOON GROUND CLOVES
½	ONION, DICED
2	TEASPOONS EXTRA-VIRGIN OLIVE OIL
2	CUPS TOMATO SAUCE (SEE PAGE 775)

Stuffed Acorn Squash, see page 196

STUFFED ACORN SQUASH

YIELD: 2 SERVINGS / ACTIVE TIME: 40 MINUTES / TOTAL TIME: 2 HOURS AND 30 MINUTES

A perfect vegetarian entree—elegant, aesthetically pleasing, hearty, and delicious.

1. Preheat the oven to 425°F. Remove the top and seeds from the squash. Discard the top and set the seeds aside.

2. Rub the cut sides of the squash with the molasses and sprinkle half of the salt over them. Rub the outside of the squash with some of the olive oil and place the squash on a baking sheet, cut sides up. Place it in the oven and roast until tender, about 40 minutes.

3. While the squash is in the oven, clean the seeds, rinse them, and pat them dry. Place on a baking sheet, drizzle the remaining olive oil over them, and season with the remaining salt. Place the seeds in the oven and roast until golden brown, about 20 minutes, stirring halfway through.

4. Bring approximately 2 cups of water to a boil in a small saucepan. Add the split peas and boil them until tender, about 30 minutes. Drain and stir the peas into the rice. Add the cinnamon, cloves, nutmeg, cayenne, and butter and stir to combine.

5. Remove the squash and seeds from the oven. Fill the squash's cavities with the rice mixture, garnish each portion with the roasted seeds, and enjoy.

INGREDIENTS:

1	ACORN SQUASH
2	TABLESPOONS MOLASSES
1	TABLESPOON KOSHER SALT
2	TABLESPOONS EXTRA-VIRGIN OLIVE OIL
¼	CUP SPLIT PEAS
½	CUP COOKED BASMATI RICE
1	TEASPOON CINNAMON
½	TEASPOON GROUND CLOVES
½	TEASPOON FRESHLY GRATED NUTMEG
	PINCH OF CAYENNE PEPPER
1	TABLESPOON UNSALTED BUTTER

ZA'ATAR-CRUSTED RIBEYE

YIELD: 2 SERVINGS / ACTIVE TIME: 20 MINUTES / TOTAL TIME: 1 HOUR

If you can, try to pick up a bone-in ribeye—the boneless offerings tend to be so floppy that they become difficult to handle.

1. Preheat your gas or charcoal grill to high heat (500°F), making sure to set up the heat in a way that there is a cooler spot (400°F) available.

2. Place all of the ingredients, except for the steak, in a small bowl and stir until well combined. Apply the mixture generously to both sides of the steak.

3. Place the steak over high heat and let it cook until nicely seared, about 3 minutes. Turn the steak over and cook for another 3 minutes.

4. Move the steak over to the cooler part of the grill and cook until it is cooked to the desired level of doneness, 3 to 4 minutes for medium-rare.

5. Remove the steak from the grill and let it rest for 2 to 3 minutes before serving.

INGREDIENTS:

1	TABLESPOON BLACK PEPPER
2	TEASPOONS KOSHER SALT
1	TEASPOON DRIED THYME
1	TEASPOON SUMAC
1	TEASPOON SESAME SEEDS
1	LB. RIBEYE STEAK, AT ROOM TEMPERATURE

LAMB MEATBALLS OVER MARINATED EGGPLANT SALAD

YIELD: 4 SERVINGS / ACTIVE TIME: 45 MINUTES / TOTAL TIME: 1 HOUR

Using Greek yogurt instead of milk to soften the bread crumbs is such a tremendous upgrade that it may just become your standard operating procedure in all meatball-related preparations.

1. To begin preparations for the meatballs, place the yogurt, bread crumbs, and water in a mixing bowl and work the mixture with a fork until it is pasty. Add the lamb, mint, egg yolk, garlic, cumin, cinnamon, and cloves, season the mixture with salt and pepper, and work the mixture with your hands until well combined. Form the mixture into 12 meatballs.

2. Place the olive oil in a large skillet and warm it over medium heat. Working in batches to avoid crowding the pan, add the meatballs and cook until browned all over, about 6 minutes, turning them as needed. Remove the meatballs from the pan and set them aside.

3. To begin preparations for the sauce, place the olive oil in a medium saucepan and warm it over medium-high heat. Add the leek and cook, stirring occasionally, until it has softened, about 5 minutes. Add the garlic and cook, stirring continually, for 1 minute.

4. Add ½ cup of the stock and bring the mixture to a boil. Reduce the heat and simmer the mixture until it has reduced, about 10 minutes. Remove the pan from heat.

5. Place the remaining stock, the lemon juice, tahini, yogurt, and sesame seeds in a mixing bowl and stir until well combined. Add the mixture to the saucepan and bring the sauce to a simmer over low heat.

6. Add the meatballs to the sauce, cover the pan, and cook until they are cooked through, 8 to 10 minutes.

7. Season the sauce with salt and pepper and serve the meatballs alongside the eggplant salad.

INGREDIENTS:

FOR THE MEATBALLS

- ⅓   CUP FULL-FAT GREEK YOGURT
- 3   TABLESPOONS BREAD CRUMBS
- 2   TABLESPOONS WATER
- 1   LB. GROUND LAMB
- 2   TABLESPOONS CHOPPED FRESH MINT
- 1   EGG YOLK
- 1   GARLIC CLOVE, MINCED
- 1   TEASPOON CUMIN
- ¾   TEASPOON CINNAMON
- ⅛   TEASPOON GROUND CLOVES
-   SALT AND PEPPER, TO TASTE
- 2   TABLESPOONS EXTRA-VIRGIN OLIVE OIL
-   MARINATED EGGPLANT SALAD (SEE PAGE 398), FOR SERVING

FOR THE SAUCE

- 1   TABLESPOON EXTRA-VIRGIN OLIVE OIL
- 1   LEEK, TRIMMED, HALVED, RINSED WELL, AND SLICED THIN
- 2   GARLIC CLOVES, MINCED
- 2   CUPS CHICKEN STOCK (SEE PAGE 368)
-   JUICE OF 2 LEMONS
- 1   CUP TAHINI PASTE
- ½   CUP FULL-FAT GREEK YOGURT
- 1   TABLESPOON BLACK SESAME SEEDS
-   SALT AND PEPPER, TO TASTE

RED WINE–BRAISED OCTOPUS
WITH BULGUR-STUFFED EGGPLANTS

YIELD: 4 SERVINGS / ACTIVE TIME: 30 MINUTES / TOTAL TIME: 2 HOURS

There are a lot of tricks out there when it comes to cooking octopus, but I find this to be the most foolproof method.

---

1. Place the octopus in a medium saucepan, cover it with water by 2 inches, and bring to a boil. Reduce the heat, cover the pan, and simmer for 1 hour.

2. Remove the octopus from the pan and set it aside.

3. Place the olive oil in a medium saucepan and warm it over medium heat. Add the onion and cook, stirring occasionally, until it has softened, about 5 minutes. Add the tomato paste and garlic and cook, stirring continually, for 1 minute. Add all of the remaining ingredients, except for the parsley and stuffed eggplants, and bring to a boil. Reduce the heat and simmer for 20 minutes.

4. Strain the liquid into a clean saucepan. Add the octopus and simmer until it is tender and the braising liquid has thickened, about 20 minutes.

5. Divide the octopus among the serving plates, ladle some of the braising liquid over it, and garnish with the parsley. Serve with the stuffed eggplants and enjoy.

INGREDIENTS:

1	OCTOPUS (ABOUT 4 LBS.), MANTLE AND BODY REMOVED, TENTACLES SEPARATED
2	TABLESPOONS EXTRA-VIRGIN OLIVE OIL
1	ONION, CHOPPED
2	TABLESPOONS TOMATO PASTE
3	GARLIC CLOVES, MINCED
3	CUPS CLAM JUICE
1	SPRIG OF FRESH ROSEMARY
1	SPRIG OF FRESH THYME
1	BAY LEAF
2	CINNAMON STICKS
1	CUP DRY RED WINE
2	TABLESPOONS RED WINE VINEGAR
	SALT AND PEPPER, TO TASTE
	FRESH PARSLEY, CHOPPED, FOR GARNISH
	BULGUR-STUFFED EGGPLANTS (SEE PAGE 494), FOR SERVING

Lamb Shish Kebabs, see page 204

LAMB SHISH KEBABS

YIELD: 2 TO 4 SERVINGS / **ACTIVE TIME:** 30 MINUTES / **TOTAL TIME:** 2 HOURS

Though this is traditionally prepared outdoors on a grill, I wanted to tailor this preparation to those who, like me, live in the Northeast, where the winter significantly complicates year-round grilling.

1. Place ½ cup of the olive oil, the mint, rosemary, garlic, salt, lemon zest, lemon juice, and pepper in a blender and puree until smooth.

2. Place the lamb in a bowl, add half of the marinade, and toss to coat. Cover the bowl with plastic wrap, place the lamb in the refrigerator, and marinate for 1 hour, stirring every 15 minutes.

3. Place the vegetables in another bowl, add the remaining marinade, and toss to coat. Cover the bowl with plastic wrap and let the vegetables marinate at room temperature for 1 hour.

4. Preheat the oven to 350°F. Thread the lamb onto skewers, making sure to leave a bit of space between each piece. Thread the vegetable mixture onto skewers, making sure to alternate between the vegetables.

5. Place the skewers in a 13 x 9–inch baking dish and pour the marinade over them. Cover the dish and let the skewers marinate at room temperature for 30 minutes.

6. Remove the skewers from the marinade and pat them dry. Place 2 tablespoons of the olive oil in a large skillet and warm it over medium-high heat. Add the vegetable skewers to the pan and cook until golden brown all over, about 5 minutes, turning them as necessary.

7. Place the vegetable skewers on a baking sheet, place them in the oven, and roast until the vegetables are tender, 8 to 10 minutes. Remove the skewers from the oven and set them aside.

8. Place the remaining olive oil in a large, clean skillet and warm it over medium-high heat. Add the lamb kebabs and cook until they are browned all over and medium-rare (internal temperature of 120°F), about 8 minutes, turning them as necessary.

9. Let the cooked lamb rest for 5 minutes before serving.

INGREDIENTS:

- ¾ CUP EXTRA-VIRGIN OLIVE OIL
- ¼ CUP FRESH MINT LEAVES
- 2 TEASPOONS CHOPPED FRESH ROSEMARY
- 2 GARLIC CLOVES, SMASHED
- 1 TEASPOON KOSHER SALT, PLUS MORE TO TASTE
- ZEST AND JUICE OF 1 LEMON
- ¼ TEASPOON BLACK PEPPER, PLUS MORE TO TASTE
- 2 LBS. BONELESS LEG OF LAMB, TRIMMED AND CUT INTO 1-INCH CUBES
- 1 ZUCCHINI, CUT INTO 1-INCH CUBES
- 1 SUMMER SQUASH, CUT INTO 1-INCH CUBES
- 1 RED BELL PEPPER, STEM AND SEEDS REMOVED, CUT INTO 1-INCH CUBES
- 1 GREEN BELL PEPPER, STEM AND SEEDS REMOVED, CUT INTO 1-INCH CUBES
- 2 RED ONIONS, CUT INTO 1-INCH CUBES

WHOLE BRANZINO

YIELD: 2 SERVINGS / **ACTIVE TIME:** 20 MINUTES / **TOTAL TIME:** 40 MINUTES

Cooking a whole fish in the oven is all about proper technique and patience. But don't let yourself be intimidated: the high fat content of branzino, which is often called "fatty bass," provides a lot of leeway.

1. Preheat the oven to 425°F. Clean the fish, remove the bones, and descale it. Pat it dry with paper towels and rub the flesh with the basil leaves. Season with the salt and pepper and close the fish back up.

2. Place the olive oil in a large cast-iron skillet and warm it over high heat. Place the fish in the pan and cook until it is browned on both sides, 8 to 10 minutes.

3. Place the pan in the oven and roast the fish until the internal temperature is 145°F, about 10 minutes.

4. Remove from the oven and transfer the branzino to a large platter. Squeeze the lemon over the top and enjoy.

INGREDIENTS:

1–2   LB. WHOLE BRANZINO

2   FRESH BASIL LEAVES

1   TABLESPOON KOSHER SALT

1   TABLESPOON BLACK PEPPER

2   TABLESPOONS EXTRA-VIRGIN OLIVE OIL

½   LEMON

Whole Branzino, see page 205

SWEET & SOUR SHORT RIBS

YIELD: 4 SERVINGS / **ACTIVE TIME:** 45 MINUTES / **TOTAL TIME:** 5 HOURS

The sweet and tangy combination of apples and sumac works especially well at cutting against a rich and fatty meat like short ribs.

1. Preheat the oven to 300°F. Using a sharp knife, remove the silver skin, connective tissue, and any excess fat from the rack of ribs.

2. In a small bowl, combine the salt and pepper. Rub the mixture over the short ribs.

3. Warm a roasting pan or a very large skillet over high heat. After 5 minutes or so, add a tablespoon of the olive oil and the short ribs to the pan. Cook until they are browned all over, about 10 minutes. Remove the ribs from the pan and set them in a large baking dish or roasting pan. Keep the pan over the high heat.

4. Add the onion, garlic, apples, remaining olive oil, and sumac to the pan and cook, stirring continuously, for 1 minute.

5. Pour the mixture over the ribs and then drizzle the vinegar and honey over them. Cover the pan with foil, place the pan in the oven, and braise for 4 hours.

6. Remove the pan from the oven and check the ribs. If the meat is very tender, to where it is just about to fall off the bone, cut the ribs between the bones. If not, return the pan to the oven and continue to braise the ribs until tender, checking every 30 minutes or so.

7. To serve, spoon some of the pan juices, apples, and onion over the ribs.

INGREDIENTS:

	RACK OF SHORT RIBS (3- TO 4-BONE)
2	TABLESPOONS KOSHER SALT
3	TABLESPOONS BLACK PEPPER
¼	CUP EXTRA-VIRGIN OLIVE OIL
1	ONION, QUARTERED
8	GARLIC CLOVES, MINCED
2	APPLES, PEELED AND SLICED
1	TABLESPOON SUMAC
½	CUP WHITE VINEGAR
¼	CUP HONEY

ROSTI EGG IN A HOLE

YIELD: 4 SERVINGS / ACTIVE TIME: 30 MINUTES / TOTAL TIME: 1 HOUR

A bit of cayenne and honey–enriched yogurt ferries this classic Swiss recipe to the shores of the Mediterranean.

1. Preheat the oven to 350°F. Place the potatoes in a bowl, add the salt and pepper, and stir to combine.

2. Place 3 tablespoons of the olive oil in a large cast-iron skillet and warm it over medium-high heat. Carefully place all of the potatoes in the pan and gently press down on them. Cook until the edges of the rosti are golden brown, 8 to 10 minutes.

3. Using a large spatula, carefully flip the rosti over and then cook for another 5 minutes.

4. Place the rosti in the oven and bake until it is crispy and golden brown, about 10 minutes. Remove the rosti from the oven and let it cool. Leave the oven on.

5. Place the rosti on a cutting board and cut it into four squares. Cut a hole large enough for an egg in the center of each piece. Reserve the cut-out sections.

6. Place the remaining olive oil in a large, clean cast-iron skillet and warm it over medium heat. Place the pieces of rosti in the pan and crack an egg into each hole. Cook until the edges of the whites start to become firm, about 5 minutes.

7. Place the skillet in the oven and bake until the egg whites are cooked through, about 5 minutes. Remove from the oven, garnish with the chives, and serve with the Spiced Honey Yogurt and cut-out sections of rosti.

INGREDIENTS:

6	CUPS PEELED AND GRATED POTATOES
1	TEASPOON KOSHER SALT
½	TEASPOON BLACK PEPPER
¼	CUP EXTRA-VIRGIN OLIVE OIL
4	EGGS
1	TABLESPOON CHOPPED FRESH CHIVES, FOR GARNISH
	SPICED HONEY YOGURT (SEE RECIPE), FOR SERVING

SPICED HONEY YOGURT

¼	CUP FULL-FAT GREEK YOGURT
⅛	TEASPOON CAYENNE PEPPER
1	TEASPOON HONEY
	SALT AND PEPPER, TO TASTE

SPICED HONEY YOGURT

1. Place all of the ingredients in a mixing bowl, stir to combine, and store in the refrigerator until ready to use.

SHORT RIBS WITH BRAISED
CAULIFLOWER & STUFFED TOMATOES

YIELD: 4 SERVINGS / **ACTIVE TIME:** 45 MINUTES / **TOTAL TIME:** 4 HOURS

In truth, any of the three components here will make for an outstanding dinner. Together, they are an outright feast.

1. Preheat the oven to 300°F. Place the olive oil in a Dutch oven and warm it over medium-high heat. Season the short ribs with salt and pepper, add them to the pot, and sear them for 1 minute on each side. Remove the short ribs from the pot and set them aside.

2. Reduce the heat to medium, add the onion, carrot, and celery and cook, stirring occasionally, until they have softened, about 5 minutes. Add the garlic, tomato paste, Ras el Hanout, and thyme and cook, stirring continually, for 1 minute.

3. Add the red wine and cook until the alcohol has been cooked off, about 3 minutes, scraping up any browned bits from the bottom of the pan.

4. Add the prune juice, stock, bay leaf, and prunes and bring the mixture to a boil. Return the short ribs to the pot, cover the pot, and place it in the oven. Braise the short ribs until they are extremely tender, 3 to 4 hours.

5. Remove the pot from the oven, remove the cooked short ribs, bay leaf, and half of the prunes, and set them aside. Place the mixture remaining in the Dutch oven in a food processor and puree until smooth.

6. Place the sauce back in the Dutch oven, add the reserved prunes and short ribs, and stir in the vinegar. Bring the dish to a simmer, taste, and adjust the seasoning as necessary.

7. Garnish with cilantro and sesame seeds and serve with the Braised Cauliflower and Couscous-Stuffed Tomatoes.

INGREDIENTS:

2 TABLESPOONS EXTRA-VIRGIN OLIVE OIL

3 LBS. BONE-IN SHORT RIBS

SALT AND PEPPER, TO TASTE

1 ONION, CHOPPED

1 CARROT, PEELED AND CHOPPED

2 CELERY STALKS, CHOPPED

4 GARLIC CLOVES, MINCED

1 TABLESPOON TOMATO PASTE

1 TABLESPOON RAS EL HANOUT (SEE PAGE 747)

1 TEASPOON FRESH THYME

½ CUP RED WINE

2 CUPS PRUNE JUICE

2 CUPS BEEF STOCK (SEE PAGE 369)

1 BAY LEAF

1 CUP PRUNES

2 TEASPOON RED WINE VINEGAR

FRESH CILANTRO, CHOPPED, FOR GARNISH

SESAME SEEDS, TOASTED, FOR GARNISH

BRAISED CAULIFLOWER (SEE PAGE 466), FOR SERVING

COUSCOUS-STUFFED TOMATOES (SEE PAGE 456), FOR SERVING

SEARED SHRIMP SKEWERS
WITH AIOLI & CAULIFLOWER CAKES

YIELD: 4 SERVINGS / ACTIVE TIME: 30 MINUTES / TOTAL TIME: 2 HOURS

A meal that is as suitable for a white tablecloth dinner party as it is for an impromptu meal enjoyed on the deck during the summer.

1. Place the olive oil, garlic, lime zest, lime juice, paprika, ginger, cumin, salt, and cayenne in a mixing bowl and whisk to combine.

2. Thread the shrimp onto skewers. Place the skewers in a large resealable bag, add the marinade, and marinate in the refrigerator for 1 hour.

3. Warm a cast-iron skillet over medium-high heat. Place the shrimp skewers in the pan and cook until just browned on both sides, 3 to 4 minutes.

4. Divide the skewers among the serving plates, garnish with cilantro, and serve with the Aioli, Cauliflower Cakes, and lime wedges.

AIOLI

1. Place the egg yolks, mustard, lemon juice, and garlic in a food processor and blitz until combined.

2. With the food processor running on low, slowly drizzle in the oils until they are emulsified. If the aioli becomes too thick for your liking, stir in water 1 teaspoon at a time until it has thinned out.

3. Season the aioli with salt and pepper and use as desired.

INGREDIENTS:

⅓ CUP EXTRA-VIRGIN OLIVE OIL

5 GARLIC CLOVES, MINCED

ZEST AND JUICE OF 1 LIME

1 TEASPOON PAPRIKA

½ TEASPOON GROUND GINGER

½ TEASPOON CUMIN

½ TEASPOON KOSHER SALT

¼ TEASPOON CAYENNE PEPPER

1 LB. SHRIMP (26-30), SHELLS REMOVED, DEVEINED

FRESH CILANTRO, CHOPPED, FOR GARNISH

AIOLI (SEE RECIPE), FOR SERVING

CAULIFLOWER CAKES (SEE PAGE 495), FOR SERVING

LIME WEDGES, FOR SERVING

AIOLI

2 LARGE EGG YOLKS

2 TEASPOONS DIJON MUSTARD

2 TEASPOONS FRESH LEMON JUICE

1 GARLIC CLOVE, MASHED

¾ CUP CANOLA OIL

¼ CUP EXTRA-VIRGIN OLIVE OIL

SALT AND PEPPER, TO TASTE

FRUTTI DI MARE WITH PENNE

YIELD: 4 TO 6 SERVINGS / **ACTIVE TIME:** 30 MINUTES / **TOTAL TIME:** 1 HOUR AND 30 MINUTES

A quick and easy pasta dish that becomes something special thanks to the fruits of the sea.

1. Place 2 tablespoons of the olive oil in a medium saucepan and warm it over medium heat. Add the reserved shrimp shells and cook for 4 minutes. Add the wine, reduce the heat, and simmer for 4 minutes, scraping up any browned bits up from the bottom of the pan. Strain the stock into a bowl and set it aside.

2. Place the remaining olive oil in a large skillet and warm it over medium heat. Add the onion and cook, stirring occasionally, until it has softened, about 5 minutes. Add the garlic, tomato paste, red pepper flakes, and saffron and cook, stirring continually, for 1 minute.

3. Add the stock, tomatoes, and clam juice and bring the mixture to a boil. Reduce the heat and simmer the sauce for 20 minutes.

4. Bring water to a boil in a large saucepan. Add salt and the penne and cook until the pasta is al dente, 6 to 8 minutes. Reserve ½ cup of the pasta water and drain the pasta.

5. Add the mussels, hinges facing down, to the sauce and cover the pan. Cook until the majority of the mussels have opened, about 5 minutes. Remove the mussels using a slotted spoon, discarding any that didn't open.

6. Add the scallops and shrimp to the sauce and cook until cooked through, about 2 minutes. Remove the pan from heat, add the squid, and cover the pan. Let the pan sit until the squid is cooked through, about 2 minutes.

7. Add the mussels and penne to the sauce and toss to combine, adding pasta water as needed to get the desired consistency. Season with salt and pepper, garnish with the parsley and toasted panko, and enjoy.

INGREDIENTS:

¼	CUP EXTRA-VIRGIN OLIVE OIL
½	LB. LARGE SHRIMP, SHELLS REMOVED AND RESERVED, DEVEINED
1	CUP WHITE WINE
1	ONION, SLICED THIN
4	GARLIC CLOVES, MINCED
2	TABLESPOONS TOMATO PASTE
⅛	TEASPOON RED PEPPER FLAKES
	PINCH OF SAFFRON
1	(28 OZ.) CAN OF CHOPPED TOMATOES, WITH THEIR LIQUID
2	CUPS CLAM JUICE
	SALT AND PEPPER, TO TASTE
1	LB. PENNE
½	LB. MUSSELS, SCRUBBED AND DEBEARDED
8	SCALLOPS, FOOT REMOVED FROM EACH
½	LB. SQUID
¼	CUP CHOPPED FRESH PARSLEY, FOR GARNISH
1	CUP PANKO, TOASTED, FOR GARNISH

MOUSSAKA

YIELD: 4 SERVINGS / **ACTIVE TIME:** 1 HOUR AND 15 MINUTES / **TOTAL TIME:** 2 HOURS

Layers of lamb and eggplant and an airy custard topping team to make moussaka the height of decadence.

1. Preheat the oven to 350°F. To begin preparations for the filling, place the cold water in a bowl, add the salt, and stir. When the salt has dissolved, add the eggplant cubes and let the cubes soak for about 20 minutes. Drain the eggplants and rinse with cold water. Squeeze the cubes to remove as much water as you can, place them on a pile of paper towels, and blot them dry. Set aside.

2. While the eggplants are soaking, add a tablespoon of the olive oil to a large cast-iron skillet and warm it over medium-high heat. When the oil starts to shimmer, add the ground lamb and cook, using a wooden spoon to break it up, until it is browned, about 8 minutes. Transfer the cooked lamb to a bowl and set it aside.

3. Add 2 tablespoons of the olive oil and the eggplant cubes to the skillet and cook, stirring frequently until they start to brown, about 5 minutes. Transfer the cooked eggplants to the bowl containing the lamb and add the rest of the oil, the onions, and the garlic to the skillet. Sauté until the onions are translucent, about 3 minutes, return the lamb and eggplants to the skillet, and stir in the wine, sauce, parsley, oregano, and cinnamon. Reduce the heat to low and simmer for about 15 minutes, stirring occasionally. Season with salt, pepper, and nutmeg and remove the pan from heat.

4. To begin preparations for the crust, place the eggs in a large bowl and beat them lightly. Place a saucepan over medium heat and melt the butter. Reduce the heat to medium-low and add the flour. Stir constantly until the mixture is smooth.

5. While stirring constantly, gradually add the milk and bring the mixture to a boil. When the mixture reaches a boil, remove the pan from heat. Stir approximately half of the mixture in the saucepan into the beaten eggs. Stir the tempered eggs into the saucepan and then add the cheese and dill or parsley. Stir to combine and pour the mixture over the lamb mixture in the skillet, using a rubber spatula to smooth the top.

6. Place the skillet in the oven and bake until the crust is set and golden brown, about 35 minutes. Remove from the oven and let the moussaka rest for 5 minutes before serving.

INGREDIENTS:

FOR THE FILLING

4	CUPS COLD WATER
¼	CUP KOSHER SALT, PLUS MORE TO TASTE
3	LARGE EGGPLANTS, ENDS TRIMMED, CUT INTO CUBES
5	TABLESPOONS EXTRA-VIRGIN OLIVE OIL
2	LBS. GROUND LAMB
2	ONIONS, DICED
3	GARLIC CLOVES, MINCED
½	CUP DRY WHITE WINE
1	CUP TOMATO SAUCE (SEE PAGE 775)
2	TABLESPOONS FINELY CHOPPED FRESH PARSLEY
1	TEASPOON DRIED OREGANO
½	TEASPOON CINNAMON
	BLACK PEPPER, TO TASTE
	FRESHLY GRATED NUTMEG, TO TASTE

FOR THE CRUST

5	EGGS
6	TABLESPOONS UNSALTED BUTTER
⅓	CUP ALL-PURPOSE FLOUR
2½	CUPS MILK
⅔	CUP GRATED KEFALOTYRI CHEESE
⅓	CUP FRESH DILL OR PARSLEY, CHOPPED

STUFFED ZUCCHINI

YIELD: 4 SERVINGS / ACTIVE TIME: 25 MINUTES / TOTAL TIME: 45 MINUTES

This is a dish that will accomodate almost any whim, so don't hesitate to get creative with the stuffing.

1. Preheat the oven to 400°F. Place the zucchini on a baking sheet, cut sides down, brush with 1 tablespoon of the olive oil, and season them with salt and pepper. Place the zucchini in the oven and roast until their skins start to wrinkle, about 7 minutes. Remove the zucchini from the oven and set them aside. Leave the oven on.

2. Place 1 tablespoon of the olive oil in a medium saucepan and warm it over medium-high heat. Add the lamb, season it with salt and pepper, and cook, breaking up the meat with a wooden spoon, until it is browned, about 5 minutes. Using a slotted spoon, transfer the lamb to a bowl and set it aside.

3. Drain the fat from the saucepan, add the remaining olive oil and the shallots and cook, stirring occasionally, until they are translucent, about 3 minutes. Add the garlic and Ras el Hanout and cook, stirring continually, for 1 minute.

4. Add the stock, couscous, and apricots and bring the mixture to a boil. Remove the pan from heat, cover it, and let it stand for 5 minutes.

5. Fluff the couscous mixture with a fork, stir in the pine nuts, parsley, and lamb, and season it with salt and pepper.

6. Turn the roasted zucchini over and distribute the filling between their cavities. Place them in the oven and roast until warmed through, about 5 minutes. Remove from the oven and let the stuffed zucchini cool slightly before enjoying.

INGREDIENTS:

4	ZUCCHINI, TRIMMED AND HALVED, SEEDS SCOOPED WITH A SPOON
3	TABLESPOONS EXTRA-VIRGIN OLIVE OIL
	SALT AND PEPPER, TO TASTE
½	LB. GROUND LAMB
4	SHALLOTS, MINCED
4	GARLIC CLOVES, MINCED
1	TABLESPOON RAS EL HANOUT (SEE PAGE 747)
1	CUP CHICKEN STOCK (SEE PAGE 368)
½	CUP COUSCOUS
⅓	CUP DRIED APRICOTS, CHOPPED
3	TABLESPOONS PINE NUTS, TOASTED AND CHOPPED
2	TABLESPOONS CHOPPED FRESH PARSLEY

PAN-ROASTED MONKFISH
WITH OLIVE RELISH & BRAISED FENNEL

YIELD: 4 SERVINGS / ACTIVE TIME: 30 MINUTES / TOTAL TIME: 1 HOUR

A beautifully balanced dish that targets every single taste bud.

1. Place ¼ cup of the olive oil in a small saucepan and warm it over low heat. Add the oregano, remove the pan from heat, and cover it. Let the oil steep for 5 minutes.

2. Add the vinegar, onion, mustard, olives, capers, and parsley, season the relish with salt and pepper, and stir to combine. Transfer the relish to a bowl and set it aside.

3. Place the remaining olive oil in a large cast-iron skillet and warm it over medium-high heat. Pat the monkfish dry with paper towels and season it with salt and pepper. Place the monkfish in the pan and cook until golden brown on the bottom, 3 to 4 minutes. Turn it over and cook until it is cooked through (internal temperature of 160°F), another 3 to 4 minutes.

4. Transfer the monkfish to a serving platter, garnish it with the pine nuts and Parmesan, and serve with the olive relish, Braised Fennel, and lemon wedges.

BRAISED FENNEL

1. Place the olive oil in a Dutch oven and warm it over medium-high heat. Add the fennel and cook until golden brown on both sides, 6 to 8 minutes.

2. Add the white wine and cook until it has almost evaporated, about 3 minutes, scraping up any browned bits from the bottom of the Dutch oven.

3. Add the lemon zest, lemon juice, stock, and honey, bring to a simmer, and cover the pot. Simmer until the fennel is tender, about 10 minutes. Remove the fennel from the pot with a slotted spoon and place it in a bowl.

4. Add the radicchio to the Dutch oven and cook over medium heat, stirring frequently, until it has softened, about 5 minutes.

5. Place the radicchio on top of the fennel, season the dish with salt and pepper, and serve.

INGREDIENTS:

6	TABLESPOONS EXTRA-VIRGIN OLIVE OIL
1	TABLESPOON DRIED OREGANO
2	TABLESPOONS RED WINE VINEGAR
½	ONION, FINELY DICED
2	TEASPOONS DIJON MUSTARD
2	TABLESPOONS MINCED KALAMATA OLIVES
2	TABLESPOONS MINCED GREEN OLIVES
1	TABLESPOON MINCED CAPERS
1	TABLESPOON CHOPPED FRESH PARSLEY
	SALT AND PEPPER, TO TASTE
1½	LBS. MONKFISH FILLETS, CUT INTO 2-INCH CUBES
	PINE NUTS, TOASTED AND CHOPPED, FOR GARNISH
	PARMESAN CHEESE, SHAVED, FOR GARNISH
	BRAISED FENNEL (SEE RECIPE), FOR SERVING
	LEMON WEDGES, FOR SERVING

BRAISED FENNEL

2	TABLESPOONS EXTRA-VIRGIN OLIVE OIL
2	FENNEL BULBS, TRIMMED AND HALVED
½	CUP WHITE WINE
	ZEST AND JUICE OF ½ LEMON
2	CUPS CHICKEN STOCK (SEE PAGE 368)
1	TABLESPOON HONEY
1	RADICCHIO, CORED AND SLICED THIN
	SALT AND PEPPER, TO TASTE

Eggplant Rollatini, see page 226

EGGPLANT ROLLATINI

YIELD: 2 SERVINGS / **ACTIVE TIME:** 1 HOUR / **TOTAL TIME:** 1 HOUR AND 30 MINUTES

This rollatini has its feet planted firmly in Italy, but the addition of bright sumac means that it also looks longingly toward the east.

1. Add canola oil to a deep skillet until it is about 1 inch deep. Place the eggs in a bowl and beat until scrambled. Place the flour on a plate and the panko on another.

2. Dredge the eggplant in the flour, then the egg, then the panko, repeating until each piece is fully coated.

3. Working in batches to avoid crowding the pan, gently slip the breaded eggplant into the hot oil and fry until golden brown, about 3 minutes. Transfer the cooked slices of eggplant to a paper towel–lined plate to drain.

4. Preheat the oven to 400°F.

5. Place the remaining ingredients, except for the sauce, in a mixing bowl and stir until thoroughly combined. Place a heaping tablespoon of the mixture at the end of each slice of eggplant and then roll up the slices. Place the rolled-up eggplant in a cast-iron skillet or baking dish, seam side down.

6. Pour the sauce over the eggplant and place the pan in the oven. Bake until the filling is warmed through, about 25 minutes. Remove from the oven and serve immediately.

INGREDIENTS:

	CANOLA OIL, AS NEEDED
2	EGGS
½	CUP ALL-PURPOSE FLOUR
1	CUP PANKO
1	EGGPLANT, TRIMMED AND SLICED LENGTHWISE (¼ INCH THICK)
1	CUP RICOTTA CHEESE
1	TEASPOON SUMAC
1	TEASPOON SUGAR
1	TEASPOON FRESH LEMON JUICE
1	TABLESPOON KOSHER SALT
2	CUPS TOMATO SAUCE (SEE PAGE 775)

ORANGE CHICKEN WITH
ROASTED VEGETABLES & OLIVES

YIELD: 4 SERVINGS / **ACTIVE TIME:** 30 MINUTES / **TOTAL TIME:** 1 HOUR

Discover the magic that fennel and orange make.

1. Preheat the oven to 400°F. Place the carrots, fennel, tomatoes, 2 tablespoons of the olive oil, the garlic, rosemary, orange zest, and red wine vinegar in a bowl, season the mixture with salt and pepper, and stir to combine.

2. Transfer the vegetable mixture to a baking dish, place it in the oven, and roast until the vegetables are almost completely tender, about 40 minutes. Remove the dish from the oven and set it aside. Leave the oven on.

3. While the vegetables are roasting, season the chicken with salt and pepper, place it in a bowl, and add the orange juice. Stir until the chicken is coated and let the mixture marinate.

4. Place the remaining olive oil in a skillet and warm it over medium-high heat. When the oil starts to shimmer, add the chicken and cook until browned on both sides, about 8 minutes. Remove the chicken from the pan and place it on top of the vegetable mixture in the baking dish.

5. Place the baking dish in the oven and roast until the chicken is cooked all the way through, about 16 minutes.

6. Divide the vegetables among the serving plates, top each portion with a chicken breast, and sprinkle the olives and basil over each dish.

INGREDIENTS:

3	CARROTS, PEELED AND CHOPPED
1	SMALL FENNEL BULB, TRIMMED AND SLICED THIN
1	CUP CHERRY TOMATOES
¼	CUP EXTRA-VIRGIN OLIVE OIL
4	GARLIC CLOVES, MINCED
2	TEASPOONS FINELY CHOPPED FRESH ROSEMARY
1	TABLESPOON ORANGE ZEST
1	TABLESPOON RED WINE VINEGAR
	SALT AND PEPPER, TO TASTE
2	LBS. BONELESS, SKINLESS CHICKEN BREASTS
	JUICE OF 2 ORANGES
¼	CUP KALAMATA OLIVES, PITS REMOVED, CHOPPED, FOR GARNISH
	FRESH BASIL, FINELY CHOPPED, FOR GARNISH

BAKED ORZO

YIELD: 4 TO 6 SERVINGS / ACTIVE TIME: 30 MINUTES / TOTAL TIME: 1 HOUR AND 30 MINUTES

An invaluable recipe, one of those easy, comforting dinners that you can never really make too often.

1. Preheat the oven to 350°F. Place the orzo in a medium saucepan and toast it, stirring frequently, over medium heat until it is lightly browned, about 10 minutes. Transfer the orzo to a bowl.

2. Place 2 tablespoons of the olive oil in the saucepan and warm it over medium heat. Add the eggplant and cook, stirring occasionally, until it has browned, about 10 minutes. Remove the eggplant from the pan and place it in the bowl with the orzo.

3. Add 1 tablespoon of the olive oil to the saucepan and warm it over medium heat. Add the onion and cook, stirring occasionally, until it has softened, about 5 minutes. Add the garlic, oregano, and tomato paste and cook, stirring continually, for 1 minute.

4. Remove the pan from heat, add the stock, Parmesan, capers, orzo, and eggplant, season the mixture with salt and pepper, and stir to combine. Pour the mixture into a 10 x 8–inch baking dish.

5. Alternating rows, layer the tomatoes and zucchini on top of the orzo mixture. Season with salt and pepper.

6. Place the baking dish in the oven and bake until the orzo is tender, about 30 minutes.

7. Remove the dish from the oven, sprinkle the feta on top, and enjoy.

INGREDIENTS:

2	CUPS ORZO
3	TABLESPOONS EXTRA-VIRGIN OLIVE OIL
1	EGGPLANT, SEEDS REMOVED, CHOPPED INTO ½-INCH CUBES
1	ONION, CHOPPED
4	GARLIC CLOVES, MINCED
2	TEASPOONS DRIED OREGANO
1	TABLESPOON TOMATO PASTE
3	CUPS CHICKEN STOCK (SEE PAGE 368)
1	CUP FRESHLY GRATED PARMESAN CHEESE
2	TABLESPOONS CAPERS, DRAINED AND CHOPPED
	SALT AND PEPPER, TO TASTE
2	TOMATOES, SLICED THIN
2	ZUCCHINI, SLICED THIN
1	CUP CRUMBLED FETA CHEESE

ROASTED CHICKEN THIGHS
WITH PISTACHIO & RAISIN SAUCE

YIELD: 4 SERVINGS / **ACTIVE TIME:** 20 MINUTES / **TOTAL TIME:** 24 HOURS

Letting the chicken thighs dry out in the refrigerator overnight is key to getting the most out of them.

1. Preheat the oven to 425°F. Pat the chicken thighs dry and poke their skin all over with a skewer. Place the chicken thighs on a wire rack set in a rimmed baking sheet. Place the chicken thighs in the refrigerator and let them sit, uncovered, overnight.

2. Remove the chicken thighs from the refrigerator, brush them with the olive oil, and place them on a baking sheet. Season with salt and pepper and place them in the oven.

3. Roast the chicken thighs until they are cooked through (internal temperature is 160°F), 15 to 20 minutes. Remove the chicken thighs from the oven and let them rest for 10 minutes.

4. Spread some of the sauce over each of the serving plates, place a chicken thigh on each plate, and serve with the Marinated Cauliflower & Chickpeas.

INGREDIENTS:

4   BONE-IN, SKIN-ON CHICKEN THIGHS

2   TEASPOONS EXTRA-VIRGIN OLIVE OIL

    SALT AND PEPPER, TO TASTE

    PISTACHIO & RAISIN SAUCE (SEE PAGE 762), FOR SERVING

    MARINATED CAULIFLOWER & CHICKPEAS (SEE PAGE 480), FOR SERVING

MONKFISH TAGINE

YIELD: 4 SERVINGS / ACTIVE TIME: 15 MINUTES / TOTAL TIME: 45 MINUTES

The genius of the tagine is on full display in this seafood-based version.

1. Place the olive oil in a Dutch oven and warm it over medium-high heat. Add the onion and carrots and cook, stirring occasionally, until they are lightly browned, 8 to 10 minutes.

2. Add the tomato paste, paprika, cumin, saffron, garlic, and orange zest and cook, stirring continually, for 1 minute. Stir in the orange juice, clam juice, and chickpeas and bring to a simmer.

3. Pat the monkfish dry with paper towels and season it with salt and pepper. Nestle the monkfish into the pot and spoon some liquid over it. Cover the pot and simmer until the monkfish is cooked through (internal temperature of 160°F), about 10 minutes.

4. Add the olives, mint, and vinegar and gently stir to incorporate. Taste, adjust the seasoning as necessary, and enjoy.

INGREDIENTS:

2	TABLESPOONS EXTRA-VIRGIN OLIVE OIL
1	ONION, CHOPPED
2	CARROTS, PEELED AND CHOPPED
1	TABLESPOON TOMATO PASTE
1	TEASPOON PAPRIKA
1	TEASPOON CUMIN
¼	TEASPOON SAFFRON
4	GARLIC CLOVES, MINCED
	ZEST AND JUICE OF 1 ORANGE
1	CUP CLAM JUICE
1	(14 OZ.) CAN OF CHICKPEAS, DRAINED AND RINSED
2	LBS. MONKFISH FILLETS
	SALT AND PEPPER, TO TASTE
¼	CUP SLICED KALAMATA OLIVES
2	TABLESPOONS TORN FRESH MINT
1	TEASPOON WHITE WINE VINEGAR

CREAMY PAPPARDELLE WITH CRAB

YIELD: 8 SERVINGS / **ACTIVE TIME:** 1 HOUR AND 15 MINUTES / **TOTAL TIME:** 1 HOUR AND 40 MINUTES

Don't be intimidated by fresh pasta—it's easy to make, and noticeably better.

1. Place the flour on a work surface and make a well in the center. Pour the yolks into the well and use a fork to incorporate the flour. When enough flour has been incorporated that the egg yolks become like a paste, start kneading the mixture.

2. Incorporate the salt and olive oil and continue kneading until the mixture comes together as a dough, dusting your hands with '00' flour as necessary. Shape the dough into a square, dust it with '00' flour, cover it with plastic wrap, and chill in the refrigerator for 30 minutes.

3. Set up a station with a pasta maker, a sharp knife, parchment-lined baking sheets, a small bowl containing '00' flour, and another small bowl containing semolina flour.

4. Remove the dough from fridge and cut it in half. Cover one piece in plastic wrap and place it in a resealable plastic bag. Store it in the freezer and save for another preparation.

5. Cut the remaining piece of dough into four pieces. Set the pasta machine to the widest setting and, working with one piece of dough at a time, run it through the machine, adjusting to a narrower setting with each pass, until it is the desired thickness (about ⅛ inch thick). Cut the rolled sheets of dough in half and dust them with '00' flour. Roll the sheets into logs and slice dough into ¾-inch-wide strips. Cover the pieces of dough that you are not working on with plastic wrap, as it will prevent them from drying out.

6. Dust the cut pasta with semolina, shape them into bundles, and place them on the baking sheets.

7. Place the cut pasta in the freezer for 10 minutes.

8. Bring water to a boil in a large saucepan. Generously salt the water—it should taste like sea water. Add the pasta and stir it with a fork for 30 seconds. Cook until the pasta floats to the top, about 3 minutes.

9. Reserve ¼ cup of the pasta water and then drain the pasta. Return the pasta to the saucepan, add the crab, Parmesan, parsley, and sauce, and toss to coat, adding pasta water as needed to get the desired consistency. Serve immediately.

INGREDIENTS:

- 8 CUPS '00' PASTA FLOUR, PLUS MORE AS NEEDED
- 3⅔ CUPS EGG YOLKS
- 1 TEASPOON FINE SEA SALT, PLUS MORE TO TASTE
- 1 TABLESPOON EXTRA-VIRGIN OLIVE OIL
- SEMOLINA FLOUR, AS NEEDED
- 1 LB. LUMP CRABMEAT
- 1 CUP FRESHLY GRATED PARMESAN CHEESE
- 3 TABLESPOONS CHOPPED FRESH PARSLEY
- CREAMY BALSAMIC & MUSHROOM SAUCE (SEE PAGE 789), FOR SERVING

Ropa Vieja, see page 239

ROASTED APRICOT CHICKEN
WITH MINT & SAGE BUTTERNUT SQUASH

YIELD: 6 SERVINGS / **ACTIVE TIME:** 30 MINUTES / **TOTAL TIME:** 2 HOURS

Some time in the oven concentrates the sweet flavor of the apricots, allowing them to balance out the slight acidity from the tomatoes and the blend of earthy seasonings.

1. Preheat the oven to 375°F. Place the cinnamon, cumin, turmeric, paprika, 1 teaspoon of the salt, and the olive oil in a mixing bowl and stir until well combined. Add the chicken to the bowl and work the rub into the chicken with your hands until the entire chicken is coated.

2. Place the tomatoes, apricots, garlic, raisins, and stock in a Dutch oven and stir until combined. Place the chicken on top of the mixture and place the pot in the oven. Bake until the thickest part of the chicken's thigh reaches an internal temperature of 160°F, about 50 minutes.

3. Remove the chicken from the pot, transfer it to a cutting board, and let it rest for 15 minutes.

4. Place the Dutch oven with the veggies over medium-low heat and simmer until the liquid has been reduced by half, 10 to 15 minutes.

5. Carve the chicken and cut the meat into bite-size pieces. Stir them into the simmering sauce and serve over the Mint & Sage Butternut Squash.

INGREDIENTS:

1	TEASPOON CINNAMON
½	TEASPOON CUMIN
1	TEASPOON TURMERIC
1½	TEASPOONS SMOKED SPANISH PAPRIKA
1	TABLESPOON KOSHER SALT
1	TEASPOON EXTRA-VIRGIN OLIVE OIL
4	LB. WHOLE CHICKEN
3	PLUM TOMATOES, DICED
1	CUP CHOPPED DRIED TURKISH APRICOTS
4	LARGE GARLIC CLOVES, MINCED
¼	CUP GOLDEN RAISINS
3	CUPS CHICKEN STOCK (SEE PAGE 368)
	MINT & SAGE BUTTERNUT SQUASH (SEE PAGE 395), FOR SERVING

ROPA VIEJA

YIELD: 8 SERVINGS / ACTIVE TIME: 40 MINUTES / TOTAL TIME: 3 HOURS

Yes, this is one of Cuba's national dishes. But the recipe itself is over five hundred years old, originating in Spain.

1. Preheat the oven to 325°F. Place the flank steak, 2 of the bay leaves, the sliced garlic cloves, 1½ of the onions, and the stock in a Dutch oven and place it in the oven. Braise until the meat is tender and easy to shred with a fork, 2 to 2½ hours.

2. Remove the pot from the oven and shred the beef with a fork. Set it aside.

3. Place ¼ cup of the avocado oil in a medium saucepan and warm it over high heat. Add the peppers and cook, stirring occasionally, until soft, about 5 minutes. Add the remaining onion and cook, stirring occasionally, until the onion is translucent, about 3 minutes. Stir in the tomato puree, wine, cumin, paprika, salt, and pepper. Cover the pan, reduce the heat to medium, and cook until the sauce has thickened, about 15 minutes.

4. Add the shredded meat and remaining bay leaf to the sauce and stir to combine. Cover the pan and cook for 5 minutes. Taste and adjust the seasoning as necessary.

5. Place the remaining avocado oil in a large saucepan with the crushed garlic clove and warm over medium heat. Add the rice and stir to coat with the oil. Add 4 cups of water and season with salt.

6. Bring to a simmer, cover the pan, reduce the heat, and let the rice simmer for 15 minutes. Turn off the heat and let the pan sit for 5 minutes. Fluff the rice before serving with the ropa vieja and avocado.

INGREDIENTS:

2	LBS. FLANK STEAK
3	BAY LEAVES
4	GARLIC CLOVES, 3 SLICED, 1 CRUSHED
2	YELLOW ONIONS, SLICED
4	CUPS CHICKEN STOCK (SEE PAGE 368)
¼	CUP PLUS 1 TABLESPOON AVOCADO OIL
1	RED BELL PEPPER, STEM AND SEEDS REMOVED, SLICED
1	GREEN BELL PEPPER, STEM AND SEEDS REMOVED, SLICED
1	(28 OZ.) CAN OF TOMATO PUREE
1½	CUPS WHITE WINE
1	TEASPOON CUMIN
½	TEASPOON SMOKED PAPRIKA
1	TEASPOON KOSHER SALT, PLUS MORE TO TASTE
⅛	TEASPOON BLACK PEPPER
2	CUPS JASMINE RICE, RINSED AND DRAINED
	SLICED AVOCADO, FOR SERVING

CORNBREAD & CRAB–STUFFED BRANZINO

YIELD: 4 TO 6 SERVINGS / ACTIVE TIME: 1 HOUR / TOTAL TIME: 1 HOUR AND 45 MINUTES

Stuffing whole branzino makes this a decadent dinner that won't leave you feeling uncomfortably full.

1. Preheat the oven to 400°F. Place a wire rack in a rimmed baking sheet. Layer the stuffing, crabmeat, slices of lemon, thyme, and bay leaves inside of the branzino and tie the fish closed with kitchen twine. Season them with salt and pepper.

2. Place the olive oil in a large skillet and warm it over medium-high heat. Place the branzino in the pan, one at a time, and sear on each side for 3 to 4 minutes.

3. Place the branzino on the wire rack set in the baking sheet, place them in the oven, and roast until cooked through (internal temperature of 120°F).

4. Remove the branzino from the oven, cut off the kitchen twine, and serve them with the Charred Scallion Sauce and rice.

CORNBREAD STUFFING

1. Preheat the oven to 350°F. Line six wells in a muffin pan with paper liners. Sift the flour, baking powder, baking soda, salt, and cornmeal into a mixing bowl and set the mixture aside.

2. Place the egg, yogurt, honey, ¼ cup of the milk, and the melted butter in a separate bowl and whisk until combined. Add the wet mixture to the dry mixture and whisk until it comes together as a smooth batter.

3. Pour the batter into the paper liners, place the pan in the oven, and bake until a cake tester inserted into the center of each muffin comes out clean, 10 to 15 minutes. Remove the muffins from the oven and let them cool completely. When the muffins are cool enough to handle, chop them into bite-size pieces.

4. Coat a small skillet with butter and warm it over medium heat. Add the onion, celery, and garlic and cook, stirring frequently, until the onion has softened, about 5 minutes. Season the mixture with salt, stir in the sage and thyme, and transfer the mixture to a bowl.

5. Add the pieces of cornbread and toss to combine. Add the remaining milk, stir until incorporated, and use immediately.

INGREDIENTS:

- 2½ CUPS CORNBREAD STUFFING (SEE RECIPE)
- 1 LB. LUMP CRABMEAT
- 1 LEMON, SLICED THIN
- 4 SPRIGS OF FRESH THYME
- 4 BAY LEAVES
- 2 (1 LB.) WHOLE BRANZINO, CLEANED, SCALES REMOVED
- SALT AND PEPPER, TO TASTE
- 1 TABLESPOON EXTRA-VIRGIN OLIVE OIL
- CHARRED SCALLION SAUCE (SEE PAGE 781), FOR SERVING
- RICE, COOKED, FOR SERVING

CORNBREAD STUFFING

- ¼ CUP ALL-PURPOSE FLOUR
- 1½ TEASPOONS BAKING POWDER
- ¼ TEASPOON BAKING SODA
- ⅓ TEASPOON FINE SEA SALT, PLUS MORE TO TASTE
- ½ CUP YELLOW CORNMEAL
- 1 EGG
- 1½ TEASPOONS HONEY
- ½ CUP PLAIN YOGURT
- ½ CUP MILK
- 1½ TABLESPOONS UNSALTED BUTTER, MELTED, PLUS MORE AS NEEDED
- ¼ RED ONION, DICED
- 1 CELERY STALK, DICED
- 1 GARLIC CLOVE, MINCED
- SALT, TO TASTE
- 1 TEASPOON CHOPPED FRESH SAGE
- 1 TEASPOON CHOPPED FRESH THYME

ROAST CHICKEN WITH HARISSA & DUCK FAT

YIELD: 4 SERVINGS / ACTIVE TIME: 1 HOUR / TOTAL TIME: 25 HOURS

The real magic begins when the duck fat starts sizzling in the pan. Its richness is matched and balanced with high-heat harissa.

1. Place the garlic, sugar, coriander seeds, salt, and water in a large saucepan and bring to a boil, stirring to dissolve the sugar and salt. Transfer the brine to a large bowl and add 1 cup of ice. Let the brine cool completely.

2. Place the chicken halves in the cooled brine, cover the bowl tightly with plastic wrap, and refrigerate for 12 hours.

3. Transfer the chicken to a rimmed baking sheet or baking pan and pick off any coriander seeds. Spread the harissa all over the chicken, cover it tightly with plastic wrap, and refrigerate for at least 1 hour, and up to 12 hours.

4. Preheat the oven to 400°F.

5. Place the duck fat in a large cast-iron pan and warm it over medium heat. Carefully place the chicken halves, skin side down, in the pan, making sure all of the skin is in the fat. Cook until the skin darkens and starts to crisp up, about 5 minutes. Transfer the skillet to the oven and roast the chicken until the skin is very dark and the meat is more than halfway cooked through, 20 to 25 minutes.

6. Remove the skillet from the oven and carefully turn the chicken over. Return it to the oven and roast, skin side up, until an instant-read thermometer inserted into the thickest part of the thigh registers 165°F, 8 to 12 minutes.

7. Transfer the chicken to a large platter, skin side up. Drizzle the pan juices over the chicken and enjoy.

INGREDIENTS:

3 GARLIC CLOVES, SMASHED

⅓ CUP SUGAR

¼ CUP CORIANDER SEEDS

1 CUP KOSHER SALT, PLUS MORE TO TASTE

8 CUPS WATER

4 LB. WHOLE CHICKEN, HALVED AND BACKBONE REMOVED

1 CUP THREE-PEPPER HARISSA SAUCE (SEE PAGE 791)

¼ CUP DUCK FAT

SABICH

Falafel, burika, and shawarma are all popular sandwiches in Israel, but the sabich is arguably the most beloved.

1. Arrange the eggplant rounds in a single layer on a wire rack set in a baking sheet. Sprinkle them on both sides with the salt and let the eggplant slices stand for at least 20 minutes and up to 1 hour.

2. Preheat the oven to 425°F.

3. Pat the eggplant slices dry using a paper towel, brush both sides generously with oil, and place them on a baking sheet or two, being careful not to overcrowd either pan. Place the eggplants in the oven and roast until golden brown, about 20 minutes, turning the eggplants over halfway through.

4. Create your spread, and enjoy.

INGREDIENTS:

2   MEDIUM EGGPLANTS, SLICED INTO 1-INCH-THICK ROUNDS

2   TEASPOONS KOSHER SALT

    AVOCADO OIL, TO TASTE

SERVE WITH ANY, OR ALL, OF THE FOLLOWING:

6–8   PIECES OF PITA BREAD (SEE PAGE 532)

8   LARGE HARD-BOILED EGGS, QUARTERED

2   CUCUMBERS, CHOPPED

2   TOMATOES, CHOPPED

1   ONION, CHOPPED

1   BELL PEPPER, STEM AND SEEDS REMOVED, CHOPPED

    TAHINI SAUCE (SEE PAGE 767)

    FRESH PARSLEY, CHOPPED

    PICKLES

    OLIVES

    HOT PEPPERS

    RED ZHUG (SEE PAGE 748)

Sabich, see page 243

SEAFOOD RISOTTO

YIELD: 4 TO 6 SERVINGS / **ACTIVE TIME:** 45 MINUTES / **TOTAL TIME:** 45 MINUTES

A dding a small amount of crème fraîche makes risotto's best attribute—its creaminess—exceptional.

1. Place the stock and clam juice in a saucepan, bring the mixture to a simmer, and remove the pan from heat.

2. Place 1 tablespoon of the olive oil in a large, deep skillet and warm it over medium-high heat. Add the shallots and cook, stirring occasionally, until they start to soften, about 3 minutes.

3. Add the rice and cook, stirring frequently, for 2 minutes. Add the white wine and cook, stirring frequently, until the rice has absorbed the wine.

4. While stirring continually, add the stock-and-clam juice mixture 2 tablespoons at a time, waiting until each addition has been fully absorbed before adding more. Add the mixture until the rice is al dente, about 15 minutes.

5. Place the remaining oil in another skillet and warm it over medium-high heat. Season the scallops, squid, and shrimp with salt, place them in the pan, and sear for 1½ minutes on each side. If the scallops are large, sear those first. Transfer the seafood to a plate and set it aside.

6. Stir the tomato paste, Parmesan, and 2 tablespoons of the crème fraîche into the risotto. Season it with salt and pepper and ladle it into warmed bowls. Top each portion with the seafood, chives, and remaining crème fraîche and enjoy.

INGREDIENTS:

3–4	CUPS CHICKEN STOCK (SEE PAGE 368)
1	CUP CLAM JUICE
2	TABLESPOONS EXTRA-VIRGIN OLIVE OIL
2	SHALLOTS, MINCED
2	CUPS ARBORIO RICE
¼	CUP WHITE WINE
	SALT AND PEPPER, TO TASTE
½	LB. SCALLOPS
½	LB. SQUID, TENTACLES LEFT WHOLE, BODIES HALVED
½	LB. LARGE SHRIMP, SHELLS REMOVED, DEVEINED
2	TABLESPOONS TOMATO PASTE
1½	CUPS FRESHLY GRATED PARMESAN CHEESE
½	CUP CRÈME FRAÎCHE
¼	CUP CHOPPED FRESH CHIVES, FOR GARNISH

SPAGHETTI WITH OXTAIL RAGOUT

Behind the oxtail's tough exterior lies an unthinkable amount of flavor. Braising it for the better part of an afternoon gets you in touch with its good side.

1. Preheat the oven to 300°F. Place the olive oil in a Dutch oven and warm it over medium heat. Season the oxtails with salt and pepper, place them in the pot, and sear until golden brown all over, about 6 minutes. Remove the oxtails from the pot and set them aside.

2. Add the onion and cook, stirring occasionally, until it has softened, about 5 minutes. Add the garlic, thyme, cinnamon sticks, and cloves and cook, stirring continually, for 1 minute.

3. Add the red wine and cook until the alcohol has cooked off, about 4 minutes. Add the stock and tomatoes and bring the mixture to a boil. Return the seared oxtails to the pot, cover the pot, and place it in the oven.

4. Braise until the oxtails are falling off the bone, 3 to 4 hours.

5. Remove the ragout from the oven, remove the oxtails from the sauce, and place them on a cutting board. Let them cool slightly and then use two forks to shred the meat.

6. Remove the cinnamon sticks from the sauce and stir in the shredded oxtails.

7. Bring water to a boil in a large saucepan. Add salt and the spaghetti and cook until the pasta is al dente, 6 to 8 minutes. Drain, add the spaghetti to the ragout, and toss to combine. Garnish with Parmesan and parsley and enjoy.

INGREDIENTS:

1	TABLESPOON EXTRA-VIRGIN OLIVE OIL
1½	LBS. OXTAILS
	SALT AND PEPPER, TO TASTE
1	ONION, CHOPPED
4	GARLIC CLOVES, MINCED
1	TEASPOON FRESH THYME
2	CINNAMON STICKS
½	TEASPOON GROUND CLOVES
⅓	CUP RED WINE
4	CUPS BEEF STOCK (SEE PAGE 369)
1	(28 OZ.) CAN OF DICED TOMATOES, WITH THEIR LIQUID
1	LB. SPAGHETTI
½	CUP FRESHLY GRATED PARMESAN CHEESE, FOR GARNISH
	FRESH PARSLEY, CHOPPED, FOR GARNISH

SHAWARMA-SPICED LEG OF LAMB

YIELD: 8 SERVINGS / ACTIVE TIME: 30 MINUTES / TOTAL TIME: 30 HOURS

When cooking a leg of lamb, the bone-in version is better in terms of flavor, but a boneless, tied leg of lamb is a little more manageable and cooks more quickly.

1. To prepare the rub, use a mortar and pestle or a spice grinder to grind the cumin, caraway, and coriander seeds to a fine powder. Transfer to a small bowl and stir in the chiles, garlic, oil, paprika, and cinnamon.

2. To begin preparations for the lamb, trim any excess fat from the lamb and remove any silvery skin. Lightly score the flesh with a paring knife and pat it dry with paper towels. Season the lamb generously with salt and pepper, place it on a wire rack set in a rimmed baking sheet, and apply the rub. Refrigerate for 12 to 24 hours.

3. Preheat the oven to 450°F.

4. Place the lamb in the oven and roast until it is well browned all over, 20 to 25 minutes.

5. Remove the lamb from the oven and reduce the oven temperature to 250°F. Grind the caraway and coriander seeds into a powder and set it aside.

6. Place the avocado oil in a large Dutch oven and warm it over medium heat (if the lamb won't fit in the pot you have, set a roasting pan over two burners). Add the onion and cook, stirring occasionally, until it starts to soften, about 5 minutes.

7. Stir in the ancho chile powder, chipotle chile powder, turmeric, and cinnamon and cook, stirring continuously, until fragrant, about 2 minutes. Add the tomatoes and broth and bring to a simmer. Season the sauce lightly with salt and pepper.

8. Carefully place the lamb in the pot and add just enough water to cover it if it is not submerged. Cover the pot, place it in the oven, and braise the lamb until the meat is very tender and the bone wiggles easily in the joint, about 5 hours (if using a roasting pan, add water as needed, so the liquid comes halfway up the sides of the leg of lamb, cover the pan with foil, and turn the lamb over once during braising).

9. Remove from the oven, transfer the lamb to a platter, and tent it with foil. Place the Dutch oven over medium-high heat and bring the braising liquid to a boil. Cook, stirring often, until it has reduced by half, 25 to 30 minutes. Taste and adjust the seasoning as necessary. Spoon the sauce over the lamb and enjoy.

INGREDIENTS:

FOR THE RUB

2	TABLESPOONS CUMIN SEEDS
2	TEASPOONS CARAWAY SEEDS
2	TEASPOONS CORIANDER SEEDS
2	THAI CHILE PEPPERS, STEMS AND SEEDS REMOVED, FINELY DICED
4	GARLIC CLOVES, GRATED
½	CUP AVOCADO OIL
1	TABLESPOON PAPRIKA
½	TEASPOON CINNAMON

FOR THE LAMB

6	LB. BONE-IN LEG OF LAMB, SHANK ATTACHED, FRENCHED
	SALT AND PEPPER, TO TASTE
½	TEASPOON CARAWAY SEEDS
½	TEASPOON CORIANDER SEEDS
¼	CUP AVOCADO OIL
1	LARGE ONION, SLICED THIN
1	TABLESPOON ANCHO CHILE POWDER
1	TABLESPOON CHIPOTLE CHILE POWDER
1	TEASPOON TURMERIC
½	TEASPOON CINNAMON
1	(28 OZ.) CAN OF CRUSHED TOMATOES, DRAINED
4	CUPS LOW-SODIUM CHICKEN BROTH

DOGFISH CHRAIME

YIELD: 2 SERVINGS / ACTIVE TIME: 30 MINUTES / TOTAL TIME: 30 MINUTES

Dogfish is technically a shark, but in culinary parlance it's a tender whitefish with a texture and flavor similar to cod or haddock.

1. Place 1 tablespoon of the olive oil in a medium skillet and warm it over medium-high heat. Add the onion and garlic and cook, stirring frequently, until the onion is translucent, about 2 minutes.

2. Stir in the tomatoes, cumin, cayenne, and 1 teaspoon of the salt and bring the mixture to a simmer. Cook until the tomatoes start to break down, about 6 minutes.

3. Cut the fillet in half and season it with the pepper and remaining salt.

4. Place the remaining olive oil in a clean skillet and warm it over high heat. Place the fish in the pan, and cook until it is browned on both sides and cooked through, about 4 minutes.

5. To serve, spoon some of the sauce into a shallow bowl, place the fish on top, and spoon a little more sauce over the top.

INGREDIENTS:

2   TABLESPOONS EXTRA-VIRGIN OLIVE OIL

½   ONION, DICED

2   GARLIC CLOVES, MINCED

¾   LB DOGFISH FILLET

3   TOMATOES, DICED

    PINCH OF CUMIN

    PINCH OF CAYENNE PEPPER

2   TEASPOONS KOSHER SALT

1   TEASPOON BLACK PEPPER

ZA'ATAR-RUBBED SPATCHCOCK CHICKEN WITH HONEY-GLAZED CARROTS & ROASTED ROOT VEGETABLES

YIELD: 4 SERVINGS / ACTIVE TIME: 45 MINUTES / TOTAL TIME: 24 HOURS

Spatchcocking a chicken makes cooking it foolproof.

1. Place a wire rack in a rimmed baking sheet. Place the chicken, breast side down, on a cutting board. Using kitchen shears, cut out the chicken's backbone. Flip the chicken over so the breast side is facing up. Push down on the middle of the chicken to flatten it as much as possible. Pat the chicken dry and place it on the wire rack.

2. Place the chicken in the refrigerator and let it rest, uncovered, overnight.

3. Remove the chicken from the refrigerator and let it rest at room temperature for 1 hour.

4. Preheat the oven to 425°F.

5. Place the olive oil in a large skillet and warm it over medium heat. Add the chicken to the pan and weigh it down with a cast-iron skillet—this added weight will help the chicken cook evenly. Cook until the chicken is golden brown on each side, 15 to 20 minutes.

6. Place the chicken on a baking sheet, breast side up, sprinkle the Za'atar over the chicken, and place it in the oven. Roast the chicken until it is cooked through (internal temperature is 165°F), about 15 minutes.

7. Remove the chicken from the oven and let it rest for 10 minutes. Serve with the glazed carrots and other roasted root vegetables.

INGREDIENTS:

- 4 LB. WHOLE CHICKEN
- 2 TABLESPOONS EXTRA-VIRGIN OLIVE OIL
- 2 TABLESPOONS ZA'ATAR (SEE PAGE 766)

  HONEY-GLAZED CARROTS (SEE PAGE 484), FOR SERVING

  ROASTED ROOT VEGETABLES WITH LEMON CAPER SAUCE (SEE PAGE 488), FOR SERVING

SLOW-ROASTED LAMB SHOULDER
WITH BRUSSELS SPROUTS & CRISPY KALE

YIELD: 4 TO 6 SERVINGS / ACTIVE TIME: 30 MINUTES / TOTAL TIME: 3 HOURS AND 30 MINUTES

Roasting brassicas such as Brussels sprouts and kale and pairing them with a rich meat is the quickest way to get those who hate vegetables to reconsider.

1. Preheat the oven to 350°F. Using a mortar and pestle, grind the fennel and cumin seeds into a powder. Place the garlic, oregano, brown sugar, 1 teaspoon of the salt, the vinegar, and 2 tablespoons of the avocado oil in a mixing bowl and stir to combine.

2. Rub the lamb with the mixture and place it in a large roasting pan. Add the water and cover the roasting pan with aluminum foil.

3. Place the lamb in the oven and roast for 2 hours. Remove from the oven, remove the foil, and spoon the cooking liquid over the lamb. Return the lamb to the oven and roast until well browned, about 40 minutes.

4. While the lamb is in the oven, place the Brussels sprouts, remaining salt, the pepper, and the remaining oil in a large bowl and toss to combine. Transfer to a parchment-lined baking sheet, place it in the oven, and roast until golden brown, 15 to 20 minutes.

5. Add the almonds and kale to the pan of Brussels sprouts, return the pan to the oven, and roast until the kale is crispy, about 5 minutes.

6. Remove the lamb and vegetables from the oven and serve them together.

INGREDIENTS:

1	TABLESPOON FENNEL SEEDS
1	TABLESPOON CUMIN SEEDS
2	GARLIC CLOVES, GRATED
1	TABLESPOON FRESH OREGANO
¼	CUP BROWN SUGAR
2	TEASPOONS KOSHER SALT
¼	CUP MALT VINEGAR
¼	CUP AVOCADO OIL
4½	LB. BONE-IN LAMB SHOULDER
1	CUP WATER
1	LB. BRUSSELS SPROUTS, TRIMMED AND HALVED
½	TEASPOON BLACK PEPPER
½	CUP SMOKED ALMONDS, CHOPPED
5¼	OZ. BABY KALE LEAVES

SPAGHETTI AL TONNO

YIELD: 4 TO 6 SERVINGS / ACTIVE TIME: 20 MINUTES / TOTAL TIME: 1 HOUR

This staple of Calabrian cuisine is a salty and savory marriage of tuna, onions, and tomatoes.

1. Place the avocado oil in a medium saucepan and warm it over medium-low heat. Add the garlic and onion and cook, stirring frequently, until the onion just starts to soften, about 5 minutes.

2. Add the red pepper flakes and passata, season with salt and pepper, and stir until well combined.

3. Add about 2 cups of water to the sauce and bring it to a boil. Cover the pan, reduce the heat to medium-low, and cook until the sauce has thickened, about 45 minutes.

4. While the sauce is simmering, bring a large pot of water to a boil.

5. Salt the water, add the pasta, and cook until al dente, 6 to 8 minutes.

6. Add the drained tuna to the tomato sauce and continue to simmer for about 5 minutes.

7. Drain the pasta and toss it with some of the tomato sauce. To serve, top each portion of pasta with more sauce and some of the parsley.

INGREDIENTS:

2 TABLESPOONS AVOCADO OIL

3 GARLIC CLOVES, MINCED

1 SMALL YELLOW ONION, MINCED

⅛ TEASPOON RED PEPPER FLAKES

3 CUPS TOMATO PASSATA (STRAINED TOMATOES)

SALT AND PEPPER, TO TASTE

1 LB. SPAGHETTI

6 OZ. TUNA IN OLIVE OIL, DRAINED

4 SPRIGS OF FRESH PARSLEY, CHOPPED

SUMAC CHICKEN & RICE

YIELD: 6 SERVINGS / ACTIVE TIME: 20 MINUTES / TOTAL TIME: 1 HOUR AND 20 MINUTES

The sumac adds a surprising splash of color and flavor to this simple meal.

1. Preheat the oven to 400°F and position a rack in the middle. Place the sumac, lemon zest, 1 teaspoon of the salt, and white pepper in a small bowl and stir to combine.

2. Rub the spice mixture under the skin and on top of the chicken.

3. In a roasting pan, combine the rice, pine nuts, berberis, turmeric, remaining salt, and avocado oil until the rice is a beautiful yellow color. Press the rice down so that it's in an even layer.

4. Top the rice with the slices of red onion and lay the chicken on top of the onion. Top each piece of chicken, with a lemon slice.

5. Pour the stock around the chicken, onto the rice. Drizzle the chicken with a generous amount of avocado oil.

6. Cover the roasting pan tightly with aluminum foil and place it in the oven. Roast the chicken for 40 minutes. Remove the foil and roast until the chicken is cooked through and the rice has soaked up all of the liquid, 20 to 25 minutes. Remove from the oven and enjoy.

INGREDIENTS:

¼	CUP SUMAC
	ZEST OF 1 LEMON
1½	TEASPOONS KOSHER SALT
¼	TEASPOON WHITE PEPPER
6	BONE-IN, SKIN-ON CHICKEN LEGS
3	CUPS BASMATI OR JASMINE RICE, RINSED AND DRAINED
½	CUP PINE NUTS
3	TABLESPOONS BERBERIS, DRIED CRANBERRIES, OR CHERRIES
1	TEASPOON TURMERIC
2	TABLESPOONS AVOCADO OIL, PLUS MORE TO TASTE
1	RED ONION, HALVED AND SLICED
1	LEMON, SLICED THIN
4½	CUPS CHICKEN STOCK (SEE PAGE 368)

TOMATOES REINADOS

YIELD: 6 SERVINGS / ACTIVE TIME: 45 MINUTES / TOTAL TIME: 1 HOUR AND 15 MINUTES

This recipe has Turkish origins. The "royal" tomatoes are first stuffed with beef and then pan seared facedown, browning the meat.

1. Cut the top ¼ inch off the tomatoes. Scoop out the insides of the tomatoes.

2. Soak the loaf of bread in water for about 10 minutes and then drain.

3. Place the ground beef, bread, salt, and pepper in a mixing bowl and stir until well combined. Stuff each tomato with about 2 tablespoons of the beef mixture, using your palms to flatten the top of the stuffing.

4. Place the oil in a saucepan and warm it to 350°F over medium-high heat. Place the egg in a small bowl and beat it. Place the flour in a separate small bowl.

5. Dip the top of a tomato into the flour, shake off any excess, and then dip the top of the tomato in the beaten egg. Place the tomato on a plate and repeat with the remaining tomatoes.

6. Place the tomatoes in the pot, top down, and fry until their tops are golden brown. Transfer the fried tomatoes into another skillet, fried side up.

7. Add water to the pan until it reaches three-quarters of the way up the tomatoes. Place the pan over medium-high heat and bring the water to a boil. Reduce the heat to low, cover the pan, and cook the tomatoes until the meat is cooked, the tomatoes are tender, and about one-quarter of the water remains, about 45 minutes.

8. Remove the tomatoes from the pan and enjoy.

INGREDIENTS:

10	TOMATOES
1	LOAF OF WHITE BREAD
1	LB. GROUND BEEF
1½	TEASPOONS KOSHER SALT
¼	TEASPOON BLACK PEPPER
1	EGG
½	CUP AVOCADO OIL
½	CUP ALL-PURPOSE FLOUR

TURKISH COFFEE–RUBBED BRISKET

YIELD: 6 SERVINGS / **ACTIVE TIME:** 30 MINUTES / **TOTAL TIME:** 30 HOURS

If you love the deeply rich flavors associated with Turkish coffee, prepare to fall in love with how this rub transforms brisket. The recipe tenderizes the meat and adds a dark, smoky layer to every bite.

1. Preheat the oven to 400°F. Trim any fatty areas on the brisket so that the fat is within approximately ¼ inch of the meat, keeping in mind that it is better to leave too much fat than too little.

2. Place the onions, potatoes, carrot, fennel, and garlic in a heavy roasting pan. Add the avocado oil, 1 teaspoon of the salt, and ½ teaspoon of the pepper and toss to combine.

3. Place the coffee, cinnamon, cardamom, remaining salt, and remaining pepper in a small bowl and stir until well combined. Rub the mixture all over the brisket and nestle the brisket into the vegetables. Place the pan in the oven and roast until the vegetables are lightly browned, about 45 minutes.

4. Cover the pan tightly with aluminum foil, lower the oven's temperature to 300°F, and roast until the brisket is fork-tender, 5 to 6 hours. As the brisket cooks, check on it every 45 minutes, adding ¼ cup water to the pan if it starts to look dry.

5. Remove the roasting pan from the oven and let it cool to room temperature. Refrigerate the brisket and vegetables until the fat is solid, 8 to 24 hours.

6. Transfer the brisket to a cutting board and slice it across the grain. Skim and discard the fat in the roasting pan. Return the slices of brisket to the roasting pan with the vegetables and cooking juices.

7. Preheat the oven to 300°F. Transfer the roasting pan to the oven and heat the brisket until the liquid is starting to bubble and the brisket and vegetables are just warmed through, 15 to 20 minutes.

8. Transfer the brisket and vegetables to a serving dish, cover it with aluminum foil, and set it aside.

9. Place the roasting pan over two burners on the stovetop and simmer the liquid over medium heat until it has thickened, 10 to 15 minutes.

10. Pour the reduced liquid over the brisket and vegetables and enjoy.

INGREDIENTS:

4	LB. BEEF BRISKET
2	ONIONS, QUARTERED
2	LARGE POTATOES, SCRUBBED AND CUT INTO 1-INCH-THICK WEDGES
1	LARGE CARROT, PEELED AND CUT INTO 2-INCH-LONG PIECES
1	FENNEL BULB, TRIMMED AND CUT INTO WEDGES
1	GARLIC HEAD, HALVED CROSSWISE
2	TABLESPOONS AVOCADO OIL
1	TABLESPOON PLUS 1 TEASPOON KOSHER SALT
1½	TEASPOONS BLACK PEPPER
1	TABLESPOON VERY FINELY GROUND ARABICA COFFEE
1	TABLESPOON SMOKED CINNAMON
1	TEASPOON CARDAMOM

EGGPLANT DOLMA

YIELD: 6 TO 8 SERVINGS / ACTIVE TIME: 30 MINUTES / TOTAL TIME: 1 HOUR AND 30 MINUTES

Should you live near a Turkish market, select something from their beautiful array of dried eggplants for this dish.

1. Preheat the oven to 350°F. In a large bowl, cover the torn bread with ½ cup of the water and work the mixture with your hands until it is a paste. Add the beef, salt, cumin, and pepper and work the mixture with your hands until well combined. Set the mixture aside.

2. Remove the tops and bottoms of each eggplant, then slice each one lengthwise into ¼-inch-thick slices.

3. Place the eggs in a large bowl, season with salt and pepper, and whisk until scrambled. Add the eggplant slices and dredge them until completely coated. Transfer the slices to a colander and let them drain for 5 minutes.

4. Place the avocado oil in a large skillet and warm it over medium-high heat. Line a baking sheet with paper towels and place it by the stove. Working in batches to avoid crowding the pan, add the eggplants and fry until golden brown and softened, 4 to 6 minutes, turning them over once. Transfer the fried eggplants to the lined baking sheet. Add more avocado oil to the pan as needed.

5. Place 2 tablespoons of the beef mixture at the base of each slice of eggplant and roll them up lengthwise. Place the rolls beside each other, seam side down, in a 13 x 9–inch baking dish.

6. Place the remaining water, Tomato Sauce, tamarind concentrate, and sugar in a mixing bowl and stir to combine. Season the sauce with salt and pepper and pour it over the eggplants.

7. Place the eggplants in the oven and bake until the edges are golden brown and the filling is cooked through, 35 to 40 minutes.

8. Remove from the oven, garnish with feta and chopped parsley, and enjoy.

INGREDIENTS:

3	SLICES OF WHOLE WHEAT BREAD, CRUSTS REMOVED, ROUGHLY TORN
1	CUP WATER
2	LBS. GROUND BEEF
2	TEASPOONS KOSHER SALT, PLUS MORE TO TASTE
2	TEASPOONS CUMIN
1	TEASPOON BLACK PEPPER, PLUS MORE TO TASTE
2	EGGPLANTS (PREFERABLY WITH AN ELONGATED SHAPE)
4	EGGS
¼	CUP AVOCADO OIL, PLUS MORE AS NEEDED
1	CUP TOMATO SAUCE (SEE PAGE 775)
2	TABLESPOONS TAMARIND CONCENTRATE
1	TABLESPOON SUGAR
	FETA CHEESE, CRUMBLED, FOR GARNISH
	FRESH PARSLEY, CHOPPED, FOR GARNISH

TURMERIC CHICKEN WITH TOUM

YIELD: 2 TO 4 SERVINGS / ACTIVE TIME: 1 HOUR / TOTAL TIME: 24 HOURS

Turmeric adds not only a visual brightness to any dish, but a light and tangy zing on the palate. The health benefits of turmeric also leave you feeling properly nourished after a meal such as this.

1. Place the ground turmeric, orange peel, fennel seeds, cumin, coriander, garlic, and fresh turmeric in a bowl and stir to combine. Add the orange juice, orange blossom water, and yogurt to the bowl and stir until incorporated.

2. Season the cavity of the chicken with salt and pepper. Rub some of the marinade inside the cavity of the chicken.

3. Using kitchen twine, tie the legs together.

4. Evenly season the outside of the chicken with the salt and pepper. Place the chicken on a baking sheet and let it sit, uncovered, at room temperature for 30 minutes.

5. Rub the marinade all over the outside of the chicken; it may seem like a lot, but use it all. Place the chicken, uncovered, in the refrigerator and let it marinate overnight.

6. Remove the chicken from the refrigerator and let it sit at room temperature for 2 hours prior to cooking.

7. Preheat the oven to 450°F.

8. Place the chicken, breast side up, on a rack in a roasting pan. Place it in the oven and roast for 40 to 50 minutes, until the interior of the thickest part of the thigh reaches 160° to 165°F on an instant-read thermometer. If the chicken's skin browns too quickly in the oven, lower the heat to 375°F.

9. Remove the chicken from the oven and let it rest for 15 minutes. Serve with the Toum and enjoy.

INGREDIENTS:

1   TABLESPOON GROUND TURMERIC

2   TEASPOONS GROUND DRIED ORANGE PEEL

1   TEASPOON GROUND FENNEL SEEDS

¾   TEASPOON CUMIN

1½   TEASPOONS CORIANDER

1   GARLIC CLOVE, GRATED

    1-INCH PIECE OF FRESH TURMERIC, PEELED AND GRATED

1   TABLESPOON FRESH ORANGE JUICE

1   TABLESPOON PLUS 1 TEASPOON ORANGE BLOSSOM WATER

¾   CUP FULL-FAT GREEK YOGURT

3½   LB. WHOLE CHICKEN

1   TABLESPOON PLUS 2½ TEASPOONS SEA SALT

1   TEASPOON BLACK PEPPER

    TOUM (SEE PAGE 758), FOR SERVING

VEGETABLE TANZIA

YIELD: 6 SERVINGS / ACTIVE TIME: 45 MINUTES / TOTAL TIME: 1 HOUR AND 45 MINUTES

A sweet, lighter version of the dish that is beloved by Morocco's Jewish community.

1. Place 6 tablespoons of the avocado oil in a large skillet and warm it over medium heat. Add the onions and salt and cook, stirring frequently, until the onions are caramelized and a deep golden brown, about 30 minutes.

2. Transfer the onions to a large bowl. Add the prunes, apricots, figs, walnuts, sugar, and cinnamon and stir to combine. Season the mixture with salt and pepper.

3. Preheat the oven to 375°F.

4. Place the potatoes, turnips, and butternut squash in a roasting pan and rub them with the remaining avocado oil. Sprinkle the turmeric over the top, season the vegetables with salt and pepper, and toss to combine. Spread the vegetables in an even layer in the pan and spoon the fruit mixture over and around them.

5. Add 1½ cups of water to the pan and place it in the oven. Roast until the vegetables are well browned and cooked through, about 1 hour, stirring halfway through. Add more water if the pan starts to look dry.

6. While the vegetables are roasting, toast the almonds in a dry skillet over medium-low heat, stirring often, until lightly browned, about 6 minutes. Remove the pan from heat.

7. Remove the tanzia from the oven, sprinkle the toasted almonds on top, and enjoy.

INGREDIENTS:

- ½ CUP AVOCADO OIL
- 2 LBS. YELLOW ONIONS, SLICED THIN
- 1 TEASPOON KOSHER SALT, PLUS MORE TO TASTE
- ½ CUP PITTED PRUNES, HALVED
- ½ CUP DRIED APRICOTS, HALVED
- ½ CUP DRIED FIGS, STEMS REMOVED, HALVED
- ½ CUP SHELLED WALNUTS
- 2 TABLESPOONS SUGAR
- 1 TEASPOON CINNAMON
- BLACK PEPPER, TO TASTE
- 1 LB. SWEET POTATOES, PEELED AND CUT INTO 2-INCH-LONG PIECES
- 1 LB. TURNIPS, PEELED AND CUT INTO 2-INCH-LONG PIECES
- 2 LBS. BUTTERNUT SQUASH, PEELED, SEEDS REMOVED, CUT INTO 2-INCH-LONG PIECES
- ½ TEASPOON TURMERIC
- ½ CUP SLIVERED ALMONDS, FOR GARNISH

Vegetable Tanzia, see page 261

WHITE SHAKSHUKA

YIELD: 4 SERVINGS / **ACTIVE TIME**: 15 MINUTES / **TOTAL TIME**: 45 MINUTES

One of the beautiful things about shakshuka is that you can truly add almost anything to the pot and make it work. This version features a sauce spiked with garlic and labneh, making this a beautifully satisfying vegetarian meal.

1. Place the avocado oil in a medium skillet and warm it over medium heat. Add the onion and cook, stirring occasionally, until golden brown, 10 to 12 minutes. Add the garlic and 3 tablespoons of the hyssop and cook, stirring frequently, until fragrant, about 1 minute. Season with salt and pepper.

2. Stir in the sauce and Labneh and spread it evenly in the pan. Cook until the sauce begins to steam and bubbles form at the edges, about 15 minutes.

3. Using the back of a spoon, create eight depressions in the mixture and gently nestle an egg yolk in each one. Cook until the yolks begin to grow firm and opaque at the edges but remain soft at their centers, 3 to 5 minutes.

4. Sprinkle the remaining tablespoon of hyssop over the shakshuka, season with salt and pepper, and serve immediately with the warm pita.

INGREDIENTS:

¼   CUP AVOCADO OIL

1   LARGE YELLOW ONION, CHOPPED

4   GARLIC CLOVES, MINCED

¼   CUP CHOPPED FRESH HYSSOP LEAVES (OR A MIX OF CHOPPED FRESH MINT, OREGANO, SAGE, AND/OR THYME)

     SALT AND PEPPER, TO TASTE

1   CUP TOMATO SAUCE (SEE PAGE 775)

1   LB. LABNEH (SEE PAGE 67)

8   LARGE EGG YOLKS

     PITA BREAD (SEE PAGE 532), WARM, FOR SERVING

ZA'ATAR CHICKEN WITH GARLICKY YOGURT

YIELD: 4 SERVINGS / ACTIVE TIME: 20 MINUTES / TOTAL TIME: 1 HOUR AND 30 MINUTES

Bright and savory Za'atar-studded chicken pieces roasted and piled onto a yogurt-smeared platter with lemon wedges, roasted red onions, and roasted garlic . . . if your mouth isn't watering, check your pulse.

1. Preheat the oven to 325°F. Pat the chicken legs dry with paper towels. Arrange the chicken, onions, halved heads of garlic, and lemon in a 13 x 9–inch baking dish. Season generously with salt, drizzle the avocado oil over the mixture, and toss to coat.

2. Turn the heads of garlic, cut sides down, and nestle them in to ensure they are in contact with the baking dish.

3. Place the dish in the oven and roast until the meat is nearly falling off the bone, 50 minutes to 1 hour, rotating the dish halfway through.

4. While the chicken is in the oven, grate 1 of the garlic cloves into a small bowl. Add the yogurt, big pinch of salt, and a tablespoon of water and stir until combined. Set the yogurt sauce aside.

5. Remove the chicken from the oven and transfer the onions, garlic, and lemon to a plate. Raise the oven's temperature to 425°F, return the chicken to the oven, and roast until the skin is crispy and golden brown, 10 to 15 minutes.

6. Remove the chicken from the oven, place it on a cutting board, and let it rest for 10 minutes. Reserve the pan juices.

7. Grate the remaining garlic clove into a small bowl. Add the Za'atar, coriander, lemon zest, and lime zest and stir to combine. Add the reserved juices until you've reached a rich consistency (about ⅓ cup). Taste and adjust the seasoning as necessary.

8. Spread the yogurt sauce over a platter and arrange the chicken legs on top. Scatter the onions, roasted garlic, and lemon around the chicken, drizzle the za'atar dressing over the top, and enjoy.

INGREDIENTS:

2½ LBS. CHICKEN LEGS

2 ONIONS, CUT INTO WEDGES

2 HEADS OF GARLIC, HALVED CROSSWISE, PLUS 2 GARLIC CLOVES

1 LEMON, QUARTERED, SEEDS REMOVED

SALT, TO TASTE

⅓ CUP AVOCADO OIL

1½ CUPS FULL-FAT GREEK YOGURT

3 TABLESPOONS ZA'ATAR (SEE PAGE 766)

1 TEASPOON CORIANDER

1 TEASPOON LEMON ZEST

1 TEASPOON LIME ZEST

Stuffed Eggplants, see page 268

STUFFED EGGPLANTS

YIELD: 4 SERVINGS / ACTIVE TIME: 30 MINUTES / TOTAL TIME: 1 HOUR AND 20 MINUTES

If a vegan dinner is desired, simply forgo the lamb here—the eggplants provide more than enough flavor on their own.

1. Preheat the oven to 400°F. Place the eggplants on a baking sheet, drizzle olive oil over the top, and place them in the oven. Roast until the flesh is tender, about 30 minutes. Remove from the oven and let the eggplants cool slightly. When cool enough to handle, scoop out the flesh, mince it, and place it in a mixing bowl. Set the hollowed-out eggplants aside and leave the oven on.

2. Place the quinoa and water in a saucepan and bring to a boil over medium heat. Let the quinoa boil until it has absorbed all of the water. Remove the pan from heat, cover it, and let it steam for 5 minutes. Fluff with a fork and let it cool slightly.

3. Place the olive oil in a large skillet and warm it over medium-high heat. When the oil starts to shimmer, add the onions, garlic, and bell pepper and cook, stirring frequently, until the onions and pepper start to soften, about 5 minutes. Add the ground lamb, season it with salt and pepper, stir in the garam masala and cumin, and cook, breaking the lamb up with a fork, until it is browned, about 6 minutes. Transfer the mixture to the bowl containing the minced eggplants, add the quinoa to the bowl, and stir until the mixture is combined.

4. Fill the cavities of the hollowed-out eggplants with the lamb-and-quinoa mixture. Place the eggplants on a baking sheet, place them in the oven, and roast until they are starting to collapse, about 15 minutes. Remove from the oven and let the stuffed eggplants cool slightly before garnishing them with parsley and serving.

INGREDIENTS:

2　LARGE EGGPLANTS, HALVED

2　TABLESPOONS EXTRA-VIRGIN OLIVE OIL, PLUS MORE AS NEEDED

½　CUP QUINOA

1　CUP WATER

2　ONIONS, CHOPPED

3　GARLIC CLOVES, MINCED

2　BELL PEPPERS, STEMS AND SEEDS REMOVED, CHOPPED

1　LB. GROUND LAMB

　SALT AND PEPPER, TO TASTE

½　TEASPOON GARAM MASALA

2　TEASPOONS CUMIN

　FRESH PARSLEY, FINELY CHOPPED, FOR GARNISH

BRIAM

YIELD: 4 SERVINGS / **ACTIVE TIME**: 40 MINUTES / **TOTAL TIME**: 2 HOURS

Think of this as the Greek version of ratatouille, the celebrated Provençal dish. As it includes potatoes, expect this iteration to be a little heartier than what you're used to.

1. Preheat the oven to 400°F. Place the potatoes and zucchini in a bowl, season with salt and pepper, and then add the oregano, rosemary, parsley, garlic, and olive oil. Stir until the vegetables are evenly coated and set aside.

2. Cover the bottom of a 10-inch cast-iron skillet with half of the tomatoes. Arrange the potatoes, zucchini, and onion in rows, working in from the edge of the pan to the center and alternating the vegetables as you go. Top with the remaining tomatoes and cover with foil.

3. Place the skillet in the oven and roast for 45 minutes. Remove from the oven, remove the foil, and roast for another 40 minutes, until the vegetables are charred and tender.

4. Remove from the oven and let the briam cool slightly before enjoying.

INGREDIENTS:

3	YUKON GOLD POTATOES, PEELED AND SLICED THIN
3	ZUCCHINI, SLICED THIN
	SALT AND PEPPER, TO TASTE
1	TABLESPOON CHOPPED FRESH OREGANO
2	TEASPOONS CHOPPED FRESH ROSEMARY
½	CUP FRESH PARSLEY, CHOPPED
4	GARLIC CLOVES, MINCED
3	TABLESPOONS EXTRA-VIRGIN OLIVE OIL
4	TOMATOES, SEEDED AND CHOPPED
1	LARGE RED ONION, HALVED AND SLICED THIN

CHICKEN SOUVLAKI

YIELD: 4 SERVINGS / ACTIVE TIME: 20 MINUTES / TOTAL TIME: 2 HOURS AND 30 MINUTES

Should you want something lighter, simply serve the chicken over Greek Salad (see page 451).

1. Place the garlic, oregano, rosemary, paprika, salt, pepper, olive oil, wine, and lemon juice in a food processor and blitz to combine.

2. Place the chicken and bay leaves in a bowl or a large resealable bag, pour the marinade over the chicken, and stir so that it gets evenly coated. Marinate in the refrigerator for 2 hours.

3. Prepare a gas or charcoal grill for medium-high heat (about 450°F). If using bamboo skewers, soak them in water.

4. Remove the chicken from the refrigerator and thread the pieces onto the skewers. Make sure to leave plenty of space between the pieces of chicken, as it will provide the heat more room to operate, ensuring that the chicken cooks evenly.

5. Place the skewers on the grill and cook, turning as necessary, until the chicken is cooked through, 12 to 15 minutes. Remove the skewers from the grill and let them rest briefly before serving with the pita, Tzatziki, tomatoes, onion, and cucumbers.

INGREDIENTS:

10	GARLIC CLOVES, CRUSHED
4	SPRIGS OF FRESH OREGANO
1	SPRIG OF FRESH ROSEMARY
1	TEASPOON PAPRIKA
1	TEASPOON KOSHER SALT
1	TEASPOON BLACK PEPPER
¼	CUP EXTRA-VIRGIN OLIVE OIL, PLUS MORE AS NEEDED
¼	CUP DRY WHITE WINE
2	TABLESPOONS FRESH LEMON JUICE
2½	LBS. BONELESS, SKINLESS CHICKEN THIGHS, CHOPPED
2	BAY LEAVES
	PITA BREAD (SEE PAGE 532), WARMED, FOR SERVING
	TZATZIKI (SEE PAGE 56), FOR SERVING
2	TOMATOES, SLICED, FOR SERVING
½	ONION, SLICED, FOR SERVING
2	CUCUMBERS, SLICED, FOR SERVING

KEFTA WITH CHICKPEA SALAD

YIELD: 4 SERVINGS / **ACTIVE TIME:** 35 MINUTES / **TOTAL TIME:** 1 HOUR

Try roasting the garlic cloves before adding them to the kefta mix—that added bit of sweetness will go a long way.

1. Place all of the ingredients, except for the olive oil and the Chickpea Salad, in a mixing bowl and stir until well combined. Microwave a small bit of the mixture until cooked through. Taste and adjust the seasoning in the remaining mixture as necessary.

2. Working with wet hands, form the mixture into 18 ovals and place three meatballs on a skewer.

3. Place the olive oil in a Dutch oven and warm it over medium-high heat. Working in batches, add three skewers to the pot and sear the kefta until they are browned all over and nearly cooked through, about 10 minutes. Transfer the browned kefta to a paper towel–lined plate to drain.

4. When the kefta have been browned, return all of the skewers to the pot, cover it, and remove from heat. Let the kefta stand until cooked through, about 10 minutes.

5. When the kefta are cooked through, remove them from the skewers. Divide the salad between the serving plates, top each portion with some of the kefta, and enjoy.

INGREDIENTS:

1½ LBS. GROUND LAMB

½ LB. GROUND BEEF

½ WHITE ONION, MINCED

2 GARLIC CLOVES, GRATED

ZEST OF 1 LEMON

1 CUP FRESH PARSLEY, CHOPPED

2 TABLESPOONS CHOPPED FRESH MINT

1 TEASPOON CINNAMON

2 TABLESPOONS CUMIN

1 TABLESPOON PAPRIKA

1 TEASPOON CORIANDER

SALT AND PEPPER, TO TASTE

¼ CUP EXTRA-VIRGIN OLIVE OIL

CHICKPEA SALAD (SEE PAGE 397), FOR SERVING

GARLIC & LIME CALAMARI

YIELD: 4 SERVINGS / ACTIVE TIME: 10 MINUTES / TOTAL TIME: 20 MINUTES

Keep all of your attention on the skillet once the squid goes in, as it is very easy to overcook.

1. Pat the calamari dry and set it aside. Place the olive oil and butter in a large cast-iron skillet and warm over medium-high heat. When the butter starts to foam, add the garlic and cook, stirring continuously, until fragrant, about 1 minute.

2. Add the calamari to the pan, cook for 2 minutes, and then stir in the wine and lime juice. Cook for another 30 seconds, until warmed through, and remove the pan from heat.

3. Season with salt and pepper, stir in the cayenne and dill, and enjoy.

INGREDIENTS:

1½   LBS. SQUID, SLICED INTO RINGS

2   TABLESPOONS EXTRA-VIRGIN OLIVE OIL

1   TABLESPOON UNSALTED BUTTER

10   GARLIC CLOVES, CHOPPED

3   TABLESPOONS WHITE WINE

  JUICE OF 1½ LIMES

  SALT AND PEPPER, TO TASTE

  PINCH OF CAYENNE PEPPER

3   TABLESPOONS CHOPPED FRESH DILL

PESCE ALL'EBRAICA

YIELD: 4 SERVINGS / ACTIVE TIME: 10 MINUTES / TOTAL TIME: 30 MINUTES

If you can secure the red mullet that is traditionally used in Italy for this dish, that would be best, but red snapper makes for a more-than-acceptable substitute.

1. Preheat the oven to 400°F. Season the fish with salt and pepper and place it in a 13 x 9–inch baking dish.

2. In a small bowl, add the vinegar, honey, oil, and 1 teaspoon of salt and stir until well combined. Pour the mixture over the fish and then sprinkle the raisins and pine nuts over the top.

3. Place in the oven and bake until the fish is opaque and can be flaked easily with a fork. For a very thin piece of fish, this will only take about 10 minutes. For a thicker fillet, such as halibut, this can take up to 20 minutes. Baste the fish after 10 minutes if it is not yet ready.

4. Remove from the oven, garnish with parsley, and enjoy.

INGREDIENTS:

4   LBS. WHITEFISH

1   TEASPOON KOSHER SALT, PLUS MORE TO TASTE

     BLACK PEPPER, TO TASTE

¼   CUP APPLE CIDER VINEGAR OR RED WINE VINEGAR

1   TABLESPOON HONEY

½   CUP AVOCADO OIL

⅓   CUP GOLDEN RAISINS, CHOPPED

⅓   CUP PINE NUTS

     FRESH PARSLEY, CHOPPED, FOR GARNISH

ALICIOTTI CON INDIVIA

YIELD: 4 SERVINGS / **ACTIVE TIME:** 25 MINUTES / **TOTAL TIME:** 45 MINUTES

A classic Roman Jewish dish featuring anchovies baked in escarole or endives. The origins of this dish are linked with strict Papal laws that prohibited Roman Jews from consuming any fish besides anchovies and sardines.

1. Preheat the oven to 350°F. Coat a 13 x 9–inch baking dish with a tablespoon of the olive oil and sprinkle a teaspoon of the garlic over the dish. Place the escarole in the baking dish and sprinkle the remaining garlic over the top.

2. Slice open the anchovies from head to tail. Place a layer of anchovies, skin side up, over the escarole. Season with the salt, pepper, and red pepper flakes, drizzle the remaining olive oil over the anchovies, and cover the baking dish with aluminum foil.

3. Place the dish in the oven and bake until the escarole is tender and the anchovies have softened, about 20 minutes.

4. Remove from the oven and enjoy immediately.

INGREDIENTS:

2   TABLESPOONS EXTRA-VIRGIN OLIVE OIL

6   GARLIC CLOVES, MINCED

2   BUNCHES OF ESCAROLE, CHOPPED

36   FRESH ANCHOVIES OR ANCHOVY FILLETS IN OIL AND VINEGAR

¼   TEASPOON KOSHER SALT

⅛   TEASPOON BLACK PEPPER

⅛   TEASPOON RED PEPPER FLAKES

ALMODROTE

YIELD: 8 SERVINGS / **ACTIVE TIME:** 40 MINUTES / **TOTAL TIME:** 1 HOUR AND 45 MINUTES

Although this delicious roasted eggplant-and-cheese pie dates back to the Middle Ages, it remains perfectly comforting today.

1. Position a rack in the middle of the oven and preheat the oven to 425°F. Place the eggplants on baking sheets, cut side up, place them in the oven, and roast until they collapse, about 40 minutes. Remove from the oven and let them cool. When they are cool enough to handle, scoop the flesh into a fine-mesh sieve and let it drain.

2. Rub a baking dish with the cut sides of the garlic clove, making sure to go over the entire surface of the dish a few times. Generously coat the dish with butter and then sprinkle with the flour, making sure to coat the entire dish. Tap out any excess flour.

3. Place the eggplants in a bowl and taste them—if they are sweet, you can skip adding the zucchini; if they are a bit bitter, place the zucchini in a linen towel, and wring it to remove as much liquid as possible. Add it to the bowl.

4. Add the eggs, 2½ cups of the cheese, and salt and stir vigorously with a fork until the mixture is combined, making sure to break up the eggplants.

5. Spread the eggplant mixture evenly in the baking dish. Sprinkle the remaining cheese over the top, place the dish in the oven, and bake until well browned and crispy on top, 25 or 30 minutes.

6. Remove from the oven and serve with Greek yogurt.

INGREDIENTS:

5	EGGPLANTS, HALVED
1	GARLIC CLOVE, UNPEELED AND HALVED LENGTHWISE
	UNSALTED BUTTER, AS NEEDED
2	TABLESPOONS ALL-PURPOSE FLOUR
1	SMALL ZUCCHINI, GRATED (OPTIONAL)
2	EGGS
3	CUPS GRATED KASHKAVAL CHEESE
½	TEASPOON KOSHER SALT
	GREEK YOGURT, FOR SERVING

BULGUR WITH FRIED ONIONS

YIELD: 6 SERVINGS / **ACTIVE TIME:** 30 MINUTES / **TOTAL TIME:** 1 HOUR

Make this dish when you're too busy to make something more elaborate—chances are, you'll soon be looking to prepare it when you need a meal that's a little more special.

1. Place the avocado oil in a Dutch oven and warm it over medium heat. Add the noodles and fry, stirring constantly, until they are lightly browned, about 2 minutes.

2. Add the bulgur and salt and cover with water by ½ inch. Cover the pot and cook over medium-low heat until the bulgur is tender, 20 to 25 minutes. Remove the pot from heat and let it stand, covered, for 10 minutes.

3. Place the onions and canola oil in a saucepan and cook over high heat, stirring frequently, until the onions are softened and golden brown, about 20 minutes. If you want the onions to be a bit more charred, cook them for 5 more minutes.

4. Top the bulgur with the onions and chickpeas and serve with the Tzatziki.

INGREDIENTS:

¼ CUP AVOCADO OIL

¼ CUP THIN VERMICELLI NOODLES

2 CUPS BULGUR WHEAT

½ TEASPOON KOSHER SALT, PLUS MORE TO TASTE

4 ONIONS, SLICED

½ CUP CANOLA OIL

1 (14 OZ.) CAN OF CHICKPEAS, DRAINED AND RINSED

TZATZIKI (SEE PAGE 56), FOR SERVING

BRISKET WITH PISTACHIO GREMOLATA

YIELD: 8 SERVINGS / ACTIVE TIME: 30 MINUTES / TOTAL TIME: 30 HOURS

Tart pomegranate, acting as both marinade and sauce, brings brightness and balance to this rich brisket, while the gremolata adds a touch of herbal freshness.

1. Trim any fatty areas on the brisket so that the fat is within approximately ¼ inch of the meat, keeping in mind that it is better to leave too much fat than too little. Season the brisket all over with salt and pepper. Transfer the brisket to a large resealable plastic bag or bowl.

2. Place the garlic, walnuts, honey, and 1 cup of the pomegranate juice in a blender and puree until very smooth. Add the remaining pomegranate juice and blend until smooth. Pour the marinade over the brisket. Seal the bag or cover the bowl tightly with aluminum foil and let the brisket marinate in the refrigerator for 24 hours.

3. Transfer the brisket and marinade to a roasting pan, cover it tightly with foil, and let the brisket sit at room temperature for 1 hour.

4. Preheat the oven to 275°F. Place the covered roasting pan in the oven and braise the brisket until it is tender enough that the meat can easily be shredded with two forks, 5 to 6 hours.

5. Transfer the brisket to a cutting board and cover it loosely with aluminum foil.

6. Transfer the cooking liquid to a saucepan and spoon off as much fat as possible from the surface. Cook over medium-high heat, skimming off any fat and foam as it surfaces, until the liquid has been reduced by two-thirds, leaving you with about 2 cups of sauce. Taste and season the sauce with salt and pepper if necessary.

7. To serve, slice the brisket against the grain and transfer it to a platter. Spoon the sauce over the top and top with the gremolata.

INGREDIENTS:

7   LB. BEEF BRISKET

2   TEASPOONS KOSHER SALT, PLUS MORE TO TASTE

1   TEASPOON FRESHLY GROUND BLACK PEPPER, PLUS MORE TO TASTE

    CLOVES FROM 1 HEAD OF GARLIC

1   CUP WALNUTS

2   TABLESPOONS HONEY

3   CUPS POMEGRANATE JUICE

    PISTACHIO GREMOLATA (SEE PAGE 778), FOR SERVING

Brisket with Pistachio Gremolata, see page 279

CHICKEN WITH MEHSHI SFEEHA

YIELD: 6 SERVINGS / ACTIVE TIME: 30 MINUTES / TOTAL TIME: 3 HOURS

Chicken with stuffed eggplant has its roots in Syria. This hearty version is sure to fill up, and impress, the hungriest of diners at your table.

1. Preheat the oven to 400°F. In a large bowl, combine the beef, rice, 1 teaspoon of the allspice, 1 teaspoon of the salt, and the water and stir until well combined. Set the mixture aside.

2. To rehydrate the eggplant skins, bring 6 cups of water to a boil. Carefully place the dried eggplant skins in the water and boil until they are soft, stirring occasionally, about 5 minutes. Drain, sprinkle about ½ teaspoon of salt on each eggplant skin, and let them cool.

3. Stuff each eggplant skin with about 2 teaspoons of the meat mixture and flatten the filling at the top edge of the eggplant skins.

4. Lay the slices of fresh eggplant on paper towels and season them with salt. Let them stand for 30 minutes.

5. Pat the slices of fresh eggplant dry. Add 2 tablespoons of the avocado oil to a medium skillet and warm it over medium-high heat. Place a single layer of eggplant slices in the pan and fry until they are a deep golden brown on both sides, 4 to 8 minutes. Transfer the fried eggplant to a paper towel–lined plate and continue frying the fresh eggplant.

6. Place 1 tablespoon of oil in a Dutch oven and warm it over medium-high heat. Place the stuffed dried eggplants in a single layer on the bottom of the pot and sprinkle a teaspoon of allspice over the top. Lay the fried eggplant over the stuffed dried eggplants.

7. Place the whole chicken over the fried eggplant and rub the chicken with the remaining oil, remaining allspice, a generous amount of salt, the Ras el Hanout, paprika, and garlic. Place the chicken in the pot, breast side down. Add enough water to the pot to reach halfway up the stuffed eggplants (about ½ cup).

8. Place the Dutch oven in the oven, uncovered, and bake until the chicken is cooked through, 1½ to 2 hours. Flip the chicken over halfway through, and check to make sure that there is enough liquid in the pot.

9. Remove from the oven and let the dish rest for 15 minutes before enjoying.

INGREDIENTS:

1	LB. GROUND BEEF
¼	CUP SHORT-GRAIN RICE, RINSED AND DRAINED
1	TABLESPOON ALLSPICE
7	TEASPOONS KOSHER SALT, PLUS MORE TO TASTE
1	TABLESPOON WATER
12	DRIED EGGPLANT SKINS
1	EGGPLANT, SLICED INTO ½-INCH-THICK ROUNDS
¼	CUP AVOCADO OIL
3	LB. WHOLE CHICKEN
1	TABLESPOON RAS EL HANOUT (SEE PAGE 747)
1	TEASPOON PAPRIKA
4–6	GARLIC CLOVES, MINCED

CHARRED CHICKEN
WITH SWEET POTATOES & ORANGES

YIELD: 4 SERVINGS / ACTIVE TIME: 30 MINUTES / TOTAL TIME: 2 HOURS AND 25 MINUTES

A topping of olives and feta is a salty, bright complement to the caramelized oranges and roasted sweet potatoes in this flavor-packed chicken dinner. If you're keeping the meal dairy free, skip the cheese.

INGREDIENTS:

4	BONE-IN, SKIN-ON CHICKEN THIGHS
	SALT, TO TASTE
4	GARLIC CLOVES, GRATED
3	TABLESPOONS FRESH LEMON JUICE
5	TABLESPOONS AVOCADO OIL
1	LARGE SWEET POTATO
3	SPRIGS OF FRESH ROSEMARY
1	BLOOD ORANGE, THINLY SLICED, PLUS WEDGES FOR SERVING
1	(14 OZ.) CAN OF CHICKPEAS, DRAINED AND RINSED
½	CUP CASTELVETRANO OLIVES, PITTED
3	OZ. FETA CHEESE, CRUMBLED

1. Preheat the oven to 450°F. Place the chicken in a large bowl and season it with salt. Add the garlic, 2 tablespoons of the lemon juice, and 2 tablespoons of the avocado oil and toss to combine. Let the mixture marinate at room temperature for 30 minutes, or cover and refrigerate for up to 12 hours.

2. Remove the chicken from the marinade and drain off any excess. Discard the marinade and set the chicken aside.

3. Prick the sweet potato all over with a fork and place it on a small foil-lined baking sheet. Place it in the oven and bake until tender, about 1 hour. Remove the sweet potato from the oven and let it sit until cool enough to handle.

4. When the potato comes out of the oven, start cooking the chicken. Place 1 tablespoon of avocado oil in a large cast-iron skillet and warm it over medium-high heat. Add the chicken, skin side down, and sear until the skin is very brown, about 5 minutes.

5. Transfer the chicken to the oven and roast until it is cooked through, 18 to 22 minutes. About 1 minute before removing the chicken from the oven, toss the rosemary into the skillet.

6. Remove the chicken from the oven and transfer it to a platter, skin side up. Place the rosemary on top of the chicken.

7. Place the skillet over medium-high heat and add the blood orange slices. Cook until they have browned and softened slightly, about 30 seconds per side. Transfer to the plate with the chicken.

8. In a bowl, combine the chickpeas, olives, the remaining avocado oil, and the remaining lemon juice. Toss to combine and season with salt.

9. To serve, tear open the sweet potato and arrange big sections of its flesh on a large platter. Place the chicken, along with any accumulated juices, around the sweet potato, then top with the blood orange slices, chickpea salad, feta, and rosemary. Serve with blood orange wedges.

Charred Chicken with Sweet Potatoes
& Oranges, see page 283

CEDAR-PLANK SALMON

YIELD: 6 SERVINGS / ACTIVE TIME: 30 MINUTES / TOTAL TIME: 3 HOURS

A lovely pairing of woodsy and oceanic flavors, this salmon takes on a light smokiness from grilling on a cedar plank. A classic that adds color and simple sophistication to any table.

1. Submerge a cedar grilling plank in water for 2 hours.

2. Prepare a gas or charcoal grill for medium-high heat (450°F).

3. In a bowl, combine the mustard, honey, rosemary, lemon zest, salt, and pepper and stir until well combined. Spread the mixture on the flesh of the salmon and let it stand at room temperature for 15 minutes.

4. Place the salmon on the plank, skin side down. Grill until the salmon is just cooked through and the edges are browned, 13 to 15 minutes.

5. Remove the salmon from the grill and let it rest on the plank for 3 minutes before enjoying.

INGREDIENTS:

2   TABLESPOONS GRAINY MUSTARD

2   TABLESPOONS MILD HONEY OR PURE MAPLE SYRUP

1   TEASPOON FINELY CHOPPED FRESH ROSEMARY

1   TABLESPOON LEMON ZEST

½   TEASPOON KOSHER SALT

½   TEASPOON BLACK PEPPER

2   LB. SKIN-ON SALMON FILLET (ABOUT 1½ INCHES THICK)

ZUCCHINI FRITTATAS

YIELD: 4 SERVINGS / **ACTIVE TIME:** 20 MINUTES / **TOTAL TIME:** 1 HOUR

Unlike most egg dishes, frittatas are just as good at room temperature as they are warm, so don't be shy about making them ahead of time.

1. Preheat the oven to 350°F. Place the zucchini in a colander, season it generously with salt, and toss to coat. Let the zucchini drain for 20 minutes.

2. Place the zucchini in a linen towel and wring the towel to remove excess liquid from the zucchini.

3. Place the olive oil in a large skillet and warm it over medium heat. Add the scallions and garlic and cook, stirring continually, for 1 minute. Add the zucchini and cook until the moisture it releases has evaporated, 5 to 8 minutes. Remove the pan from heat and let the mixture cool.

4. Place the eggs and milk in a bowl and whisk until combined. Stir in the zucchini mixture, feta, and fresh herbs.

5. Coat four 6-oz. ramekins with the melted butter and dust them with the flour, knocking out any excess flour. Pour the egg mixture into the ramekins, place them on a baking sheet, and place them in the oven.

6. Bake until the centers of the frittatas feel springy, about 25 minutes. Remove the frittatas from the oven and let them rest for 10 minutes before enjoying.

INGREDIENTS:

4	CUPS GRATED ZUCCHINI
	SALT AND PEPPER, TO TASTE
2	TABLESPOONS EXTRA-VIRGIN OLIVE OIL
6	SCALLIONS, TRIMMED AND SLICED THIN
2	GARLIC CLOVES, MINCED
4	EGGS
⅓	CUP MILK
1	CUP CRUMBLED FETA CHEESE
2	TABLESPOONS CHOPPED FRESH DILL
1	TABLESPOON CHOPPED FRESH OREGANO
1	TABLESPOON CHOPPED FRESH PARSLEY
2	TABLESPOONS UNSALTED BUTTER, MELTED
2	TABLESPOONS ALL-PURPOSE FLOUR

CHERMOULA SEA BASS

YIELD: 8 SERVINGS / **ACTIVE TIME:** 20 MINUTES / **TOTAL TIME:** 45 MINUTES

C hermoula is a garlic-and-herb paste that originated in Morocco and has spread widely through the region. Have pita bread or couscous at the ready with this, as you are going to want to sop up the juices.

1. Preheat the oven to 425°F. Rub the sea bass with the chermoula. Place a 2-inch sheet of parchment paper on a work surface and fold it in half lengthwise.

2. Arrange four of the fillets along one edge of the seam. Fold the parchment over the fillets and fold in the edges to make a pouch. Repeat with a second sheet of parchment and the remaining fillets.

3. Carefully transfer the pouches to a rimmed baking sheet. Place the pan in the oven and bake until the fish is cooked through and flakes easily at the touch of a fork, 10 to 12 minutes.

4. Remove from the oven and carefully open the pouches; be careful of the steam that escapes. Serve the sea bass immediately with the lemon wedges.

INGREDIENTS:

8   MEDITERRANEAN SEA BASS FILLETS, SKIN REMOVED

3   TABLESPOONS CHERMOULA SAUCE (SEE PAGE 755)

LEMON WEDGES, FOR SERVING

ROAST CHICKEN WITH FENNEL & CARROTS

YIELD: 4 SERVINGS / ACTIVE TIME: 30 MINUTES / TOTAL TIME: 3 HOURS

Caramelized in the cooking juices released by the chicken, fennel and carrots have never tasted so good.

1. Pat the chicken dry with paper towels and season it generously with salt, inside and out. Tie the legs together with kitchen twine and let it sit at room temperature for 1 hour. If time allows, place the chicken in the refrigerator, uncovered, overnight.

2. Preheat the oven to 425°F and position a rack in the upper third of the oven. Place a large cast-iron skillet on the rack.

3. In a large bowl, combine the fennel, carrots, and 2 tablespoons of the avocado oil and toss to coat. Season the mixture with salt and pepper.

4. Pat the chicken dry with paper towels and rub it with half of the remaining oil. Drizzle the remaining oil into the hot skillet, as this helps keep the chicken from sticking. Place the chicken in the center of the skillet and arrange the vegetables around it.

5. Roast until the fennel and carrots are golden brown and an instant-read thermometer inserted into the thickest part of the breast registers 155°F, 50 to 60 minutes.

6. Remove the chicken from the oven and let it rest in the pan for 20 minutes. The internal temperature will climb to 165°F as the chicken rests.

7. Carve the chicken and serve with the vegetables.

INGREDIENTS:

4	LB. WHOLE CHICKEN
	SALT AND PEPPER, TO TASTE
2	FENNEL BULBS, EACH CUT INTO 6 WEDGES
1	LB. SMALL CARROTS, PEELED AND CUT ON A BIAS INTO 4-INCH-LONG PIECES
3	TABLESPOONS AVOCADO OIL

CHICKEN WITH TURMERIC TAHINI, CHICKPEAS & ONIONS

YIELD: 4 SERVINGS / **ACTIVE TIME:** 25 MINUTES / **TOTAL TIME:** 1 HOUR AND 30 MINUTES

Musky turmeric and rich tahini enhance the flavors of this comforting and filling dish that can be served year-round.

1. Season the chicken pieces with a generous amount of salt and pepper and place them in a large resealable plastic bag with 1 cup of the turmeric tahini sauce. Seal the bag, leaving one corner open about ½ inch. Massage the bag to coat all of the chicken pieces with sauce, then squeeze the bag to remove as much air as you can. Seal the bag and let the chicken marinate at room temperature for 30 minutes, or overnight in the refrigerator.

2. Preheat the oven to 425°F. On a large baking sheet, toss the chickpeas and half of the onion with the turmeric, cumin, coriander, and berbere. Drizzle the olive oil over the mixture, season with salt and pepper, and toss everything to coat. Push everything to the edges of the pan and place the chicken pieces in the center in a single layer.

3. Place in the oven and roast until the onion is crispy, the chicken skin is brown, and an instant-read thermometer registers 160°F when inserted into the thickest part of a thigh, about 50 minutes.

4. While the chicken is in the oven, place the remaining onion and the lemon juice in a bowl, season with salt and pepper, and stir to combine.

5. Remove the chicken from the oven and transfer it to a serving plate along with the chickpeas and onions. Drizzle the remaining tahini sauce and hot sauce over the mixture, sprinkle the onion-and-lemon mixture and cilantro over it, and enjoy.

INGREDIENTS:

3 LBS. BONE-IN, SKIN-ON CHICKEN PIECES

SALT AND PEPPER, TO TASTE

2 CUPS TURMERIC TAHINI SAUCE

2 (14 OZ.) CANS OF CHICKPEAS, DRAINED AND RINSED

1 RED ONION, SLICED THIN

1 TABLESPOON TURMERIC

1 TEASPOON CUMIN

1 TEASPOON CORIANDER

1 TEASPOON BERBERE SEASONING

2 TABLESPOONS AVOCADO OIL

1 TABLESPOON FRESH LEMON JUICE

HOT SAUCE, TO TASTE

½ BUNCH OF FRESH CILANTRO, COARSELY CHOPPED

COJADA POTATO CASSEROLE

YIELD: 6 SERVINGS / ACTIVE TIME: 30 MINUTES / TOTAL TIME: 2 HOURS

A Sephardic version of the classic Spanish tortilla, this potato-and-egg casserole is a surefire crowd-pleaser.

1. Preheat the oven to 420°F. Place the potatoes in a large pot, cover them with cold water, and add 3 tablespoons of the salt. Bring to a boil over high heat and then reduce the heat to medium-low. Simmer until the potatoes are fork-tender, 30 to 40 minutes. Drain the potatoes and let them cool.

2. Coat an 11 x 5–inch casserole dish with 1 teaspoon of the avocado oil and set it aside.

3. Place ¼ cup of avocado oil in a saucepan and warm it over medium-high heat. Add the onion and sugar and cook, stirring frequently, until the onion is golden brown, about 15 minutes. Remove the pan from heat.

4. Place the egg whites in the work bowl of a stand mixer fitted with the whisk attachment and beat on low for 2 to 3 minutes. Increase speed to medium and whip the egg whites until they hold stiff peaks, 3 to 5 minutes. Set aside.

5. Peel the potatoes, discard the skins, and mash the flesh until smooth. Place the mashed potatoes in a large mixing bowl. Add the onion, remaining salt, pepper, cumin, Ras el Hanout, nutmeg, and egg yolks and stir with a large fork until thoroughly combined. Gently fold in the egg whites.

6. Transfer the mixture to the prepared casserole dish. Smooth the top with a spatula, drizzle the remaining avocado oil over the top, and place it in the oven. Bake until the cojada is set and golden brown at the edges, about 40 minutes. Remove from the oven and enjoy warm or at room temperature.

INGREDIENTS:

3	LARGE RUSSET POTATOES
¼	CUP KOSHER SALT
¼	CUP PLUS 2 TEASPOONS AVOCADO OIL
1	LARGE YELLOW ONION, FINELY DICED
1	TEASPOON SUGAR
3	EGGS, SEPARATED
¼	TEASPOON BLACK PEPPER
¼	TEASPOON CUMIN
½	TEASPOON RAS EL HANOUT (SEE PAGE 747)
¼	TEASPOON FRESHLY GRATED NUTMEG

COLD ROAST SALMON
WITH SMASHED GREEN BEAN SALAD

YIELD: 10 SERVINGS / **ACTIVE TIME:** 20 MINUTES / **TOTAL TIME:** 1 HOUR AND 45 MINUTES

Served chilled, this entire dish can be made a day ahead, and will keep you calm, cool, and collected when the temperatures start to rise in the summer.

1. Preheat the oven to 300°F. Place the salmon on a rimmed baking sheet and rub 2 tablespoons of olive oil over each side. Season the salmon all over with black pepper, 2 teaspoons of the salt, and ¼ teaspoon of the red pepper flakes.

2. Place the salmon skin side down on the baking sheet and place it in the oven. Roast until a paring knife inserted into the side of the salmon meets with no resistance, 20 to 25 minutes. The fish should be opaque throughout and you should just be able to flake it with a fork. Remove from the oven and let it cool completely.

3. While the salmon is roasting, place the lemon juice, remaining avocado oil, remaining salt, and remaining red pepper flakes in a large bowl and whisk to combine. Set the dressing aside.

4. Working in batches, place the green beans in a large resealable plastic bag. Seal the bag and whack the beans with a rolling pin to split their skins and soften their insides without completely pulverizing them. Place them in a bowl with the lemon dressing and massage the mixture with your hands to break down the beans further. Let the mixture sit at room temperature for at least 1 hour.

5. Slice the radishes thin lengthwise. Place them in a large bowl of ice water, cover, and chill until ready to serve; this will allow you to get the prep out of the way and keep the radishes crisp and firm.

6. Just before serving, drain the radishes and toss them with the green beans. Stir in the pistachios, taste, and adjust the seasoning as necessary. Transfer to a platter, drizzle avocado oil over the top, and sprinkle the Maldon sea salt on top.

7. Using two spatulas, carefully transfer the salmon to another platter, leaving the skin behind on the baking sheet. Drizzle avocado oil over it and squeeze a lemon wedge or two over the salmon. Sprinkle Maldon over the fish and serve with more lemon wedges, the Lemony Yogurt Sauce, and the Grilled Serrano Salsa Verde.

INGREDIENTS:

1	WHOLE SIDE OF SALMON (ABOUT 3½ LBS.)
7	TABLESPOONS AVOCADO OIL, PLUS MORE FOR SERVING
	BLACK PEPPER, TO TASTE
4	TEASPOONS KOSHER SALT, PLUS MORE TO TASTE
½	TEASPOON RED PEPPER FLAKES, DIVIDED
¼	CUP FRESH LEMON JUICE
2	LBS. GREEN BEANS, TRIMMED
1	BUNCH OF RADISHES (FRENCH BREAKFAST PREFERRED), TRIMMED
1	CUP SALTED AND ROASTED PISTACHIOS, SHELLED AND COARSELY CHOPPED
	MALDON SEA SALT, TO TASTE
	LEMON WEDGES, FOR SERVING
	LEMONY YOGURT SAUCE (SEE PAGE 787), FOR SERVING
	GRILLED SERRANO SALSA VERDE (SEE PAGE 798), FOR SERVING

Jerusalem Mixed Grill, see page 296

JERUSALEM MIXED GRILL

YIELD: 4 SERVINGS / **ACTIVE TIME:** 45 MINUTES / **TOTAL TIME:** 1 HOUR

This is a traditional and immensely popular sandwich that originated from the eponymous Holy City. It typically consists of grilled chicken hearts, liver, and spleen, combined with ground lamb (or lamb fat) and onions. The mix is then seasoned with turmeric, garlic, black pepper, cumin, cilantro, and olive oil and grilled to perfection. Once ready, it is served in a baguette or pita bread as a sandwich, with a salad, hummus, and fries on the side.

1. Place 2 tablespoons of the avocado oil in a large skillet and warm it over medium heat. Add the onion and a pinch of salt and cook, stirring frequently, until the onion begins to soften, about 7 minutes.

2. Lower the heat and continue to cook the onion, stirring occasionally, until the onion is deeply caramelized, which could take up to 45 minutes. Transfer the caramelized onion to a bowl and set it aside.

3. While the onion is cooking, combine the turmeric, cumin, fenugreek, baharat, cinnamon, and the 2 teaspoons salt in a large bowl. Add the chicken and toss until fully coated with the spices.

4. Place the remaining oil in a large skillet and warm it over high heat. Add the chicken and spread it out in an even layer. Let the meat sear, undisturbed, for about 2 minutes, then lower the heat to medium-high and cook, stirring once or twice, until it is completely cooked through, about 6 minutes. Squeeze one of the lemon halves over the chicken.

5. Remove the chicken mixture from the skillet and stir it into the caramelized onion. Serve with pita, pickles, and plenty of hummus.

INGREDIENTS:

¼ CUP AVOCADO OIL

1 LARGE RED ONION, HALVED AND SLICED THIN

2 TEASPOONS KOSHER SALT, PLUS MORE TO TASTE

2 TEASPOONS TURMERIC

1 TEASPOON CUMIN

1 TEASPOON GROUND FENUGREEK

1 TEASPOON BAHARAT SEASONING BLEND

1 TEASPOON CINNAMON

2½ LBS. BONELESS, SKINLESS CHICKEN THIGHS (OR 1½ LBS. BONELESS, SKINLESS CHICKEN THIGHS, ½ LB. CHICKEN HEARTS, AND ½ LB. CHICKEN LIVERS), TRIMMED AND CUT INTO NICKEL-SIZE PIECES

1 LEMON, HALVED

PITA BREAD (SEE PAGE 532), FOR SERVING

PICKLES, FOR SERVING

MODERN HUMMUS (SEE PAGE 31), FOR SERVING

FRIED FISH WITH AGRISTADA SAUCE

YIELD: 6 SERVINGS / **ACTIVE TIME:** 30 MINUTES / **TOTAL TIME:** 1 HOUR

A Sephardic take on the Greek avgolemono, agristada is a lemon-and-egg sauce that beautifully complements fried fish—both in terms of taste and texture.

1. Place the fish in a shallow dish, pour the lemon juice over it, and sprinkle ¼ teaspoon of the salt over the top. Turn the fish in the lemon juice until it is well coated. Let the fish soak for 30 minutes, turning once or twice.

2. Transfer the fish to a colander and rinse well. Pat it dry and cut it into 1-inch cubes.

3. Add avocado oil to a Dutch oven until it reaches about halfway up the side. Warm it to 350°F over medium-high heat.

4. In a shallow bowl, combine the flour with ¼ teaspoon of the salt. Place the eggs in a separate shallow bowl with the remaining ¼ teaspoon of salt and beat until scrambled.

5. Dredge the fish in the flour mixture until coated, shake off any excess, and then dredge it in the eggs until completely coated.

6. Working in batches to avoid crowding the pot, gently slip the fish into the hot oil and fry until cooked through and golden brown, about 10 minutes, turning as necessary. Transfer the fried fish to a paper towel–lined plate.

7. When all of the fish has been fried, serve with the Agristada Sauce.

INGREDIENTS:

2	LBS. COD OR RED MULLET FILLETS
½	CUP FRESH LEMON JUICE
¾	TEASPOON KOSHER SALT
	AVOCADO OIL, AS NEEDED
1	CUP ALL-PURPOSE FLOUR
2	EGGS
	AGRISTADA SAUCE (SEE PAGE 793), FOR SERVING

SOUPS & STEWS

Outsiders tend to picture the Mediterranean as a temperate, sun-soaked region, a gloss that—between the French Riviera, Sicily, sunny old Athens, North Africa, and the Levant—is not far off the mark. As such, soup is not the dish that leaps to mind when one thinks of the food. But, remember—no cuisine is as focused on simplicity and comfort quite like that of the countries in this area. Considering this, it is only natural that some of the greatest soups and stews in the world—bouillabaisse, avgolemono, romesco de peix, sharba, and harira—number among the Mediterranean's many culinary treasures.

BOUILLABAISSE

YIELD: 6 SERVINGS / ACTIVE TIME: 25 MINUTES / TOTAL TIME: 1 HOUR AND 30 MINUTES

This soup allows you to yake a trip to Marseille, France, any time you want.

1. Place ¼ cup of the olive oil in a large saucepan and warm it over medium heat. Add the onion, leeks, celery, and fennel and cook, stirring occasionally, until the vegetables have softened, about 10 minutes.

2. Add the garlic, Bouquet Garni, orange zest, and tomato and cook, stirring continually, for 1 minute. Stir in the saffron, stocks, Pernod, and tomato paste and bring the soup to a boil. Reduce the heat and simmer the soup for 20 minutes.

3. While the soup is simmering, place the remaining olive oil in a skillet and warm it over medium heat. Add the monkfish and shrimp and cook for 2 minutes on each side. Remove the shrimp and monkfish from the pan and set them aside.

4. Add the clams to the soup and cook for 3 minutes. Add the mussels and cook until the majority of the clams and mussels have opened, 3 to 4 minutes. Discard any clams and mussels that do not open.

5. Add the monkfish and shrimp to the soup and cook until warmed through.

6. Season the soup with salt and pepper and ladle it into warmed bowls. Garnish each portion with parsley and serve with bread and Garlic Butter.

BOQUET GARNI

1. Cut a 2-inch section of kitchen twine. Tie one side of the twine around the herbs and knot it tightly.

2. To use, attach the other end of the twine to one of the pot's handles and slip the herbs into the broth. Remove before serving.

INGREDIENTS:

6	TABLESPOONS EXTRA-VIRGIN OLIVE OIL
1	ONION, CHOPPED
1	CUP CHOPPED LEEKS
½	CUP SLICED CELERY
1	CUP CHOPPED FENNEL
2	GARLIC CLOVES, MINCED
	BOUQUET GARNI (SEE RECIPE)
	ZEST OF 1 ORANGE
1	TOMATO, PEELED, SEEDS REMOVED, AND CHOPPED
	PINCH OF SAFFRON
3	CUPS FISH STOCK (SEE PAGE 372)
3	CUPS LOBSTER STOCK (SEE PAGE 373)
2	TEASPOONS PERNOD
1	TABLESPOON TOMATO PASTE
1	LB. MONKFISH, CUT INTO 1-INCH CUBES
12	SMALL SHRIMP, SHELLS REMOVED, DEVEINED
12	STEAMER CLAMS
24	MUSSELS
	SALT AND PEPPER, TO TASTE
	FRESH PARSLEY, CHOPPED, FOR GARNISH
	CRUSTY BREAD, TOASTED, FOR SERVING
	GARLIC BUTTER (SEE PAGE 806), FOR SERVING

BOUQUET GARNI

1-2	BAY LEAVES
3	SPRIGS OF FRESH THYME
3	SPRIGS OF FRESH PARSLEY

ALBONDIGAS SOUP

YIELD: 4 SERVINGS / ACTIVE TIME: 45 MINUTES / TOTAL TIME: 2 HOURS

The poached meatballs provide this soup a wonderful mouthfeel, and a saffron-enriched broth makes it refreshing and aesthetically appealing. Should Zamorana cheese prove tough to find, Manchego is a good substitute.

1. To begin preparations for the meatballs, place the bread and milk in a mixing bowl. Let the bread soak for 10 minutes.

2. Use a fork to mash the bread until it is very soft and broken down. Add the remaining ingredients and work the mixture with your hands until thoroughly combined. Cover the bowl with plastic wrap and chill it in the refrigerator for 30 minutes.

3. Line a baking sheet with parchment paper. Remove the mixture from the refrigerator and form tablespoons of it into balls. Place the meatballs on the baking sheet, cover them with plastic wrap, and refrigerate for 30 minutes.

4. To begin preparations for the soup, place the olive oil in a large saucepan and warm it over medium-high heat. Add the onion and cook, stirring frequently, for 2 minutes. Add the celery and bell peppers and cook, stirring occasionally, until the vegetables are soft, about 8 minutes.

5. Add the garlic, paprika, saffron, and red pepper flakes and cook, stirring continually, for 45 seconds. Add the wine and cook until the alcohol has been cooked off, 1 to 2 minutes. Add the stock and bring the soup to a boil.

6. Reduce the heat, add the meatballs, and simmer until they are cooked through, 15 to 20 minutes.

7. Stir in the parsley, season the soup with salt and pepper, and ladle it into warmed bowls.

INGREDIENTS:

FOR THE MEATBALLS

2	CUPS DAY-OLD BREAD PIECES, CRUST REMOVED
½	CUP MILK
½	LB. GROUND PORK
½	LB. GROUND BEEF
½	CUP FRESHLY GRATED ZAMORANA CHEESE
¼	CUP CHOPPED FRESH PARSLEY
2	TABLESPOONS MINCED SHALLOTS
2	TABLESPOONS EXTRA-VIRGIN OLIVE OIL
1	TEASPOON KOSHER SALT
½	TEASPOON BLACK PEPPER
1	EGG

FOR THE SOUP

1	TABLESPOON EXTRA-VIRGIN OLIVE OIL
1	ONION, CHOPPED
2	CELERY STALKS, CHOPPED
2	RED BELL PEPPERS, STEMS AND SEEDS REMOVED, CUT INTO ¼-INCH-WIDE STRIPS
2	GARLIC CLOVES, MINCED
1½	TEASPOONS PAPRIKA
¼	TEASPOON SAFFRON
2	PINCHES OF RED PEPPER FLAKES
½	CUP WHITE WINE
6	CUPS CHICKEN STOCK (SEE PAGE 368)
¼	CUP CHOPPED FRESH PARSLEY
	SALT AND PEPPER, TO TASTE

AVGOLEMONO

YIELD: 4 TO 6 SERVINGS / **ACTIVE TIME:** 15 MINUTES / **TOTAL TIME:** 45 MINUTES

A delightful Greek soup that takes full advantage of the unexpectedly brilliant combination of egg and lemon.

1. Place the stock in a large saucepan and bring it to a boil. Reduce the heat so that the stock simmers. Add the orzo and cook until tender, about 5 minutes.

2. Strain the stock and orzo over a large bowl. Set the orzo aside. Return the stock to the pan and bring it to a simmer.

3. Place the eggs in a mixing bowl and beat until scrambled and frothy. Stir in the lemon juice and cold water. While stirring constantly, add approximately ½ cup of the stock to the egg mixture. Stir another cup of stock into the egg mixture and then stir the tempered eggs into the saucepan. Reduce the heat to low and be careful not to let the stock come to boil once you add the egg mixture.

4. Return the orzo to the soup. Cook, stirring continually, until everything is warmed through, about 2 minutes. Season with salt and pepper, ladle the soup into warmed bowls, and garnish each portion with slices of lemon and dill.

INGREDIENTS:

- 8 CUPS CHICKEN STOCK (SEE PAGE 368)
- ½ CUP ORZO
- 3 EGGS

  JUICE OF 1 LEMON

- 1 TABLESPOON COLD WATER

  SALT AND PEPPER, TO TASTE

- 1 LEMON, SEEDS REMOVED, SLICED THIN, FOR GARNISH

  FRESH DILL, CHOPPED, FOR GARNISH

LAMB SHARBA

YIELD: 6 SERVINGS / **ACTIVE TIME:** 30 MINUTES / **TOTAL TIME:** 2 HOURS

If lamb is not your thing, this Libyan delicacy can also be made with chicken or fish serving as the protein.

1. Place half of the olive oil in a Dutch oven and warm it over medium-high heat. Add the lamb and cook, turning it as necessary, until it is browned all over, about 5 minutes. Remove the lamb with a slotted spoon and place it on a paper towel–lined plate.

2. Add the onion to the pot and cook, stirring occasionally, until it starts to soften, about 5 minutes. Add the tomato, garlic, tomato paste, mint, cinnamon sticks, turmeric, paprika, and cumin and cook, stirring continually, for 1 minute.

3. Add the stock and bring the mixture to a boil. Return the seared lamb to the pot, reduce the heat, and simmer until the lamb is tender, about 30 minutes.

4. Add the chickpeas and orzo and cook until the orzo is tender, about 10 minutes.

5. Remove the mint and discard it. Season the soup with salt and pepper and ladle it into warmed bowls. Garnish with additional mint and enjoy.

INGREDIENTS:

- 2 TABLESPOONS EXTRA-VIRGIN OLIVE OIL
- ¾ LB. BONELESS LEG OF LAMB, CUT INTO 1-INCH CUBES
- 1 ONION, CHOPPED
- 1 TOMATO, QUARTERED, SEEDS REMOVED, SLICED THIN
- 1 GARLIC CLOVE, MINCED
- 1 TABLESPOON TOMATO PASTE
- 1 BUNCH OF FRESH MINT, TIED WITH TWINE, PLUS MORE FOR GARNISH
- 2 CINNAMON STICKS
- 1¼ TEASPOONS TURMERIC
- 1¼ TEASPOONS PAPRIKA
- ½ TEASPOONS CUMIN
- 8 CUPS CHICKEN STOCK (SEE PAGE 368)
- 1 (14 OZ.) CAN OF CHICKPEAS, DRAINED AND RINSED
- ¾ CUP ORZO
- SALT AND PEPPER, TO TASTE

MOROCCAN LENTIL STEW

YIELD: 6 SERVINGS / **ACTIVE TIME**: 10 MINUTES / **TOTAL TIME**: 8 HOURS

Be generous with the mint, as its fresh, clean flavor lifts everything else.

1. Place the lentils in a fine-mesh sieve, rinse them well, and pick them over to remove any debris or shriveled lentils.

2. Place all of the ingredients, except for the cannellini beans and the garnishes, in a slow cooker. Cover and cook on low for 7½ hours.

3. After 7½ hours, stir in the cannellini beans. Cover and cook on low for 30 another minutes.

4. Ladle into warmed bowls and garnish with fresh mint and goat cheese.

INGREDIENTS:

1	CUP BROWN LENTILS
½	CUP GREEN LENTILS
4	CUPS VEGETABLE STOCK (SEE PAGE 371)
3	CARROTS, PEELED AND CHOPPED
1	LARGE YELLOW ONION, CHOPPED
3	GARLIC CLOVES, MINCED
	3-INCH PIECE OF FRESH GINGER, PEELED AND GRATED
	ZEST AND JUICE OF 1 LEMON
3	TABLESPOONS SMOKED PAPRIKA
2	TABLESPOONS CINNAMON
1	TABLESPOON CORIANDER
1	TABLESPOON TURMERIC
1	TABLESPOON CUMIN
1½	TEASPOONS ALLSPICE
2	BAY LEAVES
	SALT AND PEPPER, TO TASTE
1	(14 OZ.) CAN OF CANNELLINI BEANS, DRAINED AND RINSED
	FRESH MINT, CHOPPED, FOR GARNISH
	GOAT CHEESE, CRUMBLED, FOR GARNISH

CHICKEN & TOMATO STEW
WITH CARAMELIZED LEMON

YIELD: 4 SERVINGS / **ACTIVE TIME:** 45 MINUTES / **TOTAL TIME:** 3 HOURS

Cooking the lemon slices to the edge of burnt adds a layer of complex flavor and brightness to this comforting dish.

---

1. Pat the chicken dry and season it with salt. Let the chicken sit at room temperature for at least 15 minutes and up to 1 hour, or cover and refrigerate for up to 24 hours.

2. Place 2 tablespoons of the olive oil in a large Dutch oven and warm it over medium-high heat. Add the chicken and cook until it is a deep golden brown on both sides, about 12 minutes, adjusting the heat as necessary to avoid burning.

3. Transfer the chicken to a plate, leaving the drippings in the pan.

4. Place the onion in the pot and cook, stirring frequently, until it has softened, 6 to 8 minutes. Add the garlic and cook, stirring frequently, until the onion begins to brown around the edges, about 3 minutes. Stir in the honey, tomato paste, turmeric, and cinnamon and cook until fragrant, about 2 minutes. Add the tomatoes and their juices and smash the tomatoes with a wooden spoon until they break down into pieces no larger than 1 inch.

5. Return the chicken to the pot, add the stock (it should barely cover the chicken), and bring to a simmer. Reduce the heat to low, partially cover the pot with a lid, and gently simmer until the chicken is tender and the sauce has thickened, about 1 hour and 15 minutes.

6. While the chicken is simmering, trim the top and bottom from the lemon and cut it into quarters. Remove the seeds and the white pith in the center. Slice the quarters crosswise into quarter-moons.

7. Place the lemon pieces in a medium skillet, cover them with water, and bring to a boil. Cook for 3 minutes, drain, and pat dry with paper towels.

8. Transfer the lemon pieces to a small bowl, sprinkle the sugar over them, and toss to coat.

9. Wipe out the skillet and warm the remaining olive oil over medium-high heat. Arrange the lemon pieces in a single layer in the skillet. Cook, turning halfway through, until they are deeply browned all over, about 3 minutes. Return the lemon to the bowl and season with salt.

10. Ladle the stew into bowls, top with the caramelized lemon, sesame seeds, and mint, and serve with pitas.

INGREDIENTS:

4	BONE-IN, SKIN-ON CHICKEN LEGS
	SALT, TO TASTE
¼	CUP EXTRA-VIRGIN OLIVE OIL
1	LARGE ONION, SLICED THIN
6	GARLIC CLOVES, HALVED
2	TABLESPOONS HONEY
1	TABLESPOON TOMATO PASTE
¾	TEASPOON TURMERIC
½	TEASPOON CINNAMON
1	(14 OZ.) CAN OF WHOLE PEELED TOMATOES, WITH THEIR JUICES
3	CUPS CHICKEN STOCK (SEE PAGE 368)
1	LEMON
1½	TEASPOONS SUGAR
1	TABLESPOON TOASTED SESAME SEEDS
½	CUP TORN FRESH MINT LEAVES
	PITA BREAD (SEE PAGE 532), FOR SERVING

Chicken & Tomato Stew with Caramelized Lemon, see page 311

DRIED FAVA BEAN SOUP
WITH GRILLED HALLOUMI CHEESE

YIELD: 4 SERVINGS / ACTIVE TIME: 30 MINUTES / TOTAL TIME: 24 HOURS

The creamy, earthy flavor of fava beans makes them a natural for the comforting nature of a soup.

1. Drain the fava beans and place them in a large saucepan with the stock and garlic. Bring to a boil, reduce the heat so that the soup simmers, cover, and cook until the beans are so tender that they are starting to fall apart, about 1 hour.

2. While the soup is simmering, place ¼ cup of the olive oil in a skillet and warm it over medium heat. When the oil starts to shimmer, add the shallot and sauté until it starts to soften, about 5 minutes. Remove the pan from heat, stir in the lemon zest, and let the mixture sit for 1 hour.

3. Transfer the soup to a food processor and puree until smooth. Return the soup to a clean saucepan, season with salt and pepper, and bring to a gentle simmer. Stir in the mixture in the skillet, lemon juice, and parsley, cook until heated through, and remove the soup from heat.

4. Warm a skillet over medium heat. Place the remaining olive oil in a small bowl, add the cheese, and toss to coat. Place the cheese in the pan and cook until browned on both sides, about 2 minutes per side. Serve the Halloumi and lemon wedges alongside the soup.

INGREDIENTS:

1½ CUPS DRIED FAVA BEANS, SOAKED OVERNIGHT

6 CUPS VEGETABLE STOCK (SEE PAGE 371)

4 GARLIC CLOVES, MINCED

5 TABLESPOONS EXTRA-VIRGIN OLIVE OIL

1 SHALLOT, MINCED

ZEST AND JUICE OF 1 LEMON

SALT AND PEPPER, TO TASTE

2 TABLESPOONS FINELY CHOPPED FRESH PARSLEY

½ LB. HALLOUMI CHEESE, CUT INTO 4 PIECES

LEMON WEDGES, FOR SERVING

SPLIT PEA SOUP WITH SMOKED HAM

YIELD: 4 SERVINGS / **ACTIVE TIME:** 30 MINUTES / **TOTAL TIME:** 2 HOURS

This preparation leaves the split peas al dente. If you'd like them to be a little more tender, add a bit more stock and cook for another 30 minutes.

1. Place the butter in a large saucepan and melt it over medium heat. Add the onion, carrot, and celery and cook, stirring frequently, until they have softened, about 5 minutes.

2. Add the stock, split peas, ham, parsley, bay leaf, and thyme. Bring the soup to a boil, reduce the heat to medium-low, and simmer, stirring occasionally, until the peas are al dente, about 1 hour.

3. Remove the bay leaf and discard it. Season the soup with salt and pepper and ladle it into warmed bowls. Garnish with additional parsley and serve with lemon wedges.

INGREDIENTS:

2 TABLESPOONS UNSALTED BUTTER

1 ONION, MINCED

1 CARROT, PEELED AND MINCED

1 CELERY STALK, MINCED

5 CUPS CHICKEN STOCK (SEE PAGE 368)

1 CUP SPLIT PEAS

½ LB. SMOKED HAM, CHOPPED

2 TABLESPOONS FINELY CHOPPED FRESH PARSLEY, PLUS MORE FOR GARNISH

1 BAY LEAF

1 TEASPOON FINELY CHOPPED FRESH THYME

SALT AND PEPPER, TO TASTE

LEMON WEDGES, FOR SERVING

CHILLED WHITE TOMATO SOUP
WITH BRAISED GRAPES

YIELD: 4 SERVINGS / ACTIVE TIME: 30 MINUTES / TOTAL TIME: 24 HOURS

This soup takes some time but carries a unique flavor thanks to the tomato water—just make sure you use ripe tomatoes when preparing it.

1. Place the tomatoes in a food processor and puree them for 5 minutes.

2. Strain the puree through cheesecloth into a bowl, making sure you let gravity do its job and refrain from forcing the puree through. Strain the puree through cheesecloth again, letting it sit overnight.

3. Place 4 cups of the tomato water in a bowl. If you do not have 4 cups, add the necessary amount of water. Add the bread and let it soak for 5 minutes.

4. Place the almonds in a food processor and blitz until they are finely ground.

5. Remove the bread from the tomato water, gently squeeze the bread, and add it to the food processor.

6. Measure out 3 cups of the tomato water and set it aside.

7. Add the garlic, vinegar, and cayenne to the food processor and blitz for 1 minute. With the food processor running, slowly drizzle in the almond oil and blitz until it has been thoroughly incorporated.

8. Add the tomato water and blitz the mixture for 2 minutes. Season the soup with salt and pepper, place it in the refrigerator, and chill for 4 hours.

9. Remove the soup from the refrigerator and strain it. Ladle the soup into chilled bowls, garnish each with a drizzle of olive oil, and serve with the Braised Grapes.

BRAISED GRAPES

1. Place the olive oil in a medium skillet and warm it over medium heat. Add the grapes and cook, stirring frequently, until they have been browned, 5 to 10 minutes.

2. Add the vermouth, star anise, and cinnamon sticks and cook until the vermouth has evaporated, 2 to 4 minutes.

3. Season the mixture with salt and pepper, sprinkle the almonds over the top, and let the mixture cool.

INGREDIENTS:

10	RIPE TOMATOES, STEMS REMOVED, CHOPPED
4	CUPS DAY-OLD SOURDOUGH BREAD PIECES
2	CUPS SLIVERED BLANCHED ALMONDS, TOASTED
1	GARLIC CLOVE, MINCED
4	TEASPOONS WHITE WINE VINEGAR
	PINCH OF CAYENNE PEPPER
½	CUP ALMOND OIL
	SALT AND PEPPER, TO TASTE
	EXTRA-VIRGIN OLIVE OIL, FOR GARNISH
	BRAISED GRAPES (SEE RECIPE), FOR SERVING

BRAISED GRAPES

1	TABLESPOON EXTRA-VIRGIN OLIVE OIL
2	CUPS GRAPES, STEMS REMOVED
½	CUP DRY VERMOUTH
2	STAR ANISE PODS
2	CINNAMON STICKS
	SALT AND PEPPER, TO TASTE
¼	CUP SLIVERED BLANCHED ALMONDS, TOASTED

CHAMIN

YIELD: 4 SERVINGS / ACTIVE TIME: 30 MINUTES / TOTAL TIME: 24 HOURS

A warning to those looking to cut corners: canned chickpeas will cut way down on the prep time, but you will taste the difference.

1. Preheat the oven to 250°F. Place the olive oil in a Dutch oven and warm over medium heat. Add the onion, garlic, parsnip, carrots, cumin, turmeric, and ginger and cook, stirring continually, for 2 minutes.

2. Add the brisket and lamb and cook, stirring occasionally, until both are browned all over, about 8 minutes.

3. Add the stock and bring the soup to a simmer. Stir in the chickpeas, potato, zucchini, tomatoes, lentils, bay leaf, and cilantro. Cover the pot, place it in the oven, and cook until the meat is tender, about 1 hour.

4. Remove the stew from the oven and skim the fat from the top. Season with salt and pepper and ladle into warmed bowls. Garnish with the chiles and serve with the lemon wedges and rice.

INGREDIENTS:

1½ TABLESPOONS EXTRA-VIRGIN OLIVE OIL

1 SMALL ONION, CHOPPED

5 GARLIC CLOVES, MINCED

¾ CUP CHOPPED PARSNIP

2 CARROTS, PEELED AND SLICED

1 TEASPOON CUMIN

¼ TEASPOON TURMERIC

1½-INCH PIECE FRESH GINGER, PEELED AND MINCED

½ LB. BEEF BRISKET, TRIMMED AND CHOPPED

4 OZ. LAMB SHOULDER, TRIMMED AND CHOPPED

4 CUPS BEEF STOCK (SEE PAGE 369)

½ CUP CHICKPEAS, SOAKED OVERNIGHT AND DRAINED

1 SMALL POTATO, PEELED AND CHOPPED

1 SMALL ZUCCHINI, SLICED

½ LB. TOMATOES, CHOPPED

2 TABLESPOONS BROWN LENTILS

1 BAY LEAF

½ BUNCH OF FRESH CILANTRO, CHOPPED

SALT AND PEPPER, TO TASTE

FRESH CHILE PEPPERS, STEMS AND SEEDS REMOVED, CHOPPED, FOR GARNISH

LEMON WEDGES, FOR SERVING

LONG-GRAIN RICE, COOKED, FOR SERVING

PROVENÇAL FISH SOUP

YIELD: 4 SERVINGS / **ACTIVE TIME:** 30 MINUTES / **TOTAL TIME:** 1 HOUR

This warm, revitalizing soup is bright, briny, and slightly sweet thanks to the array of seasonings and vegetables.

1. Place the olive oil in a medium saucepan and warm it over medium heat. Add the pancetta and cook, stirring occasionally, until it is crispy, about 5 minutes.

2. Add the fennel, onion, and celery and cook, stirring occasionally, until the vegetables have softened, about 8 minutes.

3. Add the garlic, herbes de Provence, bay leaf, red pepper flakes, and saffron and cook, stirring continually, for 1 minute.

4. Deglaze the pan with the vermouth and white wine, scraping up any browned bits from the bottom of the pan. Cook until the alcohol has been cooked off, about 2 minutes.

5. Add the clam juice and water and bring the soup to a boil. Reduce the heat and simmer the soup until the flavor has developed, about 15 minutes.

6. Remove the bay leaf and discard it. Add the haddock and orange zest and remove the pan from heat. Cover it and let it rest until the haddock is opaque and can be flaked with a fork, about 8 minutes.

7. Stir in the orange juice, season the soup with salt and pepper, and ladle it into warmed bowls. Garnish with the fennel fronds and enjoy.

INGREDIENTS:

1	TABLESPOON EXTRA-VIRGIN OLIVE OIL
½	LB. PANCETTA, CHOPPED
¼	CUP CHOPPED FENNEL
1	ONION, CHOPPED
2	CELERY STALKS, CHOPPED
3	GARLIC CLOVES, MINCED
1½	TEASPOONS PAPRIKA
1	TEASPOON HERBES DE PROVENCE
1	BAY LEAF
2	PINCHES OF RED PEPPER FLAKES
	PINCH OF SAFFRON
½	CUP DRY VERMOUTH
½	CUP WHITE WINE
4	CUPS CLAM JUICE
2	CUPS WATER
2	LBS. HADDOCK, SKIN REMOVED, CUT INTO 1-INCH PIECES
	ZEST AND JUICE OF 1 ORANGE
	SALT AND PEPPER, TO TASTE
	FENNEL FRONDS, FOR GARNISH

BONE MARROW & MATZO BALL SOUP

YIELD: 8 SERVINGS / ACTIVE TIME: 35 MINUTES / TOTAL TIME: 24 HOURS

This is a recipe to turn to when you are sick, or aching from a bad day.

1. Place the marrow bones in a saucepan, add a few pinches of salt, and cover the bones with cold water. Let the bones soak overnight.

2. Preheat the oven to 400°F. Pat the bones dry, arrange them on a baking sheet, and place them in the oven. Roast for 30 minutes, remove from the oven, and let the marrow bones cool slightly.

3. Using a spoon or a table knife, remove the marrow from the bones and place it in a small bowl. Continue until you have about ½ cup of marrow.

4. Place half of the marrow in a mixing bowl and mash it with a fork until it is smooth. Add the egg yolks, parsley, salt, pepper, and nutmeg and stir until combined. Add the matzo and work the mixture until it comes together as a soft dough.

5. Cover the bowl with plastic wrap and chill it in the refrigerator for 2 hours.

6. Place the egg whites in a mixing bowl and whip them until they hold soft peaks. Add them to the matzo dough and gently fold to incorporate them.

7. Place the stock in a large saucepan and stir in the garlic and the remaining marrow. Bring the stock to a simmer.

8. Form the dough into small balls and drop them into the simmering stock in batches of five. Cook each batch in the simmering stock until cooked through and tender, 10 to 15 minutes. Transfer the cooked matzo balls to a serving bowl.

9. When all of the matzo balls have been cooked, divide them among the serving bowls. Ladle the stock over each portion and enjoy.

INGREDIENTS:

4	LBS. MARROW BONES
2	TEASPOONS KOSHER SALT, PLUS MORE TO TASTE
2	EGGS, SEPARATED
2	TABLESPOONS CHOPPED FRESH PARSLEY
1	TEASPOON BLACK PEPPER
	DASH OF FRESHLY GRATED NUTMEG
1	CUP MATZO MEAL
8	CUPS CHICKEN STOCK (SEE PAGE 368)
1	GARLIC CLOVE

LAMB & CANNELLINI SOUP

YIELD: 4 SERVINGS / ACTIVE TIME: 20 MINUTES / TOTAL TIME: 24 HOURS

A soup that resides somewhere between Sicily, North Africa, and Greece.

1. Place the olive oil in a large saucepan and warm over medium heat. Add the onion and cook, stirring frequently, until it starts to soften, about 5 minutes. Stir in the garlic, cook for 2 minutes, and then add the lamb. Cook until it starts to brown, about 5 minutes, and add the carrots and celery.

2. Cook for 5 minutes, stir in the tomatoes, herbs, cannellini beans, and stock, and bring the soup to a boil. Reduce the heat to medium-low, cover the pan, and simmer for 1 hour, until the beans are tender.

3. Add the spinach and olives and cook until the spinach wilts, about 2 minutes. Season with salt and pepper, ladle into warmed bowls, and garnish with the feta cheese.

INGREDIENTS:

- 2 TABLESPOONS EXTRA-VIRGIN OLIVE OIL
- 1 ONION, CHOPPED
- 2 GARLIC CLOVES, MINCED
- 1½ LBS. GROUND LAMB
- 3 CARROTS, PEELED AND CHOPPED
- 3 CELERY STALKS, CHOPPED
- 1 (14 OZ.) CAN OF STEWED TOMATOES, DRAINED
- ¼ CUP FINELY CHOPPED FRESH PARSLEY
- 2 TABLESPOONS FINELY CHOPPED FRESH THYME
- ½ LB. DRIED CANNELLINI BEANS, SOAKED OVERNIGHT AND DRAINED
- 6 CUPS CHICKEN STOCK (SEE PAGE 368)
- ½ LB. BABY SPINACH
- ¼ CUP SLICED KALAMATA OLIVES

  SALT AND PEPPER, TO TASTE

  FETA CHEESE, CRUMBLED, FOR GARNISH

Lamb & Cannellini Soup, see page 325

VEGETABLE SOUP

YIELD: 12 SERVINGS / ACTIVE TIME: 30 MINUTES / TOTAL TIME: 2 HOURS

For when you need some veggies, but a salad simply won't do.

1. Place the avocado oil in a large saucepan and warm it over medium heat. Add the onion and cook, stirring occasionally, until it starts to soften, about 5 minutes.

2. Add the carrots, celery, parsnip, leek, and garlic and cook, stirring frequently, until fragrant, about 5 minutes.

3. Add the stock and bay leaves and bring the soup to a boil. Reduce the heat and simmer the soup until the flavor has developed nicely, about 1 hour.

4. Stir in the lemongrass, parsley, and salt and simmer for another 30 minutes.

5. Remove the bay leaves and lemongrass, ladle into warmed bowls, and serve.

INGREDIENTS:

2 TABLESPOONS AVOCADO OIL

1 LARGE ONION, CHOPPED

2 LARGE CARROTS, PEELED AND CHOPPED

2 LARGE CELERY STALKS WITH THEIR LEAVES, CHOPPED

1 PARSNIP, PEELED AND CHOPPED

1 LEEK, TRIMMED, RINSED WELL, AND CHOPPED

5 GARLIC CLOVES, SMASHED

9 CUPS VEGETABLE STOCK (SEE PAGE 371)

2 BAY LEAVES

1 LEMONGRASS STALK, CUT INTO FOUR SMALL PIECES

1 HANDFUL OF FRESH PARSLEY, CHOPPED

2 TABLESPOONS KOSHER SALT

MANSAF

YIELD: 4 SERVINGS / **ACTIVE TIME:** 30 MINUTES / **TOTAL TIME:** 1 HOUR AND 30 MINUTES

The national dish of Jordan has expanded its reach throughout the Mediterranean region.

1. Place the olive oil in a saucepan and warm over medium-high heat. Add the onion and cook, stirring frequently, until it starts to soften, about 5 minutes. Add the lamb and cook until it is browned all over, about 8 minutes.

2. Add the stock and cardamom and bring the soup to a boil. Reduce the heat to medium-low, cover the pan, and simmer until the lamb is very tender, about 1 hour.

3. Stir in the yogurt, season with salt and pepper, and remove the soup from heat. Divide the rice among the serving bowls, ladle the soup over the rice, and garnish with the pine nuts and parsley.

INGREDIENTS:

2   TABLESPOONS EXTRA-VIRGIN OLIVE OIL

1   ONION, CHOPPED

2   LBS. LAMB SHOULDER, CUBED

6   CUPS BEEF STOCK (SEE PAGE 369)

    SEEDS FROM 2 CARDAMOM PODS

1   CUP PLAIN GREEK YOGURT

    SALT AND PEPPER, TO TASTE

2   CUPS COOKED LONG-GRAIN RICE

¼   CUP PINE NUTS, TOASTED, FOR GARNISH

    FRESH PARSLEY, FINELY CHOPPED, FOR GARNISH

Mansaf, see page 329

SAFFRON & MUSSEL SOUP

YIELD: 4 SERVINGS / ACTIVE TIME: 20 MINUTES / TOTAL TIME: 45 MINUTES

Never been to Catalonia? This soup spirits you there in seconds.

1. Place the mussels and wine in a large saucepan, cover, and cook over medium heat, shaking the pan occasionally, for 4 to 5 minutes, until the majority of the mussels have opened.

2. Discard any unopened mussels. Drain, reserve the cooking liquid, and remove the meat from all but 18 of the mussels. Reserve the 18 mussels in their shells for garnish.

3. Add the butter to the saucepan and melt it over medium heat. Add the leeks, celery, fennel, carrot, and garlic and cook, stirring frequently, until the vegetables start to soften, about 5 minutes.

4. Strain the reserved liquid through a fine sieve and add it to the saucepan. Cook for 10 minutes, until the liquid has reduced by one-quarter.

5. Add the saffron and cream and bring the soup to a boil. Reduce the heat to low, season with salt and pepper, add the mussels and tomatoes, and cook gently until heated through.

6. Ladle the soup into warmed bowls, garnish with the parsley, microgreens, radish, and reserved mussels, and serve with lemon wedges.

INGREDIENTS:

- 3   LBS. MUSSELS, RINSED WELL AND DEBEARDED
- 3   CUPS WHITE WINE
- 4   TABLESPOONS UNSALTED BUTTER
- 2   LEEKS, TRIMMED, RINSED WELL, AND CHOPPED
- 2   CELERY STALKS, CHOPPED
- ¾   CUP CHOPPED FENNEL
- 1   CARROT, PEELED AND MINCED
- 2   GARLIC CLOVES, MINCED
- ⅛   TEASPOON SAFFRON
- 2   CUPS HEAVY CREAM
-    SALT AND PEPPER, TO TASTE
- 3   TOMATOES, CHOPPED
-    FRESH PARSLEY, FINELY CHOPPED, FOR GARNISH
-    MICROGREENS, FOR GARNISH
-    SHAVED RADISH, FOR GARNISH
-    LEMON WEDGES, FOR SERVING

EGGPLANT & ZUCCHINI SOUP

YIELD: 4 SERVINGS / **ACTIVE TIME:** 20 MINUTES / **TOTAL TIME:** 1 HOUR AND 15 MINUTES

Serving this soup chilled is another good option. If one goes that route, stir the Tzatziki directly into the soup and skip the other serving suggestions.

1. Preheat the oven to 425°F. Place the eggplant, zucchini, onion, and garlic in a baking dish, drizzle the olive oil over the mixture, and gently stir to coat. Place in the oven and roast for 30 minutes, removing to stir occasionally.

2. Remove from the oven and let the vegetables cool briefly.

3. Place half of the roasted vegetables in a food processor. Add the stock and blitz until pureed. Place the puree in a medium saucepan, add the remaining roasted vegetables, and bring to a boil.

4. Stir in the oregano and mint and season with salt and pepper. Cook for 2 minutes and then ladle into warmed bowls. Garnish with additional mint and serve with the Tzatziki, Pita Bread, and Minty Pickled Cucumbers.

INGREDIENTS:

- 1   LARGE EGGPLANT, PEELED AND CHOPPED
- 2   LARGE ZUCCHINI, CHOPPED
- 1   ONION, CHOPPED
- 3   GARLIC CLOVES, MINCED
- 2   TABLESPOONS EXTRA-VIRGIN OLIVE OIL
- 3   CUPS VEGETABLE STOCK (SEE PAGE 371)
- 1   TABLESPOON FINELY CHOPPED FRESH OREGANO
- 1   TABLESPOON CHOPPED FRESH MINT, PLUS MORE FOR GARNISH

    SALT AND PEPPER, TO TASTE

    TZATZIKI (SEE PAGE 56), FOR SERVING

    PITA BREAD (SEE PAGE 532), FOR SERVING

    MINTY PICKLED CUCUMBERS (SEE PAGE 414), FOR SERVING

BROCCOLI & ANCHOVY SOUP

YIELD: 4 SERVINGS / **ACTIVE TIME:** 20 MINUTES / **TOTAL TIME:** 45 MINUTES

Don't be stingy when purchasing anchovies here, as their rich, umami flavor is the key to the broth.

1. Place the olive oil and butter in a saucepan and warm over low heat. When the butter has melted, add the onion, garlic, mushrooms, chili, and anchovies and cook, stirring frequently, until the onion starts to soften, about 5 minutes.

2. Stir in the tomatoes and the white wine and simmer, stirring occasionally, for 10 minutes.

3. Add the stock, raise the heat to medium-high, and bring the soup to a boil. Reduce the heat so that the soup simmers. Add the broccoli florets and cook for 10 minutes.

4. Season with salt and pepper, ladle into warmed bowls, and garnish with Parmesan cheese.

INGREDIENTS:

1   TABLESPOON EXTRA-VIRGIN OLIVE OIL

1   TABLESPOON UNSALTED BUTTER

1   ONION, CHOPPED

1   GARLIC CLOVE, MINCED

1½ CUPS CHOPPED PORTOBELLO MUSHROOMS

1   BIRD'S EYE CHILI PEPPER, STEMS AND SEEDS REMOVED, CHOPPED

2   WHITE ANCHOVY FILLETS, MINCED

1   CUP CHOPPED TOMATOES

¼   CUP WHITE WINE

4   CUPS VEGETABLE STOCK (SEE PAGE 371)

2   CUPS BROCCOLI FLORETS

    SALT AND PEPPER, TO TASTE

    PARMESAN CHEESE, FRESHLY GRATED, FOR GARNISH

SEAFOOD & LEEK SOUP

YIELD: 4 TO 6 SERVINGS / ACTIVE TIME: 30 MINUTES / TOTAL TIME: 1 HOUR AND 30 MINUTES

This preparation brings the effortless elegance we all dream of within reach.

1. Place half of the olive oil in a medium saucepan and warm over medium heat. Add the shrimp shells and cook, stirring frequently, until the bottom of the pan starts to brown, about 4 minutes. Remove the shells from the pan and discard them.

2. Add the white wine and cook until it has evaporated, scraping any browned bits from the bottom of the pan.

3. Add the clam juice and water and bring the broth to a boil. Reduce the heat and simmer.

4. Place the remaining olive oil in a separate pan and warm it over medium-high heat. Add the leek and pancetta and cook, stirring frequently, until the leek has softened and the pancetta is lightly browned, 6 to 8 minutes.

5. Stir in the tomato paste, ginger, coriander, paprika, turmeric, and red pepper flakes and cook, stirring continually, for 1 minute. Add the mixture to the broth and simmer for 20 minutes.

6. Add the cod and cook for 2 minutes. Add the shrimp and cook for another 2 minutes.

7. Remove the pan from heat, add the squid, and cover the pan. Let the soup sit until the squid is cooked through, 4 to 6 minutes.

8. Stir in the lemon juice, season the soup with salt and pepper, and ladle it into warmed bowls. Serve with crusty bread and enjoy.

INGREDIENTS:

2	TABLESPOONS EXTRA-VIRGIN OLIVE OIL
½	LB. MEDIUM SHRIMP (41-50), SHELLS REMOVED AND RESERVED, DEVEINED
¾	CUP WHITE WINE
2	CUPS CLAM JUICE
3	CUPS WATER
1	LEEK, TRIMMED, HALVED, RINSED WELL, AND SLICED THIN
6	OZ. PANCETTA, CHOPPED
2	TABLESPOONS TOMATO PASTE
1	TEASPOON GRATED FRESH GINGER
1	TEASPOON CORIANDER
1	TEASPOON PAPRIKA
½	TEASPOON TURMERIC
2	PINCHES OF RED PEPPER FLAKES
½	LB. COD, SKIN REMOVED, CUT INTO ½-INCH CUBES
10	OZ. SQUID, HALVED IF LARGE
1	TEASPOON FRESH LEMON JUICE
	SALT AND PEPPER, TO TASTE
	CRUSTY BREAD, FOR SERVING

ARTICHOKE À LA BARIGOULE

YIELD: 4 SERVINGS / ACTIVE TIME: 30 MINUTES / TOTAL TIME: 1 HOUR AND 30 MINUTES

A Provençal preparation that originated because of a desire to preserve the sought-after globe artichoke. Typically made with whole peeled artichokes, this preparation is more refined, and can be enjoyed on its own or beside fish or poultry.

1. Place 2 tablespoons of the olive oil reserved from the artichokes in a medium saucepan and warm it over medium heat. Add the artichokes and cook, stirring occasionally, until they are lightly caramelized, about 5 minutes. Remove the pan from heat, transfer the artichokes to a plate, and let them cool.

2. Place the pan back over medium heat and add the mushrooms. Cover the pan and cook for 5 minutes. Remove the cover and cook until most of the liquid the mushrooms release has evaporated, about 5 minutes.

3. Add another tablespoon of the reserved oil and the leek and cook, stirring occasionally, until it has softened, about 5 minutes. Stir in the garlic, anchovies, and thyme and cook, stirring continually, for 1 minute.

4. Stir in the flour, cook for 1 minute, and then add the vermouth. Cook until the alcohol has been cooked off, 1 to 2 minutes.

5. While whisking, gradually add the stock. When all of the stock has been incorporated, add the celeriac and bay leaf along with the artichokes and bring the mixture to a boil. Reduce the heat and simmer until the celeriac is tender, 10 to 15 minutes, adding more stock if the level of liquid starts to look a bit too low.

6. Remove the pan from heat, remove the bay leaf, and discard it. Stir in the cream, tarragon, and vinegar, season the soup with salt and pepper, ladle it into warmed bowls, and enjoy.

INGREDIENTS:

2	CUPS BABY ARTICHOKES IN OLIVE OIL, DRAINED AND QUARTERED, OIL RESERVED
½	LB. BUTTON MUSHROOMS, SLICED THIN
1	LEEK, TRIMMED, HALVED, RINSED WELL, AND SLICED THIN
1	GARLIC CLOVE, MINCED
2	ANCHOVIES IN OLIVE OIL, DRAINED AND FINELY CHOPPED
½	TEASPOON FRESH THYME
2	TABLESPOONS ALL-PURPOSE FLOUR
¼	CUP DRY VERMOUTH
4	CUPS CHICKEN STOCK (SEE PAGE 368), PLUS MORE AS NEEDED
½	CUP PEELED AND CHOPPED CELERIAC
1	BAY LEAF
½	CUP HEAVY CREAM
1½	TABLESPOONS CHOPPED FRESH TARRAGON
1	TEASPOON CHAMPAGNE VINEGAR
	SALT AND PEPPER, TO TASTE

RUTABAGA & FIG SOUP

YIELD: 4 SERVINGS / ACTIVE TIME: 20 MINUTES / TOTAL TIME: 1 HOUR

The touch of honey perfectly balances the tart burst provided by the buttermilk.

1. Place the olive oil in a medium saucepan and warm it over medium heat. Add the onion and rutabagas and cook, stirring occasionally, until the onion is soft, about 10 minutes.

2. Stir in the honey, stock, thyme, and figs and bring the soup to a boil.

3. Reduce the heat so that the soup simmers and cook until the rutabagas are tender, about 20 minutes.

4. Transfer the soup to a food processor or blender and puree until smooth. Place the soup in a clean saucepan, add the buttermilk, and bring to a simmer.

5. Season the soup with salt and pepper, ladle into warm bowls, and serve with the Spicy Chickpeas.

SPICY CHICKPEAS

1. Bring 4 cups of water to a boil in a saucepan. Add the chickpeas, reduce heat so that the water simmers, and cook until the chickpeas are tender, 45 Minutes to 1 hour. Drain the chickpeas, place them on a paper towel–lined plate, and pat them dry.

2. Place the canola oil in a Dutch oven and warm it to 350°F over medium heat.

3. Place the remaining ingredients in a bowl, stir until thoroughly combined, and set the mixture aside.

4. Place the chickpeas in the hot oil and fry until golden brown, about 3 minutes. Remove and place in the bowl with the seasoning mixture. Toss to coat and serve.

INGREDIENTS:

2 TABLESPOONS EXTRA-VIRGIN OLIVE OIL

1 ONION, CHOPPED

4 CUPS PEELED AND CHOPPED RUTABAGAS

1 TABLESPOON HONEY

4 CUPS VEGETABLE STOCK (SEE PAGE 371)

1 TEASPOON FRESH THYME

16 FIGS

1 CUP BUTTERMILK

SALT AND PEPPER, TO TASTE

SPICY CHICKPEAS (SEE RECIPE), FOR SERVING

SPICY CHICKPEAS

1 CUP DRIED CHICKPEAS, SOAKED OVERNIGHT AND DRAINED

2 CUPS CANOLA OIL

1 TEASPOON SMOKED PAPRIKA

½ TEASPOON ONION POWDER

½ TEASPOON BROWN SUGAR

¼ TEASPOON GARLIC POWDER

¼ TEASPOON KOSHER SALT

PINCH OF CHILI POWDER

PINCH OF CAYENNE PEPPER

ROMESCO DE PEIX

YIELD: 6 SERVINGS / ACTIVE TIME: 25 MINUTES / TOTAL TIME: 40 MINUTES

If one cannot find fresh monkfish, sea bass is a good alternative.

1. Place the almonds in a large cast-iron skillet and toast them over medium heat until they are just browned. Transfer them to a food processor and pulse until they are finely ground.

2. Place the saffron and boiling water in a bowl and let the mixture steep.

3. Place the olive oil in a Dutch oven and warm over medium heat. Add the onion and bell peppers and cook, stirring occasionally, until the peppers are tender, about 15 minutes.

4. Add the sweet paprika, smoked paprika, bay leaf, and tomato paste and cook, stirring constantly, for 1 minute. Add the sherry and bring the mixture to a boil. Boil for 5 minutes and then stir in the stock, tomatoes, saffron, and the soaking liquid. Stir to combine, season with salt and pepper, and reduce the heat so that the soup simmers.

5. Add the ground almonds and cook until the mixture thickens slightly, about 8 minutes. Add the fish and mussels, stir gently to incorporate, and simmer until the fish is cooked through and a majority of the mussels have opened, about 5 minutes. Discard any mussels that do not open.

6. Ladle the mixture into warmed bowls, garnish with cilantro, and enjoy.

INGREDIENTS:

½ CUP SLIVERED ALMONDS

½ TEASPOON SAFFRON

¼ CUP BOILING WATER

½ CUP EXTRA-VIRGIN OLIVE OIL

1 LARGE YELLOW ONION, CHOPPED

2 LARGE RED BELL PEPPERS, STEMS AND SEEDS REMOVED, CHOPPED

2½ TEASPOONS SWEET PAPRIKA

1 TABLESPOON SMOKED PAPRIKA

1 BAY LEAF

2 TABLESPOONS TOMATO PASTE

½ CUP SHERRY

2 CUPS FISH STOCK (SEE PAGE 372)

1 (28 OZ.) CAN OF CHOPPED TOMATOES, WITH THEIR LIQUID

SALT AND PEPPER, TO TASTE

1½ LBS. MONKFISH FILLETS, CHOPPED INTO LARGE PIECES

1 LB. MUSSELS, RINSED WELL AND DEBEARDED

FRESH CILANTRO, FINELY CHOPPED, FOR GARNISH

TOMATO & EGGPLANT SOUP

YIELD: 4 SERVINGS / **ACTIVE TIME:** 30 MINUTES / **TOTAL TIME:** 1 HOUR AND 30 MINUTES

A simple preparation that yields an astonishingly complex and well-rounded soup.

1. Place 1 tablespoon of the olive oil in a large saucepan and warm it over medium heat. Add the eggplants, cover the pan, and cook, stirring occasionally, for 5 minutes. Remove the cover and cook, stirring occasionally, until the eggplants are browned, about 10 minutes.

2. Add 2 tablespoons of the olive oil to the pan along with the onion and cook, stirring occasionally, until the onion has softened, about 5 minutes. Stir in the garlic, Ras el Hanout, and cumin and cook, stirring continually, for 1 minute.

3. Add the stock, tomatoes, raisins, and pine nuts and bring the soup to a boil. Reduce the heat and simmer the soup until the flavor has developed to your liking, about 20 minutes.

4. Remove the pan from heat and let the soup cool for 10 minutes.

5. Place the soup in a blender and puree until smooth, adding more stock if the soup seems too thick.

6. Place the soup in a clean saucepan and warm it over medium-low heat. Stir in the lemon juice and season with salt and pepper.

7. Ladle the soup into warmed bowls, drizzle some of the remaining olive oil over each portion, and garnish with cilantro. Add a dollop of the Eggplant & Pine Nut Ragout to each bowl and enjoy.

INGREDIENTS:

½ CUP EXTRA-VIRGIN OLIVE OIL

2 EGGPLANTS, TRIMMED AND CUT INTO ¾-INCH CUBES

1 ONION, CHOPPED

2 GARLIC CLOVES, MINCED

2 TEASPOONS RAS EL HANOUT (SEE PAGE 747)

½ TEASPOON CUMIN

4 CUPS CHICKEN STOCK (SEE PAGE 368), PLUS MORE AS NEEDED

1 (14 OZ.) CAN OF CRUSHED TOMATOES, WITH THEIR LIQUID

⅓ CUP RAISINS

¼ CUP PINE NUTS, TOASTED

2 TEASPOONS FRESH LEMON JUICE

SALT AND PEPPER, TO TASTE

FRESH CILANTRO, CHOPPED, FOR GARNISH

EGGPLANT & PINE NUT RAGOUT (SEE PAGE 776), FOR SERVING

VEGETARIAN SPLIT PEA SOUP

YIELD: 10 SERVINGS / **ACTIVE TIME**: 30 MINUTES / **TOTAL TIME**: 2 HOURS

This is a love-it-or-hate-it kind of dish; some claim that it's their favorite soup, while others are reticent to even try it. This recipe will settle the score in favor of the former, once and for all.

1. Place the avocado oil in a large saucepan and warm it over medium heat. Add the onion and cook, stirring occasionally, until it has softened and is beginning to brown, about 7 minutes.

2. Add the garlic, carrots, and celery and cook, stirring frequently, for 3 minutes. Add the bay leaves and thyme and season with salt and pepper.

3. Add the split peas, lemon zest, and stock to the pot and stir to incorporate. Bring the soup to a boil, reduce the heat, and simmer until the split peas are tender, about 1½ hours.

4. Remove the soup from heat and let it cool for 15 minutes.

5. Using an immersion blender, puree the soup until it has the desired texture. Ladle it into warmed bowls and enjoy.

INGREDIENTS:

2 TABLESPOONS AVOCADO OIL

1 LARGE ONION, CHOPPED

1 GARLIC CLOVE, MINCED

2 MEDIUM CARROTS, PEELED AND DICED

2 CELERY STALKS WITH THEIR LEAVES, DICED

2 BAY LEAVES

1 TEASPOON FRESH THYME

1 TEASPOON KOSHER SALT

BLACK PEPPER, TO TASTE

1 LB. DRIED GREEN SPLIT PEAS

½ TEASPOON LEMON ZEST

8 CUPS VEGETABLE STOCK (SEE PAGE 371)

MSOKI DE PESAJ

YIELD: 6 SERVINGS / ACTIVE TIME: 45 MINUTES / TOTAL TIME: 3 HOURS

The blend of braised lamb in a tomato-based stew makes this traditional Tunisian dish a delicious dinner for cooler weather. For the fava beans, peas, and artichoke hearts, fresh is best, but frozen is more than acceptable.

1. Season the lamb with the salt and pepper. Place the olive oil in a large Dutch oven and warm it over medium-high heat. Working in batches to avoid crowding the pot, add the lamb and cook until browned all over, about 8 minutes for each batch, turning it as necessary. Using a slotted spoon, transfer the browned lamb to a bowl.

2. Add the onions, carrots, turnip, and garlic and cook, stirring frequently, until the vegetables are tender, 15 to 20 minutes.

3. Add the cinnamon stick and harissa and cook, stirring frequently, for 5 minutes.

4. Add the spinach, leeks, zucchini, fennel, and celery and cook until the fennel is tender, about 15 minutes.

5. Stir in the fava beans, peas, artichoke hearts, parsley, cilantro, mint, and orange blossom water. Add water until the liquid reaches three-quarters of the way up the mixture. Bring the stew to a simmer and let it cook, stirring occasionally, until the liquid has reduced to one-quarter the original amount.

6. Season the stew with salt and pepper, ladle it into warmed bowls, and enjoy.

INGREDIENTS:

- 2½ LBS. BONELESS LAMB SHOULDER, CUT INTO 3-INCH CUBES
- 1 TABLESPOON KOSHER SALT, PLUS MORE TO TASTE
- ½ TEASPOON BLACK PEPPER, PLUS MORE TO TASTE
- 2 TABLESPOONS AVOCADO OIL
- 2 LARGE YELLOW ONIONS, CHOPPED
- 2 CARROTS, PEELED AND CHOPPED
- 1 TURNIP, PEELED AND CHOPPED
- 1 GARLIC CLOVE, MINCED
- 1 CINNAMON STICK
- 2 TEASPOONS THREE-PEPPER HARISSA SAUCE (SEE PAGE 791)
- 2 LBS. SPINACH LEAVES, FINELY CHOPPED
- 2 LEEKS, TRIMMED, RINSED WELL, MINCED
- 1 ZUCCHINI, CHOPPED
- 1 FENNEL BULB, TRIMMED AND CHOPPED
- 3 CELERY STALKS, CHOPPED
- 1½ CUPS FAVA BEANS
- 1 CUP GREEN PEAS
- 4 ARTICHOKE HEARTS, CUT INTO WEDGES
- ¼ BUNCH OF FRESH PARSLEY, CHOPPED
- ¼ BUNCH OF FRESH CILANTRO, CHOPPED
- ¼ BUNCH OF FRESH MINT LEAVES, FINELY CHOPPED
- 2 TEASPOONS ORANGE BLOSSOM WATER

HARIRA

YIELD: 6 SERVINGS / **ACTIVE TIME:** 30 MINUTES / **TOTAL TIME:** 1 HOUR

This stew is a popular choice for Moroccan Muslims to break the fast with during Ramadan.

1. Place the butter in a Dutch oven and melt it over medium-high heat. Season the chicken thighs with salt and pepper, place them in the pot, and cook until browned on both sides, about 8 minutes. Remove the chicken from the pot and set it on a plate.

2. Add the onion and cook, stirring occasionally, until it starts to brown, about 8 minutes. Add the garlic and ginger and cook until fragrant, about 1 minute. Stir in the turmeric, cumin, cinnamon, and cayenne pepper and cook for 1 minute. Add ½ cup of the cilantro and ¼ cup of the parsley and cook for 1 minute.

3. Stir in the stock, water, chickpeas, and lentils and bring the soup to a simmer. Return the chicken to the pot, reduce the heat to medium-low, partially cover the Dutch oven, and gently simmer, stirring occasionally, until the lentils are just tender, about 20 minutes.

4. Add the tomatoes and vermicelli and simmer, stirring occasionally, until the pasta is tender, about 10 minutes.

5. Stir in the lemon juice and the remaining cilantro and parsley. Taste, adjust the seasoning as necessary, and enjoy.

INGREDIENTS:

3	TABLESPOONS UNSALTED BUTTER
1½	LBS. BONELESS, SKINLESS CHICKEN THIGHS
	SALT AND PEPPER, TO TASTE
1	LARGE ONION, FINELY DICED
5	GARLIC CLOVES, MINCED
	1-INCH PIECE OF FRESH GINGER, PEELED AND GRATED
2	TEASPOONS TURMERIC
1	TEASPOON CUMIN
½	TEASPOON CINNAMON
⅛	TEASPOON CAYENNE PEPPER
¾	CUP FINELY CHOPPED FRESH CILANTRO
½	CUP FINELY CHOPPED FRESH PARSLEY
4	CUPS CHICKEN STOCK (SEE PAGE 368)
4	CUPS WATER
1	(14 OZ.) CAN OF CHICKPEAS, DRAINED AND RINSED
1	CUP BROWN LENTILS, PICKED OVER AND RINSED
1	(28 OZ.) CAN OF CRUSHED TOMATOES, WITH THEIR LIQUID
½	CUP VERMICELLI, BROKEN INTO 2-INCH PIECES
2	TABLESPOONS FRESH LEMON JUICE, PLUS MORE TO TASTE

TUNISIAN BUTTERNUT SQUASH SOUP

YIELD: 12 SERVINGS / **ACTIVE TIME:** 30 MINUTES / **TOTAL TIME:** 2 HOURS

This Tunisian-inspired soup layers its flavors beautifully, but the harissa will help the squash stand out from the rest.

1. Preheat the oven to 400°F. Place the butternut squash on an aluminum foil–lined baking sheet, cut side up.

2. Place the harissa, salt, pepper, lemon juice, lemon zest, lime zest, and olive oil in a bowl and stir until combined.

3. Spread the mixture over the squash. Place the parsnips around the squash, drizzle the harissa mixture over them, and toss to coat.

4. Place the pan in the oven and roast until the squash and parsnips are fork-tender, about 1 hour. Remove from the oven and let the vegetables cool for 20 minutes.

5. Place the avocado oil in a large saucepan and warm it over medium heat. Add the shallots and cook, stirring frequently, until they are translucent, about 3 minutes.

6. Add the garlic and cook, stirring frequently, until fragrant, about 1 minute.

7. Scoop the squash's flesh into a food processor, add the parsnips and some of the stock, and puree until smooth.

8. Add the puree to the saucepan, add the remaining stock, and simmer until the flavor has developed to your liking, about 25 minutes.

9. Taste, adjust the seasoning as necessary, and ladle the soup into warmed bowls.

INGREDIENTS:

1	LARGE BUTTERNUT SQUASH, HALVED AND SEEDED
1	TEASPOON THREE-PEPPER HARISSA SAUCE (SEE PAGE 791)
1	TEASPOON KOSHER SALT
½	TEASPOON BLACK PEPPER
¼	CUP FRESH LEMON JUICE
1	TABLESPOON LEMON ZEST
1½	TEASPOONS LIME ZEST
2	TABLESPOONS EXTRA-VIRGIN OLIVE OIL
2	PARSNIPS, PEELED AND CUBED
2	TABLESPOONS AVOCADO OIL
3	SMALL SHALLOTS, DICED
3	GARLIC CLOVES, SLICED
8	CUPS CHICKEN STOCK (SEE PAGE 368)

TUNISIAN VEGETABLE SOUP

YIELD: 12 SERVINGS / **ACTIVE TIME:** 20 MINUTES / **TOTAL TIME:** 1 HOUR AND 15 MINUTES

An intriguing blend of spices differentiates this from your standard vegetable soup.

1. Place half each of the celeriac, carrots, and onion, and all of the garlic in a food processor and pulse until the vegetables are very finely diced.

2. Place the olive oil in a large saucepan and warm it over medium-high heat. Add the vegetable mixture and cook, stirring frequently, until the onion is starting to brown, about 10 minutes.

3. Add the tomato paste, salt, turmeric, cumin, coriander, and pepper and cook, stirring frequently, for 4 minutes.

4. Add the stock, bring the soup to a boil, and then add the remaining celery root, carrots, and onion, along with the butternut squash, parsnip, and potatoes. Reduce the heat, cover the pan, and simmer for 40 minutes.

5. Remove the pan from heat, add the mushrooms, and cover the pan. Let stand for 10 minutes before ladling the soup into warmed bowls.

INGREDIENTS:

3	CUPS CUBED CELERIAC
2	CUPS SLICED CARROTS
1	CUP CHOPPED ONION
3	GARLIC CLOVES
2	TABLESPOONS EXTRA-VIRGIN OLIVE OIL
¼	CUP TOMATO PASTE
2	TEASPOONS KOSHER SALT
2	TEASPOONS TURMERIC
1	TEASPOON CUMIN
1	TEASPOON CORIANDER
½	TEASPOON BLACK PEPPER
8	CUPS VEGETABLE STOCK (SEE PAGE 371)
1½	CUPS CUBED BUTTERNUT SQUASH
1	CUP SLICED PARSNIP
1	CUP CUBED RED BLISS POTATOES
10	OZ. ENOKI MUSHROOMS

SAFFRON, TOMATO & FENNEL SOUP

YIELD: 12 TO 16 SERVINGS / ACTIVE TIME: 5 MINUTES / TOTAL TIME: 25 MINUTES

This can be consumed hot, but it also works beautifully chilled, as a cool palate cleanser at a summer dinner party.

1. Place the olive oil in a saucepan and warm it over medium heat. Add the onions, parsnips, celery, fennel, garlic, bay leaves, salt, and pepper and cook, stirring frequently, until the onions are translucent, about 3 minutes.

2. Deglaze the pan with the wine, scraping up any browned bits from the bottom of the pan. Bring the wine to a simmer and then stir in the Saffron Water, tomato juice, and all of the fresh herbs. Return the soup to a simmer and let it cook for 10 minutes.

3. Stir in the lemon juice and vinegar, season the soup with salt and pepper, ladle it into warmed bowls, and enjoy.

INGREDIENTS:

2   TABLESPOONS EXTRA-VIRGIN OLIVE OIL

½   CUP DICED ONIONS

¼   CUP DICED PARSNIPS

¼   CUP DICED CELERY

¼   CUP DICED FENNEL (RESERVE FENNEL FRONDS AND STALK)

2   TABLESPOONS SLICED GARLIC

3   BAY LEAVES

1½   TABLESPOONS KOSHER SALT, PLUS MORE TO TASTE

1   TABLESPOON BLACK PEPPER, PLUS MORE TO TASTE

1   CUP WHITE WINE

1   TEASPOON SAFFRON WATER (SEE PAGE 151)

1   (64 OZ.) CAN OF HIGH-QUALITY TOMATO JUICE

1   TABLESPOON FRESH OREGANO

2   TABLESPOONS CHOPPED FRESH BASIL

2   TABLESPOONS CHOPPED FRESH PARSLEY

1   TABLESPOON FRESH LEMON JUICE

1   TABLESPOON RED WINE VINEGAR

CHOLENT

YIELD: 4 SERVINGS / **ACTIVE TIME:** 15 MINUTES / **TOTAL TIME:** 2 DAYS

Consider this one of the world's oldest slow-cooked dishes, created out of the necessity of doing no labor—therefore, not cooking—on the Sabbath, but still very much needing to eat. While many people think of cholent as an Eastern European dish, its origins can actually be traced back to North Africa and Spain.

1. Coat the inside of a slow cooker with nonstick cooking spray. Add the beef, marrow bones, and potatoes to the slow cooker, followed by the onion, garlic, barley, kidney beans, and the water the beans soaked in.

2. In a bowl, combine the ketchup, paprika, and 2½ cups of the water and add to the slow cooker. Stir in the salt, pepper, and garlic powder and arrange the kishke on top.

3. Set the slow cooker to low and cook overnight. Check it in the morning and add the remaining water if the stew seems too dry.

4. Ladle the stew into warmed bowls and enjoy.

INGREDIENTS:

1½	LBS. FATTY BEEF CHUCK, CUBED
4–5	MARROW BONES
2	LARGE YUKON GOLD OR RUSSET POTATOES, PEELED AND CUT INTO CHUNKS
1	WHOLE ONION, PEELED
3–4	GARLIC CLOVES, PEELED
2	CUPS PEARL BARLEY
1	CUP KIDNEY BEANS, SOAKED OVERNIGHT AND DRAINED; SOAKING WATER RESERVED
⅓	CUP KETCHUP
1	TABLESPOON PAPRIKA
3	CUPS WATER, PLUS MORE AS NEEDED
2	TEASPOONS KOSHER SALT
1	TEASPOON BLACK PEPPER
1	TEASPOON GARLIC POWDER
1	LB. PACKAGED KISHKE

CHICKEN STEW WITH POTATOES & RADISHES

YIELD: 4 SERVINGS / ACTIVE TIME: 30 MINUTES / TOTAL TIME: 2 HOURS AND 30 MINUTES

This comforting stew takes its cues from the classic chicken paprikash. Leave off the sour cream at the end if you prefer to keep the dinner dairy free.

1. Season the chicken legs generously with salt. Place the olive oil in a large Dutch oven and warm it over medium-high heat. Working in two batches, add the chicken and cook until the skin is golden brown, 8 to 10 minutes. Transfer the chicken to a plate and set it aside.

2. Add the onion and cook, stirring occasionally, until it is browned, 8 to 10 minutes. Add the garlic and cook, stirring frequently, until softened, about 1 minute. Add the paprika and cook, stirring continually, until fragrant, about 30 seconds.

3. Add the tomatoes and cook, breaking them up with a wooden spoon until no pieces are bigger than ½ inch. Bring the mixture to a simmer and cook until the liquid in the pan has thickened slightly, 6 to 8 minutes.

4. Add stock, potatoes, and chicken and return to a simmer. Cook, stirring occasionally, until the chicken is very tender and the potatoes are creamy, about 1½ hours. Add more stock to the pot as necessary to keep the potatoes submerged.

5. Remove the pot from heat and season it with salt and paprika.

6. Squeeze the lemon into a small bowl and stir in the sour cream. Season the mixture with salt. In another small bowl, combine the radishes with a pinch of salt and toss to coat.

7. To serve, ladle the stew into warmed bowls, season each portion generously with pepper, and drizzle some olive oil over the top. Serve with the sour cream and radishes.

INGREDIENTS:

4	CHICKEN LEGS
	SALT AND PEPPER, TO TASTE
2	TABLESPOONS EXTRA-VIRGIN OLIVE OIL, PLUS MORE TO TASTE
1	LARGE ONION, CHOPPED
5	GARLIC CLOVES, SLICED THIN
2	TABLESPOONS HUNGARIAN PAPRIKA (HOT OR SWEET), PLUS MORE TO TASTE
1	(28 OZ.) CAN OF WHOLE PEELED TOMATOES, WITH THEIR LIQUID
3	CUPS CHICKEN STOCK (SEE PAGE 368)
1½	LBS. BABY YUKON GOLD POTATOES
½	LEMON
¾	CUP SOUR CREAM, FOR SERVING
6	RADISHES, SLICED THIN, FOR SERVING

AVIKAS

YIELD: 6 SERVINGS / **ACTIVE TIME:** 1 HOUR / **TOTAL TIME:** 24 HOURS

The tastes of well-browned onions and caramelized tomatoes key this stew.

1. Place the olive oil in a large saucepan and warm it over medium-high heat.

2. Season the meat with 1 teaspoon of the salt, place it in the pan, and cook until well browned all over, turning it as needed. Transfer the meat to a plate and set it aside.

3. Add the onion to the pan and cook, stirring occasionally, until golden brown, about 10 minutes. Add the tomato paste and cook until it has caramelized, about 2 minutes.

4. Return the meat to the pot and stir in the beans, pepper, and remaining salt. Cover with water, bring the soup to a boil, and then reduce the heat. Cover the pan and gently simmer the soup until the soup has thickened and the beans and meat are tender, about 30 minutes.

5. Ladle the soup into warmed bowls and serve with rice.

INGREDIENTS:

- 1 TABLESPOON EXTRA-VIRGIN OLIVE OIL
- 1 LB. BEEF CHUCK, CUBED
- 1 TABLESPOON KOSHER SALT
- 1 YELLOW ONION, CHOPPED
- 1 TABLESPOON TOMATO PASTE
- ½ CUP CANNELLINI BEANS, SOAKED OVERNIGHT AND DRAINED
- ¼ TEASPOON BLACK PEPPER

  LONG-GRAIN RICE, COOKED, FOR SERVING

Avikas, see page 359

BOULETTES WITH CHICKEN & VEGETABLE SOUP

YIELD: 6 SERVINGS / **ACTIVE TIME:** 1 HOUR / **TOTAL TIME:** 2 HOURS AND 30 MINUTES

Boulettes, or "meatballs" in French, key this hearty dish that takes the comforting flavors of a chicken soup and manages to elevate them into something refined.

1. To begin preparations for the boulettes, place the onion and parsley in a food processor and blitz until the mixture is a smooth paste, about 5 minutes. Transfer the paste to a large bowl, add the beef, bread crumbs, salt, pepper, and 3 of the eggs. Work the mixture until it is well combined. Form 1½-tablespoon portions of the mixture into oval meatballs and then set them aside.

2. To prepare the sauce, place the olive oil in a large, deep skillet and warm it over medium-high heat. Add the onion and cook, stirring occasionally, until it has browned, 8 to 10 minutes. Stir in the tomato paste, water, and salt, reduce the heat to medium-low, and simmer until the tomato paste has dissolved, about 3 minutes. Remove the pan from heat and set it aside.

3. Resume preparations for the boulettes. Crack the remaining 3 eggs into a wide and shallow bowl, add the water, and beat until the eggs are scrambled. Place the flour in a wide, shallow bowl.

4. Add avocado oil to a medium saucepan until it is about ¾ inch deep and warm it over medium-high heat. While the oil is heating up, dredge the boulettes in the flour and then the eggs until they are all completely coated.

5. When the oil starts sizzling, gently slip the boulettes into it, working in batches to avoid overcrowding the pan. Fry until the boulettes are golden brown all over, 6 to 10 minutes, turning them as necessary. Transfer the fried boulettes to a paper towel–lined plate to drain.

6. When all of the boulettes have been fried, place them in the sauce and add water until the sauce covers three-quarters of the boulettes. Place the pan over medium-high heat and simmer until the sauce has reduced by half and the boulettes are cooked through, about 15 minutes. Remove the pan from heat and set the meatballs aside.

INGREDIENTS:

FOR THE BOULETTES

1	YELLOW ONION, CHOPPED
1	CUP CHOPPED FRESH PARSLEY
1½	LBS. GROUND BEEF
½	CUP BREAD CRUMBS
1	TABLESPOON KOSHER SALT
1	TEASPOON BLACK PEPPER
6	EGGS
1	TABLESPOON WATER
2	CUPS ALL-PURPOSE FLOUR
	AVOCADO OIL, AS NEEDED

FOR THE SAUCE

3	TABLESPOONS EXTRA-VIRGIN OLIVE OIL
1	YELLOW ONION, MINCED
1	TABLESPOON TOMATO PASTE
1	CUP WATER, PLUS MORE AS NEEDED
1	TEASPOON KOSHER SALT

7. To begin preparations for the soup, place the avocado oil in a large saucepan and warm it over medium heat. Add the chicken in one layer and sprinkle the minced onion around it. Cook the chicken until it is golden brown on both sides, about 10 minutes. Stir the onion occasionally as it cooks.

8. Place the coriander, cumin, salt, pepper, 2 of the cloves, tomato paste, and water in a bowl and stir until combined. Add the mixture to the saucepan, stir until the chicken and onion are coated, and cook for 3 minutes.

9. Reduce the heat to medium and add the carrots, turnips, squash, and potatoes. Peel the whole onion, press the remaining cloves into the onion, and add it to the pot.

10. Gently slip the eggs, in their shells, into the pan. Add enough water to cover the eggs, chicken, and vegetables. Bring the soup to a simmer and cook for 30 minutes.

11. Add the cilantro, zucchini, artichoke hearts, and chickpeas and cook until the chicken, vegetables, and eggs are cooked through, 15 to 20 minutes.

12. Remove the eggs from the pan and peel them. Place the hard-boiled eggs back in the soup and remove the pan from heat.

13. To serve, place a small mound of couscous in a warmed bowl. Top with 1 or 2 boulettes, a piece of chicken, a hard-boiled egg, and some vegetables. Spoon some broth and harissa over the top and enjoy.

INGREDIENTS:

FOR THE SOUP

3	TABLESPOONS AVOCADO OIL
6	CHICKEN DRUMSTICKS
2	YELLOW ONIONS, 1 MINCED, 1 LEFT WHOLE
2	TEASPOONS CORIANDER
1	TABLESPOON CUMIN
2	TEASPOONS KOSHER SALT
½	TEASPOON BLACK PEPPER
6	WHOLE CLOVES
2	TABLESPOONS TOMATO PASTE
½	CUP WATER
4	CARROTS, PEELED AND CHOPPED
3	SMALL TURNIPS, PEELED AND CHOPPED
2	CUPS CHOPPED BUTTERNUT SQUASH
4	SMALL YUKON GOLD POTATOES, PEELED AND CHOPPED
7	EGGS, LEFT WHOLE
½	CUP CHOPPED FRESH CILANTRO
3	ZUCCHINI, PEELED AND CHOPPED
6	CANNED ARTICHOKE HEARTS
2	CUPS CANNED CHICKPEAS, DRAINED AND RINSED
	COUSCOUS, FOR SERVING
	THREE-PEPPER HARISSA SAUCE (SEE PAGE 791), FOR SERVING

LAMB STEW

YIELD: 10 SERVINGS / ACTIVE TIME: 30 MINUTES / TOTAL TIME: 1 HOUR

A lamb stew that stands apart due to the heat from the berbere.

1. Place the wine, lemon juice, lemon zest, berbere, paprika, and mustard in a small bowl and stir until well combined.

2. Season the lamb with the salt and pepper. Place the olive oil in a large Dutch oven and warm it over medium-high heat. Working in two batches, add the lamb and cook until browned all over, about 8 minutes for each batch, turning it as necessary. Using a slotted spoon, transfer the browned lamb to a bowl.

3. Add the onions, garlic, rosemary, thyme, and a generous pinch of salt and pepper to the pot, reduce the heat to medium, and cook, stirring occasionally, until the onions have softened and are starting to brown, about 8 minutes.

4. Return the lamb and any juices that have accumulated to the pot along with the wine mixture, tomatoes, bell pepper, and shallot. Cook, stirring, until the bell pepper has softened and the lamb is just cooked through, about 10 minutes.

5. Taste, adjust the seasoning as necessary, and enjoy.

INGREDIENTS:

2	TABLESPOONS RED WINE
1	TABLESPOON FRESH LEMON JUICE
½	TEASPOON LEMON ZEST
1	TABLESPOON BERBERE SEASONING
1	TEASPOON SMOKED PAPRIKA
1	TEASPOON DIJON MUSTARD
3½	LBS. BONELESS LEG OF LAMB, CUBED
1	TEASPOON KOSHER SALT, PLUS MORE TO TASTE
½	TEASPOON BLACK PEPPER, PLUS MORE TO TASTE
¼	CUP EXTRA-VIRGIN OLIVE OIL
2	ONIONS, SLICED THIN
6	GARLIC CLOVES, MINCED
2	TEASPOONS CHOPPED FRESH ROSEMARY
2	TEASPOONS FRESH THYME
2	PLUM TOMATOES, DICED
1	ORANGE BELL PEPPER, STEM AND SEEDS REMOVED, DICED
1	LARGE SHALLOT, SLICED THIN

DAFINA

YIELD: 4 SERVINGS / **ACTIVE TIME:** 20 MINUTES / **TOTAL TIME:** 24 HOURS

This iconic slow-cooked Moroccan stew has a long history, during which countless variations have arisen.

1. Place the chickpeas on the bottom of a slow cooker. Place the potatoes against the wall of the slow cooker and then place the flanken meat, chicken, eggs, and dates in the center.

2. Add the remaining ingredients and stir to incorporate, making sure to keep all of the ingredients in their particular place. Add water until the mixture is covered by ¼ inch.

3. Set the slow cooker to low and cook for 24 hours.

4. Ladle the stew into warmed bowls and enjoy.

INGREDIENTS:

- 2 (14 OZ.) CANS OF CHICKPEAS, DRAINED AND RINSED
- 12 LARGE RED POTATOES, PEELED
- 2 LBS. BONE-IN FLANKEN MEAT
- 4 CHICKEN DRUMSTICKS
- 4 EGGS, LEFT WHOLE
- 4 PITTED DATES
- 1 TABLESPOON KOSHER SALT
- 1 TEASPOON BLACK PEPPER
- 1 TEASPOON PAPRIKA
- 1 TEASPOON CUMIN
- 1 TEASPOON TURMERIC
- 1 TEASPOON HONEY
- 1 TEASPOON CINNAMON
- 3 GARLIC CLOVES
- 2 TABLESPOONS AVOCADO OIL

SHORT RIB & OKRA STEW

YIELD: 6 SERVINGS / ACTIVE TIME: 30 MINUTES / TOTAL TIME: 3 HOURS

The rice will soak up all of the delicious flavors in this Egyptian stew, ensuring it will become a family favorite. When choosing okra, make sure that it is crisp and not soggy; pierce the skin of the okra with a thumbnail to test for crispiness.

1. Preheat the oven to 350°F. Slice the short ribs into 2-inch cubes and season with the salt and pepper.

2. Place ¼ cup of the avocado oil in a Dutch oven and warm it over medium-high heat. Working in batches to avoid crowding the pot, add the short ribs and cook until browned all over, about 5 minutes, turning the meat as necessary. Transfer the browned short ribs to a plate.

3. Add the garlic to the pot and cook until it is fragrant, about 1 minute. Add the tomato paste and cook for 30 seconds, stirring constantly. Add the tomatoes a little bit at a time, crushing them in your hands before adding them to the pot.

4. Add the water, lemon juice, paprika, 1 of the bay leaves, and 3 to 5 slices of the jalapeño. Return the short ribs and sprinkle the sugar over them. Reduce the heat to low and let the stew simmer while preparing the okra.

5. Add 3 tablespoons of avocado oil to a large skillet and warm it over high heat. Add the okra and cook, tossing it frequently, until it is bright green and lightly blistered, 1 to 2 minutes. Remove the pan from heat, season it with salt and lemon juice, and toss to coat.

6. Add the okra to the stew, making sure it is evenly distributed. Add 6 to 10 mint leaves, cover the pot, and place it in the oven. Braise for 2 hours, checking the stew every 30 minutes and adding water as necessary if the liquid has reduced too much.

7. After 2 hours, the meat should be fork-tender. Turn on the broiler and broil the stew until it is dark and caramelized, about 10 minutes.

8. While the stew is in the oven, place the remaining avocado oil in a small saucepan and warm it over high heat. Add the rice and toast it, stirring continuously, until the grains are too hot to touch, about 2 minutes. Add the remaining bay leaves, coriander seeds, and boiling water, bring the rice to a boil, and cover the pan. Reduce the heat and simmer the rice until it is tender, about 20 minutes.

9. Remove the rice from heat and let it stand, covered, for 10 minutes. Gently fluff the rice with a fork and cover until ready to serve.

10. Remove the stew from the oven. Season with salt and pepper and sprinkle the remaining mint over it. Serve with the rice and enjoy.

INGREDIENTS:

- 2¼ LBS. BONELESS SHORT RIBS
- 1 TEASPOON KOSHER SALT, PLUS MORE TO TASTE
- ½ TEASPOON BLACK PEPPER, PLUS MORE TO TASTE
- ¼ CUP PLUS 5 TABLESPOONS AVOCADO OIL
- 3 GARLIC CLOVES, SMASHED
- ¼ CUP TOMATO PASTE
- ¾ LB. TOMATOES, QUARTERED
- 1½ CUPS WATER
- JUICE OF 1 LEMON, PLUS MORE TO TASTE
- 1 TEASPOON SWEET PAPRIKA
- 3 BAY LEAVES
- 1 SMALL JALAPEÑO CHILE PEPPER, STEM AND SEEDS REMOVED, SLICED THIN
- 1 TEASPOON SUGAR
- 1 LB. OKRA, TRIMMED
- 1 BUNCH OF FRESH MINT
- 1 CUP BASMATI RICE
- 1 TEASPOON CORIANDER SEEDS
- 1½ CUPS BOILING WATER

CHICKEN STOCK

YIELD: 8 CUPS / **ACTIVE TIME:** 20 MINUTES / **TOTAL TIME:** 6 HOURS

Shifting from store-bought to homemade stock is the easiest way to lift what comes out of your kitchen.

1. Place the chicken bones in a stockpot and cover with cold water. Bring to a simmer over medium-high heat and use a ladle to skim off any impurities that rise to the surface.

2. Add the vegetables, thyme, peppercorns, and bay leaf, reduce the heat to low, and simmer for 5 hours, while skimming to remove any impurities that rise to the surface.

3. Strain, allow to cool slightly, and transfer to the refrigerator. Leave uncovered and let the stock cool completely. Remove layer of fat and cover. The stock will keep in the refrigerator for 3 to 5 days, and in the freezer for up to 3 months.

INGREDIENTS:

7	LBS. CHICKEN BONES, RINSED
4	CUPS CHOPPED YELLOW ONIONS
2	CUPS CHOPPED CARROTS
2	CUPS CHOPPED CELERY
3	GARLIC CLOVES, CRUSHED
3	SPRIGS OF FRESH THYME
1	TEASPOON BLACK PEPPERCORNS
1	BAY LEAF

BEEF STOCK

YIELD: 8 CUPS / **ACTIVE TIME:** 20 MINUTES / **TOTAL TIME:** 6 HOURS

If you want an extra-smooth stock, try using veal bones instead of beef bones. Lamb bones can also be used, but we recommend that you pair them with beef bones to balance the flavor.

1. Place the beef bones in a stockpot and cover with cold water. Bring to a simmer over medium-high heat and use a ladle to skim off any impurities that rise to the surface.

2. Add the vegetables, thyme, peppercorns, and bay leaf, reduce the heat to low, and simmer for 5 hours, while skimming to remove any impurities that rise to the surface.

3. Strain, let the stock cool slightly, and transfer to the refrigerator. Leave uncovered and let cool completely. Remove layer of fat and cover. The stock will keep in the refrigerator for 3 to 5 days, and in the freezer for up to 3 months.

INGREDIENTS:

7 LBS. BEEF BONES, RINSED

4 CUPS CHOPPED YELLOW ONIONS

2 CUPS CHOPPED CARROTS

2 CUPS CHOPPED CELERY

3 GARLIC CLOVES, CRUSHED

3 SPRIGS OF FRESH THYME

1 TEASPOON BLACK PEPPERCORNS

1 BAY LEAF

VEGETABLE STOCK

YIELD: 6 CUPS / ACTIVE TIME: 20 MINUTES / TOTAL TIME: 3 HOURS

A great way to make use of your vegetable trimmings. Just void starchy vegetables such as potatoes, as they will make the stock cloudy.

1. Place the olive oil and the vegetables in a large stockpot and cook over low heat until the liquid they release has evaporated. This will allow the flavor of the vegetables to become concentrated.

2. Add the garlic, parsley, thyme, bay leaf, water, peppercorns, and salt. Raise the heat to high and bring to a boil. Reduce heat so that the stock simmers and cook for 2 hours, while skimming to remove any impurities that float to the top.

3. Strain through a fine sieve, let the stock cool slightly, and place in the refrigerator, uncovered, to chill. Remove the fat layer and cover. The stock will keep in the refrigerator for 3 to 5 days, and in the freezer for up to 3 months.

INGREDIENTS:

2	TABLESPOONS EXTRA-VIRGIN OLIVE OIL
2	LARGE LEEKS, TRIMMED AND RINSED WELL
2	LARGE CARROTS, PEELED AND SLICED
2	CELERY STALKS, SLICED
2	LARGE YELLOW ONIONS, SLICED
3	GARLIC CLOVES, UNPEELED BUT SMASHED
2	SPRIGS OF FRESH PARSLEY
2	SPRIGS OF FRESH THYME
1	BAY LEAF
8	CUPS WATER
½	TEASPOON BLACK PEPPERCORNS
	SALT, TO TASTE

FISH STOCK

YIELD: 6 CUPS / **ACTIVE TIME:** 20 MINUTES / **TOTAL TIME:** 4 HOURS

You want to avoid using fish such as salmon or tuna in this stock, as their bold flavors will overwhelm it.

1. Place the olive oil in a stockpot and warm it over low heat. Add the vegetables and cook until the liquid they release has evaporated.

2. Add the whitefish bodies, the aromatics, the salt, and the water to the pot, raise the heat to high, and bring to a boil. Reduce heat so that the stock simmers and cook for 3 hours, while skimming to remove any impurities that float to the surface.

3. Strain the stock through a fine sieve, let it cool slightly, and place in the refrigerator, uncovered, to chill. When the stock is completely cool, remove the fat layer from the top and cover. The stock will keep in the refrigerator for 3 to 5 days, and in the freezer for up to 3 months.

INGREDIENTS:

¼ CUP EXTRA-VIRGIN OLIVE OIL

1 LEEK, TRIMMED, RINSED WELL, AND CHOPPED

1 LARGE YELLOW ONION, UNPEELED, ROOT CLEANED, CHOPPED

2 LARGE CARROTS, CHOPPED

1 CELERY STALK, CHOPPED

¾ LB. WHITEFISH BODIES

4 SPRIGS OF FRESH PARSLEY

3 SPRIGS OF FRESH THYME

2 BAY LEAVES

1 TEASPOON BLACK PEPPERCORNS

1 TEASPOON KOSHER SALT

8 CUPS WATER

LOBSTER STOCK

YIELD: 8 CUPS / **ACTIVE TIME:** 30 MINUTES / **TOTAL TIME:** 4 HOURS AND 30 MINUTES

When straining this stock, be sure to press on the lobster bodies with a ladle or wooden spoon to extract every last bit of flavor.

1. Preheat the oven to 350°F. Place the lobster bodies and shells on two baking sheets, place them in the oven, and roast for 30 to 45 minutes. Remove the roasted bodies and shells from the oven and set them aside.

2. While the lobster bodies and shells are in the oven, place the olive oil in a large stockpot and warm it over medium heat. Add the carrots and onions and cook, stirring occasionally, until the onions start to brown, about 10 minutes. Remove the pan from heat.

3. Add the lobster bodies and shells, tomatoes, V8, fresh herbs, garlic, and white wine to the stockpot. Add enough water to cover the mixture, raise the heat to high, and bring to a boil. Reduce the heat and simmer the stock for at least 2 hours, occasionally skimming to remove any impurities that rise to the surface.

4. When the flavor of the stock has developed to your liking, strain it through a fine-mesh sieve or a colander lined with cheesecloth. Place the stock in refrigerator and chill until it is completely cool.

5. Remove the fat layer from the top of the cooled stock and discard. Use immediately, refrigerate, or freeze.

INGREDIENTS:

5	LBS. LOBSTER SHELLS AND BODIES
2	TABLESPOONS EXTRA-VIRGIN OLIVE OIL
½	LB. CARROTS, PEELED AND CHOPPED
½	LB. ONIONS, CHOPPED
10	TOMATOES, CHOPPED
1	CUP V8
5	SPRIGS OF FRESH THYME
5	SPRIGS OF FRESH PARSLEY
5	SPRIGS OF FRESH TARRAGON
5	SPRIGS OF FRESH DILL
1	GARLIC CLOVE
2	CUPS WHITE WINE

SALADS & SIDES

While the inhabitants of Mediterranean are magnificent at using time, the region's surfeit of quality produce, and centuries of accrued knowledge to create dishes that are exceptionally wholesome and flavorful, this powerful alignment is not always available in the modern world. At times, all you have time for is tossing a protein in a skillet, in the oven, or on the grill. You don't have to turn your back on the Mediterranean completely, though. While your piece of chicken or fish is cooking, simply whip up one of these vegetable-forward preparations to round out your table and remain in touch with the balanced, wholesome approach to eating that is by now second nature in the region.

SALADE NIÇOISE

YIELD: 4 SERVINGS / **ACTIVE TIME:** 45 MINUTES / **TOTAL TIME:** 1 HOUR

A classic dish from the French Riviera.

1. Prepare an ice bath. Place the potatoes in a large saucepan and cover them with water. Season the water with salt and bring the potatoes to a boil. Add the eggs and cook for 10 minutes.

2. Remove the eggs and place them in the ice bath for 5 minutes. Remove the eggs from the ice bath and peel them when you have a moment.

3. Cook the potatoes until tender and then remove them with a strainer or slotted spoon. Add the potatoes to the ice bath.

4. Add the green beans to the boiling water and cook for 3 minutes. Remove the green beans from the pot and place them in the ice bath. When the green beans are cool, drain the potatoes and green beans and pat them dry.

5. Place the lettuce in a mixing bowl and add enough of the dressing to lightly coat the lettuce. Toss to coat, season with salt and pepper, and place on the serving platter.

6. Add the tomatoes, Confit Tuna, potatoes, and blanched green beans to the bowl, add some dressing, and toss to coat.

7. Place the salad on a platter, top with the hard-boiled eggs, red onion, olives, and capers, and enjoy.

CONFIT TUNA

1. Place the tuna and olive oil in a small saucepan. The tuna needs to be completely covered by the olive oil; if it is not, add more olive oil as needed.

2. Add the remaining ingredients and warm over low heat. Cook until the internal temperature of the tuna is 135°F.

3. Remove the tuna from the oil and let it cool. Store in the refrigerator until needed.

INGREDIENTS:

1	LB. BABY RED POTATOES, QUARTERED
	SALT AND PEPPER, TO TASTE
2	EGGS
2	CUPS TRIMMED GREEN BEANS
2	HEADS OF BIBB LETTUCE
	DIJON DRESSING (SEE PAGE 788)
2	SMALL TOMATOES, CUT INTO ½-INCH WEDGES
	CONFIT TUNA (SEE RECIPE)
½	RED ONION, SLICED THIN
¼	CUP PITTED KALAMATA OLIVES
1	TABLESPOON CAPERS, DRAINED

CONFIT TUNA

½	LB. YELLOW FIN TUNA
1	CUP EXTRA-VIRGIN OLIVE OIL, PLUS MORE AS NEEDED
	ZEST OF 1 ORANGE
1	GARLIC CLOVE
1	BAY LEAF
5	BLACK PEPPERCORNS

CHILLED CALAMARI SALAD

YIELD: 4 TO 6 SERVINGS / **ACTIVE TIME:** 15 MINUTES / **TOTAL TIME:** 45 MINUTES

This can work as part of a meal composed of small plates, a first course, or a light lunch.

1. Bring approximately 8 cups of water to a boil in a large saucepan and prepare an ice bath. Season the boiling water generously with salt, add the tentacles of the squid, and cook for 1 minute. Add the bodies, cook for another minute, and use a slotted spoon to transfer the squid to the ice bath.

2. Drain the squid, pat it dry, and store in the refrigerator.

3. Place the red wine vinegar, harissa, and mustard in a salad bowl and whisk to combine. While whisking, slowly drizzle in the olive oil until it has emulsified.

4. Add the chilled calamari, oranges, bell pepper, and celery and gently toss until combined.

5. Season the salad with salt and pepper, top with the hazelnuts and mint, and enjoy.

INGREDIENTS:

SALT AND PEPPER, TO TASTE

1½ LBS. SMALL SQUID, BODIES AND TENTACLES SEPARATED, RINSED WELL

3 TABLESPOONS RED WINE VINEGAR

2 TABLESPOONS THREE-PEPPER HARISSA SAUCE (SEE PAGE 791)

1½ TEASPOONS DIJON MUSTARD

⅓ CUP EXTRA-VIRGIN OLIVE OIL

2 ORANGES, PEELED AND CUT INTO SEGMENTS

1 RED BELL PEPPER, STEM AND SEEDS REMOVED, CUT INTO STRIPS

2 CELERY STALKS, CHOPPED

¼ CUP HAZELNUTS, TOASTED

¼ CUP SHREDDED FRESH MINT

PANZANELLA

YIELD: 4 SERVINGS / **ACTIVE TIME:** 30 MINUTES / **TOTAL TIME:** 1 HOUR

One of my favorite salads, thanks to the texture of the vinaigrette-softened bread.

1. Preheat the oven to 375°F. Place the bread and 2 tablespoons of the olive oil in a mixing bowl, season the mixture with salt and pepper, and toss to coat.

2. Place the bread on a baking sheet, place it in the oven, and bake until it is golden brown, 8 to 10 minutes, stirring frequently. Remove the bread from the oven and let it cool.

3. Place the vinegar in a salad bowl. While whisking, slowly drizzle in the remaining olive oil. As this is a split vinaigrette, the oil will not emulsify. Add the herbs, tomatoes, beans, and onion to the vinaigrette and toss to coat.

4. Add the bread and baby arugula to the salad bowl, stir gently until combined, and season the salad with salt and pepper. Garnish with the Parmesan and enjoy.

INGREDIENTS:

4   CUPS CUBED CRUSTY BREAD

6   TABLESPOONS EXTRA-VIRGIN OLIVE OIL

     SALT AND PEPPER, TO TASTE

2   TABLESPOONS RED WINE VINEGAR

2   TABLESPOONS CHOPPED FRESH BASIL

2   TABLESPOONS CHOPPED FRESH OREGANO

1   LB. CHERRY TOMATOES, HALVED

1   (14 OZ.) CAN OF CANNELLINI BEANS, DRAINED AND RINSED

½   RED ONION, SLICED THIN

4   CUPS BABY ARUGULA

     PARMESAN CHEESE, SHAVED, FOR GARNISH

ROASTED RADICCHIO

YIELD: 2 SERVINGS / ACTIVE TIME: 10 MINUTES / TOTAL TIME: 30 MINUTES

A very simple side with a very complex flavor profile.

1. Preheat the oven to 450°F. Cut the head of radicchio in half and remove the stem. Separate the leaves and place them in a mixing bowl. Add the olive oil and salt and toss to coat.

2. Arrange the radicchio on a baking sheet in a single layer. Place it in the oven and roast until the radicchio is brown and slightly wilted, 10 to 15 minutes. Remove from the oven and leave the oven on.

3. Distribute the vinegar and capers over the radicchio and return it to the oven. Roast until the vinegar starts to bubble, 5 to 10 minutes.

4. Remove the radicchio from the oven and place it in a serving dish. Sprinkle the feta over the top and enjoy.

INGREDIENTS:

1	HEAD OF RADICCHIO
¼	CUP EXTRA-VIRGIN OLIVE OIL
1	TEASPOON KOSHER SALT
¼	CUP BALSAMIC VINEGAR
1	TABLESPOON CAPERS, DRAINED AND RINSED
¼	CUP CRUMBLED FETA CHEESE

SEARED EGGPLANT

YIELD: 4 SERVINGS / **ACTIVE TIME:** 10 MINUTES / **TOTAL TIME:** 30 MINUTES

A simple, but refined way to prepare a flavorful side of eggplant.

1. Place the wood chips in a small cast-iron skillet and light them on fire. Place the cast-iron pan into a roasting pan and place the onion beside the skillet. Cover the roasting pan with aluminum foil and smoke the onion for 20 minutes.

2. Transfer the onion to a food processor and puree until smooth. Add 1 teaspoon of the salt, stir to combine, and set the puree aside.

3. Place the avocado oil in a large skillet and warm it over high heat. Add the eggplant, season it with the remaining salt, and sear it for 1 minute. Turn the eggplant over, add the bell pepper, and cook for another minute.

4. Add the balsamic vinegar and toss to coat.

5. To serve, spoon the onion puree onto the serving plates and top with the vegetables.

INGREDIENTS:

1	CUP WOOD CHIPS
1	ONION, QUARTERED
2	TEASPOONS KOSHER SALT
¼	CUP AVOCADO OIL
1	SMALL EGGPLANT, TRIMMED AND CUBED
1	RED BELL PEPPER, STEM AND SEEDS REMOVED, DICED
¼	CUP BALSAMIC VINEGAR

Seared Eggplant, see page 385

ROASTED TOMATO CAPRESE

YIELD: 2 SERVINGS / **ACTIVE TIME:** 25 MINUTES / **TOTAL TIME:** 45 MINUTES

Roasting the tomatoes concentrates their sweetness and adds a note of char that is lovely amidst all that freshness.

1. Preheat the oven to 450°F. Place the basil, spinach, garlic, 7 tablespoons of the olive oil, and Parmesan cheese in a food processor and blitz until smooth. Set the mixture aside.

2. Place the vinegar in a small saucepan and bring it to a simmer over medium-high heat. Reduce the heat to medium and cook the vinegar until it has been reduced by half, 6 to 8 minutes. Remove the pan from heat and let the reduction cool completely.

3. Cut the tomatoes into ⅛-inch-thick slices and place them on a baking sheet in a single layer. Drizzle the remaining olive oil over the top.

4. Distribute the mozzarella around the tomatoes, place the pan in the oven, and bake until the cheese and tomatoes start to brown, about 10 minutes. Remove the pan from the oven and let the tomatoes and mozzarella cool.

5. To serve, arrange the tomatoes and mozzarella on a plate, spoon the pesto over them, and drizzle the balsamic reduction over the top.

INGREDIENTS:

½   CUP FRESH BASIL

½   CUP FRESH SPINACH

2   GARLIC CLOVES

½   CUP EXTRA-VIRGIN OLIVE OIL

½   CUP FRESHLY GRATED PARMESAN CHEESE

½   CUP BALSAMIC VINEGAR

2   TOMATOES

6   OZ. FRESH MOZZARELLA CHEESE, TORN

GRAPEFRUIT & FENNEL SALAD

YIELD: 4 SERVINGS / **ACTIVE TIME:** 20 MINUTES / **TOTAL TIME:** 20 MINUTES

The grapefruit is the key here, as its tang ties the array of other flavors together.

1. Using a mandoline or sharp knife, cut the onion, fennel stalks, and apple into very thin slices. Chop the fennel fronds. Place these items in a bowl.

2. Add the fresh herbs, honey, and white vinegar and toss to combine.

3. Trim the top and bottom from the grapefruit and then cut along the contour of the fruit to remove the pith and peel. Cut one segment, lengthwise, between the pulp and the membrane. Make a similar slice on the other side of the segment and then remove the pulp. Set aside and repeat with the remaining segments. This technique is known as "supreming," and it can be used for all citrus fruits.

4. Add the segments to the salad bowl along with the jalapeño, toss to combine, and enjoy.

INGREDIENTS:

½   WHITE ONION

2   FENNEL STALKS, FRONDS REMOVED AND RESERVED

1   APPLE

1   TEASPOON CHOPPED FRESH DILL

1   TEASPOON CHOPPED FRESH MINT

1   TABLESPOON CHOPPED FRESH PARSLEY

1   TABLESPOON HONEY

3   TABLESPOONS WHITE VINEGAR

1   GRAPEFRUIT

1   JALAPEÑO CHILE PEPPER, STEM AND SEEDS REMOVED, SLICED THIN

Grapefruit & Fennel Salad, see page 389

SPINACH, FENNEL & APPLE SALAD
WITH SMOKED TROUT

YIELD: 4 SERVINGS / ACTIVE TIME: 15 MINUTES / TOTAL TIME: 30 MINUTES

A well-balanced salad that gets sweetness from the apple, anise from the fennel, and salt and freshness from the trout.

1. Place the vinegar, lemon juice, mustard, and honey in a salad bowl and whisk to combine. While whisking continually, slowly drizzle in the olive oil until it has emulsified. Stir in the shallot and tarragon and season the vinaigrette with salt and pepper.

2. Add the spinach, apples, and fennel to the salad bowl and toss to coat.

3. To serve, plate the salad, top each portion with some of the smoked trout, and enjoy.

INGREDIENTS:

2   TABLESPOONS WHITE WINE VINEGAR

1   TABLESPOON FRESH LEMON JUICE

1   TABLESPOON GRAINY MUSTARD

1   TEASPOON HONEY

½   CUP EXTRA-VIRGIN OLIVE OIL

1   SHALLOT, MINCED

2   TEASPOONS CHOPPED FRESH TARRAGON

    SALT AND PEPPER, TO TASTE

4   CUPS BABY SPINACH

2   GRANNY SMITH APPLES, HALVED, SEEDS REMOVED, SLICED THIN

1   FENNEL BULB, TRIMMED, CORED, AND SLICED THIN

½   LB. SMOKED TROUT, SKIN REMOVED, FLAKED

OLIVE SALAD

YIELD: 6 SERVINGS / ACTIVE TIME: 15 MINUTES / TOTAL TIME: 15 MINUTES

Tart and briny, with a slight sweetness and a surprising burst of freshness thanks to the mint, this simple salad is something of a wonder.

1. Place the olives, garlic, and pomegranate seeds in a bowl and stir until well combined.

2. Place the pomegranate juice, mint, and olive oil in a separate bowl and stir until combined.

3. Pour the dressing over the olive mixture and stir until evenly coated. Add the salt and pepper, garnish with the walnuts and additional mint, and enjoy.

INGREDIENTS:

2	CUPS GREEN OLIVES, PITS REMOVED
2	GARLIC CLOVES, MINCED
1	CUP POMEGRANATE SEEDS
⅓	CUP POMEGRANATE JUICE
⅓	CUP CHOPPED FRESH MINT, PLUS MORE FOR GARNISH
⅓	CUP EXTRA-VIRGIN OLIVE OIL
1	TEASPOON KOSHER SALT
¼	TEASPOON BLACK PEPPER
	ROASTED WALNUTS, CRUSHED, FOR GARNISH

MINT & SAGE BUTTERNUT SQUASH

YIELD: 4 TO 6 SERVINGS / ACTIVE TIME: 10 MINUTES / TOTAL TIME: 25 MINUTES

Spiking the sweetness of roasted butternut squash with the fresh taste of mint and earthy, peppery sage makes for a memorable side.

1. Preheat the oven to 350°F. Peel the squash, halve it, and remove the seeds. Dice the squash into small cubes and place them in a mixing bowl.

2. Add the avocado oil, sage, and mint and toss to coat.

3. Spread the squash on a baking sheet in a single layer. Place the squash in the oven and bake until it is fork-tender, about 15 minutes.

4. Remove the squash from the oven and enjoy.

INGREDIENTS:

1	BUTTERNUT SQUASH
1	TEASPOON AVOCADO OIL
1	TABLESPOON CHOPPED FRESH SAGE
1	TABLESPOON CHOPPED FRESH MINT

SMOKED POTATO PUREE

YIELD: 4 SERVINGS / **ACTIVE TIME:** 30 MINUTES / **TOTAL TIME:** 1 HOUR AND 15 MINUTES

B y adding a bit of smoke to this creamy puree, it acquires a depth of flavor that surprises everyone who encounters it.

1. Preheat the oven to 250°F. Place the wood chips in a cast-iron skillet and place the pan over high heat. When the wood chips start to smoke, place the skillet in a deep roasting pan. Set the sweet potatoes and potato in the roasting pan (not in the skillet) and cover the roasting pan with aluminum foil. Place it in the oven and smoke for 30 minutes.

2. While the potatoes are smoking in the oven, bring water to a boil in a large saucepan.

3. Remove the potatoes from the oven, add the salt to the boiling water, and then add the potatoes. Cook until they are fork-tender, 20 to 25 minutes. Drain, place the potatoes in a mixing bowl, and add the remaining ingredients. Mash until smooth, season with salt, and serve immediately.

INGREDIENTS:

½   CUP WOOD CHIPS

2   SWEET POTATOES, PEELED AND CHOPPED

1   YUKON GOLD POTATO, PEELED AND CHOPPED

2   TEASPOONS KOSHER SALT, PLUS MORE TO TASTE

½   CUP HEAVY CREAM

2   TABLESPOONS UNSALTED BUTTER

CHICKPEA SALAD

YIELD: 4 SERVINGS / ACTIVE TIME: 20 MINUTES / TOTAL TIME: 24 HOURS

A good option when you need something light yet flavorful beside a particularly savory dish. It is also lovely with some tuna folded in.

1. Drain the chickpeas, place them in a saucepan, and add the stock. Bring to a boil, reduce the heat, and simmer until the chickpeas are tender, about 45 minutes.

2. Drain the chickpeas and let them cool completely.

3. Place the chickpeas and the remaining ingredients in a small mixing bowl, toss until combined, and enjoy.

INGREDIENTS:

2 CUPS DRIED CHICKPEAS, SOAKED OVERNIGHT

4 CUPS CHICKEN STOCK (SEE PAGE 368)

1 ONION, CHOPPED

1 CUP CHOPPED FRESH CILANTRO

¼ CUP EXTRA-VIRGIN OLIVE OIL

¼ CUP FRESH LEMON JUICE

¼ TEASPOON SAFFRON

1 TABLESPOON CUMIN

1 TEASPOON CINNAMON

1 TEASPOON RED PEPPER FLAKES

SALT AND PEPPER, TO TASTE

MARINATED EGGPLANT SALAD

YIELD: 4 SERVINGS / **ACTIVE TIME:** 30 MINUTES / **TOTAL TIME:** 2 HOURS AND 30 MINUTES

This super acidic, herbaceous salad is a complete change of pace from a traditional eggplant salad.

1. Warm a cast-iron skillet over high heat. Brush the eggplant with the olive oil, place it in the pan, and cook until lightly charred on each side, about 6 minutes.

2. Transfer the eggplant to a salad bowl, add the garlic, fresh herbs, salt, vinegar, and any remaining olive oil, and stir to combine.

3. Add the tomatoes and shallots, toss to combine, and refrigerate for at least 2 hours before serving.

INGREDIENTS:

1   EGGPLANT, SLICED INTO ½-INCH-THICK ROUNDS

½   CUP EXTRA-VIRGIN OLIVE OIL

4   GARLIC CLOVES, MINCED

1   TABLESPOON CHOPPED FRESH DILL

1   TABLESPOON CHOPPED FRESH BASIL

1   TABLESPOON KOSHER SALT

½   CUP WHITE VINEGAR

1   CUP CHERRY TOMATOES, HALVED

2   SHALLOTS, JULIENNED

FRIED BRUSSELS SPROUTS
WITH TAHINI & FETA

YIELD: 4 SERVINGS / ACTIVE TIME: 15 MINUTES / TOTAL TIME: 15 MINUTES

The tahini goes perfectly with the nutty flavor of fried Brussels sprouts, while the feta cuts against the richness. If you get large Brussels sprouts, halve them before adding to the oil.

1. Add canola oil to a Dutch oven until it is about 2 inches deep and warm it to 350°F.

2. Gently slip the Brussels sprouts into the oil, working in batches to avoid crowding the pot. Fry the Brussels sprouts until golden brown, about 4 minutes, turning them as necessary. Remove one Brussels sprout to test that it is done—let it cool briefly and see if the inside is tender enough. Transfer the fried Brussels sprouts to a paper towel–lined plate.

3. Place the Brussels sprouts, tahini, and feta in a mixing bowl and stir until combined. Sprinkle the salt over the dish and enjoy.

INGREDIENTS:

CANOLA OIL, AS NEEDED

3 CUPS SMALL BRUSSELS SPROUTS, TRIMMED

2 TABLESPOONS TAHINI SAUCE (SEE PAGE 767)

½ CUP CRUMBLED FETA CHEESE

PINCH OF KOSHER SALT

Fried Brussels Sprouts with Tahini & Feta, see page 399

MUJADARA

YIELD: 4 SERVINGS / ACTIVE TIME: 20 MINUTES / TOTAL TIME: 1 HOUR

A classic Middle Eastern recipe dressed up with the Spiced Yogurt Sauce.

1. Place the garlic, bay leaves, cumin, and a few generous pinches of salt in a Dutch oven. Season with pepper, add 5 cups water, and bring to a boil over high heat.

2. Stir in the rice and reduce the heat to medium. Cover the pot and cook, stirring occasionally, for 10 minutes.

3. Add the lentils, return the mixture to a simmer, and cover the pot. Cook until the lentils are tender and the rice has absorbed all of the liquid, about 20 minutes.

4. Place the olive oil in a large skillet and warm it over medium-high heat. Add the onions and cook, stirring frequently, until they are deeply caramelized, about 20 minutes. Remove the onions from the pan with a slotted spoon and transfer them to a paper towel–lined plate. Season with salt and pepper and set the onions aside.

5. Uncover the Dutch oven, remove the bay leaves, and discard them. Stir half of the scallions and the cilantro into the rice mixture. Season with salt and pepper, transfer to a serving dish, and top with the caramelized onions and the remaining scallions. Serve with the Spiced Yogurt Sauce and enjoy.

INGREDIENTS:

4	GARLIC CLOVES, MINCED
2	BAY LEAVES
1	TABLESPOON CUMIN
	SALT AND PEPPER, TO TASTE
1	CUP BASMATI RICE
1	CUP BROWN OR GREEN LENTILS
⅓	CUP EXTRA-VIRGIN OLIVE OIL
2	ONIONS, HALVED AND SLICED THIN
½	CUP SLICED SCALLIONS
½	CUP CHOPPED FRESH CILANTRO
	SPICED YOGURT SAUCE (SEE PAGE 803), FOR SERVING

TARO ULASS

YIELD: 4 SERVINGS / ACTIVE TIME: 25 MINUTES / TOTAL TIME: 40 MINUTES

Taro is a popular root vegetable in Egypt, and its buttery texture makes it deserving of a much larger audience.

1. Place the stock, lemon juice, and taro in a saucepan, bring to a simmer over medium heat, and cook until the taro is tender, about 8 minutes. Remove the pan from heat and set it aside.

2. Place the chard leaves and cilantro in a pan containing approximately ¼ cup water. Cook over medium heat until the chard is wilted and most of the liquid has evaporated. Transfer the mixture to a food processor and blitz until pureed.

3. Place the olive oil in a large skillet and warm it over medium heat. Add the garlic and the chard stems and cook, stirring frequently, until the garlic starts to brown slightly, about 1½ minutes.

4. Stir in the taro mixture and the chard puree, cook until heated through, and enjoy.

INGREDIENTS:

½   CUP VEGETABLE STOCK (SEE PAGE 371)

     JUICE FROM ½ LEMON

1   LB. TARO ROOT, PEELED AND CUBED

1   LARGE BUNCH OF RED CHARD, STEMS AND LEAVES SEPARATED AND CHOPPED

½   BUNCH OF FRESH CILANTRO, CHOPPED

1   TABLESPOON EXTRA-VIRGIN OLIVE OIL

2   GARLIC CLOVES, CHOPPED

ENSALADA DE PULPO

YIELD: 8 SERVINGS / **ACTIVE TIME:** 30 MINUTES / **TOTAL TIME:** 2 HOURS AND 30 MINUTES

The key to cooking octopus is to get the tentacles very tender before searing them.

1. Fill a pot, large enough to fully submerge the octopus under water, with water and bring it to a simmer. Add the octopus and cover the pot. Simmer until the octopus is very tender, 45 minutes to 1 hour. Remove the tentacles from the octopus and let them cool.

2. While the octopus is boiling, place the radishes and half of the salt in a bowl and toss to coat. Cover the radishes with some of the vinegar and let them sit.

3. Place the pear in a separate bowl, sprinkle the remaining salt over it, and toss to coat. Cover the pear with some of the white vinegar and let it sit.

4. Warm a large cast-iron skillet over high heat. Brush the pan with the olive oil, pat the octopus tentacles dry, place them in the pan, and sear until slightly charred all over, 3 to 4 minutes.

5. To serve, spread some of the salsa on a plate and place a full tentacle alongside it. Put some of the greens in a small pile beside the tentacle, sprinkle the radishes and pear on top, and enjoy.

INGREDIENTS:

1	WHOLE OCTOPUS, FROZEN
3	RADISHES, SLICED THIN
2	TEASPOONS KOSHER SALT
1	CUP WHITE VINEGAR
1	PEAR, CORED AND SLICED
1	TABLESPOON EXTRA-VIRGIN OLIVE OIL
½	CUP GRILLED SERRANO SALSA VERDE (SEE PAGE 798)
2	CUPS MESCLUN GREENS

BAMIES

YIELD: 4 SERVINGS / **ACTIVE TIME:** 15 MINUTES / **TOTAL TIME:** 40 MINUTES

This side of stewed vegetables is a classic in Greek cuisine.

1. Place the olive oil in a medium skillet and warm it over medium heat. Add the onion and cook, stirring occasionally, until it starts to brown, about 8 minutes.

2. Add the okra and potato and cook, stirring frequently, until they start to brown, about 5 minutes.

3. Add the garlic and cook for 1 minute. Add the tomatoes, wine, stock, parsley, and sugar and stir to incorporate.

4. Cook until the tomatoes have collapsed and the okra and potato are tender, about 8 minutes.

5. Season with salt, garnish with feta, and enjoy.

INGREDIENTS:

2   TABLESPOONS EXTRA-VIRGIN OLIVE OIL

1   ONION, CHOPPED

1   LB. OKRA, RINSED WELL AND CHOPPED

1   POTATO, PEELED AND MINCED

1   GARLIC CLOVE, MINCED

2   TOMATOES, CHOPPED

3   TABLESPOONS WHITE WINE

½   CUP VEGETABLE STOCK (SEE PAGE 371)

2   TABLESPOONS CHOPPED FRESH PARSLEY

2   TEASPOONS SUGAR

    SALT, TO TASTE

    FETA CHEESE, CRUMBLED, FOR GARNISH

TURKISH EGGPLANT SALAD

YIELD: 4 SERVINGS / **ACTIVE TIME:** 30 MINUTES / **TOTAL TIME:** 1 HOUR AND 30 MINUTES

A salad that highlights the best of Turkish cuisine: unapologetically garlic heavy, smoky, and earthy.

1. Preheat the oven to 450°F. Poke a few holes in the eggplants, place them on a baking sheet, and place them in the oven. Roast until completely tender and starting to collapse, 40 minutes to 1 hour. Remove the eggplants from the oven and let them cool completely.

2. Place the oil in a large skillet and warm it over high heat. Add the tomatoes and onion and cook until the onion is translucent, about 4 minutes. Add the remaining ingredients, except for the parsley, and cook for approximately 20 minutes, stirring occasionally. Transfer the mixture to a mixing bowl.

3. Halve the eggplants and scoop the flesh into the tomato mixture. Stir to combine, adding the parsley as you go. Let the mixture cool to room temperature before serving.

INGREDIENTS:

2	LARGE EGGPLANTS
2	TABLESPOONS EXTRA-VIRGIN OLIVE OIL
3	TOMATOES, DICED
1	WHITE ONION, JULIENNED
4	GARLIC CLOVES, MINCED
1	TABLESPOON PAPRIKA
1	TEASPOON KOSHER SALT
1	TEASPOON CUMIN
1	TEASPOON CAYENNE PEPPER
½	CUP CHOPPED FRESH PARSLEY

Turkish Eggplant Salad, see page 407

BROCCOLINI SALAD

YIELD: 10 SERVINGS / ACTIVE TIME: 15 MINUTES / TOTAL TIME: 15 MINUTES

Blanching is a cooking process in which a food, usually a vegetable or fruit, is scalded in boiling water and salt, removed after a brief, timed interval, and finally plunged into iced water or placed under cold running water to halt the cooking process and retain the vegetable's crisp character.

1. Bring salted water to a boil in a large saucepan and prepare an ice bath. Add the broccolini and cook for 4 minutes.

2. Transfer the broccolini to the ice bath and let it cool. Pat the broccolini dry and chop it into bite-size pieces.

3. Place the broccolini in a large salad bowl, add all of the remaining ingredients, except for the oil and garlic, and toss to combine. Set the salad aside.

4. Place the olive oil in a medium skillet and warm it over medium heat. Add the garlic and cook, stirring continuously, until it is golden brown, about 1½ minutes.

5. Pour the mixture over the salad and toss to incorporate. Taste, adjust the seasoning as necessary, and enjoy.

INGREDIENTS:

2	TABLESPOONS KOSHER SALT, PLUS MORE TO TASTE
2	LBS. BROCCOLINI, BLANCHED AND COARSELY CHOPPED
1	CUP DRIED CRANBERRIES
1	CUP SLICED ALMONDS, TOASTED
½	CUP CRUMBLED FETA OR GOAT CHEESE
1	CUP BLUEBERRIES
½	CUP CHAMPAGNE VINAIGRETTE (SEE PAGE 804)
2	CUPS SLICED RED GRAPES
1	TABLESPOON BLACK PEPPER, PLUS MORE TO TASTE
¼	CUP CHOPPED FRESH HERBS (PARSLEY, MINT, BASIL, AND OREGANO RECOMMENDED)
¼	CUP EXTRA-VIRGIN OLIVE OIL
½	CUP MINCED GARLIC

SHAVED SNAP PEA SALAD

YIELD: 2 SERVINGS / ACTIVE TIME: 20 MINUTES / TOTAL TIME: 50 MINUTES

A vibrant mix of sweet and tangy, herby and fresh, tender and crunchy.

1. Using a sharp knife, stack 4 snap peas and cut them into thin slices on a bias. Transfer them to a bowl and repeat with the remaining snap peas.

2. Add the remaining ingredients and toss until well combined.

3. Let the salad rest for 30 minutes before serving.

INGREDIENTS:

1   LB. SNAP PEAS

1   TABLESPOON CHOPPED FRESH DILL

1   TABLESPOON CHOPPED FRESH BASIL

1   TABLESPOON CHOPPED FRESH MINT

2   TEASPOONS HONEY

¼   CUP WHITE VINEGAR

1   TEASPOON KOSHER SALT

1   TABLESPOON CRUSHED TOASTED WALNUTS

Shaved Snap Pea Salad, see page 411

MINTY PICKLED CUCUMBERS

YIELD: 2 CUPS / **ACTIVE TIME:** 20 MINUTES / **TOTAL TIME:** 3 HOURS

Absolutely brilliant beside a braised or barbecued piece of lamb.

1. Place all of the ingredients, except for the cucumbers, in a small saucepan and bring to a boil, stirring to dissolve the sugar.

2. Place the cucumbers in a large mason jar. Remove the pan from heat and pour the brine over the cucumbers.

3. Let cool completely before using or storing in the refrigerator, where the pickles will keep for 1 week.

INGREDIENTS:

½   CUP SUGAR

½   CUP WATER

½   CUP RICE VINEGAR

2   TABLESPOONS DRIED MINT

1   TABLESPOON CORIANDER SEEDS

1   TABLESPOON MUSTARD SEEDS

2   CUCUMBERS, SLICED

PICKLED GREEN BEANS

YIELD: 4 SERVINGS / **ACTIVE TIME:** 15 MINUTES / **TOTAL TIME:** 2 DAYS

Perfect beside any protein that gets roasted in the oven or cooked on the grill. When the green beans are placed in the oven, the liquid can be reused to pickle another vegetable.

1. Place the green beans, dill, garlic, salt, and sugar in a large mason jar. Pour the vinegar over the mixture, cover the jar, and shake to combine. Chill the green beans in the refrigerator for 48 hours.

2. Preheat the oven to 450°F. Remove the green beans from the liquid and place them on a baking sheet. Drizzle the olive oil over them and toss to coat.

3. Place the green beans in the oven and roast until browned, about 20 minutes.

4. Remove the green beans from the oven, drizzle the honey over them, and enjoy.

INGREDIENTS:

1	LB. GREEN BEANS, TRIMMED
2	TABLESPOONS CHOPPED FRESH DILL
2	GARLIC CLOVES, MINCED
1	TABLESPOON KOSHER SALT
1	TABLESPOON SUGAR
2	CUPS WHITE VINEGAR
1	TABLESPOON EXTRA-VIRGIN OLIVE OIL
1	TABLESPOON HONEY

Pickled Green Beans, see page 415

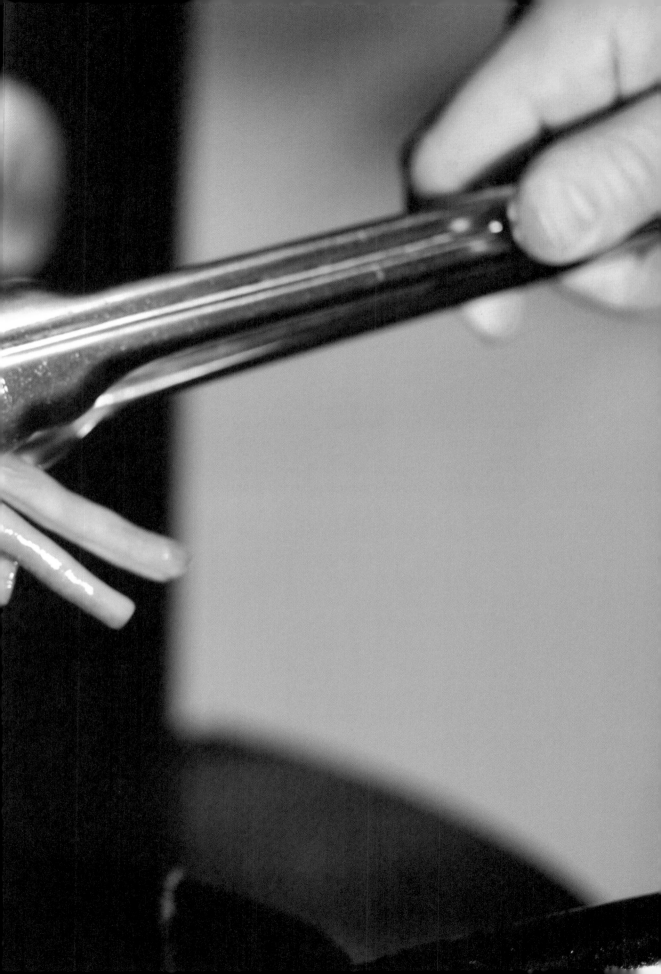

CONCIA

YIELD: 4 SERVINGS / ACTIVE TIME: 1 HOUR / TOTAL TIME: 6 HOURS

Both earthy and refreshing, concia is a perfect accompaniment to a heavier meal, and can also work as a starter.

1. Season the zucchini slices with salt and pepper on both sides, place them on a paper towel–lined baking sheet, and let them rest for 10 minutes.

2. Pat the zucchini dry and replace the paper towels on the baking sheet. Add avocado oil to a large saucepan until it is ½ inch deep and warm it over medium heat. Working in batches of 6 slices, gently slip the zucchini into the hot oil, making sure that the pieces all lie flat and do not overlap. Fry the zucchini until golden brown all over, about 10 minutes, turning as necessary. Transfer the fried zucchini to the paper towel–lined baking sheet and let it drain.

3. Place all of the fried zucchini in a mixing bowl. Season it with salt and pepper, add the garlic, basil, and vinegar, and gently stir until the zucchini is evenly coated.

4. Cover the bowl with plastic wrap and chill it in the refrigerator for 5 hours before enjoying. To serve, let the concia come to room temperature.

INGREDIENTS:

- 3   ZUCCHINI, SLICED LENGTHWISE INTO ¼-INCH-THICK PIECES
-     SALT AND PEPPER, TO TASTE
-     AVOCADO OIL, AS NEEDED
- 6   GARLIC CLOVES, MINCED
- ½   BUNCH OF FRESH BASIL LEAVES, CHOPPED
- ¼   CUP WHITE WINE VINEGAR

PEPPERY GLAZED ASPARAGUS

YIELD: 2 SERVINGS / ACTIVE TIME: 10 MINUTES / TOTAL TIME: 20 MINUTES

Roasted asparagus makes a beautiful and nimble side.

1. Preheat the broiler on the oven to high. Place the lemon juice, sugar, olive oil, salt, and garlic in a bowl, stir until well combined, and then add the asparagus. Toss until the asparagus is coated.

2. Place the asparagus on a baking sheet and sprinkle the pepper over it. Place the asparagus in the oven and broil until the asparagus is beautifully browned, approximately 10 minutes.

3. Remove the asparagus from the oven, garnish with the Parmesan, and enjoy.

INGREDIENTS:

- JUICE OF 1 LEMON
- 1 TABLESPOON SUGAR
- 1 TABLESPOON EXTRA-VIRGIN OLIVE OIL
- 1 TEASPOON KOSHER SALT
- 2 GARLIC CLOVES, MINCED
- 10 ASPARAGUS STALKS, TRIMMED
- 1 TEASPOON BLACK PEPPER
- PARMESAN CHEESE, SHAVED, FOR GARNISH

Peppery Glazed Asparagus, see page 419

CRUNCHY POMEGRANATE SALAD

YIELD: 16 SERVINGS / **ACTIVE TIME:** 30 MINUTES / **TOTAL TIME:** 30 MINUTES

The pop of each pomegranate seed when bitten into, followed by the mouth-puckering tartness, is an experience that simply can't be recreated by any other ingredient.

1. Place the cream in the work bowl of a stand mixer fitted with the whisk attachment and beat until it starts to thicken.

2. Add the sugar and vanilla and beat until the mixture holds stiff peaks.

3. Fold in the pomegranate seeds and apples, sprinkle the pecans over the top, and serve immediately.

INGREDIENTS:

2	CUPS HEAVY CREAM
¼	CUP SUGAR
2	TEASPOONS PURE VANILLA EXTRACT
2½	CUPS POMEGRANATE SEEDS
2	APPLES, PEELED, CORED, AND CUBED
1	CUP CHOPPED PECANS, TOASTED

GLAZED OKRA

YIELD: 2 SERVINGS / **ACTIVE TIME:** 30 MINUTES / **TOTAL TIME:** 30 MINUTES

When shopping, try to avoid any okra with brown spots, as they have been sitting for a bit.

1. Place the olive oil in a large cast-iron pan and warm it over high heat. Add the okra, season it with salt and pepper, and cook until the okra is browned all over, turning it as necessary.

2. Remove the okra from the pan and set it aside. Turn off the heat, but leave the pan on the stove.

3. Place the brown sugar and vinegar in the pan and stir until the mixture is syrupy.

4. Spread the goat cheese on a serving plate, arrange the okra in a line on top of it, drizzle the glaze over the top, and enjoy.

INGREDIENTS:

2	TABLESPOONS EXTRA-VIRGIN OLIVE OIL
12	OKRA PODS
1	TEASPOON KOSHER SALT
1	TEASPOON BLACK PEPPER
1	TEASPOON BROWN SUGAR
1	TEASPOON WHITE VINEGAR
¼	CUP CRUMBLED GOAT CHEESE

Glazed Okra, see page 423

ARUGULA SALAD
WITH CANDIED WALNUTS

YIELD: 4 SERVINGS / **ACTIVE TIME:** 30 MINUTES / **TOTAL TIME:** 1 HOUR AND 30 MINUTES

The sweetness of the candied walnuts brings everything into balance here, playing off the peppery arugula, rich prosciutto, and umami-laden Parmesan.

1. Preheat the oven to 350°F. Place the prosciutto on a baking sheet lined with a Silpat mat, place it in the oven, and bake until crispy and golden brown, about 10 minutes. Remove the prosciutto from the oven and let it cool. When it is cool enough to handle, chop it into bite-size pieces.

2. Place the arugula in a salad bowl, add some of the vinaigrette, and toss to coat. Add the Parmesan, season the salad with salt and pepper, and toss to combine. Top with the Candied Walnuts and prosciutto.

3. Spread some of the fig jam on each serving plate. Top with the salad, serve with the remaining vinaigrette, and enjoy.

CANDIED WALNUTS

1. Line a baking sheet with parchment paper. Place the walnuts and maple syrup in a small saucepan and bring to a boil. Reduce the heat and simmer for 5 minutes.

2. Transfer the walnuts to the baking sheet. Using a fork, separate the walnuts so that they don't stick together when cool. Let the walnuts cool completely.

3. Place the canola oil in a Dutch oven and warm it to 350°F. Working in batches to avoid crowding the pot, add the walnuts and fry until golden brown. Transfer the fried walnuts to a paper towel–lined plate to drain and season them with salt as they cool.

INGREDIENTS:

4   OZ. THINLY SLICED PROSCIUTTO

6   CUPS FRESH ARUGULA

     FIG VINAIGRETTE (SEE PAGE 752)

2   OZ. PARMESAN CHEESE, SHAVED

     SALT AND PEPPER, TO TASTE

1   CUP CANDIED WALNUTS (SEE RECIPE)

2   TABLESPOONS FIG JAM

CANDIED WALNUTS

1   CUP WALNUTS

1   CUP MAPLE SYRUP

2   CUPS CANOLA OIL

2   TABLESPOONS SUGAR

1   TEASPOON KOSHER SALT

HEART-BEET SALAD

YIELD: 1 SERVING / **ACTIVE TIME:** 20 MINUTES / **TOTAL TIME:** 20 MINUTES

Beets and goat cheese are a classic combination, but the addition of truffle flavor and hazelnuts elevates this salad to something special.

1. Place the arugula, kale, beets, orange, and vinaigrette in a bowl and gently toss to combine.

2. Spread the truffle goat cheese spread over a chilled plate. Top it with the salad, garnish with tarragon, pomegranate seeds, hazelnuts, and hemp hearts, and enjoy.

INGREDIENTS:

1	OZ. ARUGULA
1	OZ. KALE, TORN
4	OZ. ROASTED BEETS, DICED
4	ORANGE SEGMENTS
1	OZ. POMEGRANATE VINAIGRETTE (SEE PAGE 754)
3	TABLESPOONS TRUFFLE GOAT CHEESE SPREAD
	FRESH TARRAGON, FOR GARNISH
	POMEGRANATE SEEDS, FOR GARNISH
	TOASTED HAZELNUTS, CRUSHED, FOR GARNISH
	HEMP HEARTS, FOR GARNISH

SUMAC & APPLE CAULIFLOWER

YIELD: 4 SERVINGS / **ACTIVE TIME:** 15 MINUTES / **TOTAL TIME:** 1 HOUR AND 15 MINUTES

Roasting the cauliflower in a covered pan allows it to get very tender and crispy, while also helping it better absorb the flavor of the onion, apple, and sumac.

1. Preheat the oven to 400°F. Place the apple, onion, sumac, salt, sugar, and water in a food processor and pulse until combined.

2. Place the cauliflower in a roasting pan and pour the apple-and-sumac mixture over it. Cover the pan with aluminum foil, place it in the oven, and roast until the cauliflower is fork-tender, about 45 minutes.

3. Raise the oven's temperature to 450°F and remove the aluminum foil. Roast the cauliflower until crispy, about 10 minutes.

4. Remove the cauliflower from the oven, drizzle the honey and tahini over the top, and enjoy.

INGREDIENTS:

1	APPLE, PEELED AND QUARTERED
1	ONION, QUARTERED
1	TABLESPOON SUMAC
1	TABLESPOON KOSHER SALT
1	TABLESPOON SUGAR
½	CUP WATER
1	HEAD OF CAULIFLOWER, TRIMMED
2	TABLESPOONS HONEY
2	TABLESPOONS TAHINI PASTE

Sumac & Apple Cauliflower, see page 429

ROASTED BEET & LEEK RISOTTO

YIELD: 4 SERVINGS / ACTIVE TIME: 45 MINUTES / TOTAL TIME: 1 HOUR

Beets, leeks, and rice are humble ingredients that are elevated to new heights in this beautiful side dish.

1. Place the avocado oil in a large skillet and warm it over medium heat. Add the onion and leeks and cook, stirring occasionally, until they have softened, about 5 minutes.

2. Add the beet and cook, stirring occasionally, until they have softened, about 10 minutes.

3. Reduce the heat to low, add the rice, and stir to combine. Cook until the skillet has a nutty fragrance.

4. Deglaze the pan with the wine, stirring constantly. Cook until the rice has absorbed all of the wine.

5. Gradually add the warm stock, waiting until the rice has absorbed one addition before adding another, and stirring constantly.

6. Add the beet juice, stirring vigorously and continually.

7. When the beet juice has been absorbed, remove the pan from heat, stir in the butter and herbes de Provence, and enjoy.

INGREDIENTS:

2	TABLESPOONS AVOCADO OIL
½	LARGE SPANISH ONION, MINCED
2	LEEKS, TRIMMED, RINSED WELL, AND MINCED
1	RED BEET, PEELED AND DICED
1	CUP ARBORIO RICE
½	CUP DRY WHITE WINE
2	CUPS CHICKEN OR VEGETABLE STOCK (SEE PAGE 368 OR 371), WARM
½	CUP BEET JUICE
1	TABLESPOON UNSALTED BUTTER
1	TEASPOON HERBES DE PROVENCE

MOROCCAN CARROTS

YIELD: 2 SERVINGS / ACTIVE TIME: 15 MINUTES / TOTAL TIME: 15 MINUTES

Waking up your palate can be as simple as searing some carrots and pairing them with a few straightforward flavors.

1. Cut the carrots into matchsticks that are approximately ½ inch wide and 3 inches long.

2. Place the avocado oil in a large skillet and warm it over high heat. Add the carrots to the pan, making sure to leave as much space between them as possible. Sprinkle the Ras el Hanout over the carrots and sear them until lightly charred all over, about 6 minutes, turning them as necessary.

3. Transfer the carrots to a paper towel–lined plate to drain.

4. Divide the carrots between the serving plates and drizzle the honey and tahini over each portion. Garnish with the sesame seeds and enjoy.

INGREDIENTS:

2	LARGE CARROTS, PEELED
1	TABLESPOON AVOCADO OIL
1	TABLESPOON RAS EL HANOUT (SEE PAGE 747)
2	TEASPOONS HONEY, FOR TOPPING
2	TEASPOONS TAHINI PASTE
2	PINCHES OF WHITE SESAME SEEDS, FOR GARNISH

Moroccan Carrots, see page 433

ROASTED BEETS WITH
CILANTRO & BASIL PESTO

YIELD: 2 SERVINGS / ACTIVE TIME: 20 MINUTES / TOTAL TIME: 1 HOUR

With the cilantro-basil pesto, the humble beetroot gets an Italian twist in what's sure to become a new favorite.

1. Preheat the oven to 400°F. Wrap the beets in foil and use a fork to pierce a few holes in each beet.

2. Place the beets on a baking sheet, place them in the oven, and roast until a knife easily pierces through them, about 40 minutes.

3. Remove from the oven and let the beets cool.

4. Place the remaining ingredients, except for the olive oil, in a food processor and blitz until the mixture is a thick paste. With the food processor running, slowly drizzle in the olive oil and blitz until smooth. Set the pesto aside.

5. When the beets have cooled, peel them and slice them into ¼-inch-thick rounds. Place them in a bowl and drizzle the pesto over the top. Toss to coat and enjoy.

INGREDIENTS:

2	BUNCHES OF BEETS, SCRUBBED AND TRIMMED
1	CUP FRESH CILANTRO LEAVES
2	CUPS FRESH BASIL LEAVES
¼	CUP FRESHLY GRATED PARMESAN CHEESE
¼	CUP PINE NUTS
2	GARLIC CLOVES
½	TEASPOON KOSHER SALT
½	CUP EXTRA-VIRGIN OLIVE OIL

BEETS WITH WALNUT DUKKAH

YIELD: 2 SERVINGS / ACTIVE TIME: 30 MINUTES / TOTAL TIME: 1 HOUR AND 30 MINUTES

Dukkah is a seed-and-nut blend that, in Egypt, is often eaten in the same way that modern Americans might eat trail mix. Using its crunch to add a contrasting texture to this dish makes for a unique preparation.

1. Place the beet and salt in a saucepan with at least 5 cups of water and bring to a boil. Cook the beet until a knife can easily pass through it, 30 to 40 minutes.

2. Drain the beet, run it under cold water, and peel off the skin and stem; it is easiest to do this while the beet is still hot.

3. Cut the peeled beet into ¾-inch cubes and set them aside.

4. Place the nuts in a resealable bag and use a rolling pin to crush them. Transfer to a small bowl, add the black pepper and seeds, and stir to combine. Set the dukkah aside.

5. Place the avocado oil in a large skillet and warm it over high heat. Place the beet in the pan and sear until well browned all over, about 5 minutes, turning the cubes as necessary. Transfer the beet to a paper towel–lined plate to drain.

6. To serve, spread the Labneh across a shallow bowl, pile the beet cubes on top, and sprinkle the dukkah over the dish. Grate the cinnamon stick over the dish and enjoy.

INGREDIENTS:

1	LARGE BEET, UNPEELED
	PINCH OF KOSHER SALT
1	TABLESPOON CHOPPED WALNUTS
1	TABLESPOON CHOPPED HAZELNUTS
1	TEASPOON BLACK PEPPER
1	TEASPOON POPPY SEEDS
1	TEASPOON BLACK SESAME SEEDS
1	TABLESPOON AVOCADO OIL
¼	CUP LABNEH (SEE PAGE 67)
1	CINNAMON STICK

Beets with Walnut Dukkah, see page 437

STRAWBERRY FIELDS SALAD

YIELD: 1 SERVING / **ACTIVE TIME:** 15 MINUTES / **TOTAL TIME:** 15 MINUTES

Do yourself a favor and hold off on making this salad until strawberries are in season.

1. Place all of the ingredients in a mixing bowl, toss to coat, and enjoy.

INGREDIENTS:

3	OZ. ARUGULA
½	OZ. TUSCAN KALE, TORN
½	OZ. CHERRY TOMATOES, HALVED
½	OZ. FENNEL, SHAVED
1	OZ. STRAWBERRIES, HULLED AND SLICED
½	OZ. GOAT CHEESE, CRUMBLED
3	KALAMATA OLIVES, PITTED AND HALVED LENGTHWISE
1½	OZ. CHAMPAGNE VINAIGRETTE (SEE PAGE 804)
1	TEASPOON CHOPPED FRESH HERBS (TARRAGON, PARSLEY, CHIVES, AND CILANTRO RECOMMENDED)
	POMEGRANATE MOLASSES, TO TASTE

GRILLED ROMAINE & SWEET POTATO

YIELD: 2 SERVINGS / ACTIVE TIME: 30 MINUTES / TOTAL TIME: 30 MINUTES

The apple can be dressed and stored in the refrigerator overnight, or even a couple of days ahead.

1. Prepare a gas or charcoal grill for high heat (about 500°F). Add canola oil to a small saucepan until it is about 2 inches deep and warm it to 350°F. Add the sweet potato skins and fry until golden brown and crispy, about 1 minute. Remove the fried sweet potato skins from the oil and place them on a paper towel–lined plate. Season the potato skins with 1 teaspoon of the salt and 1 teaspoon of the pepper.

2. Cut the apple into ½-inch slices, leaving the skin on. Place the apple in a small bowl, add the white vinegar and 1 teaspoon of the salt, and toss to coat. Set the mixture aside.

3. Cut off the stem from the heart of romaine, separate the leaves, and place them in a bowl. Add the olive oil, remaining salt, and remaining pepper and toss to coat.

4. Place the lettuce on the grill and cook until slightly charred on both sides, but before it starts to wilt, about 1 minute.

5. Arrange the lettuce on a plate, crumble the fried sweet potato skins over them, and distribute the apple on top. Drizzle the balsamic over the dish, sprinkle the feta on top, and enjoy.

INGREDIENTS:

	CANOLA OIL, AS NEEDED
1	CUP SHREDDED SWEET POTATO SKINS
1	TABLESPOON KOSHER SALT
2	TEASPOONS BLACK PEPPER
½	GREEN APPLE
½	CUP WHITE VINEGAR
1	HEART OF ROMAINE LETTUCE
2	TEASPOONS EXTRA-VIRGIN OLIVE OIL
1	TABLESPOON BALSAMIC VINEGAR
2	TABLESPOONS CRUMBLED FETA CHEESE

Grilled Romaine & Sweet Potato, see page 441

FIG & GOAT CHEESE SALAD

YIELD: 2 SERVINGS / **ACTIVE TIME:** 30 MINUTES / **TOTAL TIME:** 30 MINUTES

Fresh figs and goat cheese is a classic combination, and slightly smoky fruit with cheese is super Mediterranean.

1. Prepare a charcoal or gas grill for high heat (about 500°F).

2. Place the wine and sugar in a small saucepan and warm the mixture over medium-high heat, stirring until the sugar has dissolved. Simmer until the mixture has reduced to a syrupy consistency. Remove the pan from heat and set it aside.

3. Place the orange slices on the grill and cook until they're caramelized on each side, about 2 minutes. Remove them from heat and set them aside.

4. Place the figs on the grill, cut side down, and cook until they are lightly browned and soft, about four minutes.

5. To serve, place the orange slices on a plate, place the figs on top of the orange slices, sprinkle the goat cheese over the dish, and then drizzle the reduction over the top.

INGREDIENTS:

1	CUP PINOT NOIR
¼	CUP SUGAR
4	ORANGE SLICES
6	FRESH FIGS, HALVED
2	TABLESPOONS CRUMBLED GOAT CHEESE

RED CABBAGE, DATE & BEET SALAD

YIELD: 6 SERVINGS / ACTIVE TIME: 30 MINUTES / TOTAL TIME: 1 HOUR AND 30 MINUTES

This salad is a beautiful burst of deep reds and savory-sweet ingredients.

1. Preheat the oven to 400°F. Line a baking sheet with parchment paper and cover it with the salt.

2. Set the beets on the bed of salt, place them in the oven, and roast them until fork-tender, 45 minutes to 1 hour.

3. Remove the beets from the oven and let them cool for 30 minutes. Discard the salt.

4. Peel the beets, cut them into 2-inch-long slices that are ⅛ inch thick, and place them in a bowl. You can also grate the beets.

5. Add all of the remaining ingredients to the bowl and stir until well combined. Taste, adjust the seasoning as necessary, and enjoy.

INGREDIENTS:

- 2 CUPS KOSHER SALT
- 6 LARGE RED BEETS
- ½ HEAD OF RED CABBAGE, CORED AND SLICED THIN
- 5 DRIED MEDJOOL DATES, PITTED AND SLICED THIN LENGTHWISE
- ½ CUP TAHINI SAUCE (SEE PAGE 767)
- ⅓ CUP CHOPPED FRESH CILANTRO
- ⅓ CUP CHOPPED FRESH MINT
- ⅓ CUP CHOPPED SCALLIONS
- ¼ CUP EXTRA-VIRGIN OLIVE OIL
- ¼ CUP FRESH LEMON JUICE

MEDITERRANEAN GRILLED CHICKEN SALAD

YIELD: 4 SERVINGS / **ACTIVE TIME**: 30 MINUTES / **TOTAL TIME**: 45 MINUTES

A lovely, simple salad that will make a wonderful dinner for some summer evening when it's too hot to even think about cooking indoors.

1. Prepare a gas or charcoal grill for medium-high heat (about 450°F). Season the chicken with salt and pepper and let it rest at room temperature.

2. Place the peppers on the grill and cook until they are charred all over, turning them as necessary, about 10 minutes. Place the peppers in a bowl, cover it with plastic wrap, and let the peppers steam for 10 minutes. Remove the stems and seeds from the peppers, slice them, and place them in a salad bowl.

3. Place the chicken on the grill and cook until it is cooked through and seared on both sides, about 10 minutes, turning it over only once as it cooks. Remove the chicken from the grill, let it rest for 10 minutes, and then slice it into strips. Add the chicken to the salad bowl.

4. While the chicken is resting, place the zucchini on the grill and cook until it is lightly charred on both sides, about 4 minutes. Place the zucchini in the salad bowl.

5. Add the red onion, arugula, and half of the vinaigrette to the salad bowl and gently toss to combine. Add the feta and toss until it has been evenly distributed. Garnish the salad with the toasted slivered almonds and serve with the remaining vinaigrette on the side.

INGREDIENTS:

2   LBS. BONELESS, SKINLESS CHICKEN BREASTS

    SALT AND PEPPER, TO TASTE

2   RED BELL PEPPERS

2   ZUCCHINI, SLICED INTO ROUNDS

½   RED ONION, HALVED AND SLICED

5   OZ. ARUGULA

    CHAMPAGNE VINAIGRETTE (SEE PAGE 804)

½   CUP CRUMBLED FETA CHEESE

    SLIVERED ALMONDS, TOASTED, FOR GARNISH

Crispy Salmon Rice, see page 450

CRISPY SALMON RICE

Use the largest pan you have available in this preparation, as the amount of surface area is critical.

1. Place the avocado oil in a large skillet and warm it over high heat. Add the onion, scallions, parsley, and salt and cook, stirring frequently, until the onion is translucent, about 3 minutes.

2. Add the rice and cook, stirring frequently, until the rice is crispy, 3 to 5 minutes. Add the salmon, reduce the heat to medium-high, and cook until the salmon is cooked through, about 4 minutes.

3. Place the pomegranate molasses and vinegar in a small bowl and whisk to combine. Add this mixture to the pan and stir until incorporated.

4. Remove the pan from heat and enjoy immediately.

INGREDIENTS:

2	TABLESPOONS AVOCADO OIL
½	WHITE ONION, MINCED
¼	CUP SLICED SCALLIONS
¼	CUP CHOPPED FRESH PARSLEY
2	TEASPOONS KOSHER SALT
2	CUPS LEFTOVER WHITE RICE
6	OZ. SALMON BELLY, CHOPPED
1	TABLESPOON POMEGRANATE MOLASSES
1	TABLESPOON APPLE CIDER VINEGAR

GREEK SALAD

YIELD: 4 SERVINGS / ACTIVE TIME: 10 MINUTES / TOTAL TIME: 10 MINUTES

You know that it's great on the side. But don't hesitate to take it further and use it as a filling for stuffed peppers or tomatoes.

1. Place the vinegar, oregano, garlic, mustard, and lemon juice in a mixing bowl and whisk to combine.

2. While whisking continually, slowly drizzle in the olive oil until it has emulsified.

3. Season the dressing with salt and pepper, add the cucumber, onion, tomatoes, and pepper, and toss to combine. Let the salad marinate for 15 minutes.

4. Stir in the olives, parsley, and mint, taste, and adjust the seasoning as necessary. Top the salad with the feta and enjoy.

INGREDIENTS:

1 TABLESPOON RED WINE VINEGAR

1 TABLESPOON CHOPPED FRESH OREGANO

1 GARLIC CLOVE, MINCED

1 TEASPOON DIJON MUSTARD

1 TEASPOON FRESH LEMON JUICE

⅓ CUP EXTRA-VIRGIN OLIVE OIL

SALT AND PEPPER, TO TASTE

1 CUCUMBER, PEELED, HALVED, SEEDS REMOVED, SLICED THIN

½ RED ONION, SLICED THIN

1 PINT OF CHERRY TOMATOES, HALVED

1 GREEN BELL PEPPER, STEM AND SEEDS REMOVED, SLICED THIN

½ CUP KALAMATA OLIVES, PITS REMOVED, SLICED THIN

2 TABLESPOONS CHOPPED FRESH PARSLEY

2 TABLESPOONS CHOPPED FRESH MINT

1 CUP CRUMBLED FETA CHEESE

Greek Salad, see page 451

VEGETABLE KEBABS

YIELD: 4 SERVINGS / ACTIVE TIME: 30 MINUTES / TOTAL TIME: 1 HOUR AND 30 MINUTES

This dish is meant to be prepared indoors, but feel free to take them out to the grill.

1. Place ¼ cup of the olive oil, the mustard, garlic, vinegar, honey, and rosemary in a mixing bowl and whisk to combine. Season the dressing with salt and pepper and set it aside.

2. Thread the vegetables onto skewers and place them on a baking sheet. Pour the dressing over the skewers, cover them with plastic wrap, and let them marinate at room temperature for 1 hour, stirring occasionally.

3. Place the remaining olive oil in a large skillet and warm it over medium-high heat. Remove the vegetable skewers from the dressing and reserve the dressing. Add the skewers to the pan and cook until golden brown all over and tender, about 8 minutes, turning them as necessary.

4. Place the skewers in a serving dish, pour the reserved dressing over them, and enjoy.

INGREDIENTS:

- ¼ CUP PLUS 1 TABLESPOON EXTRA-VIRGIN OLIVE OIL
- 2 TEASPOONS DIJON MUSTARD
- 2 GARLIC CLOVES, MINCED
- 2 TEASPOONS RED WINE VINEGAR
- 2 TEASPOONS HONEY
- 1 TEASPOON CHOPPED FRESH ROSEMARY

  SALT AND PEPPER, TO TASTE
- 2 PORTOBELLO MUSHROOMS, STEMS REMOVED, CUT INTO 1-INCH CUBES
- 2 ZUCCHINI, CUT INTO CUT INTO 1-INCH CUBES
- 1 RED BELL PEPPER, STEM AND SEEDS REMOVED, CUT INTO 1-INCH CUBES
- 1 GREEN BELL PEPPER, STEM AND SEEDS REMOVED, CUT INTO 1-INCH CUBES

COUSCOUS-STUFFED TOMATOES

YIELD: 4 SERVINGS / ACTIVE TIME: 30 MINUTES / TOTAL TIME: 1 HOUR AND 30 MINUTES

Rice, bulgur, and farro are other grains worth using as the foundation of the stuffing.

1. Preheat the oven to 350°F. Cut the top ½ inch off the tomatoes and scoop out their insides. Sprinkle the sugar and some salt into the tomatoes, turn them upside down, and place them on a wire rack. Let the tomatoes drain for 30 minutes.

2. Place 1 teaspoon of the olive oil in a large skillet and warm it over medium heat. Add the panko and cook, stirring continually, until golden brown, about 3 minutes. Remove the panko from the pan, place it in a bowl, and let it cool.

3. Stir half of the cheese into the cooled panko and set the mixture aside.

4. Place 1 tablespoon of the olive oil in a clean large skillet and warm it over medium-high heat. Add the onion and cook, stirring occasionally, until it has softened, about 5 minutes. Add the garlic and red pepper flakes and cook, stirring continually, for 1 minute.

5. Add the spinach and cook until it has wilted, about 2 minutes. Add the couscous and stock and bring the mixture to a simmer. Cover the pan, remove it from heat, and let it sit until the couscous is tender, about 7 minutes.

6. Fluff the couscous with a fork, add the olives, vinegar, and remaining cheese, and fold until incorporated. Season the stuffing with salt and pepper and set it aside.

7. Place the remaining olive oil in a baking dish. Add the tomatoes, cavities facing up, and fill them with the stuffing. Top with the toasted panko mixture and place the tomatoes in the oven. Roast until the tomatoes are tender, about 20 minutes.

8. Remove the tomatoes from the oven and let them cool slightly before enjoying.

INGREDIENTS:

4	TOMATOES
2	TEASPOONS SUGAR
	SALT AND PEPPER, TO TASTE
2	TABLESPOONS PLUS 1 TEASPOON EXTRA-VIRGIN OLIVE OIL
¼	CUP PANKO
1	CUP FRESHLY GRATED MANCHEGO CHEESE
1	ONION, CHOPPED
2	GARLIC CLOVES, MINCED
⅛	TEASPOON RED PEPPER FLAKES
4	CUPS BABY SPINACH
¾	CUP COUSCOUS
1½	CUPS CHICKEN STOCK (SEE PAGE 368)
2	TABLESPOONS CHOPPED KALAMATA OLIVES
2	TEASPOONS RED WINE VINEGAR

Lentil Salad, *see page 460*

LENTIL SALAD

YIELD: 6 SERVINGS / **ACTIVE TIME:** 15 MINUTES / **TOTAL TIME:** 2 HOURS AND 30 MINUTES

Lentils are hearty enough that this salad could serve as an entree in a pinch.

1. Place the water, lentils, 1 tablespoon of the vinegar, the garlic, herbes de Provence, and bay leaf in a slow cooker and season with salt. Cover and cook on high until the lentils are tender, about 2 hours.

2. Drain the lentils, discard the bay leaf, transfer to a large salad bowl, and let the lentils cool completely.

3. Stir in all of the remaining ingredients, except for the pepper and feta, and toss to combine. Season with salt and pepper, sprinkle the feta on top of the salad, and enjoy.

INGREDIENTS:

4	CUPS WATER
1	CUP LENTILS, PICKED OVER AND RINSED
2½	TABLESPOONS WHITE WINE VINEGAR
3	GARLIC CLOVES, MINCED
1	TEASPOON HERBES DE PROVENCE
1	BAY LEAF
	SALT AND PEPPER, TO TASTE
1	(14 OZ.) CAN OF CHICKPEAS, DRAINED AND RINSED
¾	LB. CHERRY TOMATOES, HALVED
1	RED ONION, SLICED
½	CUP FRESH PARSLEY, CHOPPED
¼	CUP EXTRA-VIRGIN OLIVE OIL
2	CUPS BABY SPINACH
½	CUP CRUMBLED FETA CHEESE

TABBOULEH

YIELD: 4 CUPS / **ACTIVE TIME:** 15 MINUTES / **TOTAL TIME:** 30 MINUTES

This can also work well as an appetizer, but I like to think of it as a freshness-packed salad.

1. Place the bulgur in a bowl and add the boiling water, salt, and half of the lemon juice. Cover and let sit for about 20 minutes, until the bulgur has absorbed all of the liquid and is tender. Drain any excess liquid if necessary. Let the bulgur cool completely.

2. When the bulgur has cooled, add the parsley, cucumber, tomatoes, scallions, mint, olive oil, black pepper, and remaining lemon juice and stir until well combined.

3. Top with the feta and enjoy.

INGREDIENTS:

½ CUP BULGUR WHEAT

1½ CUPS BOILING WATER

½ TEASPOON KOSHER SALT, PLUS MORE TO TASTE

½ CUP FRESH LEMON JUICE

2 CUPS FRESH PARSLEY, CHOPPED

1 CUP PEELED, SEEDED, AND DICED CUCUMBER

2 TOMATOES, DICED

6 SCALLIONS, TRIMMED

1 CUP FRESH MINT LEAVES, CHOPPED

2 TABLESPOONS EXTRA-VIRGIN OLIVE OIL

BLACK PEPPER, TO TASTE

½ CUP CRUMBLED FETA CHEESE

Tabbouleh, see page 461

COUSCOUS & SHRIMP SALAD

YIELD: 6 SERVINGS / ACTIVE TIME: 40 MINUTES / TOTAL TIME: 50 MINUTES

Regular couscous will also work here, but the toasted nuttiness of Israeli couscous is strongly preferred.

1. Place the shrimp, mint, and garlic in a Dutch oven and cover with water. Bring to a simmer over medium heat and cook until the shrimp are pink and cooked through, about 5 minutes after the water comes to a simmer.

2. Drain, cut the shrimp in half lengthwise, and set them aside. Discard the mint and garlic cloves.

3. Place the stock in the Dutch oven and bring to a boil. Add the couscous, reduce the heat so that the stock simmers, cover, and cook until the couscous is tender and has absorbed the stock, 7 to 10 minutes. Transfer the couscous to a salad bowl.

4. Fill the pot with water and bring it to a boil. Add the asparagus and cook until it has softened, 1 to 1½ minutes. Drain, rinse the asparagus under cold water, and chop into bite-size pieces. Pat the asparagus dry.

5. Add all of the remaining ingredients, except for the feta, to the salad bowl containing the couscous. Add the asparagus and stir to incorporate. Top with the shrimp, sprinkle the feta over the salad, and serve.

INGREDIENTS:

- ¾ LB. SHRIMP, SHELLS REMOVED, DEVEINED
- 6 BUNCHES OF FRESH MINT
- 10 GARLIC CLOVES, PEELED
- 3½ CUPS CHICKEN STOCK (SEE PAGE 368)
- 3 CUPS ISRAELI COUSCOUS
- 1 BUNCH OF ASPARAGUS, TRIMMED
- 3 PLUM TOMATOES, DICED
- 1 TABLESPOON FINELY CHOPPED FRESH OREGANO
- ½ ENGLISH CUCUMBER, DICED
- ZEST AND JUICE OF 1 LEMON
- ½ CUP DICED RED ONION
- ½ CUP SUN-DRIED TOMATOES IN OLIVE OIL, DRAINED AND SLICED THIN
- ¼ CUP CHOPPED KALAMATA OLIVES
- ⅓ CUP EXTRA-VIRGIN OLIVE OIL
- SALT AND PEPPER, TO TASTE
- ½ CUP CRUMBLED FETA CHEESE

BRAISED CAULIFLOWER

YIELD: 4 SERVINGS / ACTIVE TIME: 20 MINUTES / TOTAL TIME: 40 MINUTES

A dish that will get you thinking about just how versatile a vegetable cauliflower is.

1. Place the olive oil in a Dutch oven and warm it over medium heat. Season the cauliflower with salt and pepper, place it in the Dutch oven, and cook until golden brown all over, about 6 minutes, turning it as necessary. Remove the cauliflower from the pot and set it aside.

2. Add the garlic, red pepper flakes, and sumac and cook, stirring continually, for 1 minute. Add the wine and cook until the alcohol has been cooked off, about 2 minutes. Add the bay leaf, return the cauliflower to the pot, and add stock until the cauliflower is covered. Bring the mixture to a simmer and cook until the stem of the cauliflower is tender, about 10 minutes.

3. Transfer the cauliflower to a serving dish, garnish with the scallions, and enjoy.

INGREDIENTS:

- ¼ CUP EXTRA-VIRGIN OLIVE OIL
- 1 HEAD OF CAULIFLOWER, TRIMMED AND HALVED THROUGH THE STEM
- SALT AND PEPPER, TO TASTE
- 2 GARLIC CLOVES, MINCED
- ⅛ TEASPOON RED PEPPER FLAKES
- 1 TEASPOON SUMAC
- ½ CUP WHITE WINE
- 1 HEAD OF CAULIFLOWER, TRIMMED AND HALVED THROUGH THE STEM
- 1 BAY LEAF
- 6-8 CUPS VEGETABLE STOCK (SEE PAGE 371)
- 2 SCALLIONS, TRIMMED AND SLICED ON A BIAS, FOR GARNISH

CUCUMBER, TOMATO & MANGO RELISH

YIELD: 10 SERVINGS / ACTIVE TIME: 10 MINUTES / TOTAL TIME: 10 MINUTES

An essential preparation if you've got a table full of fatty meats and heavy starches.

1. Place the ingredients in a large mixing bowl and stir until combined.

2. Taste, adjust the seasoning as necessary, and enjoy.

INGREDIENTS:

6   CUPS HALVED HEIRLOOM CHERRY TOMATOES

4   CUPS SEEDED AND DICED PERSIAN CUCUMBERS

2   SMALL MANGOES, PITTED AND DICED

1   CUP DICED RED ONION

2   TABLESPOONS RED WINE VINEGAR

¼   CUP FRESH LEMON JUICE

2   TABLESPOONS ZA'ATAR (SEE PAGE 766)

1   TABLESPOON SUMAC

¼   CUP KOSHER SALT, PLUS MORE TO TASTE

2   TABLESPOONS BLACK PEPPER

¼   CUP CHOPPED FRESH DILL

½   CUP EXTRA-VIRGIN OLIVE OIL

PICKLED CUCUMBER SALAD

YIELD: 8 SERVINGS / ACTIVE TIME: 10 MINUTES / TOTAL TIME: 25 MINUTES

Everything a salad should be—easy, refreshing, and delicious.

1. Place the sugar and vinegar in a small saucepan and bring it to a simmer, stirring to dissolve the sugar.

2. Place the cucumbers and onion in a shallow bowl and pour the vinegar mixture over it. Let it sit until completely cool.

3. Season the salad with salt and pepper, sprinkle the parsley over it, and enjoy.

INGREDIENTS:

1	TEASPOON SUGAR
¼	CUP RICE VINEGAR
2	LARGE CUCUMBERS, PEELED AND SLICED INTO THIN ROUNDS
½	MEDIUM RED ONION, SLICED THIN
	SALT AND PEPPER, TO TASTE
1	TABLESPOON CHOPPED FRESH PARSLEY

CUCUMBER, MINT & SUMAC SALAD

YIELD: 4 SERVINGS / **ACTIVE TIME:** 15 MINUTES / **TOTAL TIME:** 15 MINUTES

Cucumber and mint are sure to lighten any warm-weather meal, and sumac adds an extra layer of brightness and acidity.

1. Place the cucumbers, 1 tablespoon of the sumac, the olive oil, lemon juice, and salt in a large bowl and toss to combine.

2. Transfer the salad to a serving bowl, taste, and adjust the seasoning as necessary. Sprinkle the remaining sumac on top, garnish with the mint, and enjoy.

INGREDIENTS:

12	PERSIAN CUCUMBERS, QUARTERED LENGTHWISE ON A BIAS
1½	TABLESPOONS SUMAC
¼	CUP EXTRA-VIRGIN OLIVE OIL
¼	CUP FRESH LEMON JUICE
1	TEASPOON KOSHER SALT, PLUS MORE TO TASTE
¼	CUP FRESH MINT LEAVES, FOR GARNISH

FAVA BEANS WITH POMEGRANATES

YIELD: 4 SERVINGS / ACTIVE TIME: 20 MINUTES / TOTAL TIME: 30 MINUTES

Young fava beans and plenty of fresh herbs make this spring in a dish.

1. Place the onion, sumac, and red wine vinegar in a bowl, season with salt, and let the mixture sit until the onion turns bright red and becomes slightly pickled.

2. Place the avocado oil in a large saucepan and warm it over medium-low heat. Add the garlic and fava beans and cook, stirring occasionally, until the fava beans are bright green in color. Season with the salt, pepper, Za'atar, and lemon juice and stir to combine.

3. Remove the pan from heat and stir in the fresh herbs and pomegranate seeds.

4. Transfer to a serving bowl, garnish with the onions, pomegranate molasses, olive oil, and Labneh, and enjoy.

INGREDIENTS:

½   RED ONION, SLICED THIN

1   TEASPOON SUMAC

1   TEASPOON RED WINE VINEGAR

½   TEASPOON KOSHER SALT, PLUS MORE TO TASTE

2   TABLESPOONS AVOCADO OIL

2   GARLIC CLOVES, CHOPPED

1½   LBS. FRESH YOUNG FAVA BEANS, PODS AND INNER SHELLS REMOVED

¼   TEASPOON BLACK PEPPER

1   TEASPOON ZA'ATAR (SEE PAGE 766)

   JUICE OF ½ LEMON

½   CUP CHOPPED FRESH PARSLEY

¼   CUP CHOPPED FRESH DILL

¼   CUP FRESH MINT LEAVES

¼   CUP POMEGRANATE SEEDS

1   TEASPOON POMEGRANATE MOLASSES, FOR GARNISH

2   TABLESPOONS EXTRA-VIRGIN OLIVE OIL, FOR GARNISH

2   TABLESPOONS LABNEH (SEE PAGE 67), FOR GARNISH

ROASTED CAULIFLOWER

YIELD: 20 SERVINGS / ACTIVE TIME: 15 MINUTES / TOTAL TIME: 1 HOUR

Cauliflower turns into something decadent in this recipe that is a combination of charred, fresh, sweet, and tangy.

1. Preheat the oven to 375°F and position a rack in the middle of the oven.

2. Place the heads of cauliflower directly on the rack in the middle and roast until they are golden brown, about 45 minutes.

3. Remove the cauliflower from the oven and let it cool. Trim the cauliflower so that only the florets are left and then set them aside.

4. Place a large skillet over medium-high heat, add the mustard seeds, and toast them until fragrant, about 30 seconds. Add the olive oil, Za'atar, turmeric, sumac, salt, and pepper, stir to combine, and remove the pan from heat. Allow the oil to infuse for 2 minutes.

5. Place the pan over medium heat and warm the mixture. Add the onion and cook it for just 15 seconds, then add the dates and cauliflower florets and stir to combine.

6. Stir the herbs, lemon juice, and lemon zest into the mixture, taste, and adjust the seasoning as necessary. Transfer to a serving dish and enjoy.

INGREDIENTS:

8	HEADS OF CAULIFLOWER
1	TEASPOON BROWN MUSTARD SEEDS
¼	CUP EXTRA-VIRGIN OLIVE OIL
3	TABLESPOONS ZA'ATAR (SEE PAGE 766)
2	TEASPOONS TURMERIC
1	TEASPOON SUMAC
2	TEASPOONS KOSHER SALT, PLUS MORE TO TASTE
1	TEASPOON BLACK PEPPER, PLUS MORE TO TASTE
1	SMALL RED ONION, SLICED
4	OZ. MEDJOOL DATES, PITS REMOVED, DICED
¼	CUP CHOPPED FRESH HERBS (TARRAGON, PARSLEY, CHIVES, AND CILANTRO RECOMMENDED)
¼	CUP FRESH LEMON JUICE
1	TABLESPOON LEMON ZEST

FUL MEDAMES

YIELD: 5 SERVINGS / **ACTIVE TIME:** 15 MINUTES / **TOTAL TIME:** 30 MINUTES

Hummus certainly deserves its worldwide popularity, but it sometimes means dishes like ful don't get the recognition they deserve. Think of it as hummus made with fava beans instead of chickpeas—it's usually chunkier, containing more cumin and topped with fresh herbs, onion, and chiles. Originally Egyptian, it has made its way all around the Mediterranean.

1. Place the avocado oil in a large skillet and warm it over medium heat. Add the the onion and garlic and cook, stirring frequently, until the onion is translucent, about 4 minutes.

2. Add the tomatoes and cook for another 4 minutes. Stir in the fava beans, cumin, Ras el Hanout, and cayenne pepper, reduce the heat to medium-low, and cook for 10 minutes.

3. Remove the pan from the heat and mash the fava beans lightly, right in the skillet, until most of the beans are mashed. Scoop into a serving bowl, stir in the lemon juice and parsley, season with salt, and enjoy.

INGREDIENTS:

1	TABLESPOON AVOCADO OIL
1	ONION, CHOPPED
3	GARLIC CLOVES, MINCED
2	TOMATOES, CHOPPED
2	(14 OZ.) CANS OF FAVA BEANS, DRAINED AND RINSED; OR 3 CUPS COOKED AND SHELLED FAVA BEANS
1	TEASPOON CUMIN
1	TABLESPOON RAS EL HANOUT (SEE PAGE 747)
¼	TEASPOON CAYENNE PEPPER
3	TABLESPOONS FRESH LEMON JUICE
¼	CUP FRESH PARSLEY, CHOPPED
	SALT, TO TASTE

Ful Medames, see page 475

KEMIA DE REMOLACHAS

YIELD: 6 SERVINGS / **ACTIVE TIME:** 15 MINUTES / **TOTAL TIME:** 45 MINUTES

This cold beet salad is often served alongside its cucumber and carrot counterparts.

1. Place the beets and 1 tablespoon salt in a pot and cover with cold water. Bring to a boil and cook until the beets are fork-tender, about 30 minutes. Drain and let the beets cool slightly.

2. Peel the beets and cut them into 1-inch cubes.

3. Place the olive oil in a skillet and warm it over medium heat. Add the beets, cumin, remaining salt, and pepper and cook, stirring frequently, for 3 minutes.

4. Transfer to a serving dish and enjoy warm or at room temperature.

INGREDIENTS:

3	BEETS
1	TABLESPOON PLUS 2 TEASPOONS KOSHER SALT
1	TABLESPOON EXTRA-VIRGIN OLIVE OIL
2	TEASPOONS CUMIN
¼	TEASPOON BLACK PEPPER

KEMIA DE ZANAHORIAS

YIELD: 6 SERVINGS / ACTIVE TIME: 10 MINUTES / TOTAL TIME: 20 MINUTES

Whether served warm or at room temperature, the spicy harissa pulls together this salad of cooked carrots and sautéed garlic.

1. Bring a large pot of water to a boil. Add the tablespoon of salt and the carrots and cook until the carrots are fork-tender, about 5 minutes. Drain the carrots and set them aside.

2. Place the olive oil in a large skillet and warm it over medium-high heat. Add the garlic and cook, stirring frequently, until golden brown. Add the cooked carrots, harissa, and paprika and cook, stirring frequently, for 3 minutes.

3. Transfer the mixture to a mixing bowl, stir in the caraway seeds, vinegar, and remaining salt, and enjoy.

INGREDIENTS:

1   TABLESPOON PLUS 1 TEASPOON KOSHER SALT

6   CARROTS, CUT INTO ¼-INCH-THICK ROUNDS

3   TEASPOONS EXTRA-VIRGIN OLIVE OIL

5   GARLIC CLOVES, SLICED THIN

1   TEASPOON THREE-PEPPER HARISSA SAUCE (SEE PAGE 791)

1   TEASPOON PAPRIKA

1   TEASPOON CARAWAY SEEDS

1   TABLESPOON WHITE WINE VINEGAR

MARINATED CAULIFLOWER & CHICKPEAS

YIELD: 4 SERVINGS / **ACTIVE TIME:** 20 MINUTES / **TOTAL TIME:** 45 MINUTES

It's better to pull the cauliflower from the boiling water too soon rather than too early, as you really want it to be crunchy.

1. Prepare an ice bath. Bring salted water to a boil in a medium saucepan. Add the cauliflower and cook until it has softened, about 4 minutes. Transfer the cauliflower to the ice bath, let it cool, and drain.

2. Place 1 tablespoon of the olive oil in a large, clean saucepan and warm it over medium heat. Add the garlic and cook, stirring continually, for 1 minute. Add the sugar, paprika, rosemary, and remaining olive oil and cook, stirring continually, for 1 minute.

3. Remove the pan from heat, stir in the saffron, and let the mixture cool.

4. Add the vinegar, chickpeas, and blanched cauliflower and stir to combine. Season the dish with salt and pepper, garnish with parsley, and serve with lemon wedges.

INGREDIENTS:

	SALT AND PEPPER, TO TASTE
1	HEAD OF CAULIFLOWER, TRIMMED AND CUT INTO FLORETS
½	CUP EXTRA-VIRGIN OLIVE OIL
4	GARLIC CLOVES, MINCED
1	TEASPOON SUGAR
1	TEASPOON PAPRIKA
2	TEASPOONS CHOPPED FRESH ROSEMARY
¼	TEASPOON SAFFRON
2	TABLESPOONS WHITE WINE VINEGAR
1	(14 OZ.) CAN OF CHICKPEAS, DRAINED AND RINSED
	FRESH PARSLEY, CHOPPED, FOR GARNISH
	LEMON WEDGES, FOR SERVING

ROASTED BRUSSELS SPROUTS
WITH WARM HONEY GLAZE

YIELD: 4 SERVINGS / ACTIVE TIME: 30 MINUTES / TOTAL TIME: 1 HOUR

By preheating the baking sheet, you'll ensure that every sprout in this goes-with-anything side has that irresistible crispy edge.

1. Postion a rack in the bottom third of the oven and set a rimmed baking sheet on it. Preheat the oven to 450°F.

2. In a large bowl, combine the Brussels sprouts and oil, toss to coat, and season with salt and pepper.

3. Carefully remove the baking sheet from the oven. Using tongs, arrange the Brussels sprouts, cut side down, on the hot baking sheet. Place it back on the low rack and roast the Brussels sprouts until they are tender and deeply browned, 20 to 25 minutes.

4. While the Brussels sprouts are roasting, place the honey in a small saucepan and bring to a simmer over medium-high heat. Reduce the heat to medium-low and cook, stirring frequently, until the honey is a deep amber color but not burnt (it will be foamy), about 3 minutes. Remove from heat, carefully add the vinegar and red pepper flakes, and stir until incorporated.

5. Place the saucepan back over medium heat, stir in the butter and ½ teaspoon salt, and cook, whisking constantly, until the glaze is glossy, bubbling, and has thickened, about 4 minutes.

6. Remove the Brussels sprouts from the oven, transfer them to a large bowl, and add the glaze. Toss to coat, top with the scallions and lemon zest, and enjoy.

INGREDIENTS:

- 1½ LBS. BRUSSELS SPROUTS, TRIMMED AND HALVED
- ¼ CUP AVOCADO OIL
- ½ TEASPOON SEA SALT, PLUS MORE TO TASTE
- BLACK PEPPER, TO TASTE
- ¼ CUP HONEY
- ⅓ CUP SHERRY VINEGAR OR RED WINE VINEGAR
- ¾ TEASPOON CRUSHED RED PEPPER FLAKES
- 3 TABLESPOONS UNSALTED BUTTER
- 3 SCALLIONS, TRIMMED AND SLICED THIN ON A BIAS
- 1 TEASPOON LEMON ZEST

HONEY-GLAZED CARROTS

YIELD: 8 SERVINGS / ACTIVE TIME: 15 MINUTES / TOTAL TIME: 30 MINUTES

Dark honeys, like buckwheat, bring a touch of malty sweetness to these lightly glazed beauties, which are perfect for serving with a crispy roasted chicken.

1. Place the carrots, butter, orange juice, honey, and salt in a saucepan, cover the pan, and cook over medium heat until the carrots are tender, about 10 minutes.

2. Uncover the pan and continue to cook the carrots, stirring occasionally, until the sauce reduces slightly, about 10 minutes.

3. Remove the pan from heat, stir in the lemon juice and cayenne, and transfer the carrots and sauce to a serving dish. Enjoy immediately.

INGREDIENTS:

5	LBS. CARROTS, PEELED
4	TABLESPOONS UNSALTED BUTTER
⅓	CUP ORANGE JUICE
1	TABLESPOON BUCKWHEAT HONEY
1½	TEASPOONS KOSHER SALT
2	TABLESPOONS FRESH LEMON JUICE
⅛	TEASPOON CAYENNE PEPPER

ARUGULA SALAD WITH PICKLED BEETS & PRESERVED LEMON VINAIGRETTE

YIELD: 4 SERVINGS / **ACTIVE TIME:** 20 MINUTES / **TOTAL TIME:** 3 HOURS AND 45 MINUTES

This bright salad is perfect for almost any time of the year, although peppery arugula is usually at its best in spring and fall. The real treat here is the vinaigrette, which enlivens all of the other ingredients.

1. Place each beet in its own small saucepan, cover with water, and simmer until a knife can easily pierce them, about 30 minutes.

2. Drain and let the beets cool. Peel the beets, slice them into thin half-moons, and place each one in a separate bowl to ensure that the red beet doesn't stain the golden one.

3. Place the vinegar, sugar, and 1 cup water in a small saucepan, bring it to a boil, and then remove the pan from heat. Divide the hot brine between the beets and let them sit at room temperature until pickled, 3 to 4 hours.

4. Preheat the oven to 300°F.

5. In a small mixing bowl, whip the egg white until frothy. Add the pistachios and Cajun seasoning, toss to coat, and spread the pistachios on a parchment-lined baking sheet. Place the pistachios in the oven and roast until they are golden and fragrant, about 15 minutes. Remove from the oven and let the pistachios cool.

6. Place the preserved lemon, olive oil, lemon juice, red pepper flakes, thyme, and salt in a bowl and whisk until well combined. Add the arugula to the vinaigrette and toss until coated.

7. Arrange the pickled beets on a serving platter and place the dressed arugula on top. Sprinkle the pistachios over the dish, drizzle the balsamic over the top, season with black pepper, and enjoy.

INGREDIENTS:

1	LARGE RED BEET, SCRUBBED
1	LARGE GOLDEN BEET, SCRUBBED
1	CUP RICE VINEGAR
1	CUP SUGAR
1	EGG WHITE
½	CUP SHELLED RAW PISTACHIOS
½	TABLESPOON CAJUN SEASONING
1	TABLESPOON MINCED PRESERVED LEMON
6	TABLESPOONS EXTRA-VIRGIN OLIVE OIL
2	TABLESPOONS FRESH LEMON JUICE
¼	TEASPOON RED PEPPER FLAKES
	LEAVES FROM 1 SPRIG FRESH THYME
	PINCH OF KOSHER SALT
5	OZ. ARUGULA
2	TABLESPOONS QUALITY AGED BALSAMIC VINEGAR
	BLACK PEPPER, TO TASTE

ROASTED ROOT VEGETABLES
WITH LEMON CAPER SAUCE

YIELD: 4 SERVINGS / ACTIVE TIME: 15 MINUTES / TOTAL TIME: 50 MINUTES

Get in the habit of whipping up a big batch of this regularly—it'll make planning meals for the rest of the week a cinch.

1. Preheat the oven to 425°F. Place the parsnips, celeriac, Brussels sprouts, potatoes, shallots, garlic, thyme, rosemary, honey, and ¼ cup of the olive oil in a mixing bowl and toss to coat. Season the mixture with salt and pepper and spread the mixture on a baking sheet in a single layer.

2. Place the vegetables in the oven and roast until golden brown and tender, 30 to 35 minutes. Remove the vegetables from the oven and let them cool.

3. Place the parsley, capers, lemon zest, lemon juice, and remaining olive oil in a mixing bowl and whisk to combine.

4. Drizzle the sauce over the roasted vegetables, toss to coat, and enjoy.

INGREDIENTS:

½   LB. PARSNIPS, PEELED, TRIMMED, AND CUT INTO 1-INCH CUBES

1   CELERIAC, TRIMMED, PEELED, AND CUT INTO 1-INCH CUBES

½   LB. BRUSSELS SPROUTS, TRIMMED AND HALVED

1   LB. NEW POTATOES

6   SHALLOTS, PEELED AND QUARTERED

4   GARLIC CLOVES, MINCED

2   TEASPOONS FRESH THYME

1   TEASPOON CHOPPED FRESH ROSEMARY

1   TABLESPOON HONEY

6   TABLESPOONS EXTRA-VIRGIN OLIVE OIL

   SALT AND PEPPER, TO TASTE

2   TABLESPOONS CHOPPED FRESH PARSLEY

1   TABLESPOON CAPERS, DRAINED AND CHOPPED

   ZEST AND JUICE OF 1 LEMON

ROMANO BEANS WITH
MUSTARD VINAIGRETTE & WALNUTS

YIELD: 8 SERVINGS / ACTIVE TIME: 15 MINUTES / TOTAL TIME: 30 MINUTES

If Romano beans are not available, green beans can be substituted.

1. Preheat the oven to 350°F. Place the walnuts on a rimmed baking sheet, place them in the oven, and toast until browned and fragrant, about 8 to 10 minutes, tossing halfway through.

2. Remove the walnuts from the oven and let them cool. When the walnuts have cooled slightly, chop them and set aside.

3. Bring salted water to a boil in a large saucepan and prepare an ice bath. Place the beans in the boiling water and cook until bright green and tender, 8 to 10 minutes. Using a slotted spoon, transfer them to the ice bath and let them cool. Drain, pat the beans dry, and set them aside.

4. Place the vinegar, mustard, garlic, and olive oil in a large mixing bowl and whisk until thoroughly combined. Let the dressing rest for 10 minutes.

5. Add the walnuts and beans to the dressing. Sprinkle the lemon zest and parsley over the beans, season with salt and pepper, and toss to coat. Transfer to a platter, drizzle more olive oil over the top, and enjoy.

INGREDIENTS:

1	CUP WALNUTS
	SALT AND PEPPER, TO TASTE
3	LBS. ROMANO BEANS, TRIMMED
3	TABLESPOONS RED WINE VINEGAR
2	TABLESPOONS DIJON MUSTARD
1	GARLIC CLOVE, FINELY GRATED
2	TABLESPOONS EXTRA-VIRGIN OLIVE OIL, PLUS MORE TO TASTE
	ZEST OF ½ LEMON
¾	CUP CHOPPED FRESH PARSLEY

BRAISED LEEKS

YIELD: 12 SERVINGS / **ACTIVE TIME:** 20 MINUTES / **TOTAL TIME:** 1 HOUR

This wonderful, straightforward dish will set your mind to work on all the other ways you can incorporate leeks into your cooking.

1. Preheat the oven to 400°F. Place the olive oil in a large skillet and warm it over medium-high heat. Season the leeks with salt and pepper, place them in the pan, cut side down, and sear until golden brown, about 5 minutes.

2. Season the leeks with salt and pepper, turn them over, and cook until browned on that side, about 2 minutes. Transfer the leeks to a baking dish.

3. Place the avocado oil in the skillet and warm it over medium-high heat. Add the shallots and cook until they start to brown, about 5 minutes.

4. Add the garlic, thyme, lemon zest, salt, and pepper to the pan and cook until just fragrant, about 1 minute.

5. Add the wine and cook until it has reduced by half, about 10 minutes.

6. Add the stock and bring the mixture to a boil. Remove the pan from heat and pour the mixture over the leeks until they are almost, but not quite, submerged.

7. Place the dish in the oven and braise the leeks until tender, about 30 minutes.

8. Remove from the oven, transfer to a serving dish, and enjoy.

INGREDIENTS:

½	CUP EXTRA-VIRGIN OLIVE OIL
6	LARGE LEEKS, TRIMMED, RINSED WELL, AND HALVED LENGTHWISE
	SALT AND PEPPER, TO TASTE
2	TABLESPOONS AVOCADO OIL
4	SHALLOTS, CHOPPED
2	GARLIC CLOVES, MINCED
1	TEASPOON DRIED THYME
1	TEASPOON LEMON ZEST
½	CUP WHITE WINE
2	CUPS VEGETABLE STOCK (SEE PAGE 371)

BULGUR-STUFFED EGGPLANTS

YIELD: 4 SERVINGS / ACTIVE TIME: 30 MINUTES / TOTAL TIME: 1 HOUR AND 15 MINUTES

By removing the meat and swapping quinoa out for bulgur, the stuffed eggplant becomes a festive side fit for a vegetarian feast.

1. Preheat the oven to 375°F. Score the flesh of each eggplant and brush them with 1 tablespoon of the olive oil. Season the eggplants with salt and pepper, place them on a baking sheet, cut side down, and place them in the oven. Roast until they have collapsed and are tender, about 45 minutes.

2. While the eggplants are in the oven, place the bulgur in a mixing bowl and add 2 tablespoons of boiling water. Cover the bowl and let the bulgur sit until it has absorbed the water, about 30 minutes.

3. Place the remaining olive oil in a large skillet and warm it over medium-high heat. Add the onion and cook, stirring occasionally, until it has softened, about 5 minutes.

4. Add the garlic, oregano, and cinnamon and cook, stirring continually, for 1 minute. Remove the pan from heat and stir in the bulgur, tomatoes, ½ cup of the Parmesan, the pine nuts, and vinegar. Season the mixture with salt and pepper and set it aside.

5. Remove the eggplants from the oven. Leave the oven on. Using a fork, gently push the eggplants' flesh to the sides and press down on it to make a cavity for the filling.

6. Fill the eggplants with the bulgur mixture and place them on the baking sheet. Top with the remaining Parmesan, place the eggplants in the oven, and roast until the cheese has melted, about 8 minutes.

7. Remove the eggplants from the oven and enjoy.

INGREDIENTS:

2	EGGPLANTS, HALVED LENGTHWISE
2	TABLESPOONS EXTRA-VIRGIN OLIVE OIL
	SALT AND PEPPER, TO TASTE
¼	CUP BULGUR, RINSED
1	ONION, CHOPPED
2	GARLIC CLOVES, MINCED
1	TEASPOON DRIED OREGANO
¼	TEASPOON CINNAMON
4	PLUM TOMATOES, SEEDS REMOVED, CHOPPED
1	CUP FRESHLY GRATED PARMESAN CHEESE
¾	CUP PINE NUTS, TOASTED
1	TEASPOON RED WINE VINEGAR

CAULIFLOWER CAKES

YIELD: 4 SERVINGS / ACTIVE TIME: 30 MINUTES / TOTAL TIME: 1 HOUR AND 30 MINUTES

Another preparation that shows off cauliflower's incredible versatility.

1. Preheat the oven to 425°F. Place the cauliflower in a mixing bowl, add 2 tablespoons of the olive oil, the turmeric, coriander, ginger, salt, and pepper, and toss to coat. Place the cauliflower on a baking sheet in a single layer, place it in the oven, and roast until it is tender and lightly browned, about 10 minutes.

2. Remove the cauliflower from the oven, transfer it to a mixing bowl, and mash until it is smooth. Let the mashed cauliflower cool.

3. Add the goat cheese, scallions, egg, garlic, and lemon zest to the cauliflower and gently fold until they have been incorporated and evenly distributed. Add the flour and stir to incorporate.

4. Divide the batter into four pieces and shape each one into a ½-inch-thick patty. Place the patties on a plate, cover them with plastic wrap, and refrigerate for 30 minutes.

5. Place the remaining olive oil in a large skillet and warm it over medium heat. Add the cauliflower patties and cook until golden brown on both sides, about 10 minutes. Remove the cauliflower cakes from the pan and serve immediately.

INGREDIENTS:

1	HEAD OF CAULIFLOWER, TRIMMED AND CUT INTO SMALL FLORETS
¼	CUP EXTRA-VIRGIN OLIVE OIL
1	TEASPOON TURMERIC
½	TEASPOON CORIANDER
¼	TEASPOON GROUND GINGER
1	TEASPOON KOSHER SALT
¼	TEASPOON BLACK PEPPER
6	OZ. GOAT CHEESE
3	SCALLIONS, TRIMMED AND SLICED THIN
1	EGG, BEATEN
2	GARLIC CLOVES, MINCED
	ZEST OF 1 LEMON
⅓	CUP ALL-PURPOSE FLOUR

BRAISED GREEN BEANS

YIELD: 2 TO 4 SERVINGS / **ACTIVE TIME:** 20 MINUTES / **TOTAL TIME:** 45 MINUTES

The added sweetness of the baby potatoes ties this salubrious side together.

1. Preheat the oven to 450°F. Place 1 tablespoon of the olive oil in a Dutch oven and warm it over medium-high heat. Add the onion and cook, stirring occasionally, until it has softened, about 5 minutes.

2. Add the oregano and garlic and cook, stirring continually, for 1 minute. Add the green beans, potatoes, and 1 cup water and bring to a boil. Reduce the heat and simmer for 10 minutes.

3. Stir in the tomatoes and tomato paste, cover the pot, and place it in the oven. Braise until the potatoes are tender and the sauce has thickened, 15 to 20 minutes.

4. Remove the pot from the oven, season the dish with salt and pepper, and stir in the lemon juice. Drizzle the remaining olive oil over the dish, garnish with the basil, and enjoy.

INGREDIENTS:

2 TABLESPOONS EXTRA-VIRGIN OLIVE OIL

1 ONION, CHOPPED

1 TEASPOON DRIED OREGANO

2 GARLIC CLOVES, MINCED

½ LB. GREEN BEANS, TRIMMED AND CUT INTO 2-INCH-LONG PIECES

½ LB. BABY POTATOES

1 (14 OZ.) CAN OF DICED TOMATOES, DRAINED

1 TABLESPOON TOMATO PASTE

  SALT AND PEPPER, TO TASTE

1 TEASPOON FRESH LEMON JUICE

¼ CUP FRESH BASIL LEAVES, TORN, FOR GARNISH

AUTUMN KALE SALAD

YIELD: 6 SERVINGS / ACTIVE TIME: 25 MINUTES / TOTAL TIME: 1 HOUR

The sweet golden raisins contrast the dark, vegetal kale, and a pungent roasted garlic dressing provides a savory kick.

1. Preheat the oven to 400°F. Trim the top 1 inch away from the head of the garlic, exposing the cloves. Drizzle 1 teaspoon of the olive oil over the garlic and rub it into the cloves. Wrap the garlic in aluminum foil, place it on a baking sheet, and place it in the oven. Roast the garlic until the cloves are completely soft, 30 to 40 minutes. Remove the garlic from the oven and set it aside.

2. While the garlic is roasting, prepare the squash. Place it in a bowl with 2 tablespoons of the olive oil, 1 teaspoon of the salt, and the black pepper. Toss to coat, place the squash on a large baking sheet, and place it in the oven. Roast the squash until browned and cooked through, about 20 minutes, turning it over halfway through. Remove the squash from the oven and let it cool.

3. Place the remaining olive oil, the vinegar, lemon juice, honey, remaining salt, and the cayenne in a bowl and stir to combine. Squeeze the roasted garlic cloves into the dressing and stir to combine, breaking up the garlic. Set the dressing aside.

4. Slice the kale into thin strips, place it in a large bowl, and add the dressing a bit at a time, using your hands to massage the kale leaves until they have softened and look shiny; there may be dressing left over. Add the raisins, nuts, and squash and toss to combine.

5. Garnish with the shaved Parmesan and enjoy.

INGREDIENTS:

- ½ HEAD OF GARLIC
- 6 TABLESPOONS PLUS 1 TEASPOON EXTRA-VIRGIN OLIVE OIL
- 1 SMALL DELICATA SQUASH, SEEDS REMOVED, SLICED THIN
- 2 TEASPOONS KOSHER SALT
- PINCH OF BLACK PEPPER
- 2 TABLESPOONS APPLE CIDER VINEGAR
- 2 TABLESPOONS FRESH LEMON JUICE
- 1 TEASPOON HONEY
- PINCH OF CAYENNE PEPPER
- 1 LARGE HEAD OF LACINATO KALE, THICKEST RIBS REMOVED
- ½ CUP GOLDEN RAISINS
- ½ CUP CHOPPED HAZELNUTS OR ALMONDS, TOASTED
- PARMESAN CHEESE, SHAVED, FOR GARNISH

HAND-ROLLED COUSCOUS

YIELD: 6 SERVINGS / ACTIVE TIME: 30 MINUTES / TOTAL TIME: 1 HOUR AND 15 MINUTES

Giving a bit of extra love and attention to this staple is well worth the effort.

1. Place the semolina into a large mixing bowl. Place the water in a spray bottle and use it to moisten the semolina. Begin by spraying the surface while stirring the mixture with your hand, pressing down and moving your palm in a circular motion. It is better to have too little moisture than too much, because you don't want to create a dough. Continue to spray and mix until the water is evenly incorporated into the semolina; it should form tiny granules without clumping—it is not necessary to use all of the water.

2. Depending on the texture of the mixture, sift it for uniformity and to remove any small clumps. To sift it, shake the moistened semolina through a strainer or colander with holes about ⅛ inch in diameter (better slightly larger than smaller) into another mixing bowl. After most of the mixture has passed through, stir to continue to pass it through, then press down on it to get as much through as possible. There may be a small amount of the mixture that won't go through the strainer—as much as ⅓ cup—and this may be discarded.

3. Bring 5 inches of water to a boil in a saucepan. Place the couscous in a steaming basket or tray, place it over the boiling water, and steam it, uncovered, for 10 minutes, stirring the couscous every 30 seconds to prevent clumping.

4. After 10 minutes, the mixture won't clump any more. Cover the steaming basket and steam for another 30 minutes, stirring every 10 minutes.

5. Transfer the couscous to a bowl, season it with the salt, and drizzle the avocado oil over it. Stir gently with a fork. The couscous may be covered and refrigerated at this point for up to 3 days.

6. Bring the stock to a boil, remove the pan from heat, and set it aside.

7. Bring 5 inches of water to a boil in a saucepan, place the couscous in a steaming basket or tray, and place it over the boiling water. Steam the couscous, covered, for 15 to 20 minutes.

8. Transfer the couscous to a bowl and add 1 to 2 cups of the stock—you want the couscous to be moist, not wet. Fluff with a fork and either serve immediately or pass it through the sieve or colander once more before enjoying.

INGREDIENTS:

- 2 CUPS SEMOLINA FLOUR
- ½ CUP WATER
- 1½ TEASPOONS KOSHER SALT
- ⅓ CUP AVOCADO OIL
- 2 CUPS BEEF OR CHICKEN STOCK (SEE PAGE 369 OR 368)

Hand-Rolled Couscous, *see page 499*

ONION MAHSHI

YIELD: 4 SERVINGS / ACTIVE TIME: 30 MINUTES / TOTAL TIME: 1 HOUR AND 30 MINUTES

This dish can be found throughout the Middle East, but is generally considered to be of Lebanese origin. The onions are generously stuffed with beef and rice, then roasted to aromatic perfection.

1. Fill a large saucepan halfway with water and bring it to a boil.

2. Peel the onions and trim away the root ends. Make a lengthwise slit to reach the center of the onions, cutting only halfway through them.

3. Place the onions in the boiling water and cook until the onions start to soften and their layers start to separate, 10 to 15 minutes. Drain the onions and let them cool.

4. Place the beef, allspice, rice, and 1½ tablespoons of the salt in a mixing bowl and work the mixture until it is well combined.

5. Gently separate the onions into individual layers, making sure each layer stays intact and does not tear.

6. Spoon 1 to 2 tablespoons of the meat mixture into one end of a piece of onion and roll it up to seal. Repeat until all of the onions have been filled with the meat mixture. Pack the stuffed onions tightly into a baking dish, stacking them in two layers if necessary.

7. Preheat the oven to 350°F.

8. Place the pomegranate molasses, water, remaining salt, and the sugar in a bowl and whisk until combined. Pour the sauce over the onions and then add water until the liquid reaches three-quarters of the way up the onions.

9. Cover the dish with aluminum foil and bake until the rice is tender and the meat is cooked through, about 30 minutes. Remove the foil and cook until the sauce thickens, 15 to 20 minutes. Transfer to a serving dish and enjoy.

INGREDIENTS:

4	LARGE YELLOW ONIONS
1	LB. GROUND BEEF
1	TABLESPOON ALLSPICE
¾	CUP ARBORIO RICE
1½	TABLESPOONS PLUS 1 TEASPOON KOSHER SALT
½	CUP POMEGRANATE MOLASSES
½	CUP WATER
1	TEASPOON SUGAR

WARM COUSCOUS SALAD

YIELD: 4 SERVINGS / **ACTIVE TIME:** 15 MINUTES / **TOTAL TIME:** 15 MINUTES

A versatile dish that can work well beside both braised chicken legs and roasted seafood.

1. Place the water and 1 tablespoon of the olive oil in a saucepan, season the mixture with salt, and bring it to a boil. Add the couscous and cook for 8 minutes.

2. Place the lemon juice, garlic, mustard, and honey in a mixing bowl and whisk until combined. While whisking continually, slowly drizzle in the remaining olive oil until it has emulsified.

3. Drain the couscous and place it in a serving bowl. Add dressing to taste, season the salad with salt and pepper, and toss to combine. Garnish with mint and parsley and enjoy.

INGREDIENTS:

1¾   CUPS WATER

7   TABLESPOONS EXTRA-VIRGIN OLIVE OIL

SALT AND PEPPER, TO TASTE

1½   CUPS ISRAELI COUSCOUS

1½   TABLESPOONS FRESH LEMON JUICE

1   GARLIC CLOVE, MINCED

2   TEASPOONS MUSTARD

1   TEASPOON HONEY

FRESH MINT, CHOPPED, FOR GARNISH

FRESH PARSLEY, CHOPPED, FOR GARNISH

CELERY SLAW WITH SEEDS & DATES

YIELD: 8 SERVINGS / **ACTIVE TIME:** 1 HOUR / **TOTAL TIME:** 3 HOURS

Even the most skeptical celery eaters will be surprised by the cool, sweet, crunchy, chewy, and savory flavors and textures that are packed into this side.

1. Place the mustard seeds in a mason jar. Place ⅓ cup of the vinegar, 2 tablespoons of the sugar, and the salt in a small saucepan and bring the mixture to a simmer, stirring to dissolve the sugar and salt. Pour the brine over the mustard seeds and let the mixture sit until cool, about 2 hours. Drain the mustard seeds and set them aside.

2. Place the olive oil and shallot in a small saucepan and cook over medium heat for 1 minute, making sure that the shallot doesn't take on any color. Remove the pan from heat and let the oil cool.

3. Strain the oil into a small bowl through a fine-mesh sieve. Discard the shallot or save it for another preparation.

4. Add the soy sauce and remaining vinegar and sugar to the shallot oil and whisk to combine. Season the vinaigrette with salt and set it aside.

5. Trim the cucumbers and use a mandoline to slice them into long, thin ribbons.

6. Place the cucumbers, arugula, celery, celery leaves, and dates in a salad bowl and toss to combine.

7. Drizzle half of the vinaigrette over the slaw and add 2 tablespoons of the mustard seeds. Toss to coat, taste, and adjust the seasoning as necessary.

8. Garnish with the sesame seeds and serve with the remaining vinaigrette.

INGREDIENTS:

¼ CUP BROWN MUSTARD SEEDS

⅓ CUP PLUS ¼ CUP RICE VINEGAR

2 TABLESPOONS PLUS 1 TEASPOON SUGAR

½ TEASPOON KOSHER SALT, PLUS MORE TO TASTE

⅓ CUP EXTRA-VIRGIN OLIVE OIL

1 SMALL SHALLOT, SLICED THIN

2 TABLESPOONS SOY SAUCE

2 PERSIAN CUCUMBERS

5 OZ. ARUGULA, TOUGH STEMS REMOVED

4 CELERY STALKS, SLICED THIN ON A BIAS

1 CUP CELERY LEAVES

10 MEDJOOL DATES, PITTED AND SLICED

SESAME SEEDS, TOASTED, FOR GARNISH

COUSCOUS WITH SEVEN VEGETABLES

YIELD: 6 SERVINGS / ACTIVE TIME: 20 MINUTES / TOTAL TIME: 50 MINUTES

A dish that could serve as an avatar for the autumn harvest.

1. Place the avocado oil in a Dutch oven and warm it over medium heat. Add the onion and cook, stirring occasionally, until it has softened, about 5 minutes.

2. Season the onion with salt and pepper, add the garlic and tomatoes, and cook, stirring frequently, until the tomatoes start to collapse, about 5 minutes. Stir in the tomato paste, cumin, paprika, ginger, cinnamon, and cayenne and cook, stirring frequently, until the mixture is fragrant, 2 to 3 minutes.

3. Add the peppers, zucchini, turnips, carrots, squash, and stock and bring to a boil. Reduce the heat, cover the pan, and simmer until the vegetables are tender, 10 to 15 minutes.

4. Remove the cover and add the chickpeas. Simmer until the chickpeas are warmed through and the stew has thickened, 5 to 10 minutes.

5. Meanwhile, make the couscous according to the directions on the package.

6. Stir the Ras el Hanout into the stew, taste, and adjust the seasoning as necessary.

7. To serve, spread the couscous on a platter. Spoon the vegetable stew over the couscous, garnish with the parsley and slivered almonds, and enjoy.

INGREDIENTS:

3	TABLESPOONS AVOCADO OIL
1	LARGE YELLOW ONION, DICED
	SALT AND PEPPER, TO TASTE
2	GARLIC CLOVES, MINCED
2	TOMATOES, SEEDS REMOVED, DICED
1	TABLESPOON TOMATO PASTE
2	TEASPOONS CUMIN
1	TEASPOON PAPRIKA
1	TEASPOON GROUND GINGER
1	TEASPOON CINNAMON
¼	TEASPOON CAYENNE PEPPER
2	BELL PEPPERS, STEMS AND SEEDS REMOVED, CHOPPED
2	ZUCCHINI, HALVED AND CHOPPED
2	SMALL TURNIPS, PEELED AND CHOPPED
1	BUNCH OF CARROTS, TRIMMED, PEELED, AND CHOPPED
1	BUTTERNUT SQUASH, PEELED AND CUBED
4	CUPS VEGETABLE STOCK (SEE PAGE 371)
1	(14 OZ.) CAN OF CHICKPEAS, DRAINED AND RINSED
1	BOX OF INSTANT COUSCOUS
2	TEASPOONS RAS EL HANOUT (SEE PAGE 747)
2	TABLESPOONS CHOPPED FRESH PARSLEY, FOR GARNISH
1	HANDFUL OF SLIVERED ALMONDS, FOR GARNISH

Couscous with Seven Vegetables, see page 505

CHARRED SWEET POTATOES WITH TOUM

YIELD: 4 SERVINGS / ACTIVE TIME: 1 HOUR AND 30 MINUTES / TOTAL TIME: 3 HOURS

The flavor of caramelized sweet potatoes is matched with pungent perfection when served on a bed of toum, a fluffy white garlic sauce.

1. Preheat the oven to 400°F and position a rack in the bottom third of the oven. Place the sweet potatoes in a large cast-iron skillet and poke them all over with a fork. Add just enough water to coat the bottom of the pan. Cover the pan tightly with aluminum foil, place it in the oven, and bake the sweet potatoes until fork-tender, 30 to 35 minutes.

2. Remove the sweet potatoes from the oven, place them on a cutting board, and let them cool.

3. Slice the sweet potatoes in half lengthwise.

4. Return the skillet to the oven and heat it for 20 minutes.

5. Remove the skillet from the oven, add 2 tablespoons of the butter, and swirl to coat. Place the sweet potatoes in the pan, cut side down, place them in the oven, and roast until the edges are browned and crispy, 18 to 25 minutes.

6. Remove the sweet potatoes from the oven. Spoon some of the Toum into a shallow bowl and arrange the sweet potatoes on top.

7. Place the remaining butter and the honey in the skillet and warm over medium heat. Drizzle the honey butter over the sweet potatoes, sprinkle the nigella seeds over the top, season with salt, and enjoy.

INGREDIENTS:

1½ LBS. SMALL SWEET POTATOES, SCRUBBED

4 TABLESPOONS UNSALTED BUTTER

TOUM (SEE PAGE 758)

SALT, TO TASTE

2 TABLESPOONS HONEY

2 TEASPOONS NIGELLA SEEDS

KOSHARI

YIELD: 8 SERVINGS / **ACTIVE TIME:** 1 HOUR / **TOTAL TIME:** 2 HOURS

This humble yet hearty Egyptian dish could also make an ideal main course for vegetarians, as the lentils are packed with protein.

1. Preheat the oven to 225°F. Bring salted water to a boil in a large saucepan. Add the pasta and cook until al dente, 6 to 8 minutes. Drain the pasta and set it aside.

2. Bring salted water to a boil in another saucepan and add the lentils. Cook until they are tender, about 20 minutes. Drain the lentils and set them aside.

3. Place the rice and 1 cup water in a small saucepan and bring it to a boil. Cover the pan, reduce the heat to low, cover, and cook until the rice is tender, 18 to 20 minutes. Remove the pan from heat but keep it covered to keep the rice warm.

4. Place 2 tablespoons of the avocado oil in a large skillet and warm it over medium-low heat. Add the onions and cook, stirring occasionally, until they are golden brown, about 30 minutes. Transfer the onions to a bowl and place it in the oven to keep warm.

5. Add ½ tablespoon of the avocado oil and the cooked pasta to the skillet and cook over medium heat, without stirring, until the bottom of the pasta is crispy, about 2 minutes. Stir and cook for another 2 minutes. Transfer the pasta to a serving dish.

6. Add ½ tablespoon of the avocado oil to the skillet. Add the lentils and cook until they are slightly crispy, 1 to 2 minutes. Spoon the lentils over the pasta. Add the rice to the serving dish.

7. Add the remaining avocado oil to the skillet. Add the chickpeas and cook until they are warmed through, about 2 minutes. Spoon the chickpeas into the serving dish.

8. Spoon the caramelized onions into the serving dish. Drizzle the sauce over the top or serve it alongside the koshari.

INGREDIENTS:

SALT, TO TASTE

6 OZ. FARFALLE OR ELBOW PASTA

½ CUP LENTILS, PICKED OVER AND RINSED

½ CUP WHITE RICE

3½ TABLESPOONS AVOCADO OIL, DIVIDED

2 LARGE ONIONS, SLICED

1 CUP CANNED CHICKPEAS, DRAINED AND RINSED

TOMATO SAUCE (SEE PAGE 775), FOR SERVING

Koshari, see page 509

FARRO SALAD WITH OLIVE & WHOLE LEMON VINAIGRETTE

YIELD: 8 SERVINGS / ACTIVE TIME: 15 MINUTES / TOTAL TIME: 1 HOUR

Look for Castelvetrano olives for this recipe; their buttery flesh and mild flavor will convert the most olive averse among us.

1. Place the farro in a large, wide saucepan and toast it over medium heat, stirring frequently, until it is golden brown and fragrant, about 4 minutes. Remove the pan from heat, cover the farro by 1 inch with cold water, and add a generous handful of salt.

2. Place the pan over medium-high heat and bring to a boil. Reduce the heat and simmer the farro, skimming any foam from the surface, until it is tender but still has some bite, 25 to 35 minutes. Drain and transfer the farro to a large bowl.

3. Crush the olives to break them up into large, craggy pieces. Discard the pits and place the olives in a large bowl.

4. Halve the lemon, remove the seeds, and finely dice the entire lemon, peel and all. Add the lemon and shallots to the olives, toss to combine, and season with salt and pepper. Let the dressing stand for 5 minutes to allow the flavors to meld.

5. Place the olive oil in a small saucepan and warm it over medium heat. Add the dressing and cook, swirling the pan occasionally, until the dressing is warmed through and the shallots have softened slightly, about 4 minutes.

6. Add the dressing to the farro and toss to combine. Taste and season with salt, pepper, and lemon juice. Add the fresh herbs, fold to incorporate them, and enjoy.

INGREDIENTS:

2	CUPS FARRO
	SALT AND PEPPER, TO TASTE
2	CUPS GREEN OLIVES
1	LEMON
2	SHALLOTS, MINCED
½	CUP EXTRA-VIRGIN OLIVE OIL
	FRESH LEMON JUICE, TO TASTE
2	CUPS CHOPPED FRESH MINT OR CILANTRO
2	CUPS CHOPPED FRESH PARSLEY

GREEN BEANS WITH ZA'ATAR & LEMON

YIELD: 8 SERVINGS / **ACTIVE TIME:** 15 MINUTES / **TOTAL TIME:** 30 MINUTES

L ife's too short; prep your green beans quickly. Stack a handful of them together on a cutting board and trim the stem ends off all of them at the same time for this delicious side dish.

1. Place the stock in a large skillet and bring it to a simmer over medium-high heat. Add the green beans, cover the pan, and cook, tossing occasionally, until the green beans are just tender, 5 to 7 minutes.

2. Uncover the pan, add the butter, and toss to coat the green beans.

3. Remove the pan from heat and stir in the Za'atar and lemon zest. Season with salt and pepper and enjoy.

INGREDIENTS:

- ¼ CUP CHICKEN STOCK (SEE PAGE 368)
- 2 LBS. GREEN BEANS, TRIMMED
- 2 TABLESPOONS UNSALTED BUTTER
- 1 TABLESPOON ZA'ATAR (SEE PAGE 766)

  ZEST OF 1 LEMON

  SALT AND PEPPER, TO TASTE

Green Beans with Za'atar &
Lemon, see page 513

HONEY-ROASTED VEGETABLE SALAD

YIELD: 4 SERVINGS / **ACTIVE TIME:** 30 MINUTES / **TOTAL TIME:** 1 HOUR

Top with yogurt sauce and chopped mint, and prepare to amaze with this sweet, sour, and savory salad.

1. Preheat the oven to 400°F. Line a large roasting pan with parchment paper.

2. Using a sharp knife, carefully peel the pumpkin and chop it into ¾-inch cubes. Discard the seeds.

3. Trim and cut the cauliflower into florets, halving any large ones.

4. Trim and gently scrub the carrots.

5. Place the vegetables in the roasting pan and drizzle the olive oil and honey over them. Season with the cumin, salt, and pepper and toss to coat.

6. Place the vegetables in the oven and roast until tender and golden brown, 25 to 30 minutes.

7. Remove the pan from the oven, add the spinach and mint, and stir to combine.

8. Place the yogurt and lemon juice in a small bowl, season with salt and pepper, and stir to combine.

9. Transfer the vegetables to a serving dish or salad bowl, drizzle the yogurt over the top, garnish with additional mint, and enjoy.

INGREDIENTS:

1¾	LB. PUMPKIN
1	SMALL HEAD OF CAULIFLOWER
1	BUNCH OF HEIRLOOM BABY CARROTS
2	TABLESPOONS EXTRA-VIRGIN OLIVE OIL
1	TABLESPOON HONEY
1	TEASPOON CUMIN
	SALT AND PEPPER, TO TASTE
4	CUPS BABY SPINACH
1	CUP FRESH MINT LEAVES, PLUS MORE FOR GARNISH
½	CUP PLAIN GREEK YOGURT
1	TABLESPOON FRESH LEMON JUICE

ROASTED PEPPER SALAD

YIELD: 6 SERVINGS / ACTIVE TIME: 10 MINUTES / TOTAL TIME: 30 MINUTES

A classic Moroccan dish that will fit right in at a summer barbecue.

1. Roast the peppers on a grill or over the flame of a gas burner until they are charred all over and tender. Place the peppers in a baking dish, cover it with plastic wrap, and let them steam for 10 minutes.

2. Remove the charred skins and the seed pods from the peppers and discard them. Slice the roasted peppers into strips and set them aside.

3. Place 1 tablespoon of the avocado oil in a saucepan and warm it over medium heat. Add the onion and cook, stirring occasionally, until it has softened, about 5 minutes. Remove the pan from heat and let the onion cool.

4. Place the peppers, onion, remaining avocado oil, vinegar, salt, pepper, cumin, and cilantro in a bowl, stir until combined, and enjoy.

INGREDIENTS:

3	RED BELL PEPPERS
2	YELLOW BELL PEPPERS
1	GREEN BELL PEPPER
½	CUP PLUS 1 TABLESPOON AVOCADO OIL
½	ONION, SLICED THIN
1	TEASPOON WHITE VINEGAR
¼	TEASPOON KOSHER SALT
⅛	TEASPOON BLACK PEPPER
½	TEASPOON CUMIN
¼	BUNCH OF FRESH CILANTRO, CHOPPED

ROASTED PLUMS WITH TAHINI DRESSING

YIELD: 4 SERVINGS / **ACTIVE TIME:** 30 MINUTES / **TOTAL TIME:** 2 HOURS AND 30 MINUTES

The rich and incredibly creamy tahini and lemon dressing pairs perfectly with the dessert-worthy sweetness of the roasted plums.

1. Preheat the oven to 400°F and line a baking sheet with parchment paper. Arrange the plums, cut side up, on the baking sheet, drizzle the avocado oil over them, and sprinkle the kosher salt, pepper, and herbs over them. Toss to coat.

2. Place the baking sheet in the oven and reduce the heat to 250°F. Roast until the plums are very soft and starting to caramelize, about 2 hours. Remove the plums from the oven and let them cool slightly.

3. Place the lemon juice, tahini, ¾ cup water, a few pinches of salt, and the ice cube in a mixing bowl and whisk vigorously until the dressing comes together. It should lighten in color and thicken enough that it holds an edge when the whisk is dragged through it. Remove the ice cube, if any of it remains, and discard it. Taste the dressing and adjust the seasoning as necessary.

4. Arrange the plums on a serving dish, drizzle the dressing over the top, and sprinkle the flaky sea salt—preferably Maldon—over the top.

INGREDIENTS:

2   LBS. PLUMS, HALVED AND PITTED

2   TABLESPOONS AVOCADO OIL

1½   TEASPOONS KOSHER SALT, PLUS MORE TO TASTE

¼   TEASPOON BLACK PEPPER

1   TABLESPOON FRESH THYME OR OREGANO

3   TABLESPOONS FRESH LEMON JUICE, PLUS MORE TO TASTE

1   CUP TAHINI SAUCE (SEE PAGE 767)

1   ICE CUBE

   FLAKY SEA SALT (MALDON RECOMMENDED), TO TASTE

ROASTED SQUASH & FETA SALAD

YIELD: 4 SERVINGS / **ACTIVE TIME**: 15 MINUTES / **TOTAL TIME**: 40 MINUTES

Feta and bread get roasted alongside winter squash, then tossed with pleasantly bitter greens for a salad that's equal parts warm and cold, soft and crunchy, and sweet and savory.

1. Preheat the oven to 400°F. Halve the squash lengthwise, remove the seeds and discard them, and cut the squash into ¼-inch-thick slices.

2. Place the squash on a baking sheet, season it with 1 teaspoon of salt and the black pepper, drizzle 2 tablespoons of the avocado oil over it, and toss to coat. Place the squash in the oven and roast until it is beginning to brown on one side, about 15 minutes.

3. Remove the baking sheet from the oven, turn the squash over, and then sprinkle the bread and feta over the squash. Return the pan to the oven and roast until the bread is lightly toasted and the feta is soft and warmed through, about 10 minutes.

4. Place the vinegar, honey, thyme, remaining avocado oil, and remaining salt in a large bowl and whisk until thoroughly combined.

5. In a small bowl, combine the paprika and cayenne and set the mixture aside.

6. Add the radicchio and warm squash mixture to the dressing and toss to coat.

7. Transfer to a serving dish, sprinkle the paprika-and-cayenne blend over the dish, and enjoy.

INGREDIENTS:

1½	LB. ACORN SQUASH
1½	TEASPOONS KOSHER SALT
¼	TEASPOON BLACK PEPPER
½	CUP AVOCADO OIL
4	CUPS CUBED FRENCH BREAD
½	LB. FETA CHEESE, CRUMBLED
¼	CUP SHERRY VINEGAR
1	TEASPOON HONEY
1	TEASPOON FRESH THYME
½	TEASPOON SWEET HUNGARIAN PAPRIKA
½	TEASPOON CAYENNE PEPPER
1	HEAD OF RADICCHIO, LEAVES SEPARATED AND TORN INTO LARGE PIECES

Roasted Squash & Feta Salad, see page 519

SHAVED RADISH SALAD
WITH WALNUTS & MINT

YIELD: 6 SERVINGS / ACTIVE TIME: 20 MINUTES / TOTAL TIME: 1 HOUR AND 20 MINUTES

The mandoline was made for recipes like this, as the extra-thin slices it produces will make this simple fall salad look like the work of a pro.

1. Preheat the oven to 375°F. Rinse the beets under cold water and trim away the tops and bottoms. Cut the beets in half, place them in a bowl, and add the olive oil. Season with salt and pepper and toss to coat.

2. Lay out a large piece of aluminum foil, top it with a piece of parchment paper, and wrap the beets in the packet. Place the packet in the oven and roast the beets until they are fork-tender, about 1 hour. Remove the beets from the oven.

3. Reduce the oven's temperature to 350°F.

4. Using rubber gloves or paper towels, rub the beets so that the skins slide right off. Set the beets aside and let them cool.

5. Place the walnuts on a baking sheet, place them in the oven, and toast until golden brown and fragrant, about 10 minutes, tossing them halfway through.

6. Remove the walnuts from the oven and let them cool. Crush the walnuts into small pieces.

7. Place the lemon juice, mustard, lemon zest, honey, and poppy seeds in a blender and pulse until combined. Taste, adjust the seasoning as necessary, and set the dressing aside.

8. Layer the radishes and beets on a large plate and top with the walnuts, Parmesan cheese, mint, and lime zest. Drizzle the dressing over the top and enjoy.

INGREDIENTS:

1	CHIOGGIA BEET
1	GOLDEN BEET
¾	CUP EXTRA-VIRGIN OLIVE OIL, PLUS MORE AS NEEDED
	SALT AND PEPPER, TO TASTE
¼	CUP WALNUTS
¼	CUP FRESH LEMON JUICE
1	TABLESPOON DIJON MUSTARD
1½	TEASPOONS LEMON ZEST
1	TABLESPOON HONEY
1	TABLESPOON POPPY SEEDS
1	WATERMELON RADISH, SLICED THIN
3	RADISHES, SLICED THIN
½	CUP SHAVED PARMESAN CHEESE
1	BUNCH OF CHOCOLATE MINT
1½	TEASPOONS LIME ZEST

SLOW-COOKED CHERRY TOMATOES
WITH CORIANDER & ROSEMARY

YIELD: 6 SERVINGS / **ACTIVE TIME:** 10 MINUTES / **TOTAL TIME:** 1 HOUR

A particularly good preparation for cherry tomatoes from the store as opposed to the garden or farmstand, as the long roasting time amplifies the flavor and sweetness.

1. Preheat the oven to 350°F and position a rack in the middle.

2. Place the tomatoes, garlic, rosemary, avocado oil, coriander seeds, sugar, and salt in a baking dish and toss to coat. Turn the garlic cut side down, place the dish in the oven, and then roast until the tomatoes are browned and very tender, about 50 minutes, tossing them 2 or 3 times as they cook.

3. Remove the dish from the oven and let it cool slightly.

4. Add the vinegar, stir to combine, and enjoy.

INGREDIENTS:

1½   LBS. HEIRLOOM CHERRY
     TOMATOES

½   HEAD OF GARLIC

2   SPRIGS OF FRESH
     ROSEMARY

½   CUP AVOCADO OIL

¾   TEASPOON CORIANDER
     SEEDS

½   TEASPOON SUGAR

¾   TEASPOON KOSHER SALT

1   TABLESPOON RED WINE
     VINEGAR

Slow-Cooked Cherry Tomatoes with Coriander & Rosemary, see page 523

ZA'ATAR OKRA & LEMONS

YIELD: 4 SERVINGS / ACTIVE TIME: 20 MINUTES / TOTAL TIME: 20 MINUTES

If you've ever been put off by slimy okra, try this high-heat recipe that keeps the pods crispy.

1. Place the avocado oil in a large skillet and warm it over high heat. Add the okra and lemon wedges, season with salt, and cook, stirring frequently, until the okra and lemon begin to char.

2. Remove the pan from heat and stir in the Za'atar. Place the mixture in a serving bowl, garnish with parsley, and enjoy.

INGREDIENTS:

2   TABLESPOONS AVOCADO OIL

1   LB. OKRA, TRIMMED

1   LEMON, CUT INTO WEDGES

SALT, TO TASTE

ZA'ATAR (SEE PAGE 766), TO TASTE

FRESH PARSLEY, CHOPPED, FOR GARNISH

BREADS

By now, everyone is familiar with the pita. Beyond that, bread in the Mediterranean tends to be a shadowy subject for many, obscured by the trendy low-carb diets that have latched on to the balanced, salubrious diet enjoyed in the area. In truth, wheat is a foundational crop in the Mediterranean, essential to its culinary traditions and the civilizations that have thrived there. Not buying it? Don't forget that Naples—home of Neapolitan pizza, aka the food that took over the world—sits on the Mediterranean. As you can see, the region's genius for simple, delicious dishes does not except this essential category.

PITA BREAD

YIELD: 8 SERVINGS / ACTIVE TIME: 1 HOUR / TOTAL TIME: 3 HOURS

A foundational preparation in Mediterranean cuisine. If you get in the habit of making this at home, a satisfying dinner is never far away.

1. In a large mixing bowl, combine the water, yeast, and sugar. Let the mixture sit until it starts to foam, about 10 minutes.

2. Add the flours and salt to the mixing bowl and work the mixture until it comes together as a smooth dough. Cover the bowl with a linen towel and let it rise for about 15 minutes.

3. Preheat the oven to 500°F and place a baking stone on the floor of the oven.

4. Divide the dough into eight pieces and form them into balls. Place the balls on a flour-dusted work surface, press them down, and roll them until they are about ¼ inch thick.

5. Working with one pita at a time, place the pita on the baking stone and bake until it is puffy and brown, about 8 minutes.

6. Remove the pita from the oven and serve warm or at room temperature.

INGREDIENTS:

1	CUP LUKEWARM WATER (90°F)
1	TABLESPOON ACTIVE DRY YEAST
1	TABLESPOON SUGAR
1¾	CUPS ALL-PURPOSE FLOUR, PLUS MORE AS NEEDED
1	CUP WHOLE WHEAT FLOUR
1	TABLESPOON KOSHER SALT

LAVASH WITH ARUGULA, EGGPLANT & OLIVES

YIELD: 10 SERVINGS / ACTIVE TIME: 30 MINUTES / TOTAL TIME: 2 HOURS

Lavash is a flatbread that typically accompanies a dish—in this one, it's the star.

1. To begin preparations for the lavash, place all of the ingredients in the work bowl of a stand mixer fitted with the dough hook and mix on low speed until the mixture comes together as a dough. Raise the speed to medium and work the dough for about 10 minutes, until it no longer sticks to the side of the work bowl.

2. Remove the dough from the work bowl and place it on a flour-dusted work surface. Knead the dough by hand for 2 minutes.

3. Coat a bowl with olive oil and place the dough in it, seam side down. Cover the dough with plastic wrap and let it sit in a naturally warm spot until it has doubled in size, about 1 hour.

4. Line a baking sheet with parchment paper. Divide the dough into 10 pieces, shape each one into a ball, and place the balls on the baking sheet. Cover the dough with a linen towel and let it rest for 10 minutes.

5. Warm a cast-iron skillet over medium-high heat. Working with one ball of dough at a time, place the dough on a flour-dusted work surface and roll it out into a 6-inch circle. Place the dough in the dry skillet, reduce the heat to medium, and cook until it starts to bubble and brown around the edge, about 2 minutes. Turn the lavash over and cook for another minute.

6. Remove the cooked lavash from the pan, place them on a wire rack, and let them cool.

7. Preheat the oven to 450°F. To begin preparations for the topping, warm a large cast-iron skillet over medium heat. Add the olive oil and eggplant and cook, stirring occasionally, until the eggplant starts to collapse, about 5 minutes. Add the bell pepper and cook, stirring occasionally, for another 5 minutes.

8. Add the garlic, tomato paste, and red pepper flakes and cook, stirring continually, for 1 minute. Add the arugula and cook, stirring frequently, until it has wilted, about 2 minutes.

9. Remove the pan from heat and fold in the olives. Season the mixture with salt and pepper and spread it over the lavash, leaving ½ inch border around the edge.

INGREDIENTS:

FOR THE LAVASH

7	TABLESPOONS WARM WATER (105°F)
7	TABLESPOONS MILK, WARMED
2	TEASPOONS EXTRA-VIRGIN OLIVE OIL, PLUS MORE AS NEEDED
¼	TEASPOON SUGAR
½	TEASPOON FINE SEA SALT
1½	TEASPOONS ACTIVE DRY YEAST
1¾	CUPS ALL-PURPOSE FLOUR, PLUS MORE AS NEEDED

FOR THE TOPPING

1	TABLESPOON EXTRA-VIRGIN OLIVE OIL
2	CUPS CHOPPED EGGPLANT
½	RED BELL PEPPER, SLICED THIN
2	GARLIC CLOVES, MINCED
1	TABLESPOON TOMATO PASTE
½	TEASPOON RED PEPPER FLAKES
2	CUPS ARUGULA
½	CUP GREEN OLIVES, PITS REMOVED AND SLICED THIN
	SALT AND PEPPER, TO TASTE
½	CUP FRESHLY GRATED PARMESAN CHEESE

Continued . . .

10. Place the lavash on a parchment-lined baking sheet and sprinkle some Parmesan over each one. Place them in the oven and bake until the edges of the lavash are golden brown, about 5 minutes.

11. Remove from the oven and enjoy immediately.

PIDES

YIELD: 4 PIDES / ACTIVE TIME: 45 MINUTES / TOTAL TIME: 1 HOUR AND 30 MINUTES

This Turkish entry into the world of flatbreads is one of its most visually appealing.

1. To begin preparations for the dough, place all of the ingredients in the work bowl of a stand mixer fitted with the dough hook attachment and work the mixture on low until it comes together as a smooth dough. Increase the speed to medium and work the dough until it no longer sticks to the side of the bowl.

2. Coat a bowl with olive oil. Place the dough on a flour-dusted work surface and knead it for 2 minutes. Form the dough into a ball and place it, seam side down, in the greased bowl. Cover the bowl with a linen towel and let the dough rise in a naturally warm spot until it has doubled in size, about 1 hour.

3. To begin preparations for the filling, place 2 tablespoons of the olive oil in a large saucepan and warm it over medium heat. Add the eggplant and cook, stirring occasionally, until it has browned and is soft, about 5 minutes. Remove the pan from heat and set the eggplant aside.

4. Place 1 tablespoon of the olive oil in a clean large saucepan and warm it over medium heat. Add the onion and pepper and cook, stirring occasionally, until they have softened, about 5 minutes. Add the garlic, red pepper flakes, and paprika and cook, stirring continually, for 1 minute.

5. Add the tomatoes and bring the mixture to a boil. Reduce the heat and simmer the mixture until the tomatoes start to collapse, about 10 minutes, mashing the tomatoes with a wooden spoon as they cook.

6. Stir in the eggplant and cook until warmed through. Season the mixture with salt and pepper, remove the pan from heat, and let the mixture cool.

7. Preheat the oven to 450°F. Line two baking sheets with parchment paper. Cut four 12 x 4–inch strips of parchment paper. Divide the dough into four pieces and place each one on a piece of parchment paper. Roll out the dough until each piece extends ½ inch over the strips of parchment on all sides.

INGREDIENTS:

FOR THE DOUGH

2	CUPS PLUS 2 TABLESPOONS BREAD FLOUR, PLUS MORE AS NEEDED
1	TEASPOON SUGAR
¼	TEASPOON INSTANT YEAST
⅔	CUP PLUS 2 TABLESPOONS WARM WATER (105°F)
1	TEASPOON FINE SEA SALT
2	TEASPOONS EXTRA-VIRGIN OLIVE OIL, PLUS MORE AS NEEDED

FOR THE FILLING

¼	CUP EXTRA-VIRGIN OLIVE OIL
4	CUPS DICED EGGPLANT (¼-INCH CUBES)
2	TABLESPOONS WHITE WINE
1	ONION, CHOPPED
½	RED BELL PEPPER, DICED
2	GARLIC CLOVES, MINCED
⅛	TEASPOON RED PEPPER FLAKES
½	TEASPOON PAPRIKA
1	(28 OZ.) CAN OF WHOLE PEELED SAN MARZANO TOMATOES, DRAINED
	SALT AND PEPPER, TO TASTE
1	CUP CRUMBLED FETA CHEESE
1	TEASPOON MALDON SEA SALT
	FRESH MINT, CHOPPED, FOR GARNISH

Continued . . .

8. Spread the eggplant mixture over the pieces of dough, leaving a 1 inch border on the sides. Sprinkle the crumbled feta over the eggplant mixture and brush the border of dough with some of the remaining olive oil.

9. Pinch the tops of the pides to secure them. Fold each side toward the center, leaving about a 1 inch of the filling exposed. Pinch the bottoms of the pides to secure them, brush the dough with some of the remaining olive oil, and sprinkle the Maldon sea salt over the top.

10. Place the pides in the oven and bake until the edges are crispy and golden brown, about 12 minutes.

11. Remove the pides from the oven and let them cool slightly before enjoying.

WHOLE WHEAT COQUES

YIELD: 2 FLATBREADS / ACTIVE TIME: 45 MINUTES / TOTAL TIME: 24 HOURS

This Spanish flatbread is as versatile as any in the region.

1. To begin preparations for the dough, place all of the ingredients in the work bowl of a stand mixer fitted with the dough hook and work the mixture on low until it comes together as a smooth dough. Increase the speed to medium and work the dough until it no longer sticks to the side of the bowl.

2. Coat a bowl with olive oil. Dust a work surface with bread flour. Place the dough on the work surface and knead it for 30 seconds. Form the dough into a ball and place it, seam side down, in the bowl. Cover the bowl with plastic wrap and place it in the refrigerator overnight.

3. To begin preparations for the topping, place 2 tablespoons of the olive oil in a skillet and warm it over medium heat. Add the onion, peppers, and sugar and cook, stirring occasionally, until the onion and peppers are golden brown, about 10 minutes.

4. Add the oregano, garlic, and red pepper flakes and cook, stirring continually, for 1 minute. Stir in the vinegar and pine nuts, season the mixture with salt and pepper, and remove the pan from heat. Let the mixture cool.

5. Remove the dough from the refrigerator and let it sit at room temperature for 1 hour.

6. Preheat oven to 450°F. Line two baking sheets with parchment paper. Divide the dough in half and place it on a flour-dusted work surface. Roll them out into 12 x 4–inch rectangles. Brush the coques with 1 tablespoon of the olive oil and prick them all over with a fork.

7. Place the coques on the baking sheets, place them in the oven, and bake for 6 minutes. Remove the coques from the oven, brush them with the remaining olive oil, and distribute the pepper-and-onion mixture over the top.

8. Return the coques to the oven and bake until the pine nuts and edges are golden brown, about 10 minutes, rotating the pans halfway through.

9. Remove the coques from the oven and let them cool for 5 minutes. Garnish with the parsley and enjoy.

INGREDIENTS:

FOR THE DOUGH

½ CUP BREAD FLOUR, PLUS MORE AS NEEDED

1 CUP WHOLE WHEAT FLOUR

2 TEASPOONS SUGAR

½ TEASPOON INSTANT YEAST

½ CUP PLUS 2 TABLESPOONS WARM WATER (105°F)

1 TABLESPOON EXTRA-VIRGIN OLIVE OIL, PLUS MORE AS NEEDED

1 TEASPOON FINE SEA SALT

FOR THE TOPPING

¼ CUP EXTRA-VIRGIN OLIVE OIL

1 RED ONION, HALVED AND SLICED THIN

1¼ CUPS THINLY SLICED ROASTED RED PEPPERS

1 TABLESPOON SUGAR

1 TEASPOON DRIED OREGANO

2 GARLIC CLOVES, MINCED

PINCH OF RED PEPPER FLAKES

1 TABLESPOON SHERRY VINEGAR

⅓ CUP PINE NUTS

SALT AND PEPPER, TO TASTE

¼ CUP FRESH CHOPPED PARSLEY, FOR GARNISH

VEGETARIAN MUSAKHAN

YIELD: 4 FLATBREADS / ACTIVE TIME: 30 MINUTES / TOTAL TIME: 2 HOURS

This flatbread is traditionally made with chicken, but this vegetarian spin will still hit the mark, thanks to the beguiling notes added by the sumac.

1. To begin preparations for the dough, place all of the ingredients in the work bowl of a stand mixer fitted with the dough hook attachment and work the mixture on low until it comes together as a dough. Increase the speed to medium and work the dough until it no longer sticks to the side of the bowl, about 10 minutes.

2. Coat a bowl with olive oil. Place the dough on a bread flour–dusted work surface and knead it for 2 minutes. Form the dough into a ball and place it, seam side down, in the bowl. Cover the bowl with a linen towel and let the dough rise in a naturally warm spot until it has doubled in size, about 1 hour.

3. To begin preparations for the topping, place 1 tablespoon of the olive oil in a large skillet and warm it over medium heat. Working in batches to avoid crowding the pan, add the mushrooms and sear them until browned, about 5 minutes. Turn them over and sear until browned on that side, about 5 minutes. Transfer the mushrooms to a paper towel–lined plate.

4. Place 1 tablespoon of the olive oil in a large, clean skillet and warm it over medium heat. Add the onions and cook, stirring occasionally, until they have softened, about 5 minutes. Add the carrot and cook, stirring occasionally, for 2 minutes.

5. Add the oregano, garlic, sumac, cinnamon, cardamom, nutmeg, and saffron and cook, stirring continually, for 1 minute. Stir in the brown sugar, season the mixture with salt and pepper, and remove the pan from heat. Let the mixture cool.

6. Place the mixture in a food processor, add the remaining olive oil, and blitz until smooth.

7. Preheat the oven to 400°F and position a baking stone on a rack in the middle. Dust a work surface with bread flour. Divide the dough into four pieces, place them on the work surface, and roll each one into a 10 x 4–inch rectangle. Spread the puree over each musakhan, leaving a ½-inch crust. Sprinkle the pine nuts and mushrooms over the puree.

8. Using a flour-dusted peel or the back of a baking sheet, slide the musakhan onto the baking stone one at a time. Bake until the crust is golden brown, about 10 minutes.

9. Remove the musakhan from the oven and let them cool slightly before enjoying.

INGREDIENTS:

FOR THE DOUGH

1	CUP BREAD FLOUR, PLUS MORE AS NEEDED
½	CUP WHOLE WHEAT FLOUR
2	TEASPOONS HONEY
½	TEASPOON INSTANT YEAST
¾	CUP WARM WATER (105°F)
1	TABLESPOON EXTRA-VIRGIN OLIVE OIL, PLUS MORE AS NEEDED
1	TEASPOON FINE SEA SALT

FOR THE TOPPING

5	TABLESPOONS EXTRA-VIRGIN OLIVE OIL
½	LB. PORTOBELLO MUSHROOMS, SLICED
1	CUP CHOPPED ONIONS
1	CARROT, PEELED AND GRATED
2	TABLESPOONS CHOPPED FRESH OREGANO
2	GARLIC CLOVES, MINCED
¾	TEASPOON SUMAC
⅛	TEASPOON CINNAMON
⅛	TEASPOON CARDAMOM
	PINCH OF FRESHLY GRATED NUTMEG
	PINCH OF SAFFRON
2	TEASPOONS LIGHT BROWN SUGAR
	SALT AND PEPPER, TO TASTE
¼	CUP PINE NUTS

LAHMACUN

YIELD: 1 FLATBREAD / **ACTIVE TIME:** 10 MINUTES / **TOTAL TIME:** 30 MINUTES

This translates to "dough with meat." The flavor is more dynamic than that, but retains the simple, straightforward character suggested by that definition.

1. Preheat the oven to 410°F and place a baking stone in the oven as it warms. Place the dough on a piece of parchment paper and gently stretch the dough into a very thin round. Cover the dough with the Lahmacun Spread.

2. Using a peel or a flat baking sheet, transfer the flatbread to the heated baking stone in the oven. Bake for about 10 minutes, until the crust is golden brown and starting to char.

3. Remove and top with the lemon juice, sumac, onion, tomato, cucumber, and feta. Drizzle olive oil over the top, garnish with fresh mint leaves, and enjoy.

LAHMACUN SPREAD

1. Place all of the ingredients in a food processor or blender and puree until the mixture is a smooth paste.

INGREDIENTS:

1	BALL OF PIZZA DOUGH
3	TABLESPOONS LAHMACUN SPREAD (SEE RECIPE)
	JUICE OF 1 LEMON WEDGE
	SUMAC, TO TASTE
¼	SMALL RED ONION, SLICED
3	SLICES OF TOMATO
¼	CUCUMBER, PEELED AND JULIENNED
1	TABLESPOON CRUMBLED FETA CHEESE
	EXTRA-VIRGIN OLIVE OIL, TO TASTE
	FRESH MINT LEAVES, FOR GARNISH

LAHMACUN SPREAD

¾	LB. GROUND BEEF
½	LARGE ONION, CHOPPED
½	GREEN BELL PEPPER, CHOPPED
1	TOMATO, CHOPPED
1	BUNCH OF FRESH PARSLEY
1½	TEASPOONS TAHINI PASTE
1	TABLESPOON TOMATO PASTE
¼	TEASPOON RED PEPPER FLAKES
¼	TEASPOON BLACK PEPPER
¼	TEASPOON GROUND NUTMEG
½	TEASPOON CINNAMON
½	TEASPOON ALLSPICE
½	TEASPOON SUMAC
½	TEASPOON DRIED THYME
	SALT, TO TASTE
	JUICE OF 1 LEMON WEDGE

SOCCA

YIELD: 4 TO 6 SERVINGS / **ACTIVE TIME:** 30 MINUTES / **TOTAL TIME:** 1 HOUR

This cross between a pancake and a flatbread is popular in Southern France.

1. Place 1 tablespoon of the olive oil in a small cast-iron skillet and warm it over medium-high heat. Add the onions, reduce the heat to low, and cook, stirring occasionally, until the onions are caramelized, about 30 minutes. Transfer the onions to a bowl and let them cool.

2. Place the chickpea flour, salt, and turmeric in a mixing bowl and whisk to combine. While whisking, slowly drizzle in 2 tablespoons of the olive oil. When the mixture comes together as a smooth batter, season it with salt and pepper.

3. Warm the cast-iron pan over medium-high heat. Add 1 tablespoon of the olive oil and then add ⅓ cup of the batter, tilting the pan to make sure the batter is evenly distributed. Reduce the heat to medium and cook until the batter starts to firm up, about 2 minutes.

4. Sprinkle some of the caramelized onions over the socca and cook until the edges are golden brown, 2 to 4 minutes. Flip the socca over and cook until golden brown and cooked through, about 2 minutes.

5. Gently remove the socca from the pan and repeat Steps 3 and 4 until all of the batter and caramelized onions have been used.

6. When all of the socca have been made, serve with Tzatziki.

INGREDIENTS:

7   TABLESPOONS EXTRA-VIRGIN OLIVE OIL

3   SMALL ONIONS, CHOPPED

1½   CUPS CHICKPEA FLOUR

½   TEASPOON KOSHER SALT

1   TEASPOON TURMERIC

1½   CUPS WATER

   SALT AND PEPPER, TO TASTE

2   TABLESPOONS CHOPPED FRESH CHIVES

   TZATZIKI (SEE PAGE 56), FOR SERVING

ZA'ATAR BREAD

YIELD: 1 LOAF / ACTIVE TIME: 30 MINUTES / TOTAL TIME: 3 HOURS

A focaccia-style bread that takes advantage of Za'atar's unique flavor.

1. Coat a bowl with olive oil. Place the flour, yeast, sugar, water, 3 tablespoons of the olive oil, and the fine sea salt in the work bowl of a stand mixer fitted with the dough hook and work the mixture on low until it comes together as a smooth dough. Increase the speed to medium and work the dough until it is a tight, elastic ball.

2. Place the dough in the bowl, cover the bowl with plastic wrap, and let the dough rise in a naturally warm spot until it has doubled in size, about 1 hour.

3. Preheat the oven to 375°F. Coat a 10 x 8–inch rimmed baking sheet with 2 tablespoons of the olive oil. Place the dough on the pan and gently stretch it to the edges of the pan. Cover the pan with plastic wrap and let it rest in the naturally warm space until it has doubled in size, about 30 minutes.

4. Place the Za'atar and the remaining olive oil in a bowl and stir to combine. Spread the mixture over the dough and sprinkle the sesame seeds on top.

5. Place the pan in the oven and bake until the bread is golden brown, about 20 minutes, rotating the pan halfway through.

6. Remove the bread from the oven and sprinkle the Maldon sea salt over the top. Let the bread cool slightly before slicing and serving.

INGREDIENTS:

- ½ CUP PLUS 1 TABLESPOON EXTRA-VIRGIN OLIVE OIL, PLUS MORE AS NEEDED
- 1¾ CUPS BREAD FLOUR, PLUS MORE AS NEEDED
- 1½ CUPS INSTANT YEAST
- 1 TEASPOON SUGAR
- ½ CUP PLUS 2 TABLESPOONS WARM WATER (105°F)
- 1 TEASPOON FINE SEA SALT
- 3 TABLESPOONS ZA'ATAR (SEE PAGE 766)
- 1 TABLESPOON SESAME SEEDS
- MALDON SEA SALT, TO TASTE

BASIC FOCACCIA DOUGH

YIELD: DOUGH FOR 1 LARGE FOCACCIA / **ACTIVE TIME:** 30 MINUTES / **TOTAL TIME:** 3 HOURS AND 30 MINUTES

This dough will give you a soft focaccia with a nice, complex texture. It takes several hours to make, but keep in mind that most of it is rising time, during which you can attend to other activities.

1. If using active dry yeast, warm 3½ tablespoons of the water until it is about 105°F. Add the water and the yeast to a bowl and gently stir. Let it sit until it starts to foam.

2. In a large bowl, combine the flours, yeast, and water. Work the mixture until it just comes together as a dough. Transfer it to a flour-dusted work surface and knead the dough until it is compact, smooth, and elastic.

3. Add the olive oil and salt and knead until the dough is developed, elastic, and extensible, about 5 minutes. Form the dough into a ball, cover it with a damp kitchen towel or greased plastic wrap, and let it rest at room temperature until it has doubled in size, 3 to 4 hours. The time for this first fermentation can be reduced if you place the dough in a naturally warm spot. In the oven with the light on is a good option if you're going to go this route.

4. Stretch and flavor the dough as desired. It will need another 1½ to 2 hours for the second rise before baking. The extra rising time can only benefit the dough, as the relatively low amount of yeast means the risk of overproofing is small.

INGREDIENTS:

½ TEASPOON INSTANT YEAST OR ¾ TEASPOON ACTIVE DRY YEAST

17⅓ OZ. WATER

21.1 OZ. BREAD FLOUR

3½ OZ. ALL-PURPOSE FLOUR, PLUS MORE AS NEEDED

2 TABLESPOONS EXTRA-VIRGIN OLIVE OIL, PLUS MORE AS NEEDED

2 TEASPOONS TABLE SALT

24-HOUR FOCACCIA DOUGH

YIELD: DOUGH FOR 1 LARGE FOCACCIA / **ACTIVE TIME:** 30 MINUTES / **TOTAL TIME:** 24 HOURS

This dough is a good introduction to bread making—you want to let time and temperature do the work for you.

1. If using active dry yeast, warm 3½ tablespoons of the water until it is about 105°F. Add the water and the yeast to a bowl and gently stir. Let it sit until it starts to foam.

2. In a large bowl, combine the flour, yeast, and water. Work the mixture until it just comes together as a dough. Transfer it to a flour-dusted work surface and knead the dough until it is compact, smooth, and elastic.

3. Add the salt and knead until the dough is developed, elastic, and extensible, about 5 minutes. Add the olive oil and knead the dough until the oil has been incorporated. Form the dough into a ball, place it in an airtight container that is at least three times bigger, cover, and refrigerate for 24 hours.

4. Remove the dough from the refrigerator and let it warm to room temperature before making focaccia.

INGREDIENTS:

¾   TEASPOON (SCANT) INSTANT YEAST OR 1 TEASPOON (SCANT) ACTIVE DRY YEAST

13   OZ. WATER

21.1 OZ. BREAD FLOUR OR "00" FLOUR, PLUS MORE AS NEEDED

2½   TEASPOONS TABLE SALT

2   TABLESPOONS EXTRA-VIRGIN OLIVE OIL

NO-KNEAD FOCACCIA DOUGH

YIELD: DOUGH FOR 1 LARGE FOCACCIA / **ACTIVE TIME:** 30 MINUTES / **TOTAL TIME:** 17 TO 21 HOURS

A rare instance when taking the easy way out won't cost you.

1. If using active dry yeast, warm 3½ tablespoons of the water until it is about 105°F. Add the water and the yeast to a bowl and gently stir. Let it sit until it starts to foam.

2. In a large bowl, combine the flour, yeast, and water. Work the mixture until it just comes together as a dough. Cover the bowl tightly with plastic wrap and let it rest at room temperature for 16 to 20 hours.

3. Coat an 18 x 13–inch baking sheet generously with olive oil and place the dough on it. Let the dough spread to the edges of the pan, helping it along by gently stretching on occasion, being careful not to deflate the dough. Let the dough rest in the pan for 1 hour, and then flavor as desired.

INGREDIENTS:

- ¼ TEASPOON INSTANT YEAST OR ¼ TEASPOON PLUS 1 PINCH ACTIVE DRY YEAST
- 18.7 OZ. WATER
- 1½ LBS. BREAD FLOUR
- 1 TABLESPOON (SCANT) TABLE SALT
- 2 TABLESPOONS EXTRA-VIRGIN OLIVE OIL, PLUS MORE AS NEEDED

FOCACCIA GENOVESE

YIELD: 1 LARGE FOCACCIA / **ACTIVE TIME:** 2 HOURS / **TOTAL TIME:** 27 HOURS

This is the focaccia that comes to mind when most people outside of Italy think of focaccia.

1. Place the dough on a flour-dusted work surface and form it into a loose ball, making sure not to compress the core of the dough and deflate it. Coat an 18 ×13–inch baking sheet with olive oil, place the dough on the pan, and gently flatten the dough into an oval. Cover the dough with a kitchen towel and let it rest at room temperature for 30 minutes to 1 hour.

2. Stretch the dough toward the edges of the baking pan. If the dough does not want to extend to the edges of the pan right away, let it rest for 15 to 20 minutes before trying again. Cover with the kitchen towel and let it rest for another 30 minutes to 1 hour.

3. Place the olive oil, water, and salt in a mixing bowl and stir to combine. Set the mixture aside. Lightly dust the focaccia with flour and press down on the dough with two fingers to make deep indentations. Cover the focaccia with half of the olive oil mixture and let it rest for another 30 minutes.

4. Preheat the oven to 450°F. Cover the focaccia with the remaining olive oil mixture and sprinkle the coarse sea salt over the top. Place in the oven and bake for 15 to 20 minutes, until the focaccia is a light golden brown. As this focaccia is supposed to be soft, it's far better to remove it too early as opposed to too late.

5. Remove the focaccia from the oven and let it cool briefly before serving.

INGREDIENTS:

	24-HOUR FOCACCIA DOUGH (SEE PAGE 553)
	ALL-PURPOSE FLOUR, AS NEEDED
2	TABLESPOONS EXTRA-VIRGIN OLIVE OIL, PLUS MORE AS NEEDED
⅔	CUP WATER
1	TEASPOON TABLE SALT
	COARSE SEA SALT, TO TASTE

MUSTAZZEDDU

YIELD: 1 LARGE FOCACCIA / ACTIVE TIME: 40 MINUTES / TOTAL TIME: 4 HOURS AND 30 MINUTES

Traditionally, this was the sustenance food of the Sardinian women who baked for their community; they used to make this focaccia to keep themselves going during the day-long process of making large batches of bread.

1. Place the tomatoes, garlic, basil leaves, and a generous amount of olive oil in a bowl, season the mixture with salt, and stir to combine. Let the mixture sit for 2 hours, drain it in a colander, and then let it drain for another hour.

2. If using active dry yeast, warm 3½ tablespoons of the water until it is about 105°F. Add the water and the yeast to a bowl and gently stir until combined. Let the mixture sit for 5 to 10 minutes. Instant yeast does not need to be proofed.

3. In a large bowl, combine the flours, the olive oil, yeast, and water until the mixture comes together as a dough. Add the salt and work the dough until it is compact, smooth, and elastic. Cover the bowl with a damp linen towel and let it rest at room temperature until it has doubled in size, about 2 hours.

4. Place the dough on a flour-dusted work surface and roll it out until it is an approximately ¾-inch-thick disk. Place it on a parchment-lined baking sheet, cover it with the linen towel, and let the dough rest for another hour.

5. Preheat the oven to 430°F and position a rack in the middle. Place the tomato mixture on the focaccia, making sure to leave some dough uncovered at the edge. Season with salt and pepper and fold the dough over the filling. You can leave the filling partially exposed or cover it completely; both are traditional in Sardinia.

6. Brush the dough with olive oil, place the pan directly on the bottom of the oven, and bake for 10 minutes. Lower the temperature to 390°F, transfer the focaccia to the middle rack, and bake for 30 to 40 minutes, until golden brown on the edges and on the bottom.

7. Remove the focaccia from the oven and let it cool slightly before serving.

INGREDIENTS:

- 1¾ LBS. CHERRY TOMATOES, CHOPPED
- 2 GARLIC CLOVES, CHOPPED
- 3–4 FRESH BASIL LEAVES
- 1 TABLESPOON EXTRA-VIRGIN OLIVE OIL, PLUS MORE AS NEEDED
- 1½ TEASPOONS TABLE SALT, PLUS MORE TO TASTE
- 1⅔ TEASPOONS INSTANT YEAST OR 2 TEASPOONS ACTIVE DRY YEAST
- 11⅔ OZ. WATER
- 12⅓ OZ. FINE SEMOLINA FLOUR
- 5⅓ OZ. BREAD FLOUR, PLUS MORE AS NEEDED

    BLACK PEPPER, TO TASTE

RIANATA

YIELD: 1 LARGE FOCACCIA / **ACTIVE TIME:** 40 MINUTES / **TOTAL TIME:** 4 HOURS AND 45 MINUTES

A simple and scrumptious focaccia loaded with tomatoes and oregano. Don't hesitate to be extravagant with the latter, as rianata means "with oregano."

1. If using active dry yeast, warm 3½ tablespoons of the water until it is about 105°F. Add the water and the yeast to a bowl and gently stir. Let the mixture sit until it starts to foam. Instant yeast does not need to be proofed.

2. In a large bowl, combine the flours, olive oil, yeast, and water until the mixture comes together as a dough. Transfer it to a flour-dusted work surface and knead the dough until it is compact, smooth, and elastic.

3. Add the salt and knead until the dough is developed, elastic, and extensible, about 5 minutes. Form the dough into a ball and place it in an airtight container that has been coated with olive oil. Let the dough rest at room temperature until it has doubled in size, about 2 hours.

4. Coat an 18 x 13–inch baking sheet with olive oil, place the dough on it, and brush the dough with more olive oil. Cover with a linen towel and let the dough rest for 30 minutes.

5. Gently stretch the dough until it covers the entire pan. Let it rest for another hour.

6. Preheat the oven to 430°F. Press the anchovies and the tomatoes into the dough, sprinkle the pecorino over the focaccia, season it with salt and the oregano, and drizzle olive oil over everything.

7. Place the focaccia in the oven and bake for 20 to 30 minutes, until the focaccia is golden brown and crispy on the edges and the bottom.

8. Remove the focaccia from the oven and let it cool slightly before serving.

INGREDIENTS:

2½ TEASPOONS ACTIVE DRY YEAST OR 2 TEASPOONS INSTANT YEAST

14.8 OZ. WATER

1 LB. BREAD FLOUR, PLUS MORE AS NEEDED

8.8 OZ. FINE SEMOLINA FLOUR

1 TABLESPOON PLUS 1 TEASPOON EXTRA-VIRGIN OLIVE OIL, PLUS MORE AS NEEDED

1 TABLESPOON TABLE SALT, PLUS MORE TO TASTE

7–8 ANCHOVIES IN OLIVE OIL, DRAINED

30 CHERRY TOMATOES, HALVED

½ LB. PECORINO CHEESE, GRATED

FRESH OREGANO, CHOPPED, TO TASTE

SFINCIONE PALERMITANO

YIELD: 1 LARGE FOCACCIA / **ACTIVE TIME:** 1 HOUR / **TOTAL TIME:** 4 HOURS AND 30 MINUTES

The soft and spongy consistency of this Sicilian focaccia's crumb makes this one of the greatest treats the Mediterranean region has to offer.

1. If using active dry yeast, warm 3½ tablespoons of the water until it is about 105°F. Add the water and the yeast to a bowl and gently stir. Let the mixture sit until it is foamy, 5 to 10 minutes. Instant yeast does not need to be proofed.

2. In a large bowl, combine the flours, yeast, and water until the mixture comes together as a dough. If kneading by hand, transfer the dough to a flour-dusted work surface. Work the dough until it is compact, smooth, and elastic.

3. Add the salt and work the dough until it is developed, elastic, and extensible, about 5 minutes. Form the dough into a ball, place it in a bowl, and cover the bowl with a damp linen towel. Let it rest at room temperature until it has doubled in size, about 2 hours.

4. Coat the bottom of a skillet with olive oil and warm it over medium-low heat. When the oil starts to shimmer, add the onions and cook, stirring frequently, until they are starting to brown, about 12 minutes. Add the tomatoes and three of the anchovies, cover the skillet, reduce the heat, and simmer until the flavor is to your liking, 20 to 30 minutes. Season with salt and pepper and let cool completely.

5. Coat an 18 x 13–inch baking pan with olive oil, place the dough on the pan, and gently stretch it until it covers the entire pan. Cover the dough with plastic wrap and let it rest for 1 hour.

6. Preheat the oven to 430°F. Top the focaccia with the cubed caciocavallo and the remaining anchovies and press down on them until they are embedded in the dough. Cover with the tomato sauce, generously sprinkle oregano over the sauce, and drizzle olive oil over everything. Sprinkle the grated caciocavallo and a generous handful of bread crumbs over the focaccia.

7. Place it in the oven and bake for 20 minutes. Lower the temperature to 180°F and bake for another 15 to 20 minutes, until the focaccia is golden brown, both on the edges and on the bottom.

8. Remove the focaccia from the oven and let it cool slightly before serving.

INGREDIENTS:

2½	TEASPOONS ACTIVE DRY YEAST OR 2 TEASPOONS INSTANT YEAST
22½	OZ. WATER
19¾	OZ. BREAD FLOUR, PLUS MORE AS NEEDED
8.4	OZ. FINE SEMOLINA FLOUR
1	TABLESPOON TABLE SALT, PLUS MORE TO TASTE
2	TABLESPOONS PLUS 2 TEASPOONS EXTRA-VIRGIN OLIVE OIL
2	ONIONS, SLICED
22.9	OZ. CRUSHED TOMATOES, WITH THEIR LIQUID
11–14	ANCHOVIES IN OLIVE OIL, DRAINED AND TORN
	BLACK PEPPER, TO TASTE
1	LB. CACIOCAVALLO CHEESE, TWO-THIRDS CUBED, ONE-THIRD GRATED
	FRESH OREGANO, CHOPPED, TO TASTE
	BREAD CRUMBS, TO TASTE

FOCACCIA DI CARNEVALE SALENTINA

YIELD: 1 SMALL FOCACCIA / ACTIVE TIME: 45 MINUTES / TOTAL TIME: 4 HOURS

This rich and delicious Apulian calzone is typical of the region of Salento, where it is presented during the Carnival.

1. If using active dry yeast, warm 3½ tablespoons of the water until it is about 105°F. Add the water and the yeast to a bowl and gently stir. Let the mixture sit until it is foamy, 5 to 10 minutes.

2. In a large bowl, combine the flour, yeast, and water until the mixture comes together as a dough. If kneading by hand, transfer the dough to a flour-dusted work surface. Work it until it is compact, smooth, and elastic.

3. Add the salt and work the dough until it is developed, elastic, and extensible, about 5 minutes. Form the dough into a ball and place it in an airtight container that has been coated with olive oil. Let the dough rest at room temperature until it has doubled in size, about 2 hours.

4. Coat the bottom of a skillet with olive oil and warm it over medium-high heat. When the oil starts to shimmer, add the onion and sausage, season with salt and pepper, and cook, stirring frequently, until the sausage is browned and the onion is soft, about 10 minutes. Remove from heat and let cool.

5. Grease a 10-inch cast-iron skillet or a round cake pan with olive oil. Transfer the dough to a flour-dusted work surface and divide it into two pieces, with one piece slightly bigger than the other. Roll out one piece into a disk that is slightly larger than the pan. Place it in the pan, top with the onion-and-sausage mixture, and distribute the tomatoes, pecorino, and mozzarella over the mixture.

6. Roll out the second piece of dough so that it will fit within the pan, place it over the filling, and crimp the edge to seal the focaccia. Brush the top of the focaccia with olive oil and use a fork to poke holes in it. Cover with olive oil–coated plastic wrap and let it rest for 1 hour.

7. Preheat the oven to 430°F. Place the focaccia in the oven and bake for 20 minutes. Lower the temperature to 350°F and bake for another 20 to 25 minutes, until golden brown, both on top and on the bottom. Remove and let cool slightly before serving.

INGREDIENTS:

- 2 TEASPOONS ACTIVE DRY YEAST OR 1⅔ TEASPOONS INSTANT YEAST
- 8.8 OZ. WATER
- 17½ OZ. ALL-PURPOSE FLOUR, PLUS MORE AS NEEDED
- 1½ TEASPOONS TABLE SALT, PLUS MORE TO TASTE
- EXTRA-VIRGIN OLIVE OIL, AS NEEDED
- 1 ONION, SLICED
- 14 OZ. ITALIAN SAUSAGE, CHOPPED
- BLACK PEPPER, TO TASTE
- 3 SMALL TOMATOES, PEELED, SEEDS REMOVED, AND SLICED
- 2½ OZ. PECORINO CHEESE, FRESHLY GRATED
- 10 OZ. FRESH MOZZARELLA CHEESE, TORN

PUDDICA SALENTINA

YIELD: 2 SMALL FOCACCIA / ACTIVE TIME: 30 MINUTES / TOTAL TIME: 4 HOURS

I n Salento, particularly in the city of Brindisi, Apulian focaccia is made without durum flour and with capers in place of olives as a topping.

1. If using active dry yeast, warm 3½ tablespoons of the water until it is about 105°F. Add the water and the yeast to a bowl and gently stir. Let the mixture sit until it is foamy, 5 to 10 minutes. Instant yeast does not need to be proofed.

2. In a large bowl, combine the flours, yeast, and water and work the mixture until it comes together as a dough. If kneading by hand, transfer the dough to a flour-dusted work surface. Work it until it is compact, smooth, and elastic.

3. Add the salt and work the dough until it is developed, elastic, and extensible, about 5 minutes. Form the dough into a ball and place it in an airtight container that has been coated with olive oil. Let the dough rest at room temperature until it has doubled in size, about 2 hours.

4. Generously coat two 10-inch cast-iron skillets or round cake pans with olive oil. Place the dough on a flour-dusted work surface and divide it in two. Place a piece of dough in each of the pans and spread them to the edges, making sure not to press down too hard and deflate the dough. Let the dough rest at room temperature for 1 hour.

5. Preheat the oven to its maximum temperature and position a rack in the middle. Top the focaccia with the capers, press the tomatoes into the dough, season with salt and oregano, and drizzle olive oil over the top. Place the pans directly on the bottom of the oven and bake for 10 minutes.

6. Transfer the pans to the middle rack and bake until the edges look brown and crunchy, 5 to 7 more minutes.

7. Remove them from the oven and let cool slightly before serving.

INGREDIENTS:

2   TEASPOONS ACTIVE DRY YEAST OR 1⅗ TEASPOONS INSTANT YEAST

14   OZ. WATER

14   OZ. BREAD FLOUR

7   OZ. ALL-PURPOSE FLOUR, PLUS MORE AS NEEDED

2½   TEASPOONS TABLE SALT, PLUS MORE TO TASTE

    EXTRA-VIRGIN OLIVE OIL, AS NEEDED

    CAPERS, DRAINED AND RINSED, TO TASTE

2   VERY RIPE TOMATOES, CHOPPED

    FRESH OREGANO, CHOPPED, TO TASTE

FOCACCIA BARESE

YIELD: 2 SMALL FOCACCIA / **ACTIVE TIME:** 30 MINUTES / **TOTAL TIME:** 4 HOURS

Bari is the birthplace of one of the most prototypical Italian focaccia, the barese. This is the most popular version—round and topped with fresh tomatoes and olives—but many variations can be found.

1. If using active dry yeast, warm 3½ tablespoons of the water until it is about 105°F. Add the water and the yeast to a bowl and gently stir. Let the mixture sit until it is foamy, 5 to 10 minutes. Instant yeast does not need to be proofed.

2. In a large bowl, combine the flours, potato, yeast, and water. Work the mixture until it comes together as a dough. If kneading by hand, transfer the dough to a flour-dusted work surface. Work it until it is compact, smooth, and elastic.

3. Add the salt and work the dough until it is developed, elastic, and extensible, about 5 minutes. Form the dough into a ball and place it in an airtight container that has been coated with olive oil. Let the dough rest at room temperature until it has doubled in size, about 2 hours.

4. Generously coat two 10-inch cast-iron skillets or round cake pans with olive oil. Place the dough on a flour-dusted work surface and divide it in two. Place the pieces of dough in the pans and spread them to the edge of each one, making sure not to press down too hard and deflate the focaccia. Let the dough rest in a warm spot for 1 hour.

5. Preheat the oven to its maximum temperature and position a rack in the middle. Top the focaccia with the tomatoes, olives, and oregano, season with salt, and drizzle olive oil over everything. Place the pans directly on the bottom of the oven and bake for 10 minutes.

6. Transfer the pans to the middle rack and bake until the edges look brown and crunchy, 5 to 7 more minutes.

7. Remove the focaccia from the oven and let them cool slightly before serving.

INGREDIENTS:

2	TEASPOONS ACTIVE DRY YEAST OR 1⅗ TEASPOONS INSTANT YEAST
14	OZ. WATER
14	OZ. BREAD FLOUR, PLUS MORE AS NEEDED
7	OZ. FINE SEMOLINA FLOUR
1	POTATO, BOILED, PEELED, AND MASHED
2½	TEASPOONS TABLE SALT, PLUS MORE TO TASTE
	EXTRA-VIRGIN OLIVE OIL, AS NEEDED
2	VERY RIPE TOMATOES, CHOPPED
	GREEN OLIVES, PITTED AND CHOPPED, TO TASTE
	FRESH OREGANO, CHOPPED, TO TASTE

PARIGINA

YIELD: 1 LARGE FOCACCIA / **ACTIVE TIME:** 20 MINUTES / **TOTAL TIME:** 3 HOURS AND 30 MINUTES

If you are walking the streets of Naples during the day you will probably stumble upon this beloved street food. Decadent and delicious, parigina typically features multiple layers of toppings, such as tomato sauce, ham, cheese, puff pastry, and heavy cream.

1. Coat an 18 x 13–inch baking sheet with olive oil, place the dough on it, and stretch it toward the edges of the pan, taking care not to tear it. Cover the dough with olive oil–coated plastic wrap and let it rest at room temperature for 2 hours. As the dough rests, stretch it toward the edges of the pan every 20 minutes until it covers the entire pan.

2. Preheat the oven to 390°F. Spread the tomatoes over the dough, making sure to leave a 1-inch border of dough at the edges. Season the tomatoes with salt. Cover with a layer of ham and top this with a layer of cheese. Cover the focaccia with the puff pastry, beat the egg yolks and cream together until combined, and brush the puff pastry with the egg wash.

3. Place the focaccia in the oven and bake until golden brown, 30 to 35 minutes.

4. Remove the focaccia from the oven and let it cool slightly before cutting into squares.

INGREDIENTS:

EXTRA-VIRGIN OLIVE OIL, AS NEEDED

24-HOUR FOCACCIA DOUGH (SEE PAGE 553)

23 OZ. CANNED WHOLE PEELED TOMATOES, DRAINED AND CRUSHED

SALT, TO TASTE

7 OZ. HAM, SLICED

14 OZ. CACIOCAVALLO CHEESE OR LOW-MOISTURE MOZZARELLA CHEESE, SLICED THIN

1 SHEET OF FROZEN PUFF PASTRY, THAWED

2 EGG YOLKS

¼ CUP HEAVY CREAM

FOCACCIA MESSINESE

YIELD: 1 LARGE FOCACCIA / **ACTIVE TIME:** 40 MINUTES / **TOTAL TIME:** 4 HOURS AND 30 MINUTES

This delicious focaccia reigns in Messina, where escarole is queen. If you're searching for some way to make salad look and taste amazing, look no further.

1. If using active dry yeast, warm 3½ tablespoons of the water until it is about 105°F. Add the water and the yeast to a bowl and gently stir. Let the mixture sit until it becomes foamy, 5 to 10 minutes. Instant yeast does not need to be proofed.

2. In a large bowl, combine the flours, olive oil, yeast, and water until the mixture comes together as a dough. If kneading by hand, transfer to a flour-dusted work surface. Work the dough until it is compact, smooth, and elastic.

3. Add the salt and work the dough until it is developed, elastic, and extensible, about 5 minutes. Form the dough into a ball and place it in an airtight container that has been coated with olive oil. Let it rest at room temperature until it has doubled in size, about 2 hours.

4. Coat an 18 x 13–inch baking sheet with olive oil, place the dough on it, and brush the dough with more olive oil. Cover the dough with a linen towel and let it rest for 30 minutes.

5. Gently stretch the dough until it covers the entire pan. Let it rest for another hour.

6. Preheat the oven to 390°F. Press the anchovies and the cubes of caciocavallo into the dough and top with the escarole and tomatoes. Season with the oregano, salt, and pepper and drizzle olive oil over the focaccia.

7. Place it in the oven and bake for 20 to 30 minutes, until golden brown and crispy on the edges and the bottom.

8. Remove the focaccia from the oven and let it cool slightly before serving.

INGREDIENTS:

2½	TEASPOONS ACTIVE DRY YEAST OR 2 TEASPOONS INSTANT YEAST
14.8	OZ. WATER
1	LB. BREAD FLOUR, PLUS MORE AS NEEDED
8.8	OZ. FINE SEMOLINA FLOUR
1	TABLESPOON PLUS 1 TEASPOON EXTRA-VIRGIN OLIVE OIL, PLUS MORE AS NEEDED
1	TABLESPOON TABLE SALT, PLUS MORE TO TASTE
12	ANCHOVIES IN OLIVE OIL, DRAINED AND TORN
21	OZ. CACIOCAVALLO CHEESE, CUBED
14	OZ. ESCAROLE, CHOPPED
3	TOMATOES, CHOPPED
	FRESH OREGANO, CHOPPED, TO TASTE
	BLACK PEPPER, TO TASTE

PIZZ'ONTA

YIELD: 12 SMALL FOCACCIA / **ACTIVE TIME:** 30 MINUTES / **TOTAL TIME:** 3 HOURS

In Abruzzi, it is very common to eat a fried crunchy focaccia called pizz'onta, or "greasy pizza." This focaccia is very easy to make at home, and it is out-of-this-world scrumptious, perfect beside cheese and cold cuts or grilled steak tips.

1. If using active dry yeast, warm 3½ tablespoons of the water until it is about 105°F. Add the water and yeast to a bowl and gently stir. Let the mixture sit until it is foamy, 5 to 10 minutes. Instant yeast does not need to be proofed.

2. In a large bowl, combine the flour, water, yeast, and sugar. Work the mixture until it just holds together. If kneading by hand, transfer the dough to a flour-dusted work surface. Work it until it is compact, smooth, and elastic.

3. Add the salt and olive oil and work the dough until it is developed, elastic, and extensible, about 5 minutes. Form the dough into a ball and place it in an airtight container that has been coated with olive oil. Let the dough rest at room temperature until it has doubled in size, about 2 hours.

4. Divide the dough into 12 pieces and form them into rounds, taking care not to overwork the dough. Cover the dough with a linen towel and let it rest for 30 minutes.

5. Add canola oil to a Dutch oven until it is approximately 2 inches deep and warm it to 350°F. Flatten the rounds and, working in batches, fry them until they are golden brown on both sides, about 4 minutes. Transfer the fried focaccia to a paper towel–lined plate to drain and season them with the salt before serving.

INGREDIENTS:

- 1¼ TEASPOONS ACTIVE DRY YEAST OR 1 TEASPOON INSTANT YEAST
- 8½ OZ. WATER
- 14 OZ. BREAD FLOUR, PLUS MORE AS NEEDED
- 2 TEASPOONS SUGAR
- 1 TEASPOON TABLE SALT, PLUS MORE TO TASTE
- 2 TABLESPOONS EXTRA-VIRGIN OLIVE OIL, PLUS MORE AS NEEDED

  CANOLA OIL, AS NEEDED

CRESCIA SFOGLIATA

YIELD: 6 SMALL FOCACCIA / **ACTIVE TIME:** 45 MINUTES / **TOTAL TIME:** 2 HOURS

As one would expect of the stylish city of Urbino in the Marche region, this focaccia is a luxurious take on the piadina. Crescia sfogliata is rumored to have been born during the Renaissance, specifically in the kitchen of the duke of Urbino. It is wonderful on its own but is at its best if accompanied by Italian soft cheeses, like crescenza or stracchino, and vegetables or cold cuts.

1. In a large bowl, combine the flour, water, lard, eggs, salt, and pepper and work the mixture until it just comes together as a dough. If kneading by hand, transfer the dough to a flour-dusted work surface. Work it until it is compact, smooth, and elastic.

2. Form the dough into a ball, cover it with plastic wrap, and let it rest at room temperature for 30 minutes.

3. Divide the dough into six pieces and form them into balls. Flatten each ball into a disk, brush it with lard, and roll it up as tightly as possible. Twist the dough into spirals, transfer to a parchment-lined baking sheet, and cover with plastic wrap. Refrigerate for 30 minutes to 1 hour.

4. Remove the spirals from the refrigerator and flatten them out into disks that are approximately ⅛ inch thick.

5. Warm a 10-inch skillet over medium heat. Working with one disk at a time, cook until dark spots appear all over, about 5 minutes per side.

6. Let the focaccia cool briefly before enjoying.

INGREDIENTS:

17⅔	OZ. ALL-PURPOSE FLOUR, PLUS MORE AS NEEDED
7	OZ. WATER
3½	OZ. LARD, PLUS MORE AS NEEDED
2	EGGS
1¾	TEASPOONS TABLE SALT
2	PINCHES OF BLACK PEPPER

FOCACCIA DI RECCO

YIELD: 1 MEDIUM FOCACCIA / **ACTIVE TIME:** 45 MINUTES / **TOTAL TIME:** 1 HOUR AND 20 MINUTES

A beloved focaccia from the town of Recco in Liguria. It is stuffed with fresh local cheeses, and the surprising contrast created by the thin, mildly flavored, crispy outside and the slightly sour melted cheese on the inside can raise goose bumps. The cheeses used in Recco, stracchino and crescenza, may be difficult to find outside of Italy, so feel free to use Taleggio in their place.

1. In a large bowl, combine the flour and salt. Add the water and work the mixture until it just comes together as a dough. If kneading by hand, transfer the dough to a flour-dusted work surface and knead it for at least 10 minutes. You want it to be very smooth and elastic. Form the dough into two balls, place them in an airtight container, and let them rest at room temperature for 30 minutes.

2. Grease a 13 x 9–inch baking pan with olive oil. Transfer one of the balls to a flour-dusted work surface and roll it into a rectangle that will fit in the pan. Stretch the dough with your hands until it is about ½5 inch thick, taking great care not to tear the dough.

3. Preheat the oven to the maximum temperature. With the help of a flat flour-dusted baking sheet or peel, transfer the rolled and stretched dough into the baking pan and cover with the cheese. Roll and stretch the other piece of dough to the same thickness and place it over the cheese. Trim away any excess dough with a sharp knife and crimp the edges of the focaccia to seal.

4. Make a few holes in different parts of the focaccia by pinching the surface with your fingers until it breaks.

5. Drizzle olive oil over the focaccia and season it with salt. Place on the top rack of the oven and bake until dark spots begin to appear on the surface, about 10 minutes.

6. Remove the focaccia from the oven and let it cool briefly before serving.

INGREDIENTS:

14	OZ. BREAD FLOUR, PLUS MORE AS NEEDED
½	TEASPOON (SCANT) TABLE SALT, PLUS MORE TO TASTE
7.8	OZ. WATER
	EXTRA-VIRGIN OLIVE OIL, AS NEEDED
28	OZ. STRACCHINO, CRESCENZA, OR TALEGGIO CHEESE, TORN

PISSALANDREA

YIELD: 1 SMALL FOCACCIA / **ACTIVE TIME:** 45 MINUTES / **TOTAL TIME:** 3 HOURS AND 30 MINUTES

Often referred to as the Ligurian take on Neapolitan pizza, this actually dates back to long before the famous pie became popular in Naples. While it does have tomato sauce, its spongy crust, olives, and anchovies put pissalandrea in a world all its own.

1. Coat a round, 10-inch cake pan with olive oil, place the dough in the pan, and flatten the dough slightly. Cover the dough with a kitchen towel and let it rest at room temperature for 1 hour.

2. Place the onion and the olive oil in a saucepan and cook, stirring frequently, over medium-high heat until the onion starts to soften, about 5 minutes. Add the tomatoes, salt, and oregano and simmer until the flavor is to your liking, about 30 minutes. Remove from heat and let the sauce cool completely.

3. Gently stretch the dough toward the edge of the pan. If the dough does not want to extend to the edge of the pan right away, let it rest for 15 to 20 minutes before trying again. When the dough is covering the pan, brush it with olive oil, cover with the linen towel, and let it rest until it looks completely risen, about 45 minutes.

4. Preheat the oven to 430°F. Spread the tomato sauce over the focaccia, taking care not to press down too hard on the dough and deflate it. Top with the anchovies, olives, garlic, and capers. Season with salt and drizzle olive oil over the focaccia.

5. Place the focaccia in the oven and bake until golden brown, 20 to 30 minutes.

6. Remove the focaccia from the oven and let it cool briefly before serving.

INGREDIENTS:

6   TABLESPOONS EXTRA-VIRGIN OLIVE OIL, PLUS MORE AS NEEDED

½   BATCH OF 24-HOUR FOCACCIA DOUGH (SEE PAGE 553)

1   ONION, SLICED THIN

21   OZ. CANNED WHOLE PEELED TOMATOES, CRUSHED, WITH THEIR LIQUID

¾   TEASPOON TABLE SALT, PLUS MORE TO TASTE

2   PINCHES OF DRIED OREGANO

2   ANCHOVIES IN OLIVE OIL, DRAINED AND CHOPPED

½   LB. BLACK OLIVES (TAGGIASCHE PREFERRED), PITTED

9   GARLIC CLOVES, UNPEELED

1   TABLESPOON CAPERS, DRAINED AND RINSED

FOCACCIA CON LE OLIVE

YIELD: 1 LARGE FOCACCIA / **ACTIVE TIME:** 20 MINUTES / **TOTAL TIME:** 3 HOURS AND 30 MINUTES

This is a typical Ligurian focaccia, but similar versions exist in other regions. You can use any type of olives, but Ligurian taggiasche olives are a great choice.

1. Place the dough on a flour-dusted work surface and form it into a loose ball, making sure not to press down too hard on the core of the dough and deflate it. Coat an 18 x 13–inch baking sheet with olive oil, place the dough on the pan, and gently flatten the dough into an oval. Cover the dough with a linen towel and let it rest at room temperature for 1 hour.

2. Stretch the dough toward the edges of the baking sheet. If the dough does not want to extend to the edges of the pan right away, let it rest for 15 to 20 minutes before trying again. Cover the dough with the linen towel and let it rest for another 30 minutes.

3. Add the olive oil, water, and salt to a mixing bowl and stir to combine. Cover the focaccia with half of the mixture and let it rest for another hour.

4. Preheat the oven to 445°F. Distribute the olives over the focaccia, pressing each of them into the dough until they don't bounce back. Brush the focaccia with the remaining olive oil mixture.

5. Place the focaccia in the oven and bake until it is golden brown, about 15 minutes. Remove the focaccia from the oven and let it cool briefly before serving.

INGREDIENTS:

24-HOUR FOCACCIA DOUGH (SEE PAGE 553)

ALL-PURPOSE FLOUR, AS NEEDED

3½ TABLESPOONS OLIVE OIL, PLUS MORE AS NEEDED

5⅓ OZ. WATER

1 TEASPOON TABLE SALT

10 OZ. GREEN OLIVES, PITTED

FORMING A PIZZA ROUND

There are several ways to create a tight "skin" around the ball of dough, so that it will better retain gases from fermentation even when pressed to form the pizza disk.

One way is to pull all of the sides of a piece of dough toward the bottom of the dough, pinching them together.

Alternatively, the piece of dough can be slightly flattened and folded in on itself from different angles a few times until it looks like a ball.

Either way, the final step is to roll the resulting ball over an unfloured counter, cupping your hand over the ball and moving it in a circular motion, counterclockwise.

NEAPOLITAN PIZZA DOUGH

YIELD: 4 BALLS OF DOUGH / **ACTIVE TIME:** 30 MINUTES / **TOTAL TIME:** 8 TO 12 HOURS

The dough that eventually took over the culinary world.

1. If using active dry yeast, warm 3½ tablespoons of the water until it is about 105°F. Add the water and the yeast to a bowl and gently stir. Let the mixture sit until it is foamy, 5 to 10 minutes.

2. In a large bowl, combine the flour, yeast, and water. Work the mixture until it just comes together as a dough. Transfer it to a flour-dusted work surface and knead the dough until it is compact, smooth, and elastic.

3. Add the salt and knead until the dough is developed and elastic, meaning it pulls back energetically when pulled. Transfer the dough to an airtight container, cover it, and let it rest for 2 to 3 hours at room temperature. For a classic Neapolitan dough, room temperature should be 77°F. If your kitchen is colder, let the dough rest longer before shaping it into rounds.

4. Divide the dough into four pieces and shape them into very tight rounds, as it is important to create tension in the outer layer of dough. Place the rounds in a baking dish with high edges, leaving enough space between rounds that they won't touch when fully risen. Cover with a kitchen towel and let rest for 6 to 8 hours, depending on the temperature in the room, before using it to make pizza.

INGREDIENTS:

- ⅛ TEASPOON PLUS 1 PINCH ACTIVE DRY YEAST OR ⅛ TEASPOON INSTANT YEAST

- 14.8 OZ. WATER

- 23.9 OZ. BREAD FLOUR, PLUS MORE AS NEEDED

- 1 TABLESPOON TABLE SALT

MARGHERITA

YIELD: 1 PIZZA / ACTIVE TIME: 15 MINUTES / TOTAL TIME: 45 MINUTES

For most, both in Italy and abroad, this is the true original Neapolitan pizza: gooey mozzarella and a tomato sauce base.

1. Preheat the oven to the maximum temperature and place a baking stone or steel on the bottom of the oven as it warms. Dust a work surface with semolina flour, place the dough on the surface, and gently stretch it into a round. Cover the dough with the sauce and top with the mozzarella and basil leaves.

2. Season the pizza with salt and drizzle olive oil over the top.

3. Dust a peel or a flat baking sheet with semolina flour and use it to transfer the pizza to the heated baking implement in the oven. Bake for about 15 minutes, until the crust is golden brown and starting to char. Remove and let cool slightly before slicing and serving.

PIZZA SAUCE

1. Place the tomatoes and their juices in a bowl, add the olive oil, and stir until it has been thoroughly incorporated.

2. Season the sauce with salt and oregano and stir to incorporate. If using within 2 hours, leave the sauce at room temperature. If storing in the refrigerator, where the sauce will keep for up to 3 days, return to room temperature before using.

INGREDIENTS:

SEMOLINA FLOUR, AS NEEDED

1   BALL OF PIZZA DOUGH

⅓   CUP PIZZA SAUCE (SEE RECIPE)

4   OZ. FRESH MOZZARELLA CHEESE, DRAINED AND CUT INTO SHORT STRIPS

FRESH BASIL LEAVES, TO TASTE

SALT, TO TASTE

EXTRA-VIRGIN OLIVE OIL, TO TASTE

PIZZA SAUCE

1   LB. PEELED, WHOLE SAN MARZANO TOMATOES, WITH THEIR LIQUID, CRUSHED BY HAND

1½   TABLESPOONS EXTRA-VIRGIN OLIVE OIL

SALT, TO TASTE

DRIED OREGANO, TO TASTE

Pizza Marinara, see page 586

PIZZA MARINARA

YIELD: 1 PIZZA / **ACTIVE TIME:** 15 MINUTES / **TOTAL TIME:** 45 MINUTES

According to the European Union, there are only two authentic Neapolitan pizzas that deserve the TSG (Traditional Speciality Guaranteed) appellation: this and the margherita. Pizza marinara is possibly the oldest variety of Neapolitan pizza still popular today, and it is surprising in its simplicity. The key to making a good version at home is to use top-notch ingredients, as that is the only way to do justice to this simple topping.

1. Preheat the oven to the maximum temperature and place a baking stone or steel on the bottom of the oven as it warms. Dust a work surface with the semolina flour, place the dough on the surface, and gently stretch it into a round. Cover the dough with the sauce and top with the garlic.

2. Season the pizza with salt and dried oregano and drizzle olive oil over the top.

3. Dust a peel or a flat baking sheet with semolina flour and use it to transfer the pizza to the heated baking implement in the oven. Bake for about 15 minutes, until the crust is golden brown and starting to char. Remove and let cool slightly before slicing and serving.

INGREDIENTS:

SEMOLINA FLOUR, AS NEEDED

1 BALL OF PIZZA DOUGH

⅓ CUP PIZZA SAUCE (SEE PAGE 582)

1 GARLIC CLOVE, SLICED THIN

SALT, TO TASTE

DRIED OREGANO, TO TASTE

EXTRA-VIRGIN OLIVE OIL, TO TASTE

ROMANA

YIELD: 1 PIZZA / **ACTIVE TIME:** 15 MINUTES / **TOTAL TIME:** 45 MINUTES

There are two different versions of this pizza: with or without mozzarella. It also has two names: it is Romana to the Neapolitans, who created the topping, and Napoli for everyone else. Whatnever changes in this pizza is the presence of tomato sauce, anchovies, capers, and oregano.

1. Preheat the oven to the maximum temperature and place a baking stone or steel on the bottom of the oven as it warms. Dust a work surface with semolina flour, place the dough on the surface, and gently stretch it into a round. Cover the dough with the sauce and top with the mozzarella, anchovies, and capers.

2. Season the pizza with salt and oregano and drizzle olive oil over the top.

3. Dust a peel or a flat baking sheet with semolina flour and use it to transfer the pizza to the heated baking implement in the oven. Bake for about 15 minutes, until the crust is golden brown and starting to char. Remove and let cool slightly before slicing and serving.

INGREDIENTS:

	SEMOLINA FLOUR, AS NEEDED
1	BALL OF PIZZA DOUGH
⅓	CUP PIZZA SAUCE (SEE PAGE 582)
2½	OZ. FRESH MOZZARELLA CHEESE, DRAINED AND CUT INTO SHORT STRIPS
4–5	ANCHOVIES IN OLIVE OIL, DRAINED AND CHOPPED
1	TABLESPOON CAPERS, DRAINED AND RINSED
	SALT, TO TASTE
	DRIED OREGANO, TO TASTE
	EXTRA-VIRGIN OLIVE OIL, TO TASTE

Romana, see page 587

PHYLLO DOUGH PIZZA

YIELD: 4 TO 6 SERVINGS / **ACTIVE TIME:** 30 MINUTES / **TOTAL TIME:** 1 HOUR AND 30 MINUTES

By putting a traditional Margherita pizza on a phyllo dough base, you get it all—comfort, and the ability to remove yourself from the couch afterward.

1. To begin preparations for the sauce, place the olive oil in a medium saucepan and warm it over medium heat. Add the tomatoes and cook, stirring occasionally, for 5 minutes

2. Add the garlic, oregano, anchovy, and red pepper flakes and bring the sauce to a boil. Reduce the heat and simmer the sauce for 10 minutes, using a wooden spoon to mash the tomatoes as they cook.

3. Remove the pan from heat and let the sauce cool for 5 minutes.

4. Place the sauce in a food processor and pulse until it is chunky. Add the Parmesan and pulse until incorporated. Season the sauce with salt and pepper and set it aside.

5. Preheat the oven to 400°F. Line two baking sheets with parchment paper. To begin preparations for the pizza, place a piece of parchment paper on a work surface and put one sheet of phyllo in the center of the parchment. Brush the phyllo with some of the olive oil, top with another sheet of phyllo, and brush it with olive oil. Repeat until you have a layer of five sheets. Sprinkle 1 teaspoon of the dried oregano on top of the layer and repeat until you have another teaspoon of oregano sandwiched between two 5-sheet layers of phyllo. Make sure you keep the phyllo you are not working with covered so that it does not dry out.

6. Repeat Step 5 until you have another crust made of phyllo.

7. Spread the sauce over the crusts and distribute the mozzarellas and basil over the pizzas. Place a pizza on each baking sheet and place them in the oven. Bake until the crust is golden brown and the cheeses have melted, about 12 minutes.

8. Remove the pizzas from the oven and let them cool slightly before serving.

INGREDIENTS:

FOR THE SAUCE

- 2 TABLESPOONS EXTRA-VIRGIN OLIVE OIL
- 1 (28 OZ.) CAN OF WHOLE PEELED SAN MARZANO TOMATOES, WITH THEIR LIQUID
- 6 GARLIC CLOVES
- 1 TEASPOON CHOPPED FRESH OREGANO
- 1 ANCHOVY IN OLIVE OIL, DRAINED AND FINELY CHOPPED
- 1 TEASPOON RED PEPPER FLAKES
- ¼ CUP FRESHLY GRATED PARMESAN CHEESE
- SALT AND PEPPER, TO TASTE

FOR THE PIZZA

- ½ LB. FROZEN PHYLLO DOUGH, THAWED
- ½ CUP EXTRA-VIRGIN OLIVE OIL
- 4 TEASPOONS DRIED OREGANO
- ½ LB. FRESH MOZZARELLA CHEESE, DRAINED AND SLICED
- ½ CUP SHREDDED LOW-MOISTURE MOZZARELLA CHEESE
- ½ CUP FRESH BASIL LEAVES

DIAVOLA

A "devilish" pie that becomes more and more tempting as the spice level rises.

1. Preheat the oven to the maximum temperature and place a baking stone or steel on the bottom of the oven as it warms. Combine the olive oil and red pepper flakes in a small bowl and set the mixture aside.

2. Dust a work surface with the semolina flour, place the dough on the surface, and gently stretch it into a round. Cover the dough with the sauce and top with the cheese and salami. Drizzle the spicy olive oil over the top and season with salt and oregano.

3. Dust a peel or a flat baking sheet with semolina flour and use it to transfer the pizza to the heated baking implement in the oven. Bake for about 15 minutes, until the crust is golden brown and starting to char. Remove and let cool slightly before slicing and serving.

INGREDIENTS:

2	TABLESPOONS EXTRA-VIRGIN OLIVE OIL, PLUS MORE TO TASTE
	RED PEPPER FLAKES, TO TASTE
	SEMOLINA FLOUR, AS NEEDED
1	BALL OF PIZZA DOUGH
1/3	CUP PIZZA SAUCE (SEE PAGE 582)
2½	OZ. CACIOCAVALLO OR PROVOLA CHEESE, CUBED
5	SLICES OF SPICY SALAMI
	SALT, TO TASTE
	DRIED OREGANO, TO TASTE

BOSCAIOLA

YIELD: 1 PIZZA / ACTIVE TIME: 25 MINUTES / TOTAL TIME: 55 MINUTES

Boscaiola means "from the woods" in Italian, referring to mushrooms and game. Here, the game component is just humble sausage, but the pizza retains its earthy and substantial promise.

1. Preheat the oven to the maximum temperature and place a baking stone or steel on the bottom of the oven as it warms. Coat the bottom of a skillet with olive oil and warm it over medium-high heat. When the oil starts to shimmer, add the sausage and cook until it is browned, about 8 minutes. Remove from heat and set aside.

2. Dust a work surface with the semolina flour, place the dough on the surface, and gently stretch it into a round. Cover the dough with the sauce and top with the mushrooms and sausage.

3. Season the pizza with salt and drizzle olive oil over the top.

4. Dust a peel or a flat baking sheet with semolina flour and use it to transfer the pizza to the heated baking implement in the oven. Bake for about 5 minutes, until the crust starts to brown. Remove the pizza, distribute the mozzarella over the top, and return the pizza to the oven. Bake for about 10 minutes, until the crust is golden brown and starting to char. Remove and let cool slightly before slicing and serving.

INGREDIENTS:

EXTRA-VIRGIN OLIVE OIL, TO TASTE

1   LINK OF ITALIAN SAUSAGE, CHOPPED

SEMOLINA FLOUR, AS NEEDED

1   BALL OF PIZZA DOUGH

⅓   CUP PIZZA SAUCE (SEE PAGE 582)

½   CUP MUSHROOMS

SALT, TO TASTE

3   OZ. FRESH MOZZARELLA CHEESE, DRAINED AND CUT INTO SHORT STRIPS

CARRETTIERA

YIELD: 1 PIZZA / ACTIVE TIME: 25 MINUTES / TOTAL TIME: 1 HOUR

The name refers to a sandwich filling popular with the Neapolitan carrettieri, who spent the day pushing around goods in a wooden trolley. Substantial and extremely tasty, this is a must, assuming one can get hold of broccoli rabe.

1. Coat the bottom of a skillet with olive oil and warm it over medium-high heat. When the oil starts to shimmer, add the garlic and broccoli rabe and cook, stirring frequently, until the broccoli rabe has softened, about 8 minutes. Season with salt and pepper, add the sausage, and cook until the sausage is browned, about 8 minutes. Remove from heat and let cool.

2. Dust a work surface with the semolina flour, place the dough on the surface, and gently stretch it into a round. Spread the sautéed broccoli rabe and sausage over the pizza and top with the mozzarella. Drizzle olive oil over the pizza.

3. Dust a peel or a flat baking sheet with semolina flour and use it to transfer the pizza to the heated baking implement in the oven. Bake for about 15 minutes, until the crust is golden brown and starting to char. Remove and let cool slightly before slicing and serving.

INGREDIENTS:

	EXTRA-VIRGIN OLIVE OIL, AS NEEDED
½	GARLIC CLOVE, MINCED
5	OZ. BROCCOLI RABE, TRIMMED
	SALT AND PEPPER, TO TASTE
1	LINK OF ITALIAN SAUSAGE, CHOPPED
	SEMOLINA FLOUR, AS NEEDED
1	BALL OF PIZZA DOUGH
3	OZ. FRESH MOZZARELLA CHEESE, DRAINED AND CUT INTO SHORT STRIPS

QUATTRO FORMAGGI

YIELD: 1 PIZZA / ACTIVE TIME: 15 MINUTES / TOTAL TIME: 45 MINUTES

As you might expect, this pizza is exceptionally gooey, and nothing short of miraculous for cheese lovers.

1. Preheat the oven to the maximum temperature and place a baking stone or steel in the oven as it warms. Dust a work surface with the semolina flour, place the dough on the surface, and gently stretch it into a round. Distribute the cheeses over the dough.

2. Season the pizza with salt and pepper and drizzle olive oil over the top.

3. Dust a peel or a flat baking sheet with semolina flour and use it to transfer the pizza to the heated baking implement in the oven. Bake for about 15 minutes, until the crust is golden brown and starting to char. Remove and let cool slightly before slicing and serving.

INGREDIENTS:

SEMOLINA FLOUR, AS NEEDED

1 BALL OF PIZZA DOUGH

2 OZ. FRESH MOZZARELLA CHEESE, DRAINED AND CUT INTO SHORT STRIPS

2 OZ. FONTINA OR PROVOLONE CHEESE, GRATED

2 OZ. GORGONZOLA CHEESE, CRUMBLED

2 OZ. PECORINO OR PARMESAN CHEESE, GRATED

SALT AND PEPPER, TO TASTE

EXTRA-VIRGIN OLIVE OIL, TO TASTE

Pescatora, see page 600

PESCATORA

YIELD: 1 PIZZA / **ACTIVE TIME**: 25 MINUTES / **TOTAL TIME**: 1 HOUR

This variation on the margherita pizza was inspired by the classic caprese salad. A perfect pie for a hot summer night.

1. Preheat the oven to the maximum temperature and place a baking stone or steel on the bottom of the oven as it warms. Coat the bottom of a skillet with olive oil and warm it over medium-high heat. When the oil starts to shimmer, add all of the seafood and the garlic. Season with salt and red pepper flakes and cook until most of the mussels have opened and the rest of the seafood is just cooked through, about 4 minutes. Remove from heat, discard any mussels that did not open, and remove the meat from those that have opened.

2. Dust a work surface with the semolina flour, place the dough on the surface, and gently stretch it into a round. Cover the dough with the sauce and season with oregano and pepper.

3. Dust a peel or a flat baking sheet with semolina flour and use it to transfer the pizza to the heated baking implement in the oven. Bake for about 5 minutes, until the crust starts to brown. Remove the pizza, distribute the seafood over it, drizzle olive oil on top, and return the pizza to the oven. Bake for about 10 minutes, until the crust is golden brown and starting to char. Remove and let cool slightly before garnishing with the parsley, slicing, and serving.

INGREDIENTS:

	EXTRA-VIRGIN OLIVE OIL, AS NEEDED
5	LARGE SHRIMP, SHELLED AND DEVEINED
	HANDFUL OF SQUID RINGS
6	MUSSELS, DEBEARDED AND RINSED WELL
	HANDFUL OF BABY OCTOPUS
½	GARLIC CLOVE, MINCED
	SALT AND PEPPER, TO TASTE
	RED PEPPER FLAKES, TO TASTE
	SEMOLINA FLOUR, AS NEEDED
1	BALL OF PIZZA DOUGH
½	CUP PIZZA SAUCE (SEE PAGE 582)
	DRIED OREGANO, TO TASTE
	FRESH PARSLEY, FOR GARNISH

CAPRESE

YIELD: 1 PIZZA / ACTIVE TIME: 15 MINUTES / TOTAL TIME: 45 MINUTES

This variation on the Margherita pizza was inspired by the classic caprese salad. A perfect pie for a hot summer night.

1. Preheat the oven to the maximum temperature and place a baking stone or steel on the bottom of the oven as it warms. Dust a work surface with the semolina flour, place the dough on the surface, and gently stretch it into a round. Cover the dough with the sauce and top with the mozzarella and tomato.

2. Season the pizza with salt, pepper, and oregano and drizzle olive oil over the top.

3. Dust a peel or a flat baking sheet with semolina flour and use it to transfer the pizza to the heated baking implement in the oven. Bake for about 15 minutes, until the crust is golden brown and starting to char. Remove and let cool slightly before garnishing with the basil, slicing, and serving.

INGREDIENTS:

SEMOLINA FLOUR, AS NEEDED

1 BALL OF PIZZA DOUGH

⅓ CUP PIZZA SAUCE (SEE PAGE 582)

4½ OZ. FRESH MOZZARELLA CHEESE, DRAINED AND SLICED

1 TOMATO, SLICED

SALT AND PEPPER, TO TASTE

DRIED OREGANO, TO TASTE

EXTRA-VIRGIN OLIVE OIL, TO TASTE

FRESH BASIL LEAVES, FOR GARNISH

DESSERTS

As with the previous chapter, the health and wellness industry's appropriation of the concept of Mediterranean cuisine tends to make people think there's not all that much going on in terms of sweets in the region. And, once again, those assumptions carry folks astray. First off, there's baklava, which stands beside pizza and fried chicken as the rare item that there is no bad version of, only varying levels of great. Second, the exceptional produce in the area (figs, lemons, honey, to name a few) leads to a predilection for confections that can satisfy without leading one awry in their quest to live a healthier life.

BAKLAVA

YIELD: 30 PIECES / **ACTIVE TIME:** 30 MINUTES / **TOTAL TIME:** 1 HOUR AND 30 MINUTES

Much like pizza and fried chicken, there is no such thing as bad baklava. There are only varying degrees of great.

1. Place 1 cup of the sugar, the water, honey, cinnamon stick, whole cloves, and half of the sea salt in a saucepan and bring the mixture to a boil, stirring to dissolve the sugar and salt. Reduce the heat and simmer until the mixture is syrupy, about 5 minutes. Remove the pan from heat and let the syrup cool. When it is cool, strain the syrup and set it aside.

2. Place the almonds in a food processor and pulse until they are finely chopped. Place the almonds in a bowl, add the walnuts to the food processor, and pulse and they are finely chopped. Add them to the bowl along with the cinnamon, ground cloves, and remaining sugar and salt and stir until combined. Set the mixture aside.

3. Preheat the oven to 300°F. Line a 10 x 8–inch baking pan with parchment paper. Place one sheet of phyllo in the pan and keep the remaining phyllo covered so that it does not dry out. Brush the sheet with some of the melted butter and place another sheet of phyllo on top. Brush the sheet with butter and repeat four more times, so that you have a layer of six buttered phyllo sheets.

4. Spread 1 cup of the nut mixture over the layer of phyllo. Top this with another layer of six buttered phyllo sheets, spread another cup of the nut mixture over it, and repeat.

5. Top the baklava with another layer of six buttered phyllo sheets. Using a serrated knife, cut the baklava into diamonds, making sure not to cut all the way through the bottom layer. Place the baklava in oven and bake until it is golden brown, about 45 minutes, rotating the pan halfway through.

6. Remove the baklava from the oven and pour the syrup over it. Let the baklava cool completely, cut it all the way through, and enjoy.

INGREDIENTS:

1	CUP PLUS 2 TABLESPOONS SUGAR
¾	CUP WATER
½	CUP HONEY
1	CINNAMON STICK
5	WHOLE CLOVES
¼	TEASPOON FINE SEA SALT
1½	CUPS SLIVERED ALMONDS
1½	CUPS WALNUTS
1	TEASPOON CINNAMON
¼	TEASPOON GROUND CLOVES
1	LB. FROZEN PHYLLO DOUGH, THAWED
1	CUP UNSALTED BUTTER, MELTED

LEMON POPPY SEED CAKE

YIELD: 1 CAKE / **ACTIVE TIME:** 30 MINUTES / **TOTAL TIME:** 24 HOURS

S oaking the poppy seeds in yogurt softens their tough outer layer, so their unique flavoring compounds can be better expressed in the cake.

1. Place the poppy seeds and yogurt in a small bowl and stir to combine. Place the mixture in the refrigerator and let it chill overnight.

2. Preheat the oven to 350°F. Coat a 6-quart Bundt pan with nonstick cooking spray and sprinkle some flour over it, knocking out any excess flour. Sift the flour, baking powder, and salt into a small bowl and set the mixture aside.

3. Place the sugar, eggs, and olive oil in the work bowl of a stand mixer fitted with the whisk attachment and whip the mixture until it is pale yellow, frothy, and comes off a rubber spatula in ribbons, about 5 minutes, scraping down the work bowl as necessary.

4. Add the poppy seed yogurt and whip until it has been incorporated. Add the dry mixture and gently fold until incorporated. Add the lemon zest and lemon juice and stir until incorporated.

5. Pour the batter into the Bundt pan, place it in the oven, and bake until a toothpick inserted into the cake's center comes out clean, about 40 minutes, rotating the pan halfway through.

6. Remove the cake from the oven and let it cool completely.

7. Invert the cake onto a platter. Pour the glaze over the cake, let it set for a few minutes, and sprinkle additional poppy seeds over the top.

LEMON GLAZE

1. Place all of the ingredients in a mixing bowl and whisk to combine.

INGREDIENTS:

- ⅔   CUP POPPY SEEDS, PLUS MORE FOR GARNISH
- 1   CUP FULL-FAT GREEK YOGURT
- 3   CUPS ALL-PURPOSE FLOUR, PLUS MORE AS NEEDED
- 1   TABLESPOON BAKING POWDER
- 1½   TEASPOONS FINE SEA SALT
- 1⅓   CUPS SUGAR
- 5   EGGS
- 1   CUP EXTRA-VIRGIN OLIVE OIL

  ZEST AND JUICE OF 2 LEMONS

  LEMON GLAZE (SEE RECIPE)

LEMON GLAZE

- 3   TABLESPOONS FRESH LEMON JUICE
- 2   TABLESPOONS FULL-FAT GREEK YOGURT
- 2   CUPS CONFECTIONERS' SUGAR

  SEEDS OF ½ VANILLA BEAN

FIG, ORANGE & ANISE HONEY BALLS

YIELD: 20 BALLS / ACTIVE TIME: 30 MINUTES / TOTAL TIME: 2 HOURS

Kataifi, a finely shredded pastry with a texture similar to phyllo dough, provides these luxurious, fig-enriched morsels with a lovely, light crunch.

1. Place ⅓ cup of the sugar, 2 tablespoons of the water, the honey, orange zest, orange juice, and vanilla seeds in a small saucepan and bring the mixture to a boil, stirring to dissolve the sugar. Reduce the heat and simmer the mixture until it is syrupy, about 5 minutes. Remove the pan from heat, let the syrup cool, and strain it. Set the syrup aside.

2. Line a baking sheet with parchment paper. Place the figs, fennel seeds, and remaining sugar and water in a saucepan and bring the mixture to a boil, stirring to dissolve the sugar. Reduce the heat and simmer the mixture until the liquid is syrupy, about 10 minutes. Remove the pan from heat and let it cool.

3. Place the cooled fig mixture in a food processor and puree until it is a paste, scraping down the sides of the work bowl frequently. Add the walnuts and Pernod and pulse until combined.

4. Form tablespoons of the mixture into balls and place them on the baking sheet. You should have about 20 balls. Place them in the refrigerator and chill for 30 minutes.

5. Preheat the oven to 350°F. Place the kataifi in a mixing bowl, slowly drizzle in the olive oil, and gently fold until the kataifi is evenly coated.

6. Grab a small amount of the kataifi and wrap it around one of the balls. Place the ball back on the baking sheet and repeat until all of the balls have been wrapped in kataifi.

7. Place the baking sheet in the oven and cook until the kataifi is golden brown, about 10 minutes, rotating the pan halfway through.

8. Remove the balls from the oven and let them cool.

9. Pour ½ tablespoon of the syrup over each ball and enjoy.

INGREDIENTS:

½	CUP PLUS ⅓ CUP SUGAR
1	CUP PLUS 2 TABLESPOONS WATER
2	TABLESPOONS HONEY
	ZEST AND JUICE OF 1 ORANGE
	SEEDS OF ½ VANILLA BEAN
2	CUPS DRIED FIGS
½	TEASPOON FENNEL SEEDS
1	CUP WALNUTS, TOASTED AND CHOPPED
1	TABLESPOON PERNOD
½	LB. FROZEN KATAIFI, THAWED
¼	CUP EXTRA-VIRGIN OLIVE OIL

ZEPPOLE WITH LEMON CURD

YIELD: 4 SERVINGS / ACTIVE TIME: 30 MINUTES / TOTAL TIME: 2 HOURS

If so inclined, fill the zeppole with the Meyer Lemon Curd. To do this, poke a hole in the zeppole once they have cooled, place the Meyer Lemon Curd in a piping bag, insert the tip into the hole, and squeeze the desired amount into the zeppole.

1. Sift the flour, baking powder, and salt into a bowl. Set the mixture aside.

2. Place the eggs and sugar in a separate bowl and whisk to combine. Add the ricotta, whisk to incorporate, and then stir in the orange zest, milk, and vanilla.

3. Gradually incorporate the dry mixture into the wet mixture until it comes together as a smooth batter. Place the batter in the refrigerator and chill for 1 hour.

4. Add canola oil to a Dutch oven until it is about 2 inches deep and warm it to 350°F. Drop tablespoons of the batter into the hot oil, taking care not to crowd the pot, and fry until the zeppole are golden brown. Transfer the fried zeppole to a paper towel–lined plate and dust them with confectioners' sugar.

5. To serve, spread some Meyer Lemon Curd on each serving plate and top with 2 or 3 zeppole.

INGREDIENTS:

1½	CUPS ALL-PURPOSE FLOUR
1	TABLESPOON PLUS 1 TEASPOON BAKING POWDER
¼	TEASPOON FINE SEA SALT
2	TABLESPOONS SUGAR
2	EGGS
2	CUPS RICOTTA CHEESE
	ZEST OF 1 ORANGE
1	CUP MILK
1	TEASPOON PURE VANILLA EXTRACT
	CANOLA OIL, AS NEEDED
¼	CUP CONFECTIONERS' SUGAR
	MEYER LEMON CURD (SEE PAGE 614)

MEYER LEMON CURD

YIELD: 3 CUPS / **ACTIVE TIME:** 25 MINUTES / **TOTAL TIME:** 2 HOURS

The floral quality present in the Meyer lemon makes this recipe an easy but unique take on the sumptuous classic.

1. Fill a small saucepan halfway with water and bring it to a gentle simmer.

2. Place the lemon juice in a small saucepan and warm it over low heat.

3. Combine the eggs, sugar, salt, and vanilla in a metal mixing bowl. Place the bowl over the simmering water and whisk the mixture continually until it is 135°F on an instant-read thermometer.

4. When the lemon juice comes to a simmer, gradually add it to the egg mixture while whisking constantly.

5. When all of the lemon juice has been incorporated, whisk the curd until it has thickened and is 155°F. Remove the bowl from heat, add the butter, and stir until thoroughly incorporated.

6. Transfer the curd to a mason jar and let it cool. Once cool, store the curd in the refrigerator, where it will keep for up to 2 weeks.

INGREDIENTS:

- ¾ CUP FRESH MEYER LEMON JUICE
- 4 EGGS
- ¾ CUP SUGAR
- ⅛ TEASPOON KOSHER SALT
- ¼ TEASPOON PURE VANILLA EXTRACT
- 4 OZ. UNSALTED BUTTER, SOFTENED

PASTELI

YIELD: 20 BARS / **ACTIVE TIME:** 20 MINUTES / **TOTAL TIME:** 1 HOUR

These bars are traditionally made with just two ingredients—sesame seeds and honey—but a bit of salt and vanilla brings out the best in both.

1. Preheat the oven to 350°F. Line a square 8-inch baking pan with parchment paper. Place the sesame seeds on a baking sheet, place them in the oven, and toast until golden brown, about 5 minutes. Remove from the oven and let the sesame seeds cool.

2. Place the honey in a small saucepan and warm it over medium-high heat. Boil the honey until it reaches 310°F.

3. Remove the pan from heat, stir in the salt, vanilla, and toasted sesame seeds, and pour the mixture into the baking pan. Let the mixture cool for 15 minutes.

4. Cut the bars into the desired shape and size; they should still be warm. Enjoy immediately or at room temperature.

INGREDIENTS:

2 CUPS SESAME SEEDS

1 CUP HONEY

½ TEASPOON KOSHER SALT

1 TEASPOON PURE VANILLA EXTRACT

POACHED PEARS WITH CANDIED HAZELNUTS, PALMIERS & CONDENSED CARAMEL

YIELD: 8 SERVINGS / ACTIVE TIME: 20 MINUTES / TOTAL TIME: 45 MINUTES

These poached pears are wonderful by themselves. When paired with a number of other simple preparations, they become sublime.

1. Place the wine, vanilla seeds, sugar, lemon zest, lemon juice, cinnamon stick, star anise, and salt in a medium saucepan and bring the mixture to a boil.

2. Peel the pears and halve them. Add the pears to the poaching liquid—make sure they are submerged so that they don't oxidize and turn brown.

3. Reduce the heat and simmer the pears until extremely tender—a toothpick should easily slip in and out of them—about 30 minutes.

4. Remove the pears from the pan and let them cool.

5. When the pears are cool, use a spoon to scoop out the seeds and cores.

6. Spread some of the Condensed Caramel over each serving dish. Arrange the pears, Palmiers, and Candied Hazelnuts in the dishes, add a dollop of the Crème Chantilly, and enjoy.

INGREDIENTS:

1	(750 ML) BOTTLE OF WHITE WINE
	SEEDS OF 1 VANILLA BEAN
⅔	CUP SUGAR
	ZEST AND JUICE OF 1 LEMON
1	CINNAMON STICK
1	STAR ANISE POD
	PINCH OF KOSHER SALT
4	PEARS
	CONDENSED CARAMEL (SEE PAGE 647)
	PALMIERS (SEE PAGE 641)
	CANDIED HAZELNUTS (SEE PAGE 658)
	CRÈME CHANTILLY (SEE PAGE 655)

YOGURT MOUSSE WITH
BLUEBERRY COMPOTE & GRANOLA

YIELD: 4 SERVINGS / **ACTIVE TIME:** 40 MINUTES / **TOTAL TIME:** 1 HOUR

This combination of flavors would typically be part of a breakfast spread, but by refining the elements just a bit, they combine to make a luxurious dessert.

1. Place the sheets of gelatin in a bowl, cover them with cold water, and let them sit.

2. Place the lemon juice, sugar, and vanilla seeds and pod in a saucepan and bring to a simmer. Remove the pan from heat.

3. Remove the sheets of gelatin from the water and squeeze them to remove excess moisture. Add them to the warm syrup and stir until they have dissolved.

4. Strain the gelatin into a bowl and let it cool until it is just slightly warm.

5. Place the cream in the work bowl of a stand mixer fitted with the whisk attachment and whip until it holds soft peaks. Set the whipped cream aside.

6. Add the yogurt to the gelatin and gently fold to combine. Add the whipped cream and fold to combine.

7. To serve, spoon the mousse into a serving dish and top each portion with some of the compote and Granola.

INGREDIENTS:

2	SHEETS OF GELATIN
2	TABLESPOONS FRESH LEMON JUICE
⅓	CUP SUGAR
	SEEDS AND POD OF ½ VANILLA BEAN
1	CUP HEAVY CREAM
1	CUP FULL-FAT GREEK YOGURT
	BLUEBERRY COMPOTE (SEE PAGE 675)
	GRANOLA (SEE PAGE 663)

PIGNOLI

YIELD: 12 COOKIES / **ACTIVE TIME:** 15 MINUTES / **TOTAL TIME:** 1 HOUR

Make sure you are using unsweetened almond paste here instead of marzipan, as the latter will make the cookies too sweet, and keep them from rising properly.

1. Preheat the oven to 325°F. Line a baking sheet with parchment paper. Place the almond paste and sugar in a food processor and blitz until the mixture is smooth. Add the ½ cup of confectioners' sugar and 1 of the egg whites and blitz until smooth.

2. Place the remaining egg white in a mixing bowl and whisk it until it is fluffy.

3. Separate the almond paste mixture into 12 balls. Dip the balls into the whipped egg white and place them on the baking sheet. Press some pine nuts into each ball and then press down to flatten the cookies slightly.

4. Place the cookies in the oven and bake until golden brown, 12 to 15 minutes.

5. Remove the cookies from the oven, transfer them to a wire rack, and let them cool.

6. Dust the cookies with the remaining confectioners' sugar and enjoy.

INGREDIENTS:

½	LB. UNSWEETENED ALMOND PASTE
3	TABLESPOONS SUGAR
½	CUP PLUS 2 TABLESPOONS CONFECTIONERS' SUGAR
2	EGG WHITES
¾	CUP PINE NUTS

Sufganiyot, see page 626

SUFGANIYOT

YIELD: 20 SUFGANIYOT / **ACTIVE TIME:** 45 MINUTES / **TOTAL TIME:** 3 HOURS

An Israeli specialty that is the most delicious take on the jelly doughnut you'll ever encounter.

1. Coat a mixing bowl with some butter and set it aside. Sift the flour into the work bowl of a stand mixer fitted with the dough hook. Add the salt, sugar, and yeast and stir to incorporate.

2. Add the egg and butter to the mixture and mix to incorporate. Gradually add the milk and work the mixture until it comes together as a soft dough, 8 to 10 minutes.

3. Form the dough into a ball and place it in the buttered mixing bowl. Cover with a linen towel and let it rise until doubled in size, about 2 hours.

4. Line two baking sheets with parchment paper. Place the dough on a flour-dusted work surface and roll it out until it is about ¾ inch thick. Cut the dough into 2-inch circles, place them on the baking sheets, and cover with a linen towel. Let them rise for another 20 minutes.

5. Add avocado oil to a Dutch oven until it is about 2 inches deep and warm it to 325°F. Add the dough in batches of 4 and fry until golden brown, about 6 minutes, turning them over halfway through.

6. Drain the sufganiyot on a paper towel–lined plate. Fill a piping bag with the jam, and make a small slit on the top of each sufganiyah. Place the piping bag in the slit and fill until you see the filling coming back out. Sprinkle with confectioners' sugar and enjoy.

INGREDIENTS:

- 3½ TABLESPOONS UNSALTED BUTTER, CHOPPED, PLUS MORE AS NEEDED
- 3½ CUPS ALL-PURPOSE FLOUR, PLUS MORE AS NEEDED
- ½ TEASPOON FINE SEA SALT
- ¼ CUP SUGAR
- 1 TABLESPOON INSTANT YEAST
- 1 EGG
- 1¼ CUPS LUKEWARM MILK (85°F)
- AVOCADO OIL, AS NEEDED
- ½ CUP STRAWBERRY OR RASPBERRY JAM
- ¼ CUP CONFECTIONERS' SUGAR

PECAN PIE BAKLAVA

YIELD: 24 SERVINGS / ACTIVE TIME: 1 HOUR / TOTAL TIME: 2 HOURS

Baklava is easy to make—time-consuming, but easy—and lends itself to all kinds of creativity.

1. Preheat the oven to 350°F. Place 1 cup of the brown sugar, the vanilla, cinnamon, cloves, pecans, and ½ cup of the melted butter in a food processor and pulse until the mixture is combined.

2. Using half a box of phyllo dough, cut the sheets to fit a 13 x 9–inch baking dish.

3. Coat a 13 x 9–inch baking dish with a thin layer of the remaining melted butter. Lay down a sheet of phyllo, spread some butter over it, and repeat until nine sheets of phyllo have been laid down and buttered.

4. Spread the pecan mixture evenly over the stack of phyllo.

5. Place a sheet of phyllo on top of the filling. Spread some butter over it and repeat with the remaining sheets of phyllo.

6. Using a very sharp knife, cut the baklava into triangles. To do this, first cut the sheet of baklava in half, then cut each section in half, and repeat until the portions are about the size you want. Cut the squares diagonally to get triangles.

7. Place the baklava in the oven and bake until golden brown, 40 to 45 minutes.

8. While the baklava is in the oven, place the water, bourbon, and remaining brown sugar in a small saucepan and bring the mixture to a boil. Reduce the heat to medium-high and cook until the mixture has reduced by one-third. Remove the syrup from heat and set it aside.

9. Remove the baklava from the oven and pour the syrup over it. Let the baklava cool to room temperature before enjoying.

INGREDIENTS:

2	CUPS BROWN SUGAR
1	TEASPOON PURE VANILLA EXTRACT
1	TEASPOON CINNAMON
	PINCH OF GROUND CLOVES
1	LB. PECANS
1	CUP UNSALTED BUTTER, MELTED
½	LB. FROZEN PHYLLO DOUGH, THAWED
1	CUP WATER
3	OZ. BOURBON

FERMENTED BANANA FRITTERS

YIELD: 2 SERVINGS / ACTIVE TIME: 25 MINUTES / TOTAL TIME: 4 TO 5 DAYS

Once you know what to watch for when fermenting bananas, it becomes a very straight-forward process.

1. Peel the bananas, slice them into ½-inch-thick rounds, and place them in a mason jar. Add the yeast and then cover the bananas with the water. It is important that the bananas are completely covered, so add more water as necessary. Cover the jar and place it in a cupboard, keeping it at roughly 70°F, for 4 to 5 days, until the bananas start to smell a little like alcohol, though not funky. Any bananas at the top that brown should be thrown away.

2. Place the bananas in a mixing bowl and mash them. Add the flour and baking powder and stir until well combined.

3. Place the sugar and cinnamon in a bowl and stir to combine.

4. Add canola oil to a medium saucepan until it is about 1 inch deep and warm it to 325°F. Scoop tablespoons of the batter and fry until they are puffy and golden brown on one side, 1½ to 2 minutes. Turn the fritters over and cook until they are puffy and golden brown all over.

5. Remove the fritters from the hot oil, place them in the cinnamon sugar, and toss to coat.

6. Place the peanut butter in a microwave-safe bowl and microwave on medium in 10-second increments until it has liquefied.

7. To serve, spread the melted peanut butter on a small plate and pile the fritters on top.

INGREDIENTS:

2   BANANAS

1   TEASPOON ACTIVE DRY YEAST

2   CUPS WATER, PLUS MORE AS NEEDED

½   CUP ALL-PURPOSE FLOUR

1   TEASPOON BAKING POWDER

2   TABLESPOONS SUGAR

1   TABLESPOON CINNAMON

      CANOLA OIL, AS NEEDED

2   TABLESPOONS PEANUT BUTTER

GOAT CHEESE & HONEY PANNA COTTA

YIELD: 4 SERVINGS / ACTIVE TIME: 30 MINUTES / TOTAL TIME: 5 HOURS

It is imperative to use in-season fruit for the garnish here, and that it be as fresh as possible.

1. Place the water in a small saucepan and warm it over medium heat. Sprinkle the gelatin over the water and stir until thoroughly combined. The mixture will very quickly become a paste—remove the pan from heat as soon as it does and set it aside.

2. Place the cream in another small saucepan and warm it over medium heat. Stir in the goat cheese and cook until it has dissolved. Add the honey and cook until it has been incorporated.

3. Place the gelatin over low heat and gradually add the cream mixture, stirring continually. When all of the cream mixture has been incorporated, raise the heat to medium and cook the mixture until it has thickened, about 10 minutes, stirring frequently.

4. Remove the pan from heat and pour the mixture into 4-oz. ramekins or mason jars. Place them in the refrigerator and chill until they have set, 4 to 5 hours.

5. To serve, garnish each portion with fresh berries and honey.

INGREDIENTS:

2   TABLESPOONS WATER

1   ENVELOPE OF UNFLAVORED GELATIN

2½   CUPS HEAVY CREAM

4   OZ. CREAMY GOAT CHEESE

½   CUP HONEY, PLUS MORE FOR GARNISH

   FRESH BERRIES, FOR GARNISH

LEMON RICE PUDDING WITH
ROASTED VANILLA CHERRIES & LEMON CRÈME

YIELD: 4 SERVINGS / ACTIVE TIME: 45 MINUTES / TOTAL TIME: 2 HOURS

Remove the pits from cherries after roasting them; this keeps them from losing too much liquid in the oven.

1. Place all of the ingredients in a saucepan and bring the mixture to a simmer over medium-low heat. Cook, stirring frequently, until the rice is cooked through and the mixture has thickened to the consistency of yogurt, 20 to 30 minutes. Remove the pan from heat and let the mixture cool.

2. To serve, divide the rice pudding between the serving bowls and top each portion with some of the roasted cherries and Lemon Crème.

ROASTED VANILLA CHERRIES

1. Place the cherries, salt, brandy, and vanilla in a bowl and let the mixture marinate at room temperature overnight.

2. Preheat the oven to 400°F. Strain the cherries, reserve the liquid, and place the cherries on a baking sheet. Sprinkle the sugar over the cherries, place them in the oven, and roast until the sugar starts to caramelize, 8 to 10 minutes, making sure that the sugar does not burn.

3. Remove the cherries from the oven, pour the reserved liquid over them, and place them back in the oven. Roast for another 5 minutes, remove the cherries from the oven, and let them cool. When they are cool enough to handle, remove the pits from the cherries. Chill the cherries in the refrigerator until ready to use.

LEMON CRÈME

1. Place the lemon zest, lemon juice, and half of the sugar in a small saucepan and bring the mixture to a boil, stirring to dissolve the sugar. Remove the pan from heat.

2. Place the sugar and eggs in a small mixing bowl and whisk until combined. While whisking vigorously, slowly pour the hot syrup into the mixture. Place the tempered mixture in the saucepan, place it over low heat, and stir until it starts to thicken, about 5 minutes.

3. Remove the pan from heat and incorporate the butter 1 tablespoon at a time. When all of the butter has been incorporated, stir in the salt and then pour the crème into a bowl. Place plastic wrap directly on the surface to prevent a skin from forming and chill the crème in the refrigerator until ready to use.

INGREDIENTS:

	SEEDS OF 1 VANILLA BEAN
4	CUPS WHOLE MILK
½	CUP SUGAR
	ZEST OF 1 LEMON
1	CUP RICE
	ROASTED VANILLA CHERRIES (SEE RECIPE)
	LEMON CRÈME (SEE RECIPE)

ROASTED VANILLA CHERRIES

24	CHERRIES
	PINCH OF FINE SEA SALT
¼	CUP BRANDY
	SEEDS OF ½ VANILLA BEAN OR 1 TEASPOON PURE VANILLA EXTRACT
2	TABLESPOONS DEMERARA SUGAR

LEMON CRÈME

	ZEST AND JUICE OF 2 LEMONS
½	CUP SUGAR
3	EGGS
6	TABLESPOONS UNSALTED BUTTER
	PINCH OF FINE SEA SALT

SPICY CHOCOLATE HALVAH

YIELD: 4 SERVINGS / **ACTIVE TIME**: 30 MINUTES / **TOTAL TIME**: 1 HOUR

Halvah is somewhat simple to make, but getting the sugar syrup the right temperature is crucial, as it drastically impacts the texture—too low, and it will be akin to an oily fudge; too high, and it becomes hard and flaky. A temperature of 265°F yields the soft but solid result you want.

1. Place the tahini in a small saucepan and warm it over medium heat.

2. Place the sugar and water in a separate small saucepan that is fitted with a candy thermometer. Bring the mixture to a boil over high heat, stirring to dissolve the sugar. Boil until the syrup is 265°F.

3. As you wait for the syrup to reach the proper temperature, add the chocolate and cayenne to the tahini and stir until the chocolate has melted.

4. Once the syrup reaches 265°F, immediately remove the pan from heat and stir the syrup into the tahini, making sure not to overwork the mixture, as this will cause the halvah to crack.

5. Pour the mixture into a container—a silicone mold, small loaf pan, or Tupperware are all acceptable. The halvah should set relatively quickly (30 minutes or less) and can be stored in the refrigerator for up to 2 weeks. Serve at room temperature.

INGREDIENTS:

1	CUP TAHINI PASTE
1	CUP SUGAR
1	CUP WATER
3	OZ. DARK CHOCOLATE
1	TEASPOON CAYENNE PEPPER

BLACK LIME & STRAWBERRY CROSTATA

YIELD: 6 SERVINGS / **ACTIVE TIME**: 30 MINUTES / **TOTAL TIME**: 2 HOURS AND 30 MINUTES

Black limes have the most interesting acidity—think of them as nature's Sour Patch Kids.

1. Place the flour, ½ cup of the sugar, and the baking powder in the work bowl of a mixer fitted with the paddle attachment and stir to combine.

2. Add the butter and 1 egg, as well as the yolk of the second egg. Reserve the egg white for the egg wash. Beat the mixture until it comes together as a soft dough. Cover it in plastic wrap and chill in the refrigerator for 30 minutes.

3. Open the black limes and pull out the sticky pith from inside. Place it in a small saucepan with the remaining sugar, water, and strawberries. Bring the mixture to a boil and cook until it has reduced and is 220°F. Remove the pan from heat and let the mixture cool.

4. Preheat the oven to 350°F. Coat an 8-inch pie plate with butter.

5. Remove the dough from the refrigerator and place it on a flour-dusted work surface. Roll it out to ⅛ inch thick and place it in the pie plate, trimming away any excess dough.

6. Fill the crust with the jam. Cut the remaining dough into strips. Lay the strips over the filling and trim any excess. To make a lattice crust, lift every other strip and fold back so you can place another strip across those strips that remain flat. Lay the folded strips back down over the cross-strip. Fold back the strips that you laid the cross-strip on top of and repeat until the lattice covers the surface of the tart. Beat the remaining egg until scrambled and brush the strips with it, taking care not to get any egg on the filling.

7. Place the crostata in the oven and bake until the crust is golden brown, about 30 minutes.

8. Remove the crostata from the oven, place it on a wire rack, and let it cool to room temperature before enjoying.

INGREDIENTS:

- 1¾ CUPS ALL-PURPOSE FLOUR, PLUS MORE AS NEEDED
- 1 CUP SUGAR
- 1 TEASPOON BAKING POWDER
- 10 TABLESPOONS UNSALTED BUTTER, SOFTENED AND CHOPPED, PLUS MORE AS NEEDED
- 2 EGGS, AT ROOM TEMPERATURE
- 2 BLACK LIMES
- 1 CUP WATER
- 1 CUP HULLED AND SLICED FRESH STRAWBERRIES

Black Lime & Strawberry Crostata, see page 633

BLUEBERRY & GINGER MALABI

Think of this as a panna cotta that originated in the Middle East.

1. Place the cream, sugar, ginger, and blueberries in a small saucepan and warm the mixture over medium heat. When the mixture begins to bubble at the edge, reduce the heat to low and let it simmer for 30 minutes.

2. Puree the mixture using an immersion blender (or a food processor). Strain the mixture, place the liquid in a clean saucepan, and warm it over medium-high heat.

3. In a small bowl, combine the water and cornstarch. While stirring continually, gradually add the slurry to the cream mixture. As the mixture starts to thicken, reduce the heat to medium. Cook until the mixture acquires a pudding-like consistency, about 5 minutes.

4. Divide the mixture among 4-oz. ramekins or mason jars, place them in the refrigerator, and chill for 4 hours before serving.

INGREDIENTS:

2	CUPS LIGHT CREAM
1	TABLESPOON SUGAR
1	TEASPOON GRATED FRESH GINGER
½	CUP BLUEBERRIES
¼	CUP COLD WATER
2	TABLESPOONS CORNSTARCH

APPLE & WALNUT BUNDT CAKE

YIELD: 12 SERVINGS / ACTIVE TIME: 20 MINUTES / TOTAL TIME: 3 HOURS

This fragrant olive oil cake stays moist and flavorful for over a week, so feel free to make it a few days before serving. The caramel glaze is not necessary, but it is highly recommended.

1. Place the eggs on a counter and let them sit at room temperature for 30 minutes to 1 hour.

2. Preheat the oven to 350°F and position a rack in the lower third.

3. Place the walnuts in an even layer on a baking sheet, place them in the oven, and toast for 5 minutes. Remove from the oven, turn the walnuts onto a clean dish towel, and rub them around to loosen their skins. Discard any loose skins and let the walnuts cool completely. When they are cool, chop them and set them aside.

4. Coat a 12-cup Bundt pan with nonstick cooking spray and sprinkle flour over it. Knock out any excess flour and set the pan aside.

5. Place the flour, baking soda, salt, and cinnamon in a mixing bowl and stir to combine.

6. Peel and core the apples, and then finely dice them.

7. Place the eggs, olive oil, brown sugar, sugar, and vanilla in the work bowl of a stand mixer fitted with the paddle attachment. Beat on medium until combined, about 1 minute.

8. Add the flour mixture and beat on low until incorporated. Scrape down the sides of the work bowl.

9. Detach the work bowl from the mixer and stir in the apples and walnuts.

10. Spoon the batter into the Bundt pan, place it in the oven, and bake until a cake tester inserted into the center comes out clean and the cake springs back when pressed lightly in the center, about 50 minutes.

11. Remove the cake from the oven, place the pan on a wire rack, and let it cool for 30 minutes.

12. Invert the cake onto a wire rack that has been lightly coated with nonstick cooking spray and let it cool completely.

13. Drizzle the Caramel Glaze over the cake and enjoy.

Continued . . .

INGREDIENTS:

- 3   LARGE EGGS
- 1   CUP WALNUT HALVES
- 2½   CUPS ALL-PURPOSE FLOUR, PLUS MORE AS NEEDED
- 1   TEASPOON BAKING SODA
- 1   TEASPOON FINE SEA SALT
- 2   TEASPOONS CINNAMON
- 4   LARGE GRANNY SMITH APPLES
- 1¼   CUPS OLIVE OIL
- ¾   CUP LIGHT BROWN SUGAR
- 1   CUP SUGAR
- 2   TEASPOONS PURE VANILLA EXTRACT
-      CARAMEL GLAZE (SEE RECIPE)

CARAMEL GLAZE

- 2   TABLESPOONS UNSALTED BUTTER
- 6   TABLESPOONS HEAVY CREAM
- 1   CUP CASTER SUGAR (SUPERFINE)
- 2   TABLESPOONS CORN SYRUP
- ⅜   TEASPOON CREAM OF TARTAR
- ¼   CUP WATER
- 2   TEASPOONS PURE VANILLA EXTRACT

CARAMEL GLAZE

1. About 30 minutes before you are going to start preparations for the glaze, cut the butter into a few pieces and let it sit at room temperature.

2. Pour the cream into a measuring cup with a spout. Warm it in the microwave and then cover it with plastic wrap.

3. Coat a 2-cup measuring glass with a spout with nonstick cooking spray and place it beside the stove.

4. Place the sugar, corn syrup, cream of tartar, and water in a nonstick saucepan fitted with a candy thermometer. Stir until the sugar is moist.

5. Bring the mixture to a boil, stirring constantly with a silicone spatula. Stop stirring and let it boil undisturbed until it turns a deep amber and the temperature reaches 370°F. Remove the pan from heat as soon as it reaches this temperature.

6. Slowly and carefully pour the hot cream into the caramel; it will bubble up furiously.

7. Use a silicone spatula or wooden spoon to stir the mixture gently, scraping the thicker part that settles on the bottom. Place the pan over very low heat and gently stir until the mixture is uniform in color and the caramel is fully liquefied.

8. Remove the caramel from heat and gently stir in the butter. The mixture will be a little streaky but will become uniform when you stir it once it has cooled.

9. Pour the caramel into the prepared measuring glass and let it cool for 3 minutes. Gently stir in the vanilla and let it cool to room temperature, stirring it gently once or twice.

PALMIERS

YIELD: 16 PALMIERS / ACTIVE TIME: 20 MINUTES / TOTAL TIME: 2 HOURS

To enjoy these on their own, dust them with a bit of cinnamon sugar. Or just use them to add a bit of crunch to frozen and creamy desserts.

1. Place the sheet of puff pastry on a piece of parchment paper. Combine the sugar and salt in a small bowl and sprinkle the mixture over the puff pastry.

2. Working from the top edge, fold puff pastry over itself continually until you get to the center of the sheet. Repeat from the bottom edge.

3. Sandwich the puff pastry together so that it is a log, cover it with plastic wrap, place it in the refrigerator, and chill for 1 hour.

4. Preheat the oven to 375°F. Place a Silpat mat on a baking sheet. Remove the palmier log from the refrigerator and cut it into ¼-inch-wide pieces. Place them on the baking sheet, place the palmiers in the oven, and cook until the tops are golden brown, about 8 minutes.

5. Remove the palmiers from the oven and flip them oven. Return to the oven and bake until golden brown, about 5 minutes.

6. Remove from the oven, transfer the palmiers to wire racks, and let them cool before enjoying.

INGREDIENTS:

1 SHEET OF FROZEN PUFF PASTRY, THAWED

1 CUP SUGAR

¾ TEASPOON FINE SEA SALT

SALTED HONEY & APPLE UPSIDE-DOWN CAKE

YIELD: 6 SERVINGS / ACTIVE TIME: 20 MINUTES / TOTAL TIME: 1 HOUR AND 20 MINUTES

Milk and honey sound good, sure, but make that honey salted, and now you're really talking.

1. Preheat the oven to 350°F.

2. Place the flour, baking powder, ½ teaspoon of the salt, and the cinnamon in a small bowl and whisk until combined.

3. Place the sour cream, avocado oil, and vanilla in a separate bowl and stir until combined.

4. Place the sugar and eggs in a separate bowl and whisk until the mixture is foamy, about 2 minutes.

5. Add half of the flour mixture to the egg mixture and gently stir to incorporate it. Stir in half of the sour cream mixture, add the the remaining flour mixture, and stir until incorporated. Add the remaining sour cream mixture and stir until the mixture just comes together. Set the batter aside.

6. Butter the bottom and sides of an 8-inch cast-iron skillet or springform pan and add the honey, swirling the pan to ensure the honey covers as much of the pan as possible. Sprinkle the remaining salt over the honey.

7. Arrange the apples on top the honey, overlapping them to fit the pan. Pour the cake batter over the apples and tap the pan on a counter a few times to remove any large bubbles.

8. Place the cake in the oven and bake until it is golden brown and springs back when gently touched with a finger, about 30 minutes.

9. Remove the cake from the oven and let it cool in the pan for 10 minutes. Run an offset spatula or knife around the pan and invert the cake onto a cooling rack (or unmold and then invert, if using a springform pan). Let the cake cool for another 20 minutes before transferring to a platter and sprinkling the Maldon sea salt over the top. Serve with additional sour cream and honey.

INGREDIENTS:

¾	CUP ALL-PURPOSE FLOUR
1	TEASPOON BAKING POWDER
¾	TEASPOON KOSHER SALT
½	TEASPOON CINNAMON
¼	CUP SOUR CREAM, PLUS MORE FOR SERVING
¼	CUP AVOCADO OIL
2	TEASPOONS PURE VANILLA EXTRACT
½	CUP SUGAR
2	EGGS
½	TABLESPOON UNSALTED BUTTER
¼	CUP HONEY, PLUS MORE FOR SERVING
1	BAKING APPLE, CORED AND SLICED INTO THIN ROUNDS
	MALDON SEA SALT, FOR GARNISH

BLACK & WHITE HALVAH

YIELD: 16 SERVINGS / ACTIVE TIME: 35 MINUTES / TOTAL TIME: 3 HOURS AND 40 MINUTES

A simple sesame-based delicacy, yet swirling black and white tahini together for a marble effect makes for an impressive presentation.

1. Lightly coat an 8 x 4–inch loaf pan with nonstick spray and line it with parchment paper, leaving a 2-inch overhang on the long sides. Place a sheet of parchment paper on a work surface and lightly coat it with nonstick cooking spray.

2. Place the white tahini and ½ teaspoon of the salt in the work bowl of a stand mixer fitted with the paddle attachment and beat on low until the mixture is smooth.

3. Place ⅔ cup of the sugar in a small saucepan. Place the remaining sugar in another small saucepan. Add ¼ cup water to each saucepan and place both saucepans over low heat. Cook, stirring to dissolve the sugar, for about 4 minutes. Keep one saucepan over low heat. Raise the heat under the other saucepan to medium-high and fit it with a thermometer. Cook the syrup, brushing down the side of the saucepan with a wet pastry brush to dissolve any crystals that form, until the syrup is 248°F, 7 to 10 minutes.

4. Remove the boiling syrup from heat.

5. With the mixer running at medium speed, gradually stream the boiling syrup into the salted tahini, aiming for the space between the side of the bowl and the paddle. Beat just until the mixture comes together in a smooth mass, less than a minute. Take care not to overwork the mixture, or it will be crumbly.

6. Working quickly, scrape the mixture onto the prepared parchment and flatten it with a spatula until it is ¾ inch thick. Invert a medium bowl over the halvah to keep it warm.

7. Rinse any hardened sugar off the candy thermometer and clip it to the second saucepan. Raise the heat to medium-high and cook the syrup, brushing down the side of the saucepan with a wet pastry brush, until the syrup is 248°F.

8. While the syrup is cooking, place the black tahini and remaining salt in the work bowl of the stand mixer (no need to clean it out, unless you have lots of hardened sugar stuck around the sides) and beat until smooth.

INGREDIENTS:

¾ CUP WHITE TAHINI PASTE

1 TEASPOON KOSHER SALT

1⅓ CUPS SUGAR

¾ CUP BLACK TAHINI PASTE

9. With the mixer running, stream in the syrup and repeat Step 4.

10. Uncover the white halvah and scrape the black halvah on top; flatten it to about the same shape as the white halvah. Using the sides of the parchment to lift the edges of the stacked halvah, fold it in half and flatten slightly. Repeat this folding and flattening motion 4 to 5 times, rotating the halvah as you work to create a marbled effect.

11. Press the halvah into the prepared loaf pan. Fold the parchment paper over the halvah and let it cool for at least 3 hours.

12. Using the parchment paper, lift the halvah out of the pan. Peel away the parchment paper and cut the halvah into ½-inch-thick slices.

13. Enjoy or store in an airtight container at room temperature for up to 3 days.

CONDENSED CARAMEL

YIELD: 1½ CUPS / **ACTIVE TIME:** 20 MINUTES / **TOTAL TIME:** 4 HOURS

A fun, and effortless, spin on the classic caramel sauce, with the decadent flavor you've grown accustomed to.

1. Remove the label from the can of condensed milk and place the can in a medium saucepan.

2. Cover the can with water and bring the water to a boil. Reduce the heat so that the water simmers. Cook for 3 hours, adding water as needed to keep the condensed milk submerged.

3. Remove the can of condensed milk from the water and let it cool completely.

4. Open the can and use the caramel as desired.

INGREDIENTS:

1   (14 OZ.) CAN OF
     CONDENSED MILK

CARAMELIZED HONEY TART

YIELD: 8 SERVINGS / ACTIVE TIME: 35 MINUTES / TOTAL TIME: 1 HOUR AND 30 MINUTES

A scrumptious combination of textures, this sweet tart has an undeniable crunch. The richness of the nuts and seeds balances the sweet honey.

1. To begin preparations for the crust, place the flour, confectioners' sugar, and salt in a food processor and pulse to combine.

2. Add the butter and pulse until the mixture is a coarse meal with a few pea-size pieces of butter remaining.

3. Place the egg yolks and water in a small bowl and beat until combined. With the food processor running, add the egg yolks to the mixture and blitz until it comes together as a dough.

4. Coat a 9-inch springform pan with butter. Using lightly flour-dusted hands, place the dough into the pan and press it about 1 inch up the side and evenly in the bottom of the pan, making sure the side of the crust is slightly thicker than the bottom. Use a flour-dusted, straight-sided measuring cup or glass to compact and smooth the dough. Place the crust in the freezer until it is solid, 15 to 20 minutes.

5. Preheat the oven to 350°F. Prick the bottom of the crust with a fork, place it in the oven, and bake until it is golden brown, 20 to 25 minutes.

6. Remove the crust from the oven and place the pan on a wire rack. Leave the oven on.

7. To begin preparations for the filling, place the honey and water in a small saucepan and bring it to a simmer over low heat, swirling the pan frequently. Simmer until the mixture has darkened and gives off a nutty fragrance, about 2 minutes.

8. Carefully add the sugar, heavy cream, butter, corn syrup, salt, and vanilla to the pan and stir until the mixture is smooth. Raise the heat to medium and bring the mixture to a boil. Cook, swirling the pan, until the caramel has darkened slightly and is thick enough to coat a wooden spoon, 5 to 8 minutes.

9. Remove the pan from heat and stir the nuts and seeds into the caramel.

10. Scrape the filling into the crust, making sure it is evenly distributed. Place the tart in the oven and bake until the filling is a deep golden brown and bubbling, 25 to 30 minutes.

11. Remove the tart from the oven and let it cool completely before serving.

INGREDIENTS:

FOR THE CRUST

- 1½   CUPS ALL-PURPOSE FLOUR, PLUS MORE AS NEEDED
- ¼   CUP CONFECTIONERS' SUGAR
- ½   TEASPOON KOSHER SALT
- 8   TABLESPOONS UNSALTED BUTTER, CHILLED AND CHOPPED, PLUS MORE AS NEEDED
- 2   LARGE EGG YOLKS
- 1   TABLESPOON WATER

FOR THE FILLING

- ¼   CUP HONEY
- 1   TABLESPOON WATER
- ¼   CUP SUGAR
- 4   CUPS HEAVY CREAM
- 4   TABLESPOONS UNSALTED BUTTER
- 2   TABLESPOONS LIGHT CORN SYRUP
- ½   TEASPOON KOSHER SALT
- ½   TEASPOON PURE VANILLA EXTRACT
- 2   CUPS UNSALTED AND ROASTED MIXED NUTS (PECANS, HAZELNUTS, PEANUTS, PISTACHIOS, AND/OR SLICED ALMONDS)
- ⅓   CUP UNSALTED AND ROASTED SUNFLOWER SEEDS

HALVAH MILLE-FEUILLES

YIELD: 4 SERVINGS / **ACTIVE TIME:** 35 MINUTES / **TOTAL TIME:** 1 HOUR

Though this recipe calls for a raspberry garnish, feel free to swap in caramelized apples or toasted pistachios. When working with phyllo dough, make sure to keep the unused phyllo sheets covered, as they tend to dry out quickly.

1. Preheat the oven to 350°F. Line two baking sheets with parchment paper. Stack the 8 sheets of phyllo and cut them in half, crosswise.

2. Brush one half sheet of phyllo with olive oil and sprinkle some sugar over it. Layer another half sheet on top and repeat with the oil and sugar until you have a stack of four half sheets, topping the top layer of the stack with oil and sugar as well.

3. Repeat the process with remaining half sheets to form three more stacks of four. Cut each stack into four equal pieces to make 16 stacks.

4. Transfer the stacks to the baking sheets, place them in the oven, and bake until golden brown, 8 to 12 minutes.

5. Remove the stacks from the oven and let them cool to room temperature, about 15 minutes.

6. Place the honey and the tahini in a small bowl and stir to combine. Set the mixture aside.

7. Place the cream in the work bowl of a stand mixer fitted with the whisk attachment and whip until it holds soft peaks. Fold in the honey-and-tahini mixture and whip until the mixture holds stiff peaks.

8. Place one phyllo stack on a plate and spread some of the whipped cream over the phyllo. Repeat the layering process with two more stacks of phyllo and the whipped cream.

9. Top the cream with a stack of phyllo. Repeat with the remaining stacks of phyllo and whipped cream to form three more servings.

10. Drizzle additional honey over each serving. Sprinkle the halvah over the top, garnish with the raspberries, and enjoy.

INGREDIENTS:

8	SHEETS OF FROZEN PHYLLO DOUGH, THAWED
	EXTRA-VIRGIN OLIVE OIL, AS NEEDED
	SUGAR, TO TASTE
⅓	CUP HONEY, PLUS MORE TO TASTE
⅓	CUP TAHINI PASTE
1	CUP HEAVY CREAM
½	CUP CRUMBLED CLASSIC HALVAH (SEE PAGE 650)
	FRESH RASPBERRIES, FOR GARNISH

CLASSIC HALVAH

YIELD: 12 SERVINGS / ACTIVE TIME: 20 MINUTES / TOTAL TIME: 36 HOURS

Any nut can be substituted for the almonds, with pistachios being the most popular alternative.

1. Coat a loaf pan with nonstick cooking spray. Place the tahini in a small saucepan.

2. Place the honey in a saucepan fitted with a candy thermometer and warm it over medium heat until it reaches 240°F. Remove the pan from heat.

3. Warm the tahini to 120°F.

4. Add the warmed tahini to the honey and stir the mixture with a wooden spoon. It will look broken at first, but after a few minutes the mixture will come together smoothly.

5. Add the nuts and continue to stir the mixture until it starts to stiffen, 6 to 8 minutes.

6. Pour the mixture into the loaf pan and let it cool to room temperature.

7. Cover the pan tightly with plastic wrap and refrigerate for 36 hours. This will allow sugar crystals to form, which will give the halvah its distinctive texture.

8. Invert the halvah to remove it from the pan and use a sharp knife to cut it into the desired portions.

INGREDIENTS:

1½ CUPS TAHINI PASTE, STIRRED WELL

2 CUPS HONEY

2 CUPS SLICED ALMONDS, TOASTED

HONEY CAKE

YIELD: 1 CAKE / ACTIVE TIME: 1 HOUR / TOTAL TIME: 4 HOURS

With its velvety chocolate glaze and snowy flakes of sea salt, this dressed-up honey cake is ready for prime time. Measure the oil and honey in a liquid measuring cup, measuring the oil first. If you measure the honey afterward, without washing the cup, the honey will slide out easily, with barely any help needed from a rubber spatula.

1. Preheat the oven to 350°F and position a rack in middle. Generously coat a 12-cup Bundt pan with nonstick cooking spray.

2. Place the flour, baking powder, baking soda, salt, and spices in a large bowl and stir to combine.

3. Place the eggs in a separate bowl and beat until scrambled. Add the sugar, avocado oil, honey, coffee, and orange zest and whisk until thoroughly combined.

4. Make a well in the center of the dry mixture and place the wet mixture in it. Whisk until the mixture comes together as a smooth batter.

5. Pour the batter into the prepared pan and place it in the oven. Bake until the cake is springy to the touch and a cake tester inserted into the center comes out clean, 45 to 50 minutes.

6. Remove the cake from the oven, place the pan on a wire rack, and let it cool for 20 minutes.

7. Loosen the cake with a thin rubber spatula. Invert the cake onto the wire rack and let it cool completely.

8. Transfer the cake to a serving platter and slowly pour the Chocolate Glaze over the top, letting it drip down the sides. Let the cake stand at room temperature until the glaze is set.

9. Sprinkle the Maldon over the glaze and serve.

CHOCOLATE GLAZE

1. Place the coconut milk and corn syrup in a small saucepan and bring to a simmer over medium heat, stirring until combined.

2. Remove the pan from heat and add the chocolate. Let the mixture stand for 1 minute. Stir until the chocolate has melted and the glaze is smooth.

3. Let the glaze stand, stirring occasionally, until it has thickened slightly but is still pourable.

INGREDIENTS:

2½   CUPS ALL-PURPOSE FLOUR

2   TEASPOONS BAKING POWDER

½   TEASPOON BAKING SODA

½   TEASPOON KOSHER SALT

2   TEASPOONS CINNAMON

¼   TEASPOON GROUND GINGER

¼   TEASPOON GROUND CLOVES

3   LARGE EGGS

1   CUP SUGAR

1¼   CUPS AVOCADO OIL

1   CUP PURE HONEY

¾   CUP LUKEWARM BREWED COFFEE

1½   TEASPOONS ORANGE ZEST

        CHOCOLATE GLAZE (SEE RECIPE)

        MALDON SEA SALT, FOR GARNISH

CHOCOLATE GLAZE

6   TABLESPOONS UNSWEETENED, FULL-FAT COCONUT MILK, STIRRED WELL

2   TEASPOONS LIGHT CORN SYRUP

4   OZ. DARK CHOCOLATE (60 PERCENT), FINELY CHOPPED

HONEY & POMEGRANATE CAKE

YIELD: 4 SERVINGS / **ACTIVE TIME:** 10 MINUTES / **TOTAL TIME:** 1 HOUR

May this be the first step toward banishing dry honey cakes from your life forever.

1. Preheat the oven to 350°F. Place the eggs and sugar in the work bowl of a stand mixer fitted with the paddle attachment and beat until the mixture is smooth. Add the olive oil, brewed tea, and honey and beat until thoroughly combined.

2. In a separate bowl, combine the flour, baking powder, and baking soda. Gradually incorporate the dry mixture into the wet mixture and beat until it comes together as a smooth batter.

3. Pour the batter into a 10-inch fluted cake pan (not a Bundt pan) that has not been greased. Place the cake in the oven and bake for 15 minutes.

4. Reduce the oven's temperature to 300°F and bake the cake until a cake tester inserted into the center comes out clean, about 45 minutes.

5. Remove the cake from the oven, place the pan on a wire rack, and let it cool completely.

6. Invert the pan to remove the cake, pour the glaze over it, and enjoy.

POMEGRANATE GLAZE

1. Place the pomegranate juice, sugar, and lemon juice in a small saucepan and bring the mixture to a boil. Reduce the heat and simmer until the mixture becomes syrupy and reduces by half, about 15 minutes.

2. Remove the pan from heat and let the glaze cool slightly.

3. Add the confectioners' sugar and whisk until the glaze is smooth.

4. Add the pomegranate seeds and stir to combine.

INGREDIENTS:

4	EGGS
1	CUP SUGAR
1	CUP EXTRA-VIRGIN OLIVE OIL
1	CUP BREWED POMEGRANATE TEA, CHILLED
1½	CUPS HONEY
3	CUPS ALL-PURPOSE FLOUR
1	TABLESPOON BAKING POWDER
½	TEASPOON BAKING SODA
	POMEGRANATE GLAZE (SEE RECIPE)

POMEGRANATE GLAZE

½	CUP POMEGRANATE JUICE
¼	CUP SUGAR
	JUICE OF ½ LEMON
¼	CUP CONFECTIONERS' SUGAR
¼	CUP POMEGRANATE SEEDS

CRÈME CHANTILLY

YIELD: 2 CUPS / ACTIVE TIME: 5 MINUTES / TOTAL TIME: 5 MINUTES

A classic, refined whipped cream that will serve you well whenever one of your desserts needs an ornament.

1. Place all of the ingredients in the work bowl of a stand mixer fitted with the whisk attachment. Whip until the mixture holds soft peaks.

2. Use immediately or store in the refrigerator until needed.

INGREDIENTS:

1   CUP HEAVY CREAM

1   TABLESPOON SUGAR

     SEEDS OF ½ VANILLA BEAN

BAKLAVA PIE

YIELD: 16 SERVINGS / ACTIVE TIME: 1 HOUR / TOTAL TIME: 1 HOUR AND 45 MINUTES

Why choose between baklava and pie when you can have both?

1. Preheat the oven to 350°F. Place the honey, cinnamon sticks, 1 cup of the sugar, and 1 cup water in a medium saucepan and bring to a boil, stirring until the sugar has dissolved. Reduce the heat to medium and simmer until the syrup has reduced to about 1½ cups, 15 to 18 minutes. Transfer to a medium bowl, stir in the bourbon, and let the syrup cool.

2. Place the pecans on a large rimmed baking sheet, place them in the oven, and toast until golden brown, 13 to 15 minutes. Remove the pecans from the oven and let them cool. Leave the oven on.

3. Place the pecans in a food processor. Add the cinnamon, orange zest, and the remaining ½ cup sugar and pulse until the mixture is combined and the pecans are coarsely chopped.

4. Place a stack of phyllo sheets on a work surface. Keep any phyllo you're not currently working with covered under a layer of plastic wrap topped with a slightly damp linen towel. Using the base of a 9-inch springform pan as a guide, and starting at the edge of the phyllo, carefully cut a 9-inch circle out of each sheet, leaving as much phyllo remaining as possible. Cover the phyllo circles with plastic wrap and a damp linen towel. Using the base of the pan as a guide, cut the remaining phyllo into 20 half circles that are each 4½ inches.

5. Place the base into the springform pan and secure the latch. Brush the base with butter. Place one full phyllo circle in the pan and brush it generously with butter. Top it with two half circles to create a full circle, and brush it with butter. Top with a full circle, brush with butter, top with two half circles at a 90° angle from the first half circle layer, and brush with butter. Top with a full circle and brush with butter. You should have five layers of phyllo, with butter spread between each layer. Spread one-fifth of the nut mixture over the phyllo. Repeat this layering process four more times. Finish with the five remaining full circles and brush the top with butter.

6. Using a sharp knife, score the top layer (do not cut through to the bottom of the pan) to divide the pie into four quadrants. Working with one quadrant at a time, make a straight cut to divide the quadrant into two even wedges. Make four more straight cuts (two each on either side of, and parallel to, the quadrant divi-

INGREDIENTS:

- ⅔ CUP HONEY
- 2 CINNAMON STICKS
- 1½ CUPS SUGAR
- 3 TABLESPOONS BOURBON
- 3 CUPS RAW PECANS
- ½ TEASPOON CINNAMON
- 1 TEASPOON FINELY GRATED ORANGE ZEST
- 20 SHEETS OF FROZEN PHYLLO DOUGH, THAWED
- 1 CUP UNSALTED BUTTER, MELTED

  ORANGE TWISTS, FOR GARNISH

sion line), spacing the cuts evenly apart. Now working within each wedge, make two cuts parallel to the outside edge of the quadrant, connecting at points with the previous cuts to form a diamond pattern. Repeat with the remaining quadrants to create a starburst pattern.

7. Place the pan on a rimmed baking sheet, place it in the oven, and bake the pie until the phyllo is golden brown, about 45 minutes.

8. Remove the pie from the oven and spoon the cooled syrup over the hot baklava in four increments. Garnish the pie with the orange twists and let it cool completely.

9. Remove the top of the springform pan, cut the pie along the scored lines, and enjoy.

CANDIED HAZELNUTS

YIELD: ½ CUP / **ACTIVE TIME:** 30 MINUTES / **TOTAL TIME:** 1 HOUR

A good recipe to get in the habit of having on hand, as its sweet crunch can elevate the most humble desserts.

1. Line a baking sheet with parchment paper. Place the hazelnuts and maple syrup in a small saucepan and bring to a boil. Reduce the heat and simmer for 5 minutes.

2. Transfer the hazelnuts to the baking sheet. Using a fork, separate the hazelnuts so that they don't stick together when cool. Let the hazelnuts cool completely.

3. Place the canola oil in a Dutch oven and warm it to 350°F. Working in batches to avoid crowding the pot, add the hazelnuts and fry until golden brown. Transfer the fried hazelnuts to a paper towel–lined plate to drain, sprinkle the sugar and salt over them, and let them cool completely.

INGREDIENTS:

½   CUP HAZELNUTS

½   CUP MAPLE SYRUP

2   CUPS CANOLA OIL

1   TABLESPOON SUGAR

½   TEASPOON FINE SEA
    SALT

CLASSIC MALABI

YIELD: 6 SERVINGS / **ACTIVE TIME:** 20 MINUTES / **TOTAL TIME:** 4 HOURS AND 20 MINUTES

This milk pudding has legendary origins dating to Sassanid Persia, and today is popular throughout the Mediterranean region.

1. To begin preparations for the pudding, place 1 cup of milk in a bowl, add the cornstarch and rose water, and stir until the mixture is smooth. Set aside.

2. Place the remaining milk, heavy cream, and sugar in a saucepan. Bring to a simmer, stirring constantly, reduce the heat to low, and stir in the cornstarch mixture.

3. Cook, stirring constantly, until the mixture starts to thicken, 3 to 4 minutes. Pour the pudding into ramekins or small mason jars, place plastic wrap directly on the surface to prevent a skin from forming, and let the pudding cool completely. When it has cooled, chill in the refrigerator for 4 hours.

4. To prepare the syrup, place the water, sugar, and rose water in a saucepan and bring to a boil, stirring to dissolve the sugar. Stir in the food coloring, boil for another 2 minutes, and remove the pan from heat. Let the syrup cool completely.

5. When the malabi has chilled for 4 hours, pour 1 to 2 tablespoons of the syrup over each portion, and garnish with peanuts or pistachios and shredded coconut.

INGREDIENTS:

FOR THE PUDDING

4	CUPS MILK
⅔	CUP CORNSTARCH
1	TEASPOON ROSE WATER
1	CUP HEAVY CREAM
½	CUP SUGAR
½	CUP ROASTED PEANUTS OR PISTACHIOS, FOR GARNISH
	SHREDDED COCONUT, FOR GARNISH

FOR THE SYRUP

½	CUP WATER
½	CUP SUGAR
1	TEASPOON ROSE WATER
2–3	DROPS OF RED FOOD COLORING

DEBLA

YIELD: 12 COOKIES / ACTIVE TIME: 20 MINUTES / TOTAL TIME: 1 HOUR

The addition of delicate orange blossom water makes this festive and fried Libyan dessert light enough to consume after a big meal.

1. Place the eggs, baking soda, and 2½ cups of the flour in a mixing bowl and work the mixture until it comes together as a dough.

2. Separate the dough into five pieces. Roll out each piece until it is paper thin.

3. Add avocado oil to a deep skillet until it is 1 inch deep and warm it to 325°F.

4. Cut the dough into strips that are 2 inches wide and about 12 inches long. Prick the strips all over with a fork.

5. Wrap a strip around one prong of a wide fork and fry it, coiling the dough around itself as it fries until it is lightly browned all over. Transfer the fried debla to a paper towel–lined colander and let it drain. Repeat with the remaining dough.

6. Place the remaining ingredients and 1½ cups water in a saucepan, cover the pan, and simmer the mixture over low heat until it is a thick syrup, about 45 minutes.

7. Stir the syrup and remove the pan from heat.

8. Dip the debla into the warm syrup, soaking them well. Place them in a colander and let them drain.

9. When the syrup has cooled and hardened, arrange the debla on a serving platter and enjoy.

INGREDIENTS:

5	LARGE EGGS, BEATEN
1	TEASPOON BAKING SODA
3	CUPS ALL-PURPOSE FLOUR
	AVOCADO OIL, AS NEEDED
2	CUPS SUGAR
⅛	TEASPOON FRESH LEMON JUICE
⅛	TEASPOON ORANGE BLOSSOM WATER
⅛	TEASPOON ROSE WATER
⅛	TEASPOON PURE VANILLA EXTRACT

GRANOLA

YIELD: 2½ CUPS / **ACTIVE TIME:** 15 MINUTES / **TOTAL TIME:** 1 HOUR AND 30 MINUTES

t's good to commit to making granola at home, as it gives you complete control over what's going in it.

1. Preheat the oven to 350°F. Line a baking sheet with a Silpat mat. Place the oats, nuts, seeds, raisins, and baking soda in a mixing bowl and stir to combine. Set the mixture aside.

2. Place the remaining ingredients in a small saucepan and bring to a boil, stirring to dissolve the sugar and salt. Remove the pan from heat and let the syrup cool.

3. Pour the syrup over the oat-and-nut mixture and stir until everything is evenly coated. Transfer the granola to the baking sheet, place it in the oven, and bake until golden brown, about 20 minutes, stirring halfway through.

4. Remove the granola from the oven and let it cool completely before enjoying.

INGREDIENTS:

1	CUP OATS
¼	CUP SLIVERED ALMONDS
¼	CUP WALNUT HALVES
¼	CUP PUMPKIN SEEDS
¼	CUP SUNFLOWER SEEDS
½	CUP RAISINS
½	TEASPOON BAKING SODA
1	TABLESPOON UNSALTED BUTTER
1	TABLESPOON SUGAR
2	TABLESPOONS HONEY
2	TABLESPOONS MAPLE SYRUP
2	TABLESPOONS CANOLA OIL
	SALT, TO TASTE

SPICED HONEY CAKE WITH COCONUT & CREAM CHEESE FROSTING

YIELD: 8 SERVINGS / ACTIVE TIME: 20 MINUTES / TOTAL TIME: 1 HOUR AND 20 MINUTES

A gluten-free cake that everyone, no matter their stance, will find toothsome.

1. Preheat the oven to 350°F. Coat a 9-inch cake pan with non-stick cooking spray and line the bottom with a circle of parchment paper.

2. Place the flour, baking powder, baking soda, salt, cinnamon, ginger, and nutmeg in a mixing bowl and stir to combine.

3. Combine the sugar, brown sugar, avocado oil, honey, egg, and egg yolk in the work bowl of a stand mixer fitted with the paddle attachment. Add the vanilla seeds and beat the mixture until it is pale and thick, about 4 minutes. Reduce the speed to medium-low and gradually pour in the orange juice and buttermilk. Beat until frothy, about 2 minutes. Reduce speed to low and gradually incorporate the dry mixture. Beat until the mixture comes together as a thin, pancake-like batter.

4. Pour the batter into the prepared pan and bake until the cake is golden brown and the center springs back when gently pressed (a cake tester inserted will not come out clean), 45 to 55 minutes.

5. Remove the cake from the oven, place the pan on a wire rack, and let the cake cool for 20 minutes. Run a knife around the edge of the cake to loosen it and invert it onto the rack. Let the cake cool completely.

6. When the cake is completely cool, cover it with the frosting and enjoy.

INGREDIENTS:

2 CUPS GLUTEN-FREE ALL-PURPOSE BAKING FLOUR

1½ TEASPOONS BAKING POWDER

½ TEASPOON BAKING SODA

½ TEASPOON SEA SALT

1½ TEASPOONS CINNAMON

½ TEASPOON GROUND GINGER

⅛ TEASPOON FRESHLY GRATED NUTMEG

⅔ CUP SUGAR

¼ CUP PACKED LIGHT BROWN SUGAR

½ CUP AVOCADO OIL

½ CUP HONEY

1 LARGE EGG

1 LARGE EGG YOLK

SEEDS FROM ½ VANILLA BEAN

½ CUP FRESH ORANGE JUICE

½ CUP BUTTERMILK

COCONUT & CREAM CHEESE FROSTING (SEE PAGE 668)

SFENJ DONUTS

YIELD: 15 SERVINGS / ACTIVE TIME: 40 MINUTES / TOTAL TIME: 3 HOURS

These miraculous Moroccan confections pair perfectly with tea or coffee.

1. Place the flour, yeast, salt, and sugar in a mixing bowl and stir to combine. Add the egg yolks and slowly drizzle in the water while mixing by hand.

2. Knead the mixture until it comes together as a sticky, smooth, and soft dough.

3. Spray the dough with nonstick cooking spray and cover the bowl with plastic wrap. Let the dough rise at room temperature for 2 hours.

4. Coat a large baking sheet with some avocado oil. Set it aside.

5. Divide the dough into 15 parts, roll each piece into a ball, and place it on the greased baking sheet. Cover the balls of dough with a slightly damp linen towel and let them rise for another 30 minutes.

6. Add avocado oil to a large, deep skillet until it is one-third to halfway full and warm it to 375°F.

7. Using your forefinger and thumb, make a hole in the center of each dough ball and gently slip them into the hot oil. Fry until lightly golden brown all over, turning the sfenj as necessary.

8. Top the fried sfenj with confectioners' sugar or honey and enjoy immediately.

INGREDIENTS:

4	CUPS ALL-PURPOSE FLOUR
2	TEASPOONS INSTANT YEAST
1	TEASPOON FINE SEA SALT
1	TABLESPOON SUGAR
2	LARGE EGG YOLKS
1½	CUPS LUKEWARM WATER (90°F)
	AVOCADO OIL, AS NEEDED
	CONFECTIONERS' SUGAR OR HONEY, FOR TOPPING

Sfenj Donuts, see page 665

COCONUT & CREAM CHEESE FROSTING

YIELD: 1 CUP / **ACTIVE TIME:** 10 MINUTES / **TOTAL TIME:** 10 MINUTES

A preparation that will open your eyes to the considerable utility of coconut cream.

1. Place the cream cheese and butter in the work bowl of a stand mixer fitted with the paddle attachment and beat until it is smooth and creamy. Add the confectioners' sugar, lemon zest, salt, and vanilla seeds and beat until the mixture is very light and thick, about 2 minutes.

2. Scrape down the work bowl. With the mixer running, add the coconut cream 1 tablespoon at a time and beat until the mixture holds very soft peaks.

INGREDIENTS:

3   OZ. CREAM CHEESE, SOFTENED

3   TABLESPOONS UNSALTED BUTTER, SOFTENED

1   CUP CONFECTIONERS' SUGAR

1   TEASPOON LEMON ZEST

    PINCH OF FINE SEA SALT

    SEEDS FROM ½ VANILLA BEAN

    CREAM FROM 1 (14 OZ.) CAN OF UNSWEETENED COCONUT MILK, AT ROOM TEMPERATURE

SUMAC, SPELT & APPLE CAKE

YIELD: 4 SERVINGS / ACTIVE TIME: 20 MINUTES / TOTAL TIME: 1 HOUR AND 20 MINUTES

There's a lot to love about this apple cake, which gets its citrusy fragrance from sumac, as well as a rustic look and nutty flavor from spelt flour. It happens to be vegan too.

1. To prepare the applesauce, place all of the ingredients in a saucepan and bring to a simmer. Cook until the apples are completely tender, 10 to 12 minutes. Remove the pan from heat and mash the apples until smooth. Set the applesauce aside.

2. Preheat the oven to 350°F. Coat a 8 x 4–inch loaf pan with cooking spray and line it with parchment paper. To begin preparations for the cake, place the flour, ground almonds, sumac, baking powder and baking soda in a mixing bowl and stir to combine.

3. Place the avocado oil, sugar, and 1½ cups of the applesauce in a separate bowl and stir to combine. Add the wet mixture to the dry mixture and gently stir until the mixture comes together as a thick batter, making sure there are no clumps of flour. Stir in the apples.

4. Pour the batter into the loaf pan, place it in the oven, and bake until a cake tester inserted into the center of the cake comes out clean, 45 to 50 minutes.

5. Remove the cake from the oven and let it cool completely in the pan.

6. Place the confectioners' sugar and lemon juice in a mixing bowl and whisk the mixture until it is thick enough to coat the back of a wooden spoon. If it's too thin, add more sugar; if too thick, add more lemon juice.

7. Drizzle the icing over the cake, top with additional sumac, and enjoy.

INGREDIENTS:

FOR THE APPLESAUCE

- 2 LARGE GRANNY SMITH APPLES, PEELED, CORED, AND CHOPPED
- 1 TABLESPOON FRESH LEMON JUICE
- ½ CUP WATER

FOR THE CAKE

- 1⅔ CUPS SPELT FLOUR
- ½ CUP GROUND ALMONDS
- 1 TABLESPOON SUMAC, PLUS MORE FOR TOPPING
- 1 TEASPOON BAKING POWDER
- 1 TEASPOON BAKING SODA
- ¼ CUP AVOCADO OIL
- ½ CUP PLUS 2 TABLESPOONS SUGAR
- 3 GOLDEN APPLES, PEELED, CORED, AND FINELY DICED
- ½ CUP CONFECTIONERS' SUGAR, PLUS MORE AS NEEDED
- 1 TABLESPOON FRESH LEMON JUICE, PLUS MORE AS NEEDED

CARDAMOM BISCOTTI

YIELD: 8 SERVINGS / **ACTIVE TIME:** 30 MINUTES / **TOTAL TIME:** 1 HOUR AND 30 MINUTES

A floral version of these beloved double-baked biscuits that are perfect for dipping into your coffee, morning, afternoon, or evening.

1. Preheat the oven to 350°F. Line a baking sheet with parchment paper. Place all of the ingredients, except for the orange zest, eggs, olive oil, and vanilla, in a mixing bowl and whisk until combined.

2. Add the remaining ingredients and work the mixture by hand until it comes together as a smooth dough. Roll the dough into a log that is about 6 inches long and about 2 inches wide. Place the log on the baking sheet, place it in the oven, and bake until golden brown, about 20 minutes.

3. Remove the biscotti from the oven and let it cool.

4. Cut the biscotti into the desired shape and size. Place the biscotti back in the oven bake until it is crispy, about 20 minutes.

5. Remove the biscotti from the oven, transfer to a wire rack, and let them cool completely before enjoying.

INGREDIENTS:

1½	CUPS ALL-PURPOSE FLOUR
¾	TEASPOON BAKING POWDER
	PINCH OF FINE SEA SALT
¼	CUP SUGAR
⅓	CUP LIGHT BROWN SUGAR
¾	TEASPOON CARDAMOM
½	TEASPOON CINNAMON
¼	TEASPOON GROUND GINGER
⅛	TEASPOON GROUND CLOVES
⅛	TEASPOON FRESHLY GRATED NUTMEG
	ZEST OF 1 ORANGE
2	EGGS
¼	CUP EXTRA-VIRGIN OLIVE OIL
1	TEASPOON PURE VANILLA EXTRACT

SFRATTI

YIELD: 6 SERVINGS / ACTIVE TIME: 30 MINUTES / TOTAL TIME: 3 HOURS

S fratti means "eviction" in Italian—which all of the Jewish people in the Tuscan village of Piti- gliano, where these rod-shaped cookies originated, faced before settling there.

1. Combine the flour, sugar, and salt in a mixing bowl. Add the butter and work the mixture with a pastry cutter until it resembles coarse crumbs. Add the wine a little at a time, mixing it in with a fork to moisten the dough. Continue adding wine until the mixture just comes together as a dough. Divide the dough in half and form each piece into a ball. Flatten the balls into disks, cover them with plastic wrap, and refrigerate for 1 hour. The dough will keep in the refrigerator for up to 3 days.

2. Remove the dough from the refrigerator and let it stand at room temperature until malleable but not soft.

3. Place the honey in a saucepan and bring to a boil. Boil for 5 minutes, lowering the heat if the honey starts to foam over the edge of the pan. Add all of the remaining ingredients, except for the egg and water, and cook, stirring constantly, for another 3 to 5 minutes, and remove the pan from heat. If the mixture begins to turn dark, it is starting to burn—remove from heat immediately and keep stirring!

4. Let the mixture stand, stirring occasionally, until it is cool enough to handle. Pour the mixture onto a flour-dusted surface, divide it into six equal portions, and shape each portion into a 14-inch-long rod.

5. Preheat the oven to 350°F. Line a large baking sheet with parchment paper.

6. On a piece of parchment paper or on a flour-dusted work surface, roll each piece of dough into a 14 x 12–inch rectangle, then cut each rectangle lengthwise into three long rectangles. Place one of the strips of filling near a long side of each rectangle, then form the dough around the filling.

7. You will have six long sticks of dough with filling in each. Cut these into 2-inch-long sticks. Place the cookies, seam side down, on the baking sheet, leaving 1 inch between the cookies.

INGREDIENTS:

3	CUPS ALL-PURPOSE FLOUR, PLUS MORE AS NEEDED
1	CUP SUGAR
	PINCH OF FINE SEA SALT
⅓	CUP UNSALTED BUTTER, CHILLED
⅔	CUP DRY WHITE WINE, CHILLED
1	CUP HONEY
2	CUPS CHOPPED WALNUTS
2	TEASPOONS ORANGE ZEST
¾	TEASPOON CINNAMON
¼	TEASPOON GROUND GINGER
	DASH OF FRESHLY GRATED NUTMEG
¼	TEASPOON BLACK PEPPER
1	LARGE EGG
1	TABLESPOON WATER

8. Place the egg and water in a cup and beat until combined. Brush the cookies with the egg wash.

9. Place the cookies in the oven and bake until golden brown, about 20 minutes.

10. Remove from the oven, transfer the cookies to a wire rack, and and let them cool completely before serving.

BLUEBERRY COMPOTE

YIELD: 4 SERVINGS / ACTIVE TIME: 10 MINUTES / TOTAL TIME: 30 MINUTES

The hints of cinnamon and star anise are enough to arouse memories of a warm day on the shores of the Mediterranean.

1. Place all of the ingredients in a small saucepan and cook over low heat, stirring occasionally, until the mixture has thickened and most of the liquid has evaporated, 5 to 7 minutes.

2. Remove the cinnamon sticks and star anise and let the compote cool.

3. When the compote has cooled, use immediately or store in the refrigerator until needed.

INGREDIENTS:

1½ CUPS FROZEN BLUEBERRIES, THAWED

2 TABLESPOONS SUGAR

JUICE OF 1 ORANGE

2 CINNAMON STICKS

1 STAR ANISE POD

BEVERAGES

In the global imagination, a mention of the Mediterranean brings to mind a peaceful, sunny balcony looking over the deep, seemingly artificial blue of the sea. That pleasant image has caused bartenders around the world to concoct a number of refreshing serves that seek to evoke and celebrate the glory of such a setting. And, for those occasions where the cold threatens to take over your whole being, a handful of warming, traditional beverages will help keep things cozy.

SPIKED LIMONANA

YIELD: 1 SERVING / **ACTIVE TIME:** 2 MINUTES / **TOTAL TIME:** 2 MINUTES

A beautiful, refreshing drink that will serve as the launching pad for many a memorable summer brunch.

1. Place all of the ingredients in a blender and puree until smooth.

2. Pour the cocktail into a wineglass, garnish with additional mint, and enjoy.

INGREDIENTS:

1½	OZ. VODKA
8	OZ. WATER
¼	CUP SUGAR
4	FRESH MINT LEAVES, PLUS MORE FOR GARNISH
2	OZ. FRESH LEMON JUICE
1	CUP ICE

ISRAELI ICED TEA

YIELD: 1 SERVING / **ACTIVE TIME:** 2 MINUTES / **TOTAL TIME:** 2 MINUTES

A spin on the Long Island Iced Tea, with arak changing the boozy original into a flavorful and herbaceous drink.

1. Combine all of the ingredients, except for the Coca-Cola and garnish, in a Collins glass.

2. Add ice and top with Coca-Cola. Gently pour the mixture into a mixing glass and then pour it back into the Collins glass.

3. Garnish with the lemon wedge and enjoy.

INGREDIENTS:

1½   OZ. ARAK

¼   OZ. GIN

¼   OZ. TEQUILA

¼   OZ. VODKA

¼   OZ. TRIPLE SEC

     JUICE OF 1 LEMON

     COCA-COLA, TO TOP

1   LEMON WEDGE, FOR
     GARNISH

HAWAIJ HOT COCOA

YIELD: 2 SERVINGS / **ACTIVE TIME:** 15 MINUTES / **TOTAL TIME:** 15 MINUTES

Hawaij is a spice blend closely associated with Yemeni cuisine that fans of Mediterranean-style flavors will take to immediately.

1. Place the milk, sugar, and chocolate in a small saucepan and warm over medium-high heat, whisking until the chocolate begins to melt.

2. Add the cocoa powder, Hawaij Spice Blend, and salt and continue to whisk until the chocolate is completely melted and the mixture just comes to a simmer.

3. Pour the cocoa into mugs, top each one with a dollop of whipped cream, and garnish with cinnamon sticks.

HAWAIJ SPICE BLEND

1. Combine all of the ingredients and store in an airtight container.

CINNAMON WHIPPED CREAM

1. Place all of the ingredients in the work bowl of a stand mixer fitted with the paddle attachment. Whip on low for 1 minute.

2. Increase the speed to high and whip until the mixture holds stiff peaks.

INGREDIENTS:

2	CUPS MILK
2	TABLESPOONS SUGAR
1	OZ. DARK CHOCOLATE CHIPS
1	TABLESPOON (SCANT) COCOA POWDER
2	TEASPOONS HAWAIJ SPICE BLEND (SEE RECIPE)
	PINCH OF KOSHER SALT
	CINNAMON WHIPPED CREAM (SEE RECIPE), FOR GARNISH
	CINNAMON STICKS, FOR GARNISH

HAWAIJ SPICE BLEND

1½	TABLESPOONS GROUND GINGER
1	TABLESPOON CINNAMON
1½	TEASPOONS CARDAMOM
½	TEASPOON GROUND CLOVES
	PINCH OF FRESHLY GRATED NUTMEG

CINNAMON WHIPPED CREAM

2	CUPS HEAVY CREAM
2	TABLESPOONS SUGAR
1	TEASPOON PURE VANILLA EXTRACT
½	TEASPOON CINNAMON

LIMONANA

YIELD: 4 SERVINGS / **ACTIVE TIME:** 5 MINUTES / **TOTAL TIME:** 5 MINUTES

This refreshing mix of icy lemonade and crushed mint is sure to cool you down.

1. Place the lemon juice, mint, sugar, and ½ cup of the water in a blender and puree until smooth.

2. Strain through a fine-mesh sieve, reserving the liquid and discarding the solids.

3. Place the remaining water in a pitcher, add the strained liquid, and stir to combine.

4. Serve over ice.

INGREDIENTS:

1½   CUPS FRESH LEMON JUICE

3   CUPS FRESH MINT LEAVES

1   CUP SUGAR

4   CUPS WATER

POMEGRANATE PROSECCO PUNCH

YIELD: 8 SERVINGS / ACTIVE TIME: 5 MINUTES / TOTAL TIME: 5 MINUTES

Sure, you could just pour a glass of sparkling Prosecco and call it a day, but turning it into a celebratory punch rich with fruity, tart pomegranate juice and citrus livens things up a bit.

1. Place the juices and sugar in a large punch bowl and stir until the sugar has dissolved.

2. Add the Prosecco, gently stir, and garnish each serving with the clementine and lime wheels.

INGREDIENTS:

4   CUPS POMEGRANATE
      JUICE, CHILLED

2   TABLESPOONS FRESH LIME
      JUICE

¼   CUP CASTER SUGAR
      (SUPERFINE)

2   (750 ML) BOTTLES OF
      PROSECCO, CHILLED

2   CLEMENTINES, SLICED
      THIN, FOR GARNISH

1   LIME, SLICED THIN, FOR
      GARNISH

SACHLAV

In Turkey, where it originated, sachlav was traditionally made using ground orchid bulbs. Today, this thick and creamy milk-based drink is served hot and commonly topped with pistachios, grated coconut, and raisins. It's perfect to keep you warm during winter months.

1. Place ¼ cup of the milk and the cornstarch in a bowl and whisk until combined.

2. Place the remaining milk, vanilla, sugar or honey, and salt in a medium saucepan and warm it over medium-low heat. When the mixture is hot but not quite simmering, whisk in the slurry.

3. Whisk the mixture until the sachlav has thickened enough to coat the back of a wooden spoon and is frothy, 3 to 5 minutes, making sure it never comes to a boil.

4. Remove the sachlav from the heat and stir in the orange blossom water. Taste, adjust the seasoning as necessary, and serve with the pistachios, coconut, and cinnamon or cardamom.

INGREDIENTS:

4   **CUPS WHOLE MILK OR COCONUT MILK**

¼   **CUP CORNSTARCH**

2   **TEASPOONS PURE VANILLA EXTRACT**

3   **TABLESPOONS SUGAR OR HONEY**

    PINCH OF KOSHER SALT

½   **TEASPOON ORANGE BLOSSOM WATER**

    ROASTED PISTACHIOS, FINELY CHOPPED, FOR SERVING

    SHREDDED COCONUT, FOR SERVING

    CINNAMON OR CARDAMOM, FOR SERVING

Sachlav, see page 689

RAPHAEL

YIELD: 1 SERVING / ACTIVE TIME: 2 MINUTES / TOTAL TIME: 2 MINUTES

If you are unsure where to turn for quality manzana verde liqueur, both Briottet and Giffard are good choices.

1. Place the strawberry puree, liqueur, and lime juice in a cocktail shaker, fill it two-thirds of the way with ice, and shake vigorously.

2. Strain over ice into a wineglass and top with Champagne.

3. Garnish with the strawberry and enjoy.

INGREDIENTS:

2   OZ. STRAWBERRY PUREE

½   OZ. MANZANA VERDE APPLE LIQUEUR

1   TABLESPOON FRESH LIME JUICE

    CHAMPAGNE, TO TOP

1   STRAWBERRY, FOR GARNISH

MACARONI COCKTAIL

YIELD: 1 SERVING / ACTIVE TIME: 2 MINUTES / TOTAL TIME: 1 HOUR

Pastis, the anise-flavored liqueur from Provence, really comes to life with the herbal qualities of vermouth.

1. Place a teacup in the freezer for 1 hour.

2. Place the ingredients in a cocktail shaker, fill it two-thirds of the way with ice, and shake vigorously.

3. Strain the cocktail into the chilled teacup and enjoy.

INGREDIENTS:

1   OZ. PASTIS

½   OZ. SWEET VERMOUTH

VALENTINE'S GRAPEFRUIT

YIELD: 1 SERVING / ACTIVE TIME: 2 MINUTES / TOTAL TIME: 2 MINUTES

Fans of cocktails residing at the bitter end of the spectrum get their dream drink with this refreshing concoction.

1. Place the vermouth, liqueurs, and bitters in a Collins glass and stir to combine.

2. Add ice and top with the club soda.

3. Garnish with the grapefruit twist and enjoy.

INGREDIENTS:

¾   OZ. CARPANO BIANCO VERMOUTH

¾   OZ. TEMPUS FUGIT GRAN CLASSICO BITTER LIQUEUR

¾   OZ. FERNET-BRANCA

2   DASHES OF SCRAPPY'S GRAPEFRUIT BITTERS

    CLUB SODA, TO TOP

1   GRAPEFRUIT TWIST, FOR GARNISH

TRIPLE MY WORTH

YIELD: 1 SERVING / ACTIVE TIME: 2 MINUTES / TOTAL TIME: 2 MINUTES

The cardamom syrup in this cocktail brings an earthiness that balances the arak and tequila.

1. Place all of the ingredients in a cocktail shaker, fill it two-thirds of the way with ice, and shake vigorously for 15 seconds.

2. Strain over ice into a tumbler and enjoy.

CARDAMOM SYRUP

1. Place the sugar and water in a small saucepan and bring to a boil, stirring to dissolve the sugar.

2. Add the cardamom pods, boil for another minute, and remove the pan from heat. Let the syrup cool completely and strain before using or storing.

INGREDIENTS:

1½   OZ. TEQUILA

1   OZ. ARAK

¼   OZ. CARDAMOM SYRUP
    (SEE RECIPE)

¼   OZ. FRESH LIME JUICE

CARDAMOM SYRUP

1   CUP SUGAR

1   CUP WATER

10   CARDAMOM PODS

DRINK OF LAUGHTER & FORGETTING

YIELD: 1 SERVING / ACTIVE TIME: 2 MINUTES / TOTAL TIME: 2 MINUTES

Cynar is an amaro made from 13 herbs and plants, with the artichoke figuring most prominently in its mysterious formula.

1. Place all of the ingredients in a cocktail shaker, fill it two-thirds of the way with ice, and shake vigorously.

2. Strain into a cocktail glass and enjoy.

INGREDIENTS:

1½   OZ. CYNAR

½   OZ. CHARTREUSE

¾   OZ. FRESH LIME JUICE

½   OZ. SIMPLE SYRUP (SEE
      PAGE 739)

14   DROPS OF ANGOSTURA
      BITTERS

Drink of Laughter & Forgetting, see page 699

THE BITTER POMELO

YIELD: 1 SERVING / **ACTIVE TIME:** 2 MINUTES / **TOTAL TIME:** 2 MINUTES

The soft fizz of Topo Chico makes this an ultrarefreshing serve.

1. Place the Cynar, grapefruit juice, and mint leaves in a mixing glass, fill it two-thirds of the way with ice, and stir until chilled.

2. Strain the cocktail over ice into a highball glass and top with Topo Chico.

3. Garnish with the sprig of mint and enjoy.

INGREDIENTS:

2 OZ. CYNAR

4 OZ. FRESH RUBY RED GRAPEFRUIT JUICE

3–5 FRESH MINT LEAVES, CRUSHED

TOPO CHICO, TO TOP

1 SPRIG OF FRESH MINT, FOR GARNISH

TOP-SHELF NEGRONI

YIELD: 1 SERVING / **ACTIVE TIME:** 2 MINUTES / **TOTAL TIME:** 2 MINUTES

As Kingsley Amis, the great English author and spirits aficionado, once said of the Negroni, "It has the power, rare with drinks and indeed with anything else, of cheering you up."

1. Place a large ice cube in a rocks glass and pour a little bit of Punt e Mes vermouth over it. Swirl to rinse the glass, then strain to remove the vermouth.

2. Place the remaining ingredients in a wineglass or brandy snifter and swirl to combine.

3. Pour the cocktail from a height into a rocks glass.

4. Stir briefly, express the strip of orange peel over the cocktail, use it as a garnish, and enjoy.

INGREDIENTS:

1 BAR SPOON OF PUNT E MES SWEET VERMOUTH, PLUS MORE TO RINSE

1 OZ. TANQUERAY NO. TEN GIN

2 BAR SPOONS OF GORDON'S LONDON DRY GIN

2 BAR SPOONS OF CAMPARI

1 BAR SPOON OF CARPANO ANTICA FORMULA SWEET VERMOUTH

3 DROPS OF ABBOTT'S BITTERS

1 STRIP OF ORANGE PEEL, FOR GARNISH

Top-Shelf Negroni, see page 701

FENNEL & OLIVE OIL GIMLET

YIELD: 1 SERVING / **ACTIVE TIME:** 2 MINUTES / **TOTAL TIME:** 2 MINUTES

The fennel comes through much more than the olive oil, which is more of a textural element.

---

1. Place all of the ingredients in a container and use an immersion blender to puree the mixture.

2. Add the puree to a cocktail shaker, fill it two-thirds of the way with ice, and shake vigorously.

3. Strain into a goblet and enjoy.

FENNEL SYRUP

1. Place the ingredinets in a blender and pulse to combine. Strain before using or storing.

INGREDIENTS:

1½	OZ. TANQUERAY NO. TEN GIN
2	BAR SPOONS OF FENNEL SYRUP (SEE RECIPE)
2	BAR SPOONS OF FRESH LIME JUICE
3	DROPS OF ORANGE-FLAVORED OLIVE OIL
1	BAR SPOON OF LIME ZEST

FENNEL SYRUP

3½	OZ. SIMPLE SYRUP (SEE PAGE 739)
2	TABLESPOONS FENNEL SEEDS

Lipstick & Rouge, see page 708

LIPSTICK & ROUGE

YIELD: 1 SERVING / ACTIVE TIME: 2 MINUTES / TOTAL TIME: 2 MINUTES

A take on the Aperol spritz that is perfect for a brunch that you wouldn't mind seeing stretch all the way into the evening.

1. Place the Aperol, Luxardo Amaretto, and lemon juice in a cocktail shaker, fill it two-thirds of the way with ice, and shake vigorously.

2. Strain over ice into a wineglass.

3. Top with the Prosecco, garnish with the orange wheel, and enjoy.

INGREDIENTS:

¾ OZ. APEROL

¾ OZ. LUXARDO AMARETTO

¾ OZ. FRESH LEMON JUICE

3 OZ. PROSECCO

1 ORANGE WHEEL, FOR GARNISH

FALUKA

YIELD: 1 SERVING / ACTIVE TIME: 2 MINUTES / TOTAL TIME: 2 MINUTES

Jellab is a combination of dates, tamarind, rose water, and pine nuts that is typically enjoyed as a beverage on its own in the Middle East. Integrating its unique flavor into a Pisco Sour transforms the classic cocktail.

1. Place all of the ingredients in a cocktail shaker, fill it two-thirds of the way with ice, and shake vigorously.

2. Strain into a rocks glass and enjoy.

INGREDIENTS:

1¾ OZ. PISCO

⅓ OZ. FRESH LIME JUICE

½ OZ. JELLAB

1 EGG WHITE

THE PROJECT

YIELD: 1 SERVING / ACTIVE TIME: 2 MINUTES / TOTAL TIME: 2 MINUTES

A perfect after-dinner drink that slips rum into the space typically reserved for Cynar and Aperol.

1. Place the rum, Cynar, Aperol, and syrup in a cocktail shaker, fill it two-thirds of the way with ice, and shake vigorously.

2. Double-strain over an ice sphere in a rocks glass, garnish with the coffee beans and torched orange peel, and enjoy.

COFFEE SYRUP

1. Place all of the ingredients in a saucepan and bring to a boil.

2. Remove the pan from heat and let the mixture steep for 4 hours. Strain before using or storing.

INGREDIENTS:

2	OZ. SANTA TERESA 1796 RUM
¼	OZ. CYNAR
1	OZ. APEROL
¼	OZ. COFFEE SYRUP (SEE RECIPE)
3	COFFEE BEANS, FOR GARNISH
1	TORCHED ORANGE PEEL, FOR GARNISH

COFFEE SYRUP

2	CUPS SUGAR
2	CUPS WATER
5	COFFEE BEANS

BIG TROUBLE SPRITZ

This low-ABV concoction can be made quickly and built in the glass, making it perfect for an all-day summer gathering.

1. Place all of the ingredients in a wineglass, add ice, and stir until chilled and combined.

2. Garnish with the grapefruit twist and enjoy.

INGREDIENTS:

1	OZ. COCCHI AMERICANO
1	OZ. BAROLO CHINATO
2	OZ. Q GRAPEFRUIT SODA
1	OZ. PROSECCO
1	GRAPEFRUIT TWIST, FOR GARNISH

SGROPPINO PLAGIATO

YIELD: 1 SERVING / **ACTIVE TIME:** 2 MINUTES / **TOTAL TIME:** 2 MINUTES

f you cannot track down Select Aperitivo, simply substitute Aperol. The drink will be slightly less vibrant, but still refreshing.

1. Place the scoop of sorbet in a goblet.

2. Pour the Select Aperitivo over the sorbet and top with the Prosecco.

3. Garnish with a flower and serve with a spoon.

TROPICAL FRUIT SORBET

1. Place the water, sugar, and lemon juice in a saucepan and bring to a simmer, stirring to dissolve the sugar.

2. Add the remaining ingredients and stir until combined. Remove the pan from heat and let the mixture cool.

3. Freeze the mixture for 24 hours and let it sit at room temperature for 5 or 10 minutes before serving. Churn the sorbet in an ice cream maker if a smoother consistency is desired.

INGREDIENTS:

1	SCOOP OF TROPICAL FRUIT SORBET (SEE RECIPE)
1¾	OZ. SELECT APERITIVO
	PROSECCO, TO TOP
1	EDIBLE FLOWER, FOR GARNISH

TROPICAL FRUIT SORBET

3½	OZ. WATER
3½	OZ. SUGAR
½	OZ. FRESH LEMON JUICE
	SEEDS OF 1 VANILLA BEAN
14	OZ. MANGO PUREE
3½	OZ. PASSION FRUIT PUREE

LADY IN RED

This cocktail has a floral and fruity finish thanks to the Strawberry Vinegar.

1. Place all of the ingredients in a mixing glass, fill it two-thirds of the way with ice, and stir until chilled.

2. Strain over a large block of ice into a coupe and enjoy.

STRAWBERRY VINEGAR

1. Place all of the ingredients in an airtight container, cover it, and let it sit for 3 days.

2. Strain and taste the vinegar to see if it is sweet enough. Add more Simple Syrup if necessary, and use as desired.

INGREDIENTS:

¾ OZ. LONDON DRY GIN

½ OZ. CAMPARI

¼ OZ. STRAWBERRY VINEGAR (SEE RECIPE)

2 OZ. SPARKLING WINE

STRAWBERRY VINEGAR

10½ OZ. FRESH STRAWBERRIES

26 OZ. APPLE CIDER VINEGAR

2 LEMONS

1 TEASPOON GRENADINE

1½ OZ. SIMPLE SYRUP (SEE PAGE 739), PLUS MORE TO TASTE

THE TOP OF OLYMPUS

YIELD: 4 SERVINGS / **ACTIVE TIME:** 2 MINUTES / **TOTAL TIME:** 2 MINUTES

A lovely winter warmer that you can take along for a walk in the woods, or sit beside the fire with.

1. Place all of the ingredients in an appropriately sized container and gently shake it until the yogurt powder has been incorporated.

2. Pour into mugs or a Thermos flask and enjoy.

SPICED TEA CORDIAL

1. Place the boiling water, sugar, and bags of tea in a container and steep for 2 minutes, stirring gently a few times.

2. Remove the tea bags, place the tea in a saucepan, add the remaining ingredients, and cook over low heat until the flavor is to your liking, about 30 to 35 minutes.

3. Strain before using or storing.

INGREDIENTS:

6	OZ. METAXA
10	OZ. SPICED TEA CORDIAL (SEE RECIPE)
½	OZ. YOGURT POWDER

SPICED TEA CORDIAL

35	OZ. BOILING WATER
7	OZ. SUGAR
10	BAGS OF ENGLISH BREAKFAST TEA
10	STAR ANISE PODS
15	WHOLE CLOVES
3	CINNAMON STICKS
2	TABLESPOONS UNSALTED BUTTER

VITAMIN SEA

YIELD: 1 SERVING / ACTIVE TIME: 2 MINUTES / TOTAL TIME: 2 MINUTES

Here is a perfect cocktail to accompany oysters.

1. Place all of the ingredients, except for the Jasmine Air, in a cocktail shaker, fill it two-thirds of the way with ice, and shake vigorously.

2. Double-strain into a coupe.

3. Spoon the Jasmine Air on top of the drink and enjoy.

LAVENDER SYRUP

1. Place all of the ingredients in a saucepan and bring to a simmer over medium heat, stirring until the sugar has dissolved.

2. Remove the pan from heat, let the syrup cool completely, and strain before using or storing.

JASMINE AIR

1. Place the ingredients in a container and stir to incorporate.

2. Strain into a large bowl and work the mixture with an immersion blender, trying to get as much air into the mixture as possible. Once the mixture is very foamy, use immediately.

INGREDIENTS:

1¼ OZ. HENDRICK'S GIN

¾ OZ. ITALICUS ROSOLIO DI BERGAMOTTO LIQUEUR

1 TEASPOON LUXARDO MARASCHINO CHERRY LIQUEUR

⅞ OZ. BERGAMOT JUICE

½ OZ. LAVENDER SYRUP (SEE RECIPE)

DASH OF GINGER BITTERS

1 SMALL SLICE OF FRESH GINGER

JASMINE AIR (SEE RECIPE), FOR GARNISH

LAVENDER SYRUP

1½ CUPS SUGAR

1 CUP WATER

1 HANDFUL OF LAVENDER

JASMINE AIR

9 OZ. STRONG JASMINE TEA, CHILLED

½ TEASPOON SOY LECITHIN

OPENING NIGHT

YIELD: 1 SERVING / ACTIVE TIME: 2 MINUTES / TOTAL TIME: 2 MINUTES

This is an opera for your palate, and probably not a bad choice to warm up your vocal cords before taking your turn on karaoke night.

1. Pour all of the ingredients, except for the olives, into a champagne flute in the order they are listed and gently stir.

2. Garnish with the olives and enjoy.

OLIVE LEAF–INFUSED GIN

1. Place the ingredients in a large mason jar and store in a cool, dark place for 5 days.

2. Strain before using or storing.

INGREDIENTS:

1 OZ. OLIVE LEAF–INFUSED GIN (SEE RECIPE)

2 TEASPOONS NARDINI ACQUA DI CEDRO

2 TEASPOONS NOILLY PRAT DRY VERMOUTH

½ TEASPOON SUZE SAVEUR D'AUTREFOIS

2 OZ. THREE CENTS GENTLEMEN'S SODA

3 KALAMATA OLIVES, FOR GARNISH

OLIVE LEAF–INFUSED GIN

1 (750 ML) BOTTLE OF GIN

4 OZ. DRIED OLIVE LEAVES

THE ESCAPE

YIELD: 1 SERVING / **ACTIVE TIME:** 10 MINUTES / **TOTAL TIME:** 10 MINUTES

Mastiha liqueur, which can only be produced on the Greek island of Chios, adds robust herbal aromas to this cocktail.

1. Pour the Ouzo into a coupe, swirl to rinse, and then chill the glass in the freezer.

2. When the glass is chilled, place the gin, liqueur, and vermouth in a mixing glass, fill it two-thirds of the way with ice, and stir until chilled.

3. Strain into the chilled coupe, garnish with the rock samphire, and enjoy.

INGREDIENTS:

3	DASHES OF OUZO
2	OZ. BEEFEATER LONDON DRY GIN
½	OZ. MASTIHA LIQUEUR
¾	OZ. DRY VERMOUTH
1	PIECE OF ROCK SAMPHIRE, FOR GARNISH

FORGET DOMANI

YIELD: 1 SERVING / **ACTIVE TIME:** 2 MINUTES / **TOTAL TIME:** 2 MINUTES

This Mediterranean twist on a Manhattan is a solid choice to get a big night started.

1. Place all of the ingredients in a mixing glass, fill it two-thirds of the way with ice, and stir until chilled.

2. Strain into a coupe and enjoy.

SUN-DRIED TOMATO & OLIVE OIL GRAPPA

1. Place the grappa and sun-dried tomatoes in a large mason jar and chill in the refrigerator for 5 days.

2. Strain the grappa into another large mason jar. Add the olive oil, cover the jar, and shake it vigorously. Store in a cool, dark place for 24 hours.

3. Place the mason jar in the freezer overnight, so that the olive oil completely separates and solidifies.

4. Remove the layer of olive oil, strain the grappa through a coffee filter, and use as desired.

BASIL-INFUSED SUZE

1. Place the ingredients in a large mason jar and refrigerate for 4 hours.

2. Strain before using or storing.

INGREDIENTS:

1	OZ. SUN-DRIED TOMATO & OLIVE OIL GRAPPA (SEE RECIPE)
¾	OZ. BASIL-INFUSED SUZE (SEE RECIPE)
1¾	TEASPOONS CHARTREUSE
¾	TEASPOON CYNAR
2	DROPS OF BITTER BASTARDS NAGA CHILLI BITTERS

SUN-DRIED TOMATO & OLIVE OIL GRAPPA

1	(750 ML) BOTTLE OF NARDINI GRAPPA BIANCA
5½	OZ. SUN-DRIED TOMATOES
¼	CUP EXTRA-VIRGIN OLIVE OIL

BASIL-INFUSED SUZE

1	(750 ML) BOTTLE OF SUZE
10	FRESH BASIL LEAVES

CHINOTTO NEGRONI

YIELD: 1 SERVING / ACTIVE TIME: 2 MINUTES / TOTAL TIME: 2 MINUTES

An extra bit of bitterness from the Quaglia Chinotto and added brightness from the lemon juice result in a crisp and drinkable variation on the old favorite.

1. Place all of the ingredients, except for the garnish, in a mixing glass, fill it two-thirds of the way with ice, and stir until chilled.

2. Strain over ice into a rocks glass, garnish with the orange twist, and enjoy.

INGREDIENTS:

⅞   OZ. BEEFEATER GIN

⅞   OZ. CAMPARI

½   OZ. CARPANO CLASSICO ROSSO SWEET VERMOUTH

½   OZ. QUAGLIA CHINOTTO LIQUEUR

1   TEASPOON FRESH LEMON JUICE

1   ORANGE TWIST, FOR GARNISH

THE CHURCH

YIELD: 1 SERVING / **ACTIVE TIME:** 2 MINUTES / **TOTAL TIME:** 2 MINUTES

The crisp flavor of Cocchi Americano makes this a cocktail worthy of worshipping.

1. Place all of the ingredients, except for the orange peel, in a cocktail shaker, fill it two-thirds of the way with ice, and shake vigorously.

2. Double-strain over a large ice cube into a double rocks glass.

3. Garnish with the strip of orange peel and enjoy.

INGREDIENTS:

1	OZ. APEROL
1	OZ. LONDON DRY GIN
1	OZ. FRESH LEMON JUICE
½	OZ. GUM SYRUP
½	OZ. COCCHI AMERICANO
1	STRIP OF ORANGE PEEL, FOR GARNISH

ITALIAN GREYHOUND

YIELD: 1 SERVING / ACTIVE TIME: 2 MINUTES / TOTAL TIME: 2 MINUTES

What vodka lacks in flavor is more than made up for by the Cappelletti.

1. Build the cocktail in a rocks glass containing a large ice cube, adding the ingredients to the glass in the order they are listed.

2. Stir until chilled, garnish with the grapefruit twist, and enjoy.

INGREDIENTS:

1 OZ. VODKA

½ OZ. CAPPELLETTI

½ OZ. ST. GEORGE BRUTO AMERICANO

 FRESH GRAPEFRUIT JUICE, TO TOP

1 GRAPEFRUIT TWIST, FOR GARNISH

ANANDA SPRITZ

YIELD: 1 SERVING / **ACTIVE TIME:** 2 MINUTES / **TOTAL TIME:** 2 MINUTES

This combination of pineapple, bourbon, and amaro makes for an intriguing spritz.

1. Place the pineapple in a cocktail shaker and muddle it. Add all of the remaining ingredients, except for the sparkling wine and garnish, fill the shaker two-thirds of the way with ice, and shake vigorously.

2. Strain into a coupe, top with sparkling wine, garnish with edible flowers, and enjoy.

INGREDIENTS:

5	PINEAPPLE CHUNKS
1½	OZ. KNOB CREEK BOURBON
1	OZ. AMARO NONINO
3	DASHES OF ANGOSTURA BITTERS
½	OZ. SIMPLE SYRUP (SEE PAGE 739, MADE WITH PALM SUGAR)
½	OZ. FRESH LEMON JUICE
½	OZ. PINEAPPLE JUICE
¾	OZ. SPARKLING WINE
	EDIBLE FLOWERS, FOR GARNISH

WHITE PEACH SANGRIA

YIELD: 6 SERVINGS / ACTIVE TIME: 10 MINUTES / TOTAL TIME: 4 HOURS

You can use any white wine here, but I've found that Pinot Grigio produces the best results.

1. Place one peach in a blender, add a splash of water, and pulse until smooth.

2. Place the peach puree in a tall pitcher. Add the remaining peach, the rum, Simple Syrup, orange blossom water, and wine. Stir until well combined and then chill the sangria in the refrigerator for at least 4 hours.

3. To serve, pour the sangria into wineglasses and top with either seltzer or sparkling wine.

INGREDIENTS:

2   LARGE PEACHES, PITTED AND SLICED

2   TABLESPOONS WHITE RUM

¼   CUP SIMPLE SYRUP (SEE PAGE 739)

2   TEASPOONS ORANGE BLOSSOM WATER

1   (750 ML) BOTTLE OF WHITE WINE

     SELTZER OR SPARKLING WINE, FOR SERVING

STRAWBERRY ROSÉ SANGRIA

YIELD: 6 SERVINGS / ACTIVE TIME: 10 MINUTES / TOTAL TIME: 4 HOURS

Go for the fruitiest Rosé you can without breaking the bank—you want something that's drinkable on its own, but not so good that a true connoisseur would view mixing it as a tragedy.

1. Place the frozen strawberries and a splash of water in a blender and pulse until smooth.

2. Place the strawberry puree, Simple Syrup, fresh strawberries, plum, rum, rose water, and wine in a tall pitcher. Stir until well combined and then chill the sangria in the refrigerator for at least 4 hours.

3. To serve, pour the sangria into wineglasses and top with either seltzer or sparkling wine.

INGREDIENTS:

1	CUP FROZEN STRAWBERRIES
½	CUP SIMPLE SYRUP (SEE PAGE 739)
1	CUP FRESH STRAWBERRIES, HALVED
1	RED PLUM, PITTED AND SLICED
2	TABLESPOONS WHITE RUM
2	TEASPOONS ROSE WATER
1	(750 ML) BOTTLE OF ROSÉ
	SELTZER OR SPARKLING WINE, FOR SERVING

Salep, see page 738

SALEP

YIELD: 2 SERVINGS / **ACTIVE TIME:** 5 MINUTES / **TOTAL TIME:** 15 MINUTES

This warming drink dates back to the height of the Ottoman Empire.

1. Place the rice flour and milk in a small saucepan and bring it to a simmer over medium heat, whisking constantly to prevent the mixture from clumping.

2. When the mixture has thickened, add the sugar and rose water and whisk until the sugar has dissolved.

3. Divide the salep between two mugs and garnish each one with cinnamon and pistachios.

INGREDIENTS:

2   TABLESPOONS GLUTINOUS RICE FLOUR

2   CUPS WHOLE MILK

4   TEASPOONS SUGAR

¼   TEASPOON ROSE WATER

   CINNAMON, FOR GARNISH

   ROASTED PISTACHIOS, FINELY CHOPPED, FOR GARNISH

ARAK SOUR

YIELD: 1 SERVING / ACTIVE TIME: 2 MINUTES / TOTAL TIME: 2 MINUTES

A Levantine entry into the family of anise-flavored spirits, arak seems poised to succeed mezcal as the next spirit craft bartenders become obsessed with.

1. Combine all of the ingredients, except for the lime wedge, in a cocktail shaker, fill it two-thirds of the way with ice, and shake vigorously.

2. Pour the contents of the shaker into a highball glass, garnish with the lime wedge, and enjoy.

SIMPLE SYRUP

1. Place the sugar and water in a small saucepan and bring to a boil, stirring to dissolve the sugar.

2. Remove the pan from heat and let the syrup cool completely before serving.

INGREDIENTS:

1½   OZ. ARAK

1½   OZ. SIMPLE SYRUP (SEE RECIPE)

½   OZ. FRESH LIME JUICE

½   OZ. GRAPEFRUIT JUICE

1   LIME WEDGE, FOR GARNISH

SIMPLE SYRUP

1   CUP SUGAR

1   CUP WATER

SAUCES, SEASONINGS & CONDIMENTS

While the majority of the recipes collected here are present because of their ties to preparations featured in the previous chapters, do not let yourself be similarly bound. In truth, the bright and dynamic flavors offered by the various cuisines that fall under the Mediterranean umbrella can lift a large percentage of one's work in the kitchen. Be generous about incorporating them into your other preparations—they are a worthy foundation to build a creative, varied, and unique approach upon.

DUKKAH

YIELD: 1½ CUPS / **ACTIVE TIME:** 1 HOUR / **TOTAL TIME:** 1 HOUR

Dukkah is a nut-and-seed mixture that is commonly used to add texture to a dish in Egypt, or enjoyed as a snack.

1. Preheat the oven to 325°F.

2. Peel the garlic cloves, trim the ends of each clove, and slice them as thinly and evenly as you can. Trim the ends of the shallot, halve it lengthwise, and slice it as thin as possible.

3. Place the garlic and shallot in a cold skillet, add the olive oil, and cook over low heat until they are a deep, even golden brown, 30 to 40 minutes, stirring occasionally to make sure the heat circulates evenly. This is long cook time allows them to build flavor without also becoming bitter, so don't try to speed it up with a higher flame.

4. While the garlic and shallot are cooking, place the pistachios on a baking sheet, place them in the oven, and roast until fragrant, 6 to 7 minutes. Remove the pistachios from the oven and let them cool.

5. Line a plate with paper towels. Strain the garlic and shallot over a clean bowl and spread them on the plate in an even layer. Wipe out the skillet and fill it with the reserved oil. Add the coriander seeds, black sesame seeds, and white sesame seeds. Toast, over low heat, until the seeds are crunchy and aromatic, about 8 minutes. Drain and place the seeds on the same plate as the shallot and garlic.

6. Place the shallot, garlic, and seeds in a large resealable plastic bag with the pistachios and the remaining ingredients. Pound the mixture with a rolling pin or mallet until everything is roughly crushed. Use immediately or store in an airtight container in the refrigerator.

INGREDIENTS:

1	HEAD OF GARLIC
1	LARGE SHALLOT
¾	CUP EXTRA-VIRGIN OLIVE OIL
1	CUP SHELLED RAW PISTACHIOS
2	TABLESPOONS CORIANDER SEEDS
2	TABLESPOONS BLACK SESAME SEEDS
2	TABLESPOONS WHITE SESAME SEEDS
1½	TABLESPOONS PINK PEPPERCORNS
1	TABLESPOON MALDON SEA SALT
2	TEASPOONS SUMAC
2	TEASPOONS ALEPPO PEPPER
1½	TABLESPOONS DRIED MINT
1½	TABLESPOONS DRIED THYME

RAS EL HANOUT

An earthy yet bright seasoning blend from Morocco that demands inclusion on your spice rack.

1. Place all of the ingredients in a bowl and whisk until combined. The spice blend will keep indefinitely in an airtight container.

INGREDIENTS:

- 1 TEASPOON TURMERIC
- 1 TEASPOON GROUND GINGER
- 1 TEASPOON CUMIN
- ¾ TEASPOON CINNAMON
- 1 TEASPOON BLACK PEPPER
- ½ TEASPOON CORIANDER
- ½ TEASPOON CAYENNE PEPPER
- ½ TEASPOON ALLSPICE
- ½ TEASPOON FRESHLY GRATED NUTMEG
- ¼ TEASPOON GROUND CLOVES
- 1 TEASPOON FINE SEA SALT

RED ZHUG

YIELD: 2½ CUPS / ACTIVE TIME: 10 MINUTES / TOTAL TIME: 10 MINUTES

Some think of this as the ketchup of the Mediterranean—it fits in almost everywhere, and carries the region's flair for vibrant flavor.

1. Place the chiles, parsley, onion, garlic, and lemon juice in a food processor and pulse until combined.

2. Add the salt, cayenne, cumin, and paprika, and, with the food processor on high, slowly pour in the olive oil. Blitz until the mixture is emulsified, adding water as needed to get the desired texture. Use immediately or store in the refrigerator.

INGREDIENTS:

4 FRESNO CHILE PEPPERS, STEMS AND SEEDS REMOVED, ROUGHLY CHOPPED

2 CUPS FRESH PARSLEY

1 ONION, QUARTERED

5 GARLIC CLOVES

   JUICE OF 1 LEMON

1 TABLESPOON KOSHER SALT

1 TEASPOON CAYENNE PEPPER

1 TABLESPOON CUMIN

2 TABLESPOONS PAPRIKA

¾ CUP EXTRA-VIRGIN OLIVE OIL

GREEN ZHUG

YIELD: 2½ CUPS / ACTIVE TIME: 10 MINUTES / TOTAL TIME: 10 MINUTES

This is great as a condiment, or as a marinade for chicken and seafood.

1. Place the jalapeños, parsley, cilantro, mint, onion, garlic, and lemon juice in a food processor and pulse until combined.

2. Add the salt, and, with the food processor on high, slowly pour in the olive oil. Blitz until the mixture is emulsified, adding water as needed to get the desired texture. Use immediately or store in the refrigerator.

INGREDIENTS:

4   JALAPEÑO CHILE PEPPERS, STEMS AND SEEDS REMOVED, ROUGHLY CHOPPED

2   CUPS FRESH PARSLEY

¾   CUP FRESH CILANTRO

6   FRESH MINT LEAVES

1   ONION, QUARTERED

5   GARLIC CLOVES

    JUICE OF LEMON

1   TABLESPOON KOSHER SALT

½   CUP EXTRA-VIRGIN OLIVE OIL

Green Zhug, see page 749

FIG VINAIGRETTE

YIELD: 1½ CUPS / ACTIVE TIME: 5 MINUTES / TOTAL TIME: 5 MINUTES

Any salad featuring peppery arugula and rich, salty cured meats will be a good spot for this vinaigrette.

1. Place the vinegar, water, jam, mustard, and shallot in a mixing bowl and whisk to combine.

2. While whisking continually, slowly drizzle in the olive oil until it has emulsified.

3. Add the figs and chives, whisk to incorporate, and season the vinaigrette with salt and pepper. Use immediately or store in the refrigerator until needed.

INGREDIENTS:

3	TABLESPOONS BALSAMIC VINEGAR
1	TABLESPOON WATER
1	FIG JAM
1	TABLESPOON DIJON MUSTARD
1	SHALLOT, MINCED
½	CUP EXTRA-VIRGIN OLIVE OIL
½	CUP DICED FIGS
2	TABLESPOONS CHOPPED FRESH CHIVES
	SALT AND PEPPER, TO TASTE

POMEGRANATE VINAIGRETTE

YIELD: 4 CUPS / ACTIVE TIME: 30 MINUTES / TOTAL TIME: 30 MINUTES

Not only does this add flavor to anything it covers, but it also provides brilliant color.

1. Place the pomegranate juice in a small saucepan and bring it to a boil over medium-high heat. Boil until it has reduced to ¼ cup. Remove the pan from heat and let it cool.

2. Place the pomegranate reduction and the remaining ingredients, except for the olive oil, in a blender and puree until smooth.

3. With the blender on, drizzle in the oil. Puree until it has emulsified. Use immediately or store in the refrigerator.

INGREDIENTS:

2 CUPS POMEGRANATE JUICE

½ CUP RED WINE VINEGAR

2 TABLESPOONS DIJON MUSTARD

2 TABLESPOONS HONEY

1 TABLESPOON ZA'ATAR (SEE PAGE 766)

2 TEASPOONS SUMAC

2 TABLESPOONS KOSHER SALT

1 TABLESPOON BLACK PEPPER

1 TABLESPOON CHOPPED FRESH OREGANO

1 TABLESPOON CHOPPED FRESH BASIL

1 TABLESPOON CHOPPED FRESH PARSLEY

1 TABLESPOON CHOPPED FRESH MINT

3 CUPS EXTRA-VIRGIN OLIVE OIL

CHERMOULA SAUCE

YIELD: 5 CUPS / **ACTIVE TIME:** 5 MINUTES / **TOTAL TIME:** 10 MINUTES

Traditionally used with fish, this flavorful North African sauce can be used on anything your palate pleases.

1. Place the saffron in ¼ cup water and let it bloom. Remove the saffron from the water and reserve the liquid for another preparation (it's really good in a tomato sauce, for example)—using it in this sauce will make it too loose.

2. Place the saffron and the remaining ingredients in a large bowl and stir until thoroughly combined. Use immediately or transfer to an airtight container and store in the refrigerator.

INGREDIENTS:

1	TABLESPOON SAFFRON
4	CUPS MAYONNAISE
1	TABLESPOON RAS EL HANOUT (SEE PAGE 747)
1	TABLESPOON BERBERE SEASONING
2	TABLESPOONS ZA'ATAR (SEE PAGE 766)
1	TABLESPOON SUMAC
2	CUPS CHOPPED FRESH HERBS (TARRAGON, PARSLEY, CHIVES, AND CILANTRO RECOMMENDED)
1	TABLESPOON DRIED OREGANO
1	TABLESPOON KOSHER SALT
1	TABLESPOON BLACK PEPPER

Chermoula Sauce, see page 755

TOUM

YIELD: 1½ CUPS / **ACTIVE TIME**: 10 MINUTES / **TOTAL TIME**: 40 MINUTES

This fluffy, garlicky sauce is plenty versatile, but at its best beside roasted or grilled vegetables.

1. Place the avocado oil in the freezer for 30 minutes. This will help the sauce emulsify.

2. Place the garlic, lemon juice, ¼ cup of the chilled avocado oil, and 1 tablespoon of the ice water in a food processor and pulse until the mixture is smooth. With the food processor running, slowly drizzle in another ½ cup of the avocado oil.

3. Scrape down the work bowl and slowly drizzle in the remaining avocado oil with the food processor running, until the mixture has emulsified and comes together as a thick sauce—it should cling to a spoon.

4. Add the remaining ice water, season the toum with salt, and pulse to incorporate. This whole process will take 8 to 10 minutes, so remain patient.

INGREDIENTS:

1	CUP AVOCADO OIL
⅓	CUP GARLIC CLOVES
2	TABLESPOONS FRESH LEMON JUICE
2	TABLESPOONS ICE WATER
	SALT, TO TASTE

BALSAMIC GLAZE

YIELD: ½ CUP / **ACTIVE TIME:** 10 MINUTES / **TOTAL TIME:** 25 MINUTES

Wonderful for adding complexity to a number of dishes, particularly those that are on the rich end of the spectrum.

1. Place the vinegar and sugar in a small saucepan and bring the mixture to a boil.

2. Reduce the heat to medium-low and simmer for 8 to 10 minutes, stirring frequently, until the mixture has thickened.

3. Remove the pan from heat and let the glaze cool for 15 minutes before using.

INGREDIENTS:

1	CUP BALSAMIC VINEGAR
¼	CUP BROWN SUGAR

SPICED HONEY

YIELD: ½ CUP / **ACTIVE TIME:** 5 MINUTES / **TOTAL TIME:** 5 MINUTES

One could argue that the trend toward adding a hint of spice to honey's familiar sweetness is a landmark achievement of the modern culinary movement.

1. Using a spice grinder or a mortar and pestle, grind the red pepper flakes until they are reduced to a fine powder.

2. Place the powder in a bowl, add the remaining ingredients, and stir to combine. Use immediately or store in an airtight container for up to 1 month.

INGREDIENTS:

1	TEASPOON RED PEPPER FLAKES
1	GARLIC CLOVE, MINCED
1	TABLESPOON EXTRA-VIRGIN OLIVE OIL
2	TABLESPOONS FRESH LEMON JUICE
	SALT, TO TASTE
6	TABLESPOONS HONEY

PISTACHIO & RAISIN SAUCE

YIELD: 1 CUP / **ACTIVE TIME:** 5 MINUTES / **TOTAL TIME:** 5 MINUTES

Try this with roasted meats and root vegetables, and over pasta dishes featuring pancetta or bacon.

1. Place the shallots, parsley, orange juice, raisins, pistachios, cinnamon, and vinegar in a food processor and blitz until the mixture is a thick paste.

2. With the food processor running, slowly drizzle in the olive oil and blitz until it has emulsified. Season the sauce with salt and pepper and use as desired.

INGREDIENTS:

2   SHALLOTS, CHOPPED

⅓   CUP CHOPPED FRESH PARSLEY

½   CUP ORANGE JUICE

⅓   CUP RAISINS

¼   CUP PISTACHIOS, SHELLS REMOVED, TOASTED

½   TEASPOON CINNAMON

1   TABLESPOON WHITE WINE VINEGAR

2   TABLESPOONS EXTRA-VIRGIN OLIVE OIL

    SALT AND PEPPER, TO TASTE

Za'atar, see page 766

ZA'ATAR

YIELD: 1½ CUPS / ACTIVE TIME: 5 MINUTES / TOTAL TIME: 5 MINUTES

There are many variations on this seasoning blend, but they all share in common a mixture of earthy dried herbs and crunchy toasted seeds. You'd be wise to double or quadruple this recipe, because once you have it in your kitchen, you'll want to try it on everything.

1. Place all of the ingredients in a large bowl and stir until thoroughly combined. Use immediately or store in an airtight container.

INGREDIENTS:

1   TABLESPOON CUMIN

1   TABLESPOON SUMAC

1   TABLESPOON THYME

2   TEASPOONS HEMP SEEDS

2   TEASPOONS CRUSHED TOASTED SUNFLOWER SEEDS

2   TABLESPOONS SESAME SEEDS

2   TABLESPOONS KOSHER SALT

1   TABLESPOON BLACK PEPPER

2   TABLESPOONS CHOPPED FRESH OREGANO

2   TABLESPOONS CHOPPED FRESH BASIL

2   TABLESPOONS CHOPPED FRESH PARSLEY

1   TABLESPOON GARLIC POWDER

1   TABLESPOON ONION POWDER

TAHINI SAUCE

An incredibly versatile sauce that can be left thick to bolster appetizers and entrees, or thinned and used as a dressing for salads.

1. Place the tahini and water in a food processor and pulse to combine. Let the mixture sit for 30 seconds.

2. Add the garlic, salt, lemon juice, and cumin. Puree on high for 2 to 3 minutes, until the sauce is creamy and smooth. Use immediately or store in the refrigerator.

INGREDIENTS:

5	OZ. TAHINI PASTE
½	CUP WATER
3	GARLIC CLOVES
1	TEASPOON KOSHER SALT
	JUICE OF 1 LEMON
	PINCH OF CUMIN

Tahini Sauce, see page 767

SMOKED EGG AIOLI

YIELD: 1 CUP / ACTIVE TIME: 20 MINUTES / TOTAL TIME: 45 MINUTES

This works as a dipping sauce for anything fried, on a sandwich, and even in some slaws.

1. Place the yolks in a metal bowl and set the bowl in a roasting pan.

2. Place the wood chips in a cast-iron skillet and warm them over high heat. Remove the pan from heat, light the wood chips on fire, and place the skillet in the roasting pan beside the bowl. Cover the roasting pan with aluminum foil and allow the smoke to flavor the yolks for 20 minutes.

3. Place the yolks and vinegar in a bowl, gently break the yolks, and let the mixture sit for 5 minutes.

4. Add the salt to the egg yolk mixture. Slowly drizzle the oil into the mixture while beating it with an electric mixer or immersion blender until it is thick. Use immediately or store in the refrigerator.

INGREDIENTS:

2	EGG YOLKS
½	CUP WOOD CHIPS
1	TABLESPOON WHITE VINEGAR
1	TEASPOON KOSHER SALT
1	CUP AVOCADO OIL

WHIPPED FETA WITH ZA'ATAR

YIELD: 2 CUPS / ACTIVE TIME: 5 MINUTES / TOTAL TIME: 5 MINUTES

Wonderful as a stuffing for chicken or pork, as a topping on salads, or spread over warm, crusty bread.

1. Place the feta and Za'atar in a food processor and puree until smooth.

2. With the mixer running, slowly drizzle in the olive oil until the mixture becomes smooth.

3. Transfer the whipped feta to a bowl and stir in the red pepper flakes and lemon juice. Use immediately or store in the refrigerator.

INGREDIENTS:

2 CUPS CRUMBLED FETA CHEESE

2 TABLESPOONS ZA'ATAR (SEE PAGE 766)

¼ CUP EXTRA-VIRGIN OLIVE OIL

1 TEASPOON RED PEPPER FLAKES

JUICE FROM ½ LEMON

Whipped Feta with Za'atar, see page 771

TOMATO SAUCE

YIELD: 4 CUPS / ACTIVE TIME: 15 MINUTES / TOTAL TIME: 45 MINUTES

Here is a standard tomato sauce that will fit perfectly in any instance where you need a bit of the tomato's bright acidity.

1. Place the avocado oil in a large saucepan and warm it over medium heat. Add the garlic and ginger and cook, stirring frequently, until fragrant, about 1 minute.

2. Add the cinnamon stick and cook for 30 seconds. Add the remaining ingredients and bring the sauce to a boil.

3. Reduce the heat and simmer the sauce until the flavor has developed to your liking, about 30 minutes.

4. Remove the cinnamon stick from the sauce and use as desired.

INGREDIENTS:

2 TABLESPOONS AVOCADO OIL

1 LARGE GARLIC CLOVE, CHOPPED

1 TEASPOON GRATED FRESH GINGER

1 CINNAMON STICK

1 (28 OZ.) CAN OF CHOPPED SAN MARZANO TOMATOES, WITH THEIR LIQUID

½ TEASPOON CUMIN

¼ TEASPOON CORIANDER

⅛ TEASPOON CAYENNE PEPPER

EGGPLANT & PINE NUT RAGOUT

YIELD: 2 CUPS / ACTIVE TIME: 20 MINUTES / TOTAL TIME: 40 MINUTES

Whether you put it over pasta or on a flatbread, this stunningly rich vegetarian sauce will make the meal.

1. Place the olive oil in a large saucepan and warm it over medium heat. Add the eggplant, cover the pan, and cook, stirring occasionally, for 5 minutes. Remove the cover and cook, stirring occasionally, until the eggplant is browned, about 10 minutes.

2. Stir in the remaining ingredients and cook, stirring occasionally, until the eggplant has collapsed and the flavor has developed to your liking, 10 to 15 minutes.

INGREDIENTS:

1   TABLESPOON EXTRA-VIRGIN OLIVE OIL

1   EGGPLANT, TRIMMED AND CUT INTO ¾-INCH CUBES

½   TEASPOON RAS EL HANOUT (SEE PAGE 747)

1   TABLESPOON RAISINS

2   TABLESPOONS PINE NUTS, TOASTED

1   TEASPOON LEMON ZEST

    SALT AND PEPPER, TO TASTE

PISTACHIO GREMOLATA

YIELD: 2 CUPS / ACTIVE TIME: 5 MINUTES / TOTAL TIME: 5 MINUTES

A twist on the classic Italian sauce that adds brightness and texture.

1. Place the mint, pistachios, garlic, lemon zest, salt, and pepper in a food processor and pulse until the mixture is combined and coarsely chopped.

2. Add the olive oil in a slow stream and pulse until the mixture is just combined, making sure not to overprocess the gremolata—you want it to have some texture. Use as desired.

INGREDIENTS:

1½ CUPS FRESH MINT LEAVES

½ CUP SHELLED ROASTED AND SALTED PISTACHIOS

2 GARLIC CLOVES

2 TEASPOONS LEMON ZEST

¼ TEASPOON KOSHER SALT

⅛ TEASPOON BLACK PEPPER

2 TABLESPOONS EXTRA-VIRGIN OLIVE OIL

SPICY HONEY MAYONNAISE

YIELD: ½ CUP / ACTIVE TIME: 5 MINUTES / TOTAL TIME: 15 MINUTES

This condiment fits with a lot of dishes, though it is particularly good on sandwiches.

1. Place all of the ingredients in a small bowl and stir until thoroughly combined.

2. Chill the mayonnaise in the refrigerator for 10 minutes before serving.

INGREDIENTS:

½   CUP MAYONNAISE

2   TABLESPOONS HONEY

1   TABLESPOON SRIRACHA

CHARRED SCALLION SAUCE

YIELD: 1 CUP / ACTIVE TIME: 10 MINUTES / TOTAL TIME: 10 MINUTES

Sambal oelek is a chili paste that makes for an excellent condiment in its own right.

1. On a grill or over an open flame on a gas stove, char the scallions all over. Remove the charred scallions from heat and let them cool.

2. Slice the charred scallions, place them in a mixing bowl, and add the remaining ingredients. Stir to combine, taste the sauce, and adjust the seasoning as necessary. Use immediately or store in the refrigerator until needed.

INGREDIENTS:

3	SCALLIONS
2	GARLIC CLOVES, MINCED
2	THAI CHILI PEPPERS, STEMS AND SEEDS REMOVED, MINCED
¼	CUP CHOPPED FRESH CILANTRO
1	TABLESPOON GRATED FRESH GINGER
1	TABLESPOON SESAME OIL
½	CUP SOY SAUCE
1	TABLESPOON SAMBAL OELEK
2	TABLESPOONS FRESH LIME JUICE
1	TEASPOON SUGAR
1	TABLESPOON SESAME SEEDS
	SALT AND PEPPER, TO TASTE

ROMESCO SAUCE

YIELD: 2 CUPS / ACTIVE TIME: 5 MINUTES / TOTAL TIME: 20 MINUTES

A Catalan sauce that is sublime with seafood, pasta, and grill-charred pieces of bread.

1. Preheat the oven to 350°F. Place the bread and almonds on separate sections of a baking sheet, place the pan in the oven, and toast until the bread and almonds are golden brown, 5 to 7 minutes. Remove from the oven and let them cool.

2. Place the toasted bread and almonds in a food processor and pulse until they are finely ground.

3. Add the peppers and pulse until combined. Add the remaining ingredients and puree until smooth.

4. Taste, adjust the seasoning as necessary, and use as desired.

INGREDIENTS:

¾ CUP DAY-OLD SOURDOUGH BREAD PIECES (½-INCH CUBES), CRUST REMOVED

2 TABLESPOONS SLIVERED ALMONDS

¾ CUP ROASTED RED PEPPERS IN OLIVE OIL, DRAINED AND CHOPPED

1 PLUM TOMATO, SEEDS REMOVED, CHOPPED

1 TABLESPOON EXTRA-VIRGIN OLIVE OIL

2 TEASPOONS RED WINE VINEGAR

1 GARLIC CLOVE, MINCED

2 PINCHES OF CAYENNE PEPPER

SALT AND PEPPER, TO TASTE

Tahini Mayonnaise, see page 786

TAHINI MAYONNAISE

YIELD: 1 CUP / **ACTIVE TIME:** 10 MINUTES / **TOTAL TIME:** 10 MINUTES

Using tahini to make mayonnaise will add a nutty zip to any sandwich, salad, or wrap.

1. Place the egg yolks, tahini, lemon juice, water, and salt in a food processor and blitz until they are combined.

2. With the food processor running, gradually add the olive oil in a slow stream. Blitz until the mayonnaise is extremely thick and velvety. Be thorough in this step; a tight emulsion is the difference between having all of those flavors hit you in equal measure or having them fall flat.

3. Use the mayonnaise immediately or store it in the refrigerator, where it will keep for a few days.

INGREDIENTS:

2   EGG YOLKS

¼   CUP TAHINI PASTE

3   TABLESPOONS FRESH LEMON JUICE

1   TABLESPOON WATER

1   TEASPOON KOSHER SALT

½   CUP EXTRA-VIRGIN OLIVE OIL

LEMONY YOGURT SAUCE

YIELD: 2½ CUPS / ACTIVE TIME: 5 MINUTES / TOTAL TIME: 5 MINUTES

The lemon juice adds a bit of brightness and grants this sauce a velvety texture.

1. Place all of the ingredients in a mixing bowl and stir until thoroughly combined. Use immediately or store in the refrigerator.

INGREDIENTS:

6   TABLESPOONS FRESH
    LEMON JUICE

1   GARLIC CLOVE, GRATED

1   TEASPOON KOSHER SALT

1   TEASPOON BLACK PEPPER

2   CUPS PLAIN FULL-FAT
    GREEK YOGURT

DIJON DRESSING

YIELD: 1 CUP / **ACTIVE TIME:** 5 MINUTES / **TOTAL TIME:** 5 MINUTES

Meant for salads, but this can also work well as a marinade or stuffing for poultry and whitefish.

1. Place the lemon juice, shallot, fresh herbs, mustard, and anchovies in a small mixing bowl and whisk until combined.

2. While whisking continually, slowly drizzle in the olive oil until it has emulsified.

3. Season the dressing with salt and pepper and use immediately or store in the refrigerator until needed.

INGREDIENTS:

JUICE OF 2 LEMONS

1 TABLESPOON MINCED SHALLOT

1 TABLESPOON CHOPPED FRESH BASIL

2 TEASPOONS FRESH THYME

2 TEASPOONS CHOPPED FRESH OREGANO

2 TEASPOONS DIJON MUSTARD

2 ANCHOVIES IN OLIVE OIL, DRAINED AND FINELY CHOPPED

2 TEASPOONS CAPERS, DRAINED AND CHOPPED

¾ CUP EXTRA-VIRGIN OLIVE OIL

SALT AND PEPPER, TO TASTE

CREAMY BALSAMIC & MUSHROOM SAUCE

YIELD: 2 CUPS / **ACTIVE TIME:** 30 MINUTES / **TOTAL TIME:** 30 MINUTES

Remain patient while browning the mushrooms, as that step is the key toward maximizing the flavor of this sauce.

1. Place 2 tablespoons of the butter in a large skillet and melt it over medium heat. Add the mushrooms and cook, stirring one or two times, until browned all over, about 10 minutes. Remove the mushrooms from the pan and set them aside.

2. Place the remaining butter in the pan, add the onions, and cook, stirring occasionally, until they have softened, about 5 minutes. Add the tomato paste and cook, stirring continually, for 2 minutes.

3. Deglaze the pan with the stock and heavy cream, scraping up any browned bits from the bottom of the pan. Cook until the liquid has been reduced by half.

4. Add the mushrooms back to the pan and season the sauce with salt and pepper. Stir in the vinegar, thyme, and parsley and let the mixture simmer.

5. Place the cornstarch in a small bowl and add a splash of water. Whisk to combine and then whisk the slurry into the sauce. Continue whisking until the sauce has thickened, about 2 minutes, and use as desired.

INGREDIENTS:

4	TABLESPOONS UNSALTED BUTTER
2	CUPS SLICED MUSHROOMS
2	ONIONS, DICED
2	TEASPOONS TOMATO PASTE
1	CUP VEGETABLE STOCK (SEE PAGE 371)
1	CUP HEAVY CREAM
	SALT AND PEPPER, TO TASTE
2	TEASPOONS BALSAMIC VINEGAR
2	TEASPOONS DRIED THYME
¼	CUP CHOPPED FRESH PARSLEY
2	TABLESPOONS CORNSTARCH

THREE-PEPPER HARISSA SAUCE

YIELD: 1 CUP / ACTIVE TIME: 10 MINUTES / TOTAL TIME: 1 HOUR

The guajillo chile is the dried form of the mirasol chile, while a chipotle is a jalapeño that has been smoked.

1. Place the guajillo and chipotle chiles in a large heatproof bowl and cover them with boiling water. Let the chiles soak until they have softened, 40 to 45 minutes.

2. Drain the chiles and set them aside.

3. Grind the nigella seeds and coriander seeds into a powder, using a spice mill or a mortar and pestle. Transfer the powder to a food processor and add the garlic, cumin, salt, and Aleppo pepper. Pulse until the garlic is very finely chopped.

4. Add the chiles and pulse until they are chopped.

5. Add the oil and vinegar and pulse until the sauce is a chunky paste. Use immediately or store in the refrigerator until needed.

INGREDIENTS:

- 3 OZ. GUAJILLO CHILE PEPPERS, STEMS AND SEEDS REMOVED, TORN
- 1 OZ. DRIED CHIPOTLE CHILE PEPPERS, STEMS AND SEEDS REMOVED, TORN
- 1 TABLESPOON NIGELLA SEEDS
- 1 TEASPOON CORIANDER SEEDS
- 2 GARLIC CLOVES
- 1 TABLESPOON CUMIN
- 1 TEASPOON KOSHER SALT
- ½ TEASPOON ALEPPO PEPPER
- ½ CUP EXTRA-VIRGIN OLIVE OIL
- 2 TABLESPOONS WHITE WINE VINEGAR

PAPRIKA OIL

YIELD: 2 CUPS / **ACTIVE TIME:** 5 MINUTES / **TOTAL TIME:** 5 MINUTES

This infused oil provides the foundation for a number of dishes in Moroccan cooking.

1. Place the paprika and avocado oil in a mason jar and shake until thoroughly combined.

2. Store the oil in a dark pantry and always shake before using.

INGREDIENTS:

½ CUP SWEET PAPRIKA

2 CUPS AVOCADO OIL

AGRISTADA SAUCE

YIELD: 2 CUPS / **ACTIVE TIME:** 10 MINUTES / **TOTAL TIME:** 20 MINUTES

This Sephardic sauce is tremendous on seafood. If you're a fan of avgolemono, you'll love this as well.

1. Place the eggs in a medium saucepan and whisk until scrambled. Set the eggs aside.

2. Place the warm water and the flour in a mixing bowl and vigorously whisk the mixture until there are no visible lumps in it. Strain the mixture into the saucepan.

3. Add the avocado oil, lemon juice, and salt and warm the mixture over medium-low heat, stirring constantly with a wooden spoon. Cook until the sauce has thickened, 10 to 12 minutes.

4. When the sauce is just about to boil, remove the pan from heat, stir for another minute, and then strain the sauce into a bowl.

5. Taste, adjust the seasoning as necessary, and place plastic wrap directly on the surface of the sauce to prevent a skin from forming. Let the sauce cool to room temperature before serving. Store it in the refrigerator, if not using immediately, once it is cool.

INGREDIENTS:

4	EGGS
2	CUPS WARM WATER (105°F)
2	TABLESPOONS ALL-PURPOSE FLOUR
¼	CUP AVOCADO OIL
⅓	CUP FRESH LEMON JUICE
½	TEASPOON KOSHER SALT

Grilled Serrano Salsa Verde, see page 798

TAHINI & YOGURT SAUCE

YIELD: 1 CUP / ACTIVE TIME: 5 MINUTES / TOTAL TIME: 5 MINUTES

Adding the sour tang of yogurt to a standard tahini sauce is as simple as good work in the kitchen gets.

1. Place the yogurt, garlic, tahini, lemon juice, and cumin in a small bowl and whisk to combine.

2. Season the sauce with salt and pepper, add the sesame seeds and olive oil, and whisk until incorporated. Use immediately or store in the refrigerator until needed.

INGREDIENTS:

¾ CUP FULL-FAT GREEK YOGURT

1 GARLIC CLOVE, MINCED

2 TABLESPOONS TAHINI PASTE

   JUICE OF 1 LEMON

½ TEASPOON CUMIN

   SALT AND PEPPER, TO TASTE

1 TABLESPOON BLACK SESAME SEEDS

1 TABLESPOON EXTRA-VIRGIN OLIVE OIL

GRILLED SERRANO SALSA VERDE

YIELD: 3 CUPS / **ACTIVE TIME**: 20 MINUTES / **TOTAL TIME**: 45 MINUTES

This is a spicy spin on the classic Italian sauce.

1. Prepare a gas or charcoal grill for medium-high heat (about 450°F).

2. Skewer the chiles and place them on the grill, turning frequently, until they are charred all over and tender, about 6 minutes. Remove from the grill and let the peppers cool. When the peppers are cool enough to handle, remove the stems.

3. Pluck the leaves from the basil and the leaves and tender stems from the cilantro and parsley. You should have about 2 cups of each herb.

4. Place the chiles, basil, cilantro, and parsley in a food processor and pulse until finely chopped. Add the olive oil, vinegar, and salt and pulse until the mixture is a thick, slightly textured sauce. Use immediately or store in the refrigerator until needed.

INGREDIENTS:

6–8	SERRANO CHILE PEPPERS
1	BUNCH OF FRESH BASIL
1	BUNCH OF FRESH CILANTRO
1	BUNCH OF FRESH PARSLEY
1¼	CUPS EXTRA-VIRGIN OLIVE OIL
½	CUP SHERRY OR RED WINE VINEGAR
2½	TEASPOONS KOSHER SALT

PICKLED APPLESAUCE

YIELD: 4 CUPS / **ACTIVE TIME**: 20 MINUTES / **TOTAL TIME**: 1 HOUR

Essentially an apple agrodolce, this sweet-and-sour sauce cuts beautifully against rich, fatty meats.

1. Place the ingredients in a large saucepan and bring to a boil over high heat.

2. Reduce the heat to medium-high and simmer until the liquid has reduced by one-third. Remove the pan from heat and let it cool to room temperature.

3. Place the applesauce in a food processor and puree on high until smooth, about 2 minutes. Serve immediately or store in the refrigerator.

INGREDIENTS:

3 LBS. GRANNY SMITH APPLES, PEELED AND SLICED

1 TEASPOON CINNAMON

PINCH OF GROUND CLOVES

½ CUP SUGAR

1½ CUPS WHITE VINEGAR

MEDITERRANEAN-STYLE HOT SAUCE

YIELD: 8 CUPS / **ACTIVE TIME:** 45 MINUTES / **TOTAL TIME:** 2 HOURS

Cilantro is a key ingredient in this hot sauce, but if you are allergic or experience cilantro as soap, definitely omit it. This hot sauce is good on pretty much anything, but it is surreal beside fried chicken.

1. Place the vinegar, chiles, cilantro, onion, garlic, cumin, and salt in a saucepan and bring to a boil over high heat. Reduce the heat to medium and simmer, stirring occasionally, for 45 minutes to 1 hour.

2. Remove the pan from heat and let the mixture cool.

3. Place the mixture in a food processor or blender and pulse until the solids are finely chopped and it is combined.

4. Strain the liquid into a bowl or mason jar and discard the solids.

5. Place the chicken fat in a small saucepan and warm it over low heat.

6. Stir the chicken fat into the sauce, giving it a velvety texture. Use immediately or store in the refrigerator until needed.

INGREDIENTS:

8   CUPS WHITE VINEGAR

4   FRESNO CHILE PEPPERS, STEMS REMOVED

1   BUNCH OF FRESH CILANTRO, CHOPPED

½   WHITE ONION, CHOPPED

4   GARLIC CLOVES

1   TEASPOON CUMIN

2   TEASPOONS KOSHER SALT

2   TABLESPOONS CHICKEN FAT

MEYER LEMON MARMALADE

YIELD: 2 CUPS / ACTIVE TIME: 45 MINUTES / TOTAL TIME: 2 HOURS

The enhanced floral character of Meyer lemons is on full display in this sweet spread.

1. Cut the lemons, rind and all, into ½-inch chunks.

2. Place all of the ingredients in a saucepan and bring the mixture to a boil over high heat. Reduce the heat to medium-high and simmer, stirring occasionally, until everything has softened, about 45 minutes.

3. Raise the heat back to high and cook until the mixture reaches 220°F.

4. Remove the pan from heat and let it cool completely. Use immediately or store in the refrigerator.

INGREDIENTS:

5   MEYER LEMONS

2   FRESNO CHILE PEPPERS, STEMS AND SEEDS REMOVED, DICED

4   GARLIC CLOVES, MINCED

1   TABLESPOON KOSHER SALT

1   TEASPOON BLACK PEPPER

1   CUP WATER

1   CUP WHITE VINEGAR

2   CUPS SUGAR

SPICED YOGURT SAUCE

YIELD: 1¼ CUPS / **ACTIVE TIME:** 5 MINUTES / **TOTAL TIME:** 5 MINUTES

Pairing two of the best condiments Mediterranean cuisine has to offer—yogurt and zhug—ends up being every bit as grand as you'd expect.

1. Place all of the ingredients in a mixing bowl and whisk until combined. Use immediately or store in the refrigerator until needed.

INGREDIENTS:

1   CUP FULL-FAT GREEK
    YOGURT

¼   CUP GREEN ZHUG (SEE
    PAGE 749)

1   TEASPOON FRESH LEMON
    JUICE

1   TEASPOON MINCED
    GARLIC

    SALT AND PEPPER, TO
    TASTE

CHAMPAGNE VINAIGRETTE

YIELD: 2½ CUPS / **ACTIVE TIME:** 5 MINUTES / **TOTAL TIME:** 5 MINUTES

Elegant simplicity in a bottle. Bring any salad or platter of roasted vegetables to life with this bright dressing.

1. Place all of the ingredients, except for the olive oil, in a bowl and whisk until well combined.

2. While whisking, add the oil in a slow stream until it has emulsified. Use immediately or store in the refrigerator.

INGREDIENTS:

- ⅔ CUP CHAMPAGNE VINEGAR
- ¼ CUP WATER
- 2 TABLESPOONS DIJON MUSTARD
- ½ TEASPOON KOSHER SALT
- ½ TEASPOON BLACK PEPPER
- 2 TABLESPOONS HONEY
- 1½ CUPS EXTRA-VIRGIN OLIVE OIL

SAFFRON & TOMATO COULIS

YIELD: 4 CUPS / **ACTIVE TIME:** 5 MINUTES / **TOTAL TIME:** 25 MINUTES

Add this to any whitefish to make a simple weeknight meal feel like you're eating in a restaurant.

1. Place the saffron in a bowl and add a cup of water. Let the saffron steep for 10 minutes.

2. Place the olive oil in a saucepan and warm it over medium heat. Add the onion, garlic, bay leaves, salt, and pepper and cook, stirring frequently, until the onion is translucent, 3 to 4 minutes.

3. Deglaze the pan with the wine and bring the mixture to a simmer.

4. Add the saffron and soaking liquid, along with the tomatoes, and cook for 5 minutes.

5. Taste, adjust the seasoning as necessary, and use as desired.

INGREDIENTS:

1	TABLESPOON SAFFRON
2	TABLESPOONS EXTRA-VIRGIN OLIVE OIL
¼	CUP MINCED ONION
¼	CUP SLICED GARLIC
3	BAY LEAVES
3	TABLESPOONS KOSHER SALT
2	TABLESPOONS BLACK PEPPER
½	CUP WHITE WINE
1	(14 OZ.) CAN OF DICED SAN MARZANO TOMATOES, DRAINED

GARLIC BUTTER

YIELD: 1¼ CUPS / ACTIVE TIME: 5 MINUTES / TOTAL TIME: 5 MINUTES

Make this a staple in your refrigerator and dinnertime will become the most anticipated part of each day.

1. Place the butter in a bowl and whisk it until it is fluffy, about 2 minutes.

2. Add the remaining ingredients, whisk to combine, and either use immediately or store in the refrigerator.

INGREDIENTS:

1   CUP UNSALTED BUTTER, SOFTENED

1½   TEASPOONS FRESH LEMON JUICE

2   GARLIC CLOVES, MINCED

3   TABLESPOONS CHOPPED FRESH PARSLEY

SALT AND PEPPER, TO TASTE

CONVERSION TABLE

WEIGHTS

1 oz. = 28 grams
2 oz. = 57 grams
4 oz. (¼ lb.) = 113 grams
8 oz. (½ lb.) = 227 grams
16 oz. (1 lb.) = 454 grams

VOLUME MEASURES

⅛ teaspoon = 0.6 ml
¼ teaspoon = 1.23 ml
½ teaspoon = 2.5 ml
1 teaspoon = 5 ml
1 tablespoon (3 teaspoons) = ½ fluid oz. = 15 ml
2 tablespoons = 1 fluid oz. = 29.5 ml
¼ cup (4 tablespoons) = 2 fluid oz. = 59 ml
⅓ cup (5 ⅓ tablespoons) = 2.7 fluid oz. = 80 ml
½ cup (8 tablespoons) = 4 fluid oz. = 120 ml
⅔ cup (10 ⅔ tablespoons) = 5.4 fluid oz. = 160 ml
¾ cup (12 tablespoons) = 6 fluid oz. = 180 ml
1 cup (16 tablespoons) = 8 fluid oz. = 240 ml

TEMPERATURE EQUIVALENTS

°F	°C	Gas Mark
225	110	¼
250	130	½
275	140	1
300	150	2
325	170	3
350	180	4
375	190	5
400	200	6
425	220	7
450	230	8
475	240	9
500	250	10

LENGTH MEASURES

1/16 inch = 1.6 mm
⅛ inch = 3 mm
¼ inch = 1.35 mm
½ inch = 1.25 cm
¾ inch = 2 cm
1 inch = 2.5 cm

IMAGE CREDITS

Pages 17, 26–27, 34, 36, 45, 54, 72–73, 80, 87, 115, 127, 128, 131, 132, 135, 139, 144, 160, 163, 173, 177, 178, 181, 186, 189, 198, 201, 211, 212, 215, 216, 220, 223, 229, 230, 233, 234, 241, 246, 249, 252, 300, 303, 304, 307, 308, 315, 316, 319, 320, 323, 326–327, 330–331, 332, 335, 336, 339, 340, 343, 347, 370, 374–375, 376, 379, 380, 383, 392, 403, 426, 454, 457, 467, 481, 485, 489, 494, 497, 534, 539, 540, 543, 544, 547, 548, 590, 602–603, 604, 607, 608, 611, 612, 616, 619, 620, 623, 630, 640, 646, 659, 662, 671, 674, 742, 745, 746, 753, 760, 763, 777, 780, 783, 797, 802, and 807 courtesy of Derek Bissonnette.

Pages 32–33, 40–41, 52, 58–59, 62–63, 65, 76–77, 79, 84–85, 88–89, 92–93, 96–97, 100–101, 104–105, 108–109, 110, 118, 136, 148–149, 156–157, 164–165, 168–169, 170, 174, 184–185, 190–191, 194–195, 206–207, 208, 224–225, 280–281, 287, 294–295, 356, 386–387, 390–391, 400–401, 408–409, 412–413, 416–417, 420–421, 424–425, 430–431, 434–435, 438–439, 442–443, 448–449, 464, 473, 476–477, 482, 490, 493, 500–501, 506–507, 520–521, 524–525, 527, 533, 615, 634–635, 639, 681, 682, 690–691, 693, 705, 710, 713, 714, 717, 718, 721, 722, 725, 728, 731, 732, 750–751, 756–757, 768–769, and 772–773 courtesy of Cider Mill Press.

Images on page 22 courtesy of the Library of Congress.

Image on Page 447 courtesy of StockFood.

All other photos used under official license from Shutterstock.

Illustration on page 13 courtesy of the New York Public Library.

All other illustrations courtesy of Christina Hess.

ABOUT THE CONTRIBUTORS

When Derek Bissonnette was 16 he landed his first kitchen gig, at a bakery in Searsport, Maine. He went on to study baking and pastry at the Culinary Institute of America, graduating in 2000. He was hired as the pastry chef at the estimable White Barn Inn in Kennebunk, Maine, jumped to the renowned Inn at Little Washington in rural Virginia, and then joined the kitchen at the elegant English countryside hotel, The Summer Lodge Country House Hotel and Spa. In 2009, he returned to Maine and the White Barn, where he was promoted to executive chef in 2015. After Bissonnette took over the White Barn kitchen, he started toting a camera to work to create a visual record of dishes he and his staff came up with. Photography clicked with him, and in 2017, he gave up his apron to pursue photography full time. He is also the author of *Soup: The Ultimate Cookbook*, *Dumplings*, and *On Board*. For more about Derek and his work, visit dbfoodphoto.com.

Kimberly Zerkel is a freelance writer. After a decade of living and teaching in Paris, she returned to the United States to live in San Francisco, California. She has regularly contributed to the *San Francisco Chronicle* and *Represent Collaborative*, amongst other publications. Kimberly currently resides in Joplin, Missouri.

INDEX

acorn squash
  Roasted Squash & Feta Salad, 519
  Stuffed Acorn Squash, 196
Agristada Sauce
  Fried Fish with Agristada Sauce, 297
  recipe, 793
Aioli
  Seared Shrimp Skewers with Aioli & Cauliflower Cakes, 214
  recipe, 214
Albondigas, 193
Albondigas Soup, 305
Aliciotti con Indivia, 276
Almodrote, 277
almond paste
  Pignoli, 622
almonds
  Baklava, 606
  Braised Grapes, 318
  Broccolini Salad, 410
  Chicken B'stilla, 130
  Chilled White Tomato Soup with Braised Grapes, 318
  Classic Halvah, 650
  Granola, 663
  Mediterranean Grilled Chicken Salad, 446
  Romesco de Peix, 345
  Slow-Roasted Lamb Shoulder with Brussels Sprouts & Crispy Kale, 254
  Sumac, Spelt & Apple Cake, 669
  Vegetable Tanzia, 261
amaretto
  Lipstick & Rouge, 708
Amaro Nonino
  Ananda Spritz, 733
Ananda Spritz, 733
anchovies
  Aliciotti con Indivia, 276
  Artichoke à la Barigoule, 341
  Broccoli & Anchovy Soup, 337
  Dijon Dressing, 788
  Focaccia Messinese, 572
  Pissalandrea, 577
  Rianata, 561
  Romana, 587
  Sfincione Palermitano, 562
anise
  about, 18
  Braised Grapes, 318
  Fig, Orange & Anise Honey Balls, 610

Spiced Tea Cordial, 719
Aperol
  The Church, 729
  Lipstick & Rouge, 708
  The Project, 711
appetizers
  Arancini, 60
  Baba Ghanoush, 39
  Beet Chips with Spicy Honey Mayonnaise, 38
  Bourekas, 47
  Caponata, 70
  Cheesy Poofs, 111
  Chicken Liver Mousse, 78
  Chickpea Poutine, 83
  Couscous Arancini, 61
  Crushed Avocado, 102
  Eggplant & Chorizo Bourekas, 46
  Eggplant Rings, 71
  Falafel, 57
  Fire-Roasted Oysters, 103
  Fried Artichokes, 117–119
  Fried Eggplant with Garlic & Ras el Hanout, 112
  Fried Eggplant with Mint Vinaigrette, 113
  Fried Feta, 90
  Goat Cheese, Olive & Fennel Phyllo Triangles, 114
  Grilled Cantaloupe, 82
  Handrajo, 51
  Keftes de Espinaca, 43
  Labneh, 67
  Lavash Crackers with Red Pepper Feta & Ricotta and Spiced Honey, 44
  Marinated Artichokes, 86
  Marinated Olives, 120
  Modern Hummus, 31
  Mussels Escabeche, 94
  Pecan Muhammara, 64
  Pomegranate-Glazed Figs & Cheese, 116
  Roasted & Stuffed Sardines, 75
  Salata Mechouia, 30
  Scallop Ceviche, 95
  Sicilian Bar Nuts, 74
  Spanakopita, 81
  Stuffed Avocados, 91
  Stuffed Grape Leaves, 55
  Sweet Potato & Tahini Dip with Spiced Honey, 106
  Sweet Potato & Tahini Dip with Za'atar, 121

Sweet Potato Börek, 34
Swordfish Crudo, 107
Taramasalata, 37
Tiropitakia, 52
Tuna Kibbeh Nayeh, 99
Turmeric & Ginger Shrimp Cocktail, 98
Tzatziki, 56
apple liqueur
  Raphael, 692
apples
  Apple & Walnut Bundt Cake, 637–638
  Crunchy Pomegranate Salad, 422
  Grapefruit & Fennel Salad, 389
  Grilled Romaine & Sweet Potato, 441
  Pickled Applesauce, 799
  Salted Honey & Apple Upside-Down Cake, 642
  Spinach, Fennel & Apple Salad with Smoked Trout, 393
  Sumac, Spelt & Apple Cake, 669
  Sumac & Apple Cauliflower, 429
  Sweet & Sour Short Ribs, 209
Applesauce, Smoked Pork Belly in Pickled, 192
apricots, dried
  Chicken Tagine with Warm Couscous Salad, 161
  Roasted Apricot Chicken with Mint & Sage Butternut Squash, 238
  Stuffed Zucchini, 221
  Vegetable Tanzia, 261
arak
  Arak Sour, 739
  Israeli Iced Tea, 683
  Triple My Worth, 696
Arancini, 60
artichokes/artichoke hearts
  Artichoke à la Barigoule, 341
  Boulettes with Chicken & Vegetable Soup, 362–363
  Fried Artichokes, 117–119
  Marinated Artichokes, 86
  Msoki de Pesaj, 350
  Roasted Eggplant Pita, 187
  Taramasalata, 37
arugula
  Arugula Salad with Candied Walnuts, 427
  Arugula Salad with Pickled Beets & Preserved Lemon Vinaigrette, 487

Celery Slaw with Seeds & Dates, 504
Heart-Beet Salad, 428
Lavash with Arugula, Eggplant & Olives, 535–536
Mediterranean Grilled Chicken Salad, 446
Panzanella, 382
Strawberry Fields Salad, 440
asiago cheese
Cheesy Poofs, 111
asparagus
Couscous & Shrimp Salad, 465
Honey-Glazed Tuna with Romesco & Warm Asparagus Salad, 162
Peppery Glazed Asparagus, 419
Autumn Kale Salad, 498
Avgolemono, 306
avgotaraho
about, 21–22
Avikas, 359
avocados
Crab Roulade, 179
Crispy Lemon & Chickpea Cakes, 188
Crushed Avocado, 102
Ropa Vieja, 239
Stuffed Avocados, 91
Tuna Kibbeh Nayeh, 99

Baba Ghanoush
about, 24
recipe, 39
Bacon & Eggs Jachnun, 175
Baked Orzo, 228
Baklava
about, 22
recipe, 606
Baklava Pie, 656–657
Balsamic Glaze
Fried Feta, 90
Grilled Cantaloupe, 82
recipe, 759
Roasted Grapes & Sausage, 167
Bamies, 406
Banana Fritters, Fermented, 628
barley, pearl
Cholent, 357
Barolo Chinato
Big Trouble Spritz, 712
Basic Focaccia Dough, 550
basil
Basil-Infused Suze, 726
Broccolini Salad, 410
Concia, 418
Forget Domani, 726
Grilled Serrano Salsa Verde, 798
Phyllo Dough Pizza, 590
Roasted Beets with Cilantro & Basil Pesto, 436
Roasted Tomato Caprese, 388
beans
Avikas, 359
Cholent, 357
Dried Fava Bean Soup with Grilled Halloumi Cheese, 314
Fava Beans with Pomegranates, 472
Ful Medames, 475

Lamb & Cannellini Soup, 325
Moroccan Lentil Stew, 310
Panzanella, 382
Romano Beans with Mustard Vinaigrette & Walnuts, 491
see also green beans; lentils
beef
Albondigas, 193
Albondigas Soup, 305
Avikas, 359
Boulettes with Chicken & Vegetable Soup, 362–363
Brisket with Pistachio Gremolata, 279
Chamin, 321
Chicken with Mehshi Sfeeha, 282
Chickpea Poutine, 83
Cholent, 357
Dafina, 365
Eggplant Dolma, 259
Kefta with Chickpea Salad, 271
Lahmacun Spread, 545
Onion Mahshi, 502
Ropa Vieja, 239
Short Rib & Okra Stew, 366
Short Ribs with Braised Cauliflower & Stuffed Tomatoes, 213
Sweet & Sour Short Ribs, 209
Tomatoes Reinados, 257
Turkish Coffee-Rubbed Brisket, 258
Za'atar-Crusted Ribeye, 197
beef bones
Beef Stock, 369
Beef Stock
Chamin, 321
Hand-Rolled Couscous, 499
Lamb Shanks with Pomegranate Sauce, 140
Leg of Lamb with Garlic & Rosemary, 147
Mansaf, 329
recipe, 369
Short Ribs with Braised Cauliflower & Stuffed Tomatoes, 213
Spaghetti with Oxtail Ragout, 248
beer
about, 23
beets
Arugula Salad with Pickled Beets & Preserved Lemon Vinaigrette, 487
Beet Chips with Spicy Honey Mayonnaise, 38
Beets with Walnut Dukkah, 437
Heart-Beet Salad, 428
Kemia de Remolachas, 478
Red Cabbage, Date & Beet Salad, 445
Roasted Beet & Leek Risotto, 432
Roasted Beets with Cilantro & Basil Pesto, 436
Shaved Radish Salad with Walnuts & Mint, 522
berberis
Sumac Chicken & Rice, 256
bergamot juice
Vitamin Sea, 720
beverages

Ananda Spritz, 733
Arak Sour, 739
Big Trouble Spritz, 712
The Bitter Pomelo, 700
Chinotto Negroni, 727
The Church, 729
Drink of Laughter & Forgetting, 697
The Escape, 724
Faluka, 709
Fennel & Olive Oil Gimlet, 704
Forget Domani, 726
Hawaij Hot Cocoa, 684
Israeli Iced Tea, 683
Italian Greyhound, 730
Lady in Red, 716
Limonana, 687
Lipstick & Rouge, 708
Macaroni Cocktail, 694
Opening Night, 723
Pomegranate Prosecco Punch, 688
The Project, 711
Raphael, 692
Sachlav, 689
Salep, 738
Sgroppino Plagiato, 715
Spiked Lemonade, 680
Strawberry Rosé Sangria, 735
The Top of Olympus, 719
Top-Shelf Negroni, 701
Triple My Worth, 696
Valentine's Grapefruit, 695
Vitamin Sea, 720
White Peach Sangria, 734
Big Trouble Spritz, 712
Biscotti, Cardamom, 670
Bitter Pomelo, The, 700
Black & White Halvah, 644–645
Black Lime & Strawberry Crostata, 633
blueberries
Blueberry & Ginger Malabi, 636
Blueberry Compote, 675
Broccolini Salad, 410
Yogurt Mousse with Blueberry Compote & Granola, 621
Blueberry Compote
recipe, 675
Yogurt Mousse with Blueberry Compote & Granola, 621
Bone Marrow & Matzo Ball Soup, 324
börek
about, 22
Sweet Potato Börek, 34
Boscaiola, 594
bottarga
about, 21–22
Bouillabaisse, 302
Boulettes with Chicken & Vegetable Soup, 362–363
Bouquet Garni
Bouillabaisse, 302
recipe, 302
bourbon
Ananda Spritz, 733
Baklava Pie, 656–657
Pecan Pie Baklava, 627

Bourekas, 47
Braised Cauliflower
  recipe, 466
  Short Ribs with Braised Cauliflower
    & Stuffed Tomatoes, 213
Braised Grapes
  Chilled White Tomato Soup with
    Braised Grapes, 318
  recipe, 318
Braised Halibut with Crispy Polenta
  Cakes, 180
Braised Leeks, 492
Braised Pork with Greek Salad &
  Skordalia, 133
brandy
  Lemon Rice Pudding with Roasted
    Vanilla Cherries & Lemon
    Crème, 631
branzino
  Cornbread & Crab-Stuffed
    Branzino, 240
  Whole Branzino, 205
bread
  about, 10–11, 25
  Basic Focaccia Dough, 550
  Boscaiola, 594
  Caprese, 601
  Carrettiera, 596
  Crescia Sfogliata, 575
  Focaccia Barese, 569
  Focaccia con le Olive, 578
  Focaccia di Carnevale Salentina,
    565
  Focaccia di Recco, 576
  Focaccia Genovese, 557
  Focaccia Messinese, 572
  Lahmacun, 545
  Lavash with Arugula, Eggplant &
    Olives, 535–536
  Margherita, 582
  Mustazzeddu, 558
  Neapolitan Pizza Dough, 581
  No-Knead Focaccia Dough, 554
  Panzanella, 382
  Parigina, 570
  Pescatora, 600
  Phyllo Dough Pizza, 590
  Pides, 537–538
  Pissalandrea, 577
  Pita Bread, 532
  Pizza Marinara, 586
  Pizz'onta, 573
  Puddica Salentina, 566
  Quattro Formaggi, 597
  Rianata, 561
  Roasted Squash & Feta Salad, 519
  Romana, 587
  Sfincione Palermitano, 562
  Socca, 546
  from southern Europe, 20
  24-Hour Focaccia Dough, 553
  Vegetarian Musakhan, 542
  Whole Wheat Coques, 541
  Za'atar Bread, 549
Briam, 269
brisket
  Brisket with Pistachio Gremolata,
    279

Chamin, 321
Broccoli & Anchovy Soup, 337
broccoli rabe
  Carrettiera, 596
Broccolini Salad, 410
Brussels sprouts
  Fried Brussels Sprouts with Tahini
    & Feta, 399
  Roasted Brussels Sprouts with
    Warm Honey Glaze, 483
  Roasted Root Vegetables with
    Lemon Caper Sauce, 488
  Slow-Roasted Lamb Shoulder with
    Brussels Sprouts & Crispy Kale,
    254
bulgur wheat
  Bulgur with Fried Onions, 278
  Bulgur-Stuffed Eggplants, 494
  Tabbouleh, 461
  Tuna Kibbeh Nayeh, 99
Butter, Garlic, 806
buttermilk
  Rutabaga & Fig Soup, 342
  Spiced Honey Cake with Coconut
    & Cream Cheese Frosting, 664
butternut squash
  Boulettes with Chicken & Vegetable
    Soup, 362–363
  Couscous with Seven Vegetables,
    505
  Mint & Sage Butternut Squash, 395
  Roasted Apricot Chicken with Mint
    & Sage Butternut Squash, 238
  Stuffed Avocados, 91
  Tunisian Butternut Squash Soup,
    352
  Tunisian Vegetable Soup, 354
  Vegetable Tanzia, 261

cabbage
  Red Cabbage, Date & Beet Salad,
    445
caciocavallo cheese
  Focaccia Messinese, 572
  Parigina, 570
  Sfincione Palermitano, 562
cakes
  Apple & Walnut Bundt Cake,
    637–638
  Honey & Pomegranate Cake, 653
  Honey Cake, 652
  Lemon Poppy Seed Cake, 609
  Salted Honey & Apple Upside-
    Down Cake, 642
  Spiced Honey Cake with Coconut
    & Cream Cheese Frosting, 664
  Sumac, Spelt & Apple Cake, 669
calamari/squid
  Chilled Calamari Salad, 381
  Frutti di Mare with Penne, 217
  Garlic & Lime Calamari, 272
  Pescatora, 600
  Seafood & Leek Soup, 338
  Seafood Risotto, 247
Campari
  Chinotto Negroni, 727
  Lady in Red, 716
  Top-Shelf Negroni, 701

Candied Hazelnuts
  Poached Pears with Candied
    Hazelnuts, Palmiers &
    Condensed Caramel, 618
  recipe, 658
Candied Walnuts
  Arugula Salad with Candied
    Walnuts, 427
  recipe, 427
cannellini beans
  Avikas, 359
  Lamb & Cannellini Soup, 325
  Moroccan Lentil Stew, 310
  Panzanella, 382
Cantaloupe, Grilled, 82
capers
  Baked Orzo, 228
  Caponata, 70
  Dijon Dressing, 788
  Pissalandrea, 577
  Puddica Salentina, 566
  Roasted Radicchio, 384
  Roasted Root Vegetables with
    Lemon Caper Sauce, 488
  Romana, 587
Caponata, 70
Cappelletti
  Italian Greyhound, 730
Caprese, 601
Caramel, Condensed, 647
Caramel Glaze
  Apple & Walnut Bundt Cake,
    637–638
  recipe, 637–638
Caramelized Honey Tart, 648
Cardamom Biscotti, 670
Cardamom Syrup
  recipe, 696
  Triple My Worth, 696
carp roe
  Taramasalata, 37
Carrettiera, 596
carrots
  Beef Stock, 369
  Boulettes with Chicken & Vegetable
    Soup, 362–363
  Braised Pork with Greek Salad &
    Skordalia, 133
  Chamin, 321
  Chicken Stock, 368
  Chicken Tagine with Warm
    Couscous Salad, 161
  Couscous with Seven Vegetables,
    505
  Fish Stock, 372
  Honey-Glazed Carrots, 484
  Honey-Roasted Vegetable Salad,
    516
  Kemia de Zanahorias, 479
  Lamb & Cannellini Soup, 325
  Lobster Stock, 373
  Moroccan Carrots, 433
  Moroccan Lentil Stew, 310
  Msoki de Pesaj, 350
  Orange Chicken with Roasted
    Vegetables & Olives, 227
  Roast Chicken with Fennel &
    Carrots, 290

Saffron & Mussel Soup, 333
Short Ribs with Braised Cauliflower & Stuffed Tomatoes, 213
Split Pea Soup with Smoked Ham, 317
Tunisian Vegetable Soup, 354
Turkish Coffee-Rubbed Brisket, 258
Vegetable Soup, 328
Vegetable Stock, 371
Vegetarian Musakhan, 542
Vegetarian Split Pea Soup, 349
Za'atar-Rubbed Spatchcock Chicken with Honey-Glazed Carrots & Roasted Root Vegetables, 253
cashews
Sicilian Bar Nuts, 74
cauliflower
Braised Cauliflower, 466
Cauliflower Cakes, 495
Honey-Roasted Vegetable Salad, 516
Marinated Cauliflower & Chickpeas, 480
Roasted Cauliflower, 474
Roasted Chicken Thighs with Saffron Cauliflower and Pistachio & Raisin Sauce, 231
Seared Shrimp Skewers with Aioli & Cauliflower Cakes, 214
Short Ribs with Braised Cauliflower & Stuffed Tomatoes, 213
Sumac & Apple Cauliflower, 429
Cedar-Plank Salmon, 286
celeriac/celery root
Artichoke à la Barigoule, 341
Roasted Root Vegetables with Lemon Caper Sauce, 488
Tunisian Vegetable Soup, 354
celery
Beef Stock, 369
Bouillabaisse, 302
Braised Pork with Greek Salad & Skordalia, 133
Caponata, 70
Celery Slaw with Seeds & Dates, 504
Chicken Stock, 368
Chilled Calamari Salad, 381
Cornbread Stuffing, 240
Fish Stock, 372
Lamb & Cannellini Soup, 325
Msoki de Pesaj, 350
Provençal Fish Soup, 322
Roasted & Stuffed Sardines, 75
Saffron, Tomato & Fennel Soup, 355
Saffron & Mussel Soup, 333
Short Ribs with Braised Cauliflower & Stuffed Tomatoes, 213
Split Pea Soup with Smoked Ham, 317
Vegetable Soup, 328
Vegetable Stock, 371
Vegetarian Split Pea Soup, 349
Chamin, 321

Champagne
Raphael, 692
Champagne Vinaigrette
Broccolini Salad, 410
Mediterranean Grilled Chicken Salad, 446
recipe, 804
Strawberry Fields Salad, 440
chard
Taro Ulass, 404
Charred Chicken with Sweet Potatoes & Oranges, 283
Charred Scallion Sauce, 781
Charred Scallion Sauce
Cornbread & Crab-Stuffed Branzino, 240
Charred Sweet Potatoes with Toum, 508
chartreuse
Drink of Laughter & Forgetting, 697
Forget Domani, 726
cheese, about, 18–19. see also individual cheese types
Cheesy Poofs, 111
Chermoula Sauce
Chermoula Sea Bass, 289
recipe, 755
cherries
Lemon Rice Pudding with Roasted Vanilla Cherries & Lemon Crème, 631
Sumac Chicken & Rice, 256
cherry liqueur
Vitamin Sea, 720
chicken
Boulettes with Chicken & Vegetable Soup, 362–363
Charred Chicken with Sweet Potatoes & Oranges, 283
Chicken & Tomato Stew with Caramelized Lemon, 311
Chicken B'stilla, 130
Chicken in Walnut Sauce with Vegetable Kebabs, 145
Chicken Souvlaki, 270
Chicken Stew with Potatoes & Radishes, 358
Chicken Stock, 368
Chicken Tagine with Warm Couscous Salad, 161
Chicken with Mehshi Sfeeha, 282
Chicken with Turmeric Tahini, Chickpeas & Onions, 291
Dafina, 365
Easy Paella, 126
Harira, 351
Jerusalem Mixed Grill, 296
Mediterranean Grilled Chicken Salad, 446
Moroccan Cornish Hens with Pine Nut Couscous, 146
Orange Chicken with Roasted Vegetables & Olives, 227
Pomegranate & Honey-Glazed Chicken, 158
Roast Chicken with Harissa & Duck Fat, 242

Roasted Apricot Chicken with Mint & Sage Butternut Squash, 238
Roasted Chicken Thighs with Saffron Cauliflower and Pistachio & Raisin Sauce, 231
Sumac Chicken & Rice, 256
Turmeric Chicken with Toum, 260
Za'atar Chicken with Garlicky Yogurt, 265
Za'atar-Rubbed Spatchcock Chicken with Honey-Glazed Carrots & Roasted Root Vegetables, 253
Chicken Liver Mousse, 78
Chicken Stock
Albondigas Soup, 305
Arancini, 60
Artichoke à la Barigoule, 341
Avgolemono, 306
Baked Orzo, 228
Bone Marrow & Matzo Ball Soup, 324
Braised Pork with Greek Salad & Skordalia, 133
Chicken & Tomato Stew with Caramelized Lemon, 311
Chicken in Walnut Sauce with Vegetable Kebabs, 145
Chicken Stew with Potatoes & Radishes, 358
Chicken Tagine with Warm Couscous Salad, 161
Chickpea Salad, 397
Couscous & Shrimp Salad, 465
Couscous-Stuffed Tomatoes, 456
Easy Paella, 126
Green Beans with Za'atar & Lemon, 513
Hand-Rolled Couscous, 499
Harira, 351
Lamb & Cannellini Soup, 325
Lamb Meatballs over Marinated Eggplant Salad, 199
Lamb Sharba, 309
Pomegranate & Honey-Glazed Chicken, 158
recipe, 368
Roasted Apricot Chicken with Mint & Sage Butternut Squash, 238
Roasted Beet & Leek Risotto, 432
Ropa Vieja, 239
Seafood Risotto, 247
Split Pea Soup with Smoked Ham, 317
Stuffed Zucchini, 221
Sumac Chicken & Rice, 256
Toasted Pasta with Crab, 176
Tomato & Eggplant Soup, 346
Tunisian Butternut Squash Soup, 352
chickpea flour
Chickpea Poutine, 83
Falafel, 57
Socca, 546
chickpeas
Boulettes with Chicken & Vegetable Soup, 362–363

Bulgur with Fried Onions, 278
Chamin, 321
Charred Chicken with Sweet
    Potatoes & Oranges, 283
Chicken Tagine with Warm
    Couscous Salad, 161
Chicken with Turmeric Tahini,
    Chickpeas & Onions, 291
Chickpea Salad, 397
Couscous with Seven Vegetables,
    505
Crispy Lemon & Chickpea Cakes,
    188
Dafina, 365
Falafel, 57
Harira, 351
Kefta with Chickpea Salad, 271
Koshari, 509
Lamb Sharba, 309
Lentil Salad, 460
Mahshi Laban, 154
Marinated Cauliflower &
    Chickpeas, 480
Modern Hummus, 31
Rutabaga & Fig Soup, 342
Spicy Chickpeas, 342
chile/chili peppers. *see* peppers, chile/
    chili
Chilled Calamari Salad, 381
Chilled White Tomato Soup with
    Braised Grapes, 318
Chinotto Negroni, 727
chives
    Chermoula Sauce, 755
    Crab Roulade, 179
    Goat Cheese, Olive & Fennel
        Phyllo Triangles, 114
    Roasted Cauliflower, 474
    Seafood Risotto, 247
    Socca, 546
chocolate
    Chocolate Glaze, 652
    Hawaij Hot Cocoa, 684
    Spicy Chocolate Halvah, 632
Chocolate Glaze
    Honey Cake, 652
    recipe, 652
Cholent, 357
chorizo/sausage
    Boscaiola, 594
    Carrettiera, 596
    Easy Paella, 126
    Eggplant & Chorizo Bourekas, 46
    Focaccia di Carnevale Salentina,
        565
    Roasted Grapes & Sausage, 167
Church, The, 729
cilantro
    Boulettes with Chicken & Vegetable
        Soup, 362–363
    Chamin, 321
    Charred Scallion Sauce, 781
    Chermoula Sauce, 755
    Chicken with Turmeric Tahini,
        Chickpeas & Onions, 291
    Chickpea Salad, 397
    Crushed Avocado, 102
    Falafel, 57

Farro Salad with Olive & Whole
    Lemon Vinaigrette, 512
Fish & Crispy Rice Cake with
    Saffron Crust, 150–151
Green Zhug, 749
Grilled Serrano Salsa Verde, 798
Harira, 351
Kuku Sabzi, 141
Mediterranean-Style Hot Sauce,
    800
Modern Hummus, 31
Msoki de Pesaj, 350
Mujadara, 402
Red Cabbage, Date & Beet Salad,
    445
Roasted Beets with Cilantro & Basil
    Pesto, 436
Roasted Cauliflower, 474
Roasted Pepper Salad, 517
Strawberry Fields Salad, 440
Taro Ulass, 404
Whitefish Poached in Pepper Sauce,
    155
Cinnamon Whipped Cream, 684
clam juice
    Frutti di Mare with Penne, 217
    Provençal Fish Soup, 322
    Seafood & Leek Soup, 338
    Seafood Risotto, 247
clams
    Bouillabaisse, 302
Classic Halvah
    Halvah Mille-Feuilles, 649
    recipe, 650
Classic Malabi, 660
clementines
    Pomegranate Prosecco Punch, 688
Cocchi Americano
    Big Trouble Spritz, 712
    The Church, 729
Cocoa, Hawaij Hot, 684
coconut/coconut milk
    Chocolate Glaze, 652
    Coconut & Cream Cheese Frosting,
        668
    Sachlav, 689
    Spiced Honey Cake with Coconut
        & Cream Cheese Frosting, 664
cod
    Fried Fish with Agristada Sauce,
        297
    Seafood & Leek Soup, 338
coffee
    Coffee Syrup, 711
    The Project, 711
    Turkish Coffee-Rubbed Brisket, 258
Cojada Potato Casserole, 292
Cold Roast Salmon with Smashed
    Green Bean Salad, 293
Concia, 418
Condensed Caramel
    Poached Pears with Candied
        Hazelnuts, Palmiers &
        Condensed Caramel, 618
    recipe, 647
Confit Tuna, 378
Coriander & Rosemary, Slow-Cooked
    Cherry Tomatoes with, 523

Cornbread & Crab-Stuffed Branzino,
    240
Cornbread Stuffing, 240
Cornish Hens with Pine Nut
    Couscous, Moroccan, 146
couscous
    about, 23–24
    Boulettes with Chicken & Vegetable
        Soup, 362–363
    Chicken Tagine with Warm
        Couscous Salad, 161
    Couscous & Shrimp Salad, 465
    Couscous Arancini, 61
    Couscous-Stuffed Tomatoes, 456
    Couscous with Seven Vegetables,
        505
    Hand-Rolled Couscous, 499
    Moroccan Cornish Hens with Pine
        Nut Couscous, 146
    Short Ribs with Braised Cauliflower
        & Stuffed Tomatoes, 213
    Stuffed Zucchini, 221
    Sumac & Lime Mahimahi, 183
    Warm Couscous Salad, 503
crab
    Cornbread & Crab-Stuffed
        Branzino, 240
    Crab Roulade, 179
    Creamy Pappardelle with Crab, 235
    Toasted Pasta with Crab, 176
cranberries, dried
    Broccolini Salad, 410
    Sumac Chicken & Rice, 256
cream cheese
    Coconut & Cream Cheese Frosting,
        668
    Spiced Honey Cake with Coconut
        & Cream Cheese Frosting, 664
Creamy Balsamic & Mushroom Sauce
    Creamy Pappardelle with Crab, 235
    recipe, 789
Creamy Pappardelle with Crab, 235
Crème Chantilly
    Poached Pears with Candied
        Hazelnuts, Palmiers &
        Condensed Caramel, 618
    recipe, 655
crème fraîche
    Crab Roulade, 179
    Seafood Risotto, 247
crescenza cheese
    Focaccia di Recco, 576
Crescia Sfogliata, 575
Crispy Lemon & Chickpea Cakes,
    188
Crispy Salmon Rice, 450
Crunchy Pomegranate Salad, 422
Crushed Avocado
    Crispy Lemon & Chickpea Cakes,
        188
    recipe, 102
cucumber
    Celery Slaw with Seeds & Dates,
        504
    Chicken Souvlaki, 270
    Couscous & Shrimp Salad, 465
    Cucumber, Mint & Sumac Salad,
        471

Cucumber, Tomato & Mango
    Relish, 469
Greek Salad, 451
Lahmacun, 545
Mahshi Laban, 154
Minty Pickled Cucumbers, 414
Pickled Cucumber Salad, 470
Sabich, 243
Tabbouleh, 461
Taramasalata, 37
Tzatziki, 56
cynar
    The Bitter Pomelo, 700
    Drink of Laughter & Forgetting, 697
    The Project, 711

Dafina, 365
dates
    Celery Slaw with Seeds & Dates,
        504
    Dafina, 365
    Red Cabbage, Date & Beet Salad,
        445
    Roasted Cauliflower, 474
David, Elizabeth, 10
Debla, 661
delicata squash
    Autumn Kale Salad, 498
desserts
    Apple & Walnut Bundt Cake,
        637–638
    Baklava, 606
    Baklava Pie, 656–657
    Black & White Halvah, 644–645
    Black Lime & Strawberry Crostata,
        633
    Blueberry & Ginger Malabi, 636
    Blueberry Compote, 675
    Candied Hazelnuts, 658
    Caramelized Honey Tart, 648
    Cardamom Biscotti, 670
    Classic Halvah, 650
    Classic Malabi, 660
    Coconut & Cream Cheese Frosting,
        668
    Condensed Caramel, 647
    Debla, 661
    Fermented Banana Fritters, 628
    Fig, Orange & Anise Honey Balls,
        610
    Goat Cheese & Honey Panna
        Cotta, 629
    Granola, 663
    Halvah Mille-Feuilles, 649
    Honey & Pomegranate Cake, 653
    Honey Cake, 652
    Lemon Poppy Seed Cake, 609
    Lemon Rice Pudding with Roasted
        Vanilla Cherries & Lemon
        Crème, 631
    Meyer Lemon Curd, 614
    Palmiers, 641
    Pasteli, 617
    Pecan Pie Baklava, 627
    Pignoli, 622
    Poached Pears with Candied
        Hazelnuts, Palmiers &
        Condensed Caramel, 618

recipe, 655
Salted Honey & Apple Upside-
    Down Cake, 642
Sfenj Donuts, 665
Sfratti, 672–673
Spiced Honey Cake with Coconut
    & Cream Cheese Frosting, 664
Spicy Chocolate Halvah, 632
Sufganiyot, 626
Sumac, Spelt & Apple Cake, 669
Yogurt Mousse with Blueberry
    Compote & Granola, 621
Zeppole with Lemon Curd, 613
Diavola, 593
Dijon Dressing
    recipe, 788
    Salade Niçoise, 378
dill
    Cucumber, Tomato & Mango
        Relish, 469
    Fava Beans with Pomegranates, 472
    Kuku Sabzi, 141
    Moussaka, 218
    Stuffed Grape Leaves, 55
Dogfish Chraime, 251
dolmas
    about, 22
Donuts, Sfenj, 665
Dried Fava Bean Soup with Grilled
    Halloumi Cheese, 314
Drink of Laughter & Forgetting, 697
Duck Breast Wellington, 182
duck fat
    Roast Chicken with Harissa &
        Duck Fat, 242
Dukkah
    about, 23
    Beets with Walnut Dukkah, 437
    recipe, 744

Easy Paella, 126
eggplants
    Almodrote, 277
    Baba Ghanoush, 39
    Baked Orzo, 228
    Bulgur-Stuffed Eggplants, 494
    Caponata, 70
    Chicken with Mehshi Sfeeha, 282
    Eggplant & Chorizo Bourekas, 46
    Eggplant & Pine Nut Ragout, 776
    Eggplant & Zucchini Soup, 334
    Eggplant Dolma, 259
    Eggplant Rings, 71
    Eggplant Rollatini, 226
    Fried Eggplant with Garlic & Ras el
        Hanout, 112
    Handrajo, 51
    Lamb Meatballs over Marinated
        Eggplant Salad, 199
    Lavash with Arugula, Eggplant &
        Olives, 535–536
    Marinated Eggplant Salad, 398
    Moussaka, 218
    Pides, 537–538
    Red Wine–Braised Octopus with
        Bulgur-Stuffed Eggplants, 200
    Roasted Eggplant Pita, 187
    Sabich, 243

Seared Eggplant, 385
Stuffed Eggplants, 268
Tomato & Eggplant Soup, 346
Turkish Eggplant Salad, 407
eggs
    Agristada Sauce, 793
    Arancini, 60
    Avgolemono, 306
    Bacon & Eggs Jachnun, 175
    Boulettes with Chicken & Vegetable
        Soup, 362–363
    Dafina, 365
    Eggplant & Chorizo Bourekas, 46
    Eggplant Dolma, 259
    Kuku Sabzi, 141
    'Nduja Shakshuka, 137
    Ratatouille with Poached Eggs, 129
    Rosti Egg in a Hole, 210
    Sabich, 243
    Salade Niçoise, 378
    Shakshuka, 172
    Smoked Egg Aioli, 770
    Sweet Potato Börek, 34
    White Shakshuka, 264
Egypt, about, 22
Ensalada de Pulpo, 405
entrees
    Albondigas, 193
    Aliciotti con Indivia, 276
    Almodrote, 277
    Bacon & Eggs Jachnun, 175
    Baked Orzo, 228
    Braised Halibut with Crispy Polenta
        Cakes, 180
    Braised Pork with Greek Salad &
        Skordalia, 133
    Briam, 269
    Brisket with Pistachio Gremolata,
        279
    Bulgur with Fried Onions, 278
    Cedar-Plank Salmon, 286
    Charred Chicken with Sweet
        Potatoes & Oranges, 283
    Chermoula Sea Bass, 289
    Chicken B'stilla, 130
    Chicken in Walnut Sauce with
        Vegetable Kebabs, 145
    Chicken Souvlaki, 270
    Chicken Tagine with Warm
        Couscous Salad, 161
    Chicken with Mehshi Sfeeha,
        282
    Chicken with Turmeric Tahini,
        Chickpeas & Onions, 291
    Cojada Potato Casserole, 292
    Cold Roast Salmon with Smashed
        Green Bean Salad, 293
    Cornbread & Crab-Stuffed
        Branzino, 240
    Crab Roulade, 179
    Creamy Pappardelle with Crab,
        235
    Crispy Lemon & Chickpea Cakes, 188
    Dogfish Chraime, 251
    Duck Breast Wellington, 182
    Easy Paella, 126
    Eggplant Dolma, 259
    Eggplant Rollatini, 226

Fish & Crispy Rice Cake with Saffron Crust, 150–151
Fried Fish with Agristada Sauce, 297
Frutti di Mare with Penne, 217
Garlic & Lime Calamari, 272
Honey-Glazed Tuna with Romesco & Warm Asparagus Salad, 162
Jerusalem Mixed Grill, 296
Kefta with Chickpea Salad, 271
Kuku Sabzi, 141
Lamb Belly Hash, 159
Lamb Meatballs over Marinated Eggplant Salad, 199
Lamb Shanks with Pomegranate Sauce, 140
Lamb Shish Kebabs, 204
Leg of Lamb with Garlic & Rosemary, 147
Mahshi Laban, 154
Marinated Lamb Heart, 171
Monkfish Tagine, 232
Moroccan Cornish Hens with Pine Nut Couscous, 146
Moussaka, 218
'Nduja Shakshuka, 137
Olive Oil-Poached Fluke, 166
Orange Chicken with Roasted Vegetables & Olives, 227
Pan-Roasted Monkfish with Olive Relish & Braised Fennel, 222
Pesce All'ebraica, 275
Pomegranate & Honey-Glazed Chicken, 158
Ratatouille with Poached Eggs, 129
Red Wine–Braised Octopus with Bulgur-Stuffed Eggplants, 200
Risi e Bisi, 138
Roast Chicken with Fennel & Carrots, 290
Roast Chicken with Harissa & Duck Fat, 242
Roasted Apricot Chicken with Mint & Sage Butternut Squash, 238
Roasted Chicken Thighs with Saffron Cauliflower and Pistachio & Raisin Sauce, 231
Roasted Eggplant Pita, 187
Roasted Grapes & Sausage, 167
Ropa Vieja, 239
Sabich, 243
Seafood Risotto, 247
Seared Shrimp Skewers with Aioli & Cauliflower Cakes, 214
Shakshuka, 172
Shawarma-Spiced Leg of Lamb, 250
Short Ribs with Braised Cauliflower & Stuffed Tomatoes, 213
Slow-Roasted Lamb Shoulder with Brussels Sprouts & Crispy Kale, 254
Smoked Pork Belly in Pickled Applesauce, 192
Spaghetti al Tonno, 255
Spaghetti with Oxtail Ragout, 248
Stuffed Acorn Squash, 196
Stuffed Eggplants, 268
Stuffed Mackerel, 134

Stuffed Zucchini, 221
Sumac & Lime Mahimahi, 183
Sumac Chicken & Rice, 256
Sweet & Sour Short Ribs, 209
Toasted Pasta with Crab, 176
Tomatoes Reinados, 257
Turkish Coffee-Rubbed Brisket, 258
Turmeric Chicken with Toum, 260
Vegetable Tanzia, 261
White Shakshuka, 264
Whitefish Poached in Pepper Sauce, 155
Whole Branzino, 205
Za'atar Chicken with Garlicky Yogurt, 265
Za'atar-Crusted Ribeye, 197
Za'atar-Rubbed Spatchcock Chicken with Honey-Glazed Carrots & Roasted Root Vegetables, 253
Zucchini Fritters, 288
Escape, The, 724
escarole
    Aliciotti con Indivia, 276
    Focaccia Messinese, 572

Falafel
    about, 23
    recipe, 57
Faluka, 709
Farro Salad with Olive & Whole Lemon Vinaigrette, 512
fava beans
    Dried Fava Bean Soup with Grilled Halloumi Cheese, 314
    Fava Beans with Pomegranates, 472
    Ful Medames, 475
fennel
    Bouillabaisse, 302
    Fennel & Olive Oil Gimlet, 704
    Goat Cheese, Olive & Fennel Phyllo Triangles, 114
    Grapefruit & Fennel Salad, 389
    Msoki de Pesaj, 350
    Orange Chicken with Roasted Vegetables & Olives, 227
    Pan-Roasted Monkfish with Olive Relish & Braised Fennel, 222
    Provençal Fish Soup, 322
    Roast Chicken with Fennel & Carrots, 290
    Saffron, Tomato & Fennel Soup, 355
    Saffron & Mussel Soup, 333
    Spinach, Fennel & Apple Salad with Smoked Trout, 393
    Strawberry Fields Salad, 440
    Turkish Coffee-Rubbed Brisket, 258
Fennel Syrup
    Fennel & Olive Oil Gimlet, 704
    recipe, 704
Fermented Banana Fritters, 628
Fernet-Branca
    Valentine's Grapefruit, 695
feta cheese
    Baked Orzo, 228
    Bamies, 406
    Broccolini Salad, 410

Charred Chicken with Sweet Potatoes & Oranges, 283
Chickpea Poutine, 83
Couscous & Shrimp Salad, 465
Couscous Arancini, 61
Eggplant Dolma, 259
Fried Brussels Sprouts with Tahini & Feta, 399
Fried Feta, 90
Greek Salad, 451
Grilled Romaine & Sweet Potato, 441
Lahmacun, 545
Lavash Crackers with Red Pepper Feta & Ricotta and Spiced Honey, 44
Lentil Salad, 460
Mediterranean Grilled Chicken Salad, 446
Pides, 537–538
Roasted Radicchio, 384
Roasted Squash & Feta Salad, 519
Shakshuka, 172
Spanakopita, 81
Stuffed Avocados, 91
Tabbouleh, 461
Tiropitakia, 52
Whipped Feta with Za'atar, 771
Zucchini Fritters, 288
fig jam
    Arugula Salad with Candied Walnuts, 427
    Fig Vinaigrette, 752
Fig Vinaigrette
    Arugula Salad with Candied Walnuts, 427
    recipe, 752
figs
    Fig, Orange & Anise Honey Balls, 610
    Fig & Goat Cheese Salad, 444
    Fig Vinaigrette, 752
    Pomegranate-Glazed Figs & Cheese, 116
    Rutabaga & Fig Soup, 342
    Vegetable Tanzia, 261
Fire-Roasted Oysters, 103
fish and seafood
    about, 19
    Aliciotti con Indivia, 276
    Bouillabaisse, 302
    Braised Halibut with Crispy Polenta Cakes, 180
    Cedar-Plank Salmon, 286
    Chermoula Sea Bass, 289
    Chilled Calamari Salad, 381
    Cold Roast Salmon with Smashed Green Bean Salad, 293
    Cornbread & Crab-Stuffed Branzino, 240
    Couscous & Shrimp Salad, 465
    Crab Roulade, 179
    Creamy Pappardelle with Crab, 235
    Crispy Salmon Rice, 450
    Dogfish Chraime, 251
    Easy Paella, 126
    Ensalada de Pulpo, 405
    Fire-Roasted Oysters, 103

Fish & Crispy Rice Cake with
Saffron Crust, 150–151
Fried Fish with Agristada Sauce,
297
Frutti di Mare with Penne, 217
Garlic & Lime Calamari, 272
Honey-Glazed Tuna with Romesco
& Warm Asparagus Salad, 162
Monkfish Tagine, 232
Mussels Escabeche, 94
Olive Oil-Poached Fluke, 166
Pan-Roasted Monkfish with Olive
Relish & Braised Fennel, 222
Pescatora, 600
Pesce All'ebraica, 275
Provençal Fish Soup, 322
Red Wine–Braised Octopus with
Bulgur-Stuffed Eggplants, 200
Roasted & Stuffed Sardines, 75
Romesco de Peix, 345
Saffron & Mussel Soup, 333
Salade Niçoise, 378
Scallop Ceviche, 95
Seafood & Leek Soup, 338
Seafood Risotto, 247
Seared Shrimp Skewers with Aioli
& Cauliflower Cakes, 214
in southern Europe, 20
Spaghetti al Tonno, 255
Spinach, Fennel & Apple Salad with
Smoked Trout, 393
Stuffed Mackerel, 134
Sumac & Lime Mahimahi, 183
Swordfish Crudo, 107
Toasted Pasta with Crab, 176
Tuna Kibbeh Nayeh, 99
Turmeric & Ginger Shrimp
Cocktail, 98
Whitefish Poached in Pepper Sauce,
155
Whole Branzino, 205
Fish Stock
Bouillabaisse, 302
recipe, 372
Romesco de Peix, 345
Fluke, Olive Oil-Poached, 166
focaccia/focaccia dough
Basic Focaccia Dough, 550
Focaccia Barese, 569
Focaccia con le Olive, 578
Focaccia di Carnevale Salentina,
565
Focaccia di Recco, 576
Focaccia Genovese, 557
Focaccia Messinese, 572
No-Knead Focaccia Dough, 554
Parigina, 570
24-Hour Focaccia Dough, 553
fontina cheese
Arancini, 60
Quattro Formaggi, 597
Sweet Potato Börek, 34
Forget Domani, 726
Fried Artichokes, 117–119
Fried Brussels Sprouts with Tahini &
Feta, 399
Fried Eggplant with Garlic & Ras el
Hanout, 112

Fried Eggplant with Mint Vinaigrette,
113
Fried Feta, 90
Fried Fish with Agristada Sauce, 297
Frutti di Mare with Penne, 217
Ful Medames
about, 23, 24
recipe, 475

garlic
Albondigas, 193
Aliciotti con Indivia, 276
Autumn Kale Salad, 498
Baba Ghanoush, 39
Baked Orzo, 228
Braised Pork with Greek Salad &
Skordalia, 133
Briam, 269
Brisket with Pistachio Gremolata,
279
Broccolini Salad, 410
Chamin, 321
Charred Chicken with Sweet
Potatoes & Oranges, 283
Charred Sweet Potatoes with Toum,
508
Chicken & Tomato Stew with
Caramelized Lemon, 311
Chicken Souvlaki, 270
Chicken Stew with Potatoes &
Radishes, 358
Chicken Tagine with Warm
Couscous Salad, 161
Chicken with Mehshi Sfeeha, 282
Cholent, 357
Concia, 418
Couscous & Shrimp Salad, 465
Dafina, 365
Dried Fava Bean Soup with Grilled
Halloumi Cheese, 314
Dukkah, 744
Easy Paella, 126
Fire-Roasted Oysters, 103
Fish & Crispy Rice Cake with
Saffron Crust, 150–151
Fried Eggplant with Garlic & Ras el
Hanout, 112
Frutti di Mare with Penne, 217
Garlic & Lime Calamari, 272
Garlic Butter, 806
Green Zhug, 749
Harira, 351
Kemia de Zanahorias, 479
Lamb Shanks with Pomegranate
Sauce, 140
Lamb Stew, 364
Leg of Lamb with Garlic &
Rosemary, 147
Marinated Artichokes, 86
Marinated Cauliflower &
Chickpeas, 480
Marinated Eggplant Salad, 398
Marinated Olives, 120
Mediterranean-Style Hot Sauce,
800
Meyer Lemon Marmalade, 801
Moroccan Cornish Hens with Pine
Nut Couscous, 146

Mujadara, 402
'Nduja Shakshuka, 137
Orange Chicken with Roasted
Vegetables & Olives, 227
Phyllo Dough Pizza, 590
Pissalandrea, 577
Ratatouille with Poached Eggs, 129
Red Zhug, 748
Roasted Apricot Chicken with Mint
& Sage Butternut Squash, 238
Roasted Root Vegetables with
Lemon Caper Sauce, 488
Ropa Vieja, 239
Saffron & Tomato Coulis, 805
Seared Shrimp Skewers with Aioli
& Cauliflower Cakes, 214
Shawarma-Spiced Leg of Lamb, 250
Short Ribs with Braised Cauliflower
& Stuffed Tomatoes, 213
Slow-Cooked Cherry Tomatoes
with Coriander & Rosemary, 523
Spaghetti with Oxtail Ragout, 248
Stuffed Zucchini, 221
Sweet & Sour Short Ribs, 209
Sweet Potato Börek, 34
Toum, 758
Turkish Coffee-Rubbed Brisket, 258
Turkish Eggplant Salad, 407
Vegetable Soup, 328
White Shakshuka, 264
Za'atar Chicken with Garlicky
Yogurt, 265
Garlic Butter
Bouillabaisse, 302
recipe, 806
gin
Chinotto Negroni, 727
The Church, 729
The Escape, 724
Fennel & Olive Oil Gimlet, 704
Israeli Iced Tea, 683
Lady in Red, 716
Opening Night, 723
Top-Shelf Negroni, 701
Vitamin Sea, 720
ginger
Blueberry & Ginger Malabi, 636
Chamin, 321
Charred Scallion Sauce, 781
Harira, 351
Moroccan Lentil Stew, 310
Turmeric & Ginger Shrimp
Cocktail, 98
Vitamin Sea, 720
Glazed Okra, 423
goat cheese
about, 19
Broccolini Salad, 410
Fig & Goat Cheese Salad, 444
Glazed Okra, 423
Goat Cheese & Honey Panna
Cotta, 629
Goat Cheese, Olive & Fennel
Phyllo Triangles, 114
'Nduja Shakshuka, 137
Strawberry Fields Salad, 440
gorgonzola cheese
Quattro Formaggi, 597

Gran Classico bitter liqueur
   Valentine's Grapefruit, 695
Granola
   recipe, 663
   Yogurt Mousse with Blueberry
      Compote & Granola, 621
Grape Leaves, Stuffed, 55
grapefruit
   Big Trouble Spritz, 712
   Grapefruit & Fennel Salad, 389
   Italian Greyhound, 730
   Valentine's Grapefruit, 695
grapefruit juice
   The Bitter Pomelo, 700
grapefruit soda
Big Trouble Spritz, 712
grapes
   about, 13–14
   Broccolini Salad, 410
   Chilled White Tomato Soup with
      Braised Grapes, 318
   Roasted Grapes & Sausage, 167
grappa
   Forget Domani, 726
Greece, about, 21–22
Greek Salad
   Braised Pork with Greek Salad &
      Skordalia, 133
   recipe, 451
green beans
   Braised Green Beans, 496
   Cold Roast Salmon with Smashed
      Green Bean Salad, 293
   Green Beans with Za'atar & Lemon,
      513
   Pickled Green Beans, 415
   Salade Niçoise, 378
   Stuffed Mackerel, 134
Green Zhug
   recipe, 749
   Spiced Yogurt Sauce, 803
Grilled Cantaloupe, 82
Grilled Romaine & Sweet Potato, 441
Grilled Serrano Salsa Verde
   Cold Roast Salmon with Smashed
      Green Bean Salad, 293
   Ensalada de Pulpo, 405
   Fried Eggplant with Garlic & Ras el
      Hanout, 112
   recipe, 798

haddock
   Provençal Fish Soup, 322
halloumi
   about, 18
   Dried Fava Bean Soup with Grilled
      Halloumi Cheese, 314
halvah
   Black & White Halvah, 644–645
   Halvah Mille-Feuilles, 649
   Spicy Chocolate Halvah, 632
ham/prosciutto
   Arugula Salad with Candied
      Walnuts, 427
   Parigina, 570
   Risi e Bisi, 138
   Split Pea Soup with Smoked Ham,
      317

Handrajo, 51
Hand-Rolled Couscous, 499
Harira, 351
harissa
   Boulettes with Chicken & Vegetable
      Soup, 362–363
   Chilled Calamari Salad, 381
   Kemia de Zanahorias, 479
   Msoki de Pesaj, 350
   Roast Chicken with Harissa &
      Duck Fat, 242
   Three-Chile Harissa Sauce, 791
   Tunisian Butternut Squash Soup,
      352
Hawaij Hot Cocoa, 684
Hawaij Spice Blend, 684
hazelnuts
   Autumn Kale Salad, 498
   Beets with Walnut Dukkah, 437
   Candied Hazelnuts, 658
   Chilled Calamari Salad, 381
   Heart-Beet Salad, 428
   Poached Pears with Candied
      Hazelnuts, Palmiers &
      Condensed Caramel, 618
health benefits, 25
Heart-Beet Salad, 428
herbs, about, 16
honey
   Baklava, 606
   Baklava Pie, 656–657
   Caramelized Honey Tart, 648
   Classic Halvah, 650
   Fig, Orange & Anise Honey Balls,
      610
   Goat Cheese & Honey Panna
      Cotta, 629
   Granola, 663
   Halvah Mille-Feuilles, 649
   Honey & Pomegranate Cake, 653
   Honey Cake, 652
   Honey-Glazed Carrots, 484
   Honey-Glazed Tuna with Romesco
      & Warm Asparagus Salad, 162
   Honey-Roasted Vegetable Salad,
      516
   Lavash Crackers with Red Pepper
      Feta & Ricotta and Spiced
      Honey, 44
   Moroccan Carrots, 433
   Pasteli, 617
   Pomegranate & Honey-Glazed
      Chicken, 158
   Roasted Brussels Sprouts with
      Warm Honey Glaze, 483
   Salted Honey & Apple Upside-
      Down Cake, 642
   Sfratti, 672–673
   Spiced Honey, 761
   Spiced Honey Cake with Coconut
      & Cream Cheese Frosting,
      664
   Spicy Honey Mayonnaise, 779
   Sweet & Sour Short Ribs, 209
   Sweet Potato & Tahini Dip with
      Spiced Honey, 106
   Za'atar-Rubbed Spatchcock
      Chicken with Honey-Glazed

Carrots & Roasted Root
   Vegetables, 253
Hot Sauce, Mediterranean-Style, 800
hummus
   about, 23, 24
   Jerusalem Mixed Grill, 296
   Modern Hummus, 31
   Roasted Eggplant Pita, 187
hyssop leaves
   White Shakshuka, 264

Israeli Iced Tea, 683
Italian Greyhound, 730
Italicus Rosolio di Bergamotto liqueur
   Vitamin Sea, 720

jalapeño chile peppers
   Falafel, 57
   Grapefruit & Fennel Salad, 389
   Green Zhug, 749
   Salata Mechouia, 30
   Scallop Ceviche, 95
   Short Rib & Okra Stew, 366
   Swordfish Crudo, 107
   see also peppers, chile/chili
Jasmine Air
   recipe, 720
   Vitamin Sea, 720
jellab
   Faluka, 709
Jerusalem Mixed Grill, 296
juniper berries
   Lamb Shanks with Pomegranate
      Sauce, 140

kale
   Autumn Kale Salad, 498
   Heart-Beet Salad, 428
   Slow-Roasted Lamb Shoulder with
      Brussels Sprouts & Crispy Kale,
      254
   Strawberry Fields Salad, 440
kashkaval cheese
   Almodrote, 277
   Bourekas, 47
kataifi
   Fig, Orange & Anise Honey Balls,
      610
kefalotyri cheese
   Moussaka, 218
   Tiropitakia, 52
Kefta with Chickpea Salad, 271
Keftes de Espinaca, 43
Kemia de Remolachas, 478
Kemia de Zanahorias, 479
kidney beans
   Cholent, 357
kishke
   Cholent, 357
Koshari
   about, 23
   recipe, 509
Kuku Sabzi, 141

Labneh
   about, 19
   Beets with Walnut Dukkah, 437
   Fava Beans with Pomegranates, 472

Handrajo, 51
Mahshi Laban, 154
recipe, 67
White Shakshuka, 264
Lady in Red, 716
Lahmacun, 545
Lahmacun Spread, 545
lamb
about, 19
Chamin, 321
Kefta with Chickpea Salad, 271
Lamb & Cannellini Soup, 325
Lamb Belly Hash, 159
Lamb Meatballs over Marinated
Eggplant Salad, 199
Lamb Shanks with Pomegranate
Sauce, 140
Lamb Sharba, 309
Lamb Shish Kebabs, 204
Lamb Stew, 364
Leg of Lamb with Garlic &
Rosemary, 147
Mansaf, 329
Marinated Lamb Heart, 171
Moussaka, 218
Msoki de Pesaj, 350
Shawarma-Spiced Leg of Lamb, 250
Slow-Roasted Lamb Shoulder with
Brussels Sprouts & Crispy Kale,
254
Stuffed Eggplants, 268
Stuffed Zucchini, 221
Lavash Crackers with Red Pepper Feta
& Ricotta and Spiced Honey, 44
Lavash with Arugula, Eggplant &
Olives, 535–536
Lavender Syrup
recipe, 720
Vitamin Sea, 720
leeks
Artichoke à la Barigoule, 341
Bouillabaisse, 302
Braised Halibut with Crispy Polenta
Cakes, 180
Braised Leeks, 492
Crispy Lemon & Chickpea Cakes,
188
Fish Stock, 372
Lamb Meatballs over Marinated
Eggplant Salad, 199
Roasted Beet & Leek Risotto, 432
Saffron & Mussel Soup, 333
Seafood & Leek Soup, 338
Vegetable Soup, 328
Vegetable Stock, 371
Leg of Lamb with Garlic & Rosemary,
147
Lemon Crème, Lemon Rice Pudding
with Roasted Vanilla Cherries
&, 631
Lemonade, Spiked, 680
lemongrass stalks
Vegetable Soup, 328
lemons, preserved
Arugula Salad with Pickled Beets &
Preserved Lemon Vinaigrette, 487
Fish & Crispy Rice Cake with
Saffron Crust, 150–151

lemons/lemon juice
Agristada Sauce, 793
Avgolemono, 306
Chicken & Tomato Stew with
Caramelized Lemon, 311
Cold Roast Salmon with Smashed
Green Bean Salad, 293
Crispy Lemon & Chickpea Cakes,
188
Crushed Avocado, 102
Cucumber, Tomato & Mango
Relish, 469
Farro Salad with Olive & Whole
Lemon Vinaigrette, 512
Fried Artichokes, 117–119
Green Beans with Za'atar & Lemon,
513
Lemon Crème, 631
Lemon Glaze, 609
Lemon Poppy Seed Cake, 609
Lemon Rice Pudding with Roasted
Vanilla Cherries & Lemon
Crème, 631
Lemony Yogurt Sauce, 787
Limonana, 687
Mahshi Laban, 154
Meyer Lemon Curd, 614
Meyer Lemon Marmalade, 801
Modern Hummus, 31
Roasted Cauliflower, 474
Roasted Root Vegetables with
Lemon Caper Sauce, 488
Salata Mechouia, 30
Tunisian Butternut Squash Soup,
352
Za'atar Chicken with Garlicky
Yogurt, 265
Za'atar Okra & Lemons, 526
Zeppole with Lemon Curd, 613
Lemony Yogurt Sauce
Cold Roast Salmon with Smashed
Green Bean Salad, 293
recipe, 787
lentils
Chamin, 321
Harira, 351
Koshari, 509
Lentil Salad, 460
Moroccan Lentil Stew, 310
Mujadara, 402
see also beans
Levant, about, 23
limes/lime juice
Black Lime & Strawberry Crostata,
633
Garlic & Lime Calamari, 272
Pomegranate Prosecco Punch, 688
Sumac & Lime Mahimahi, 183
Limonana, 687
Lipstick & Rouge, 708
Lobster Stock
Bouillabaisse, 302
recipe, 373

Macaroni Cocktail, 694
Mackerel, Stuffed, 134
Maghrebi cuisine
about, 23–24

Mahimahi, Sumac & Lime, 183
Mahshi Laban, 154
manchego cheese
Couscous-Stuffed Tomatoes, 456
mangoes/mango puree
Cucumber, Tomato & Mango
Relish, 469
Tropical Fruit Sorbet, 715
Mansaf, 329
maple syrup
Candied Hazelnuts, 658
Candied Walnuts, 427
Granola, 663
Margherita, 582
Marinated Artichokes
recipe, 86
Roasted Eggplant Pita, 187
Taramasalata, 37
Marinated Cauliflower & Chickpeas,
480
Marinated Eggplant Salad
Lamb Meatballs over Marinated
Eggplant Salad, 199
recipe, 398
Marinated Lamb Heart, 171
Marinated Olives, 120
marrow bones
Bone Marrow & Matzo Ball Soup,
324
Cholent, 357
mascarpone cheese
Pomegranate-Glazed Figs & Cheese,
116
mastiha liqueur
The Escape, 724
Matzo Ball Soup, Bone Marrow &,
324
Mediterranean Grilled Chicken Salad,
446
Mediterranean-Style Hot Sauce, 800
mesclun greens
Ensalada de Pulpo, 405
metaxa
The Top of Olympus, 719
Meyer Lemon Curd
recipe, 614
Zeppole with Lemon Curd, 613
Meyer Lemon Marmalade, 801
microgreens
Crab Roulade, 179
mint
The Bitter Pomelo, 700
Broccolini Salad, 410
Chicken & Tomato Stew with
Caramelized Lemon, 311
Chilled Calamari Salad, 381
Couscous & Shrimp Salad, 465
Cucumber, Mint & Sumac Salad,
471
Farro Salad with Olive & Whole
Lemon Vinaigrette, 512
Fava Beans with Pomegranates, 472
Fried Eggplant with Mint
Vinaigrette, 113
Honey-Roasted Vegetable Salad,
516
Lamb Sharba, 309
Lamb Shish Kebabs, 204

Limonana, 687
Mint & Sage Butternut Squash, 395
Minty Pickled Cucumbers, 414
Msoki de Pesaj, 350
Olive Salad, 394
Pistachio Gremolata, 778
Red Cabbage, Date & Beet Salad,
    445
Roasted Apricot Chicken with Mint
    & Sage Butternut Squash, 238
Shakshuka, 172
Shaved Radish Salad with Walnuts
    & Mint, 522
Short Rib & Okra Stew, 366
Spanakopita, 81
Spiked Lemonade, 680
Stuffed Grape Leaves, 55
Sweet Potato Börek, 34
Tabbouleh, 461
Minty Pickled Cucumbers
    Eggplant & Zucchini Soup, 334
    recipe, 414
Modern Hummus
    Falafel, 57
    recipe, 31
    Roasted Eggplant Pita, 187
molasses
    Stuffed Acorn Squash, 196
    see also pomegranate molasses
monkfish
    Bouillabaisse, 302
    Monkfish Tagine, 232
    Pan-Roasted Monkfish with Olive
        Relish & Braised Fennel, 222
    Romesco de Peix, 345
Moroccan Carrots, 433
Moroccan Cornish Hens with Pine
    Nut Couscous, 146
Moroccan Lentil Stew, 310
Moussaka
    about, 22
    recipe, 218
mozzarella cheese
    Boscaiola, 594
    Caprese, 601
    Carrettiera, 596
    Cheesy Poofs, 111
    Focaccia di Carnevale Salentina, 565
    Grilled Cantaloupe, 82
    Margherita, 582
    Parigina, 570
    Phyllo Dough Pizza, 590
    Quattro Formaggi, 597
    Roasted Grapes & Sausage, 167
    Roasted Tomato Caprese, 388
    Romana, 587
Msoki de Pesaj, 350
Mujadara, 402
mushrooms
    Artichoke à la Barigoule, 341
    Boscaiola, 594
    Broccoli & Anchovy Soup, 337
    Creamy Balsamic & Mushroom
        Sauce, 789
    Tunisian Vegetable Soup, 354
    Vegetable Kebabs, 455
    Vegetarian Musakhan, 542
mussels

Bouillabaisse, 302
Easy Paella, 126
Frutti di Mare with Penne, 217
Mussels Escabeche, 94
Pescatora, 600
Romesco de Peix, 345
Saffron & Mussel Soup, 333
mustard
    Braised Halibut with Crispy Polenta
        Cakes, 180
    Romano Beans with Mustard
        Vinaigrette & Walnuts, 491
Mustazzeddu, 558

'Nduja Shakshuka, 137
Neapolitan Pizza Dough, 581
No-Knead Focaccia Dough, 554
North Africa, about, 22–23
nuts
    Caramelized Honey Tart, 648
    Sicilian Bar Nuts, 74
    see also individual nut types

oats
    Granola, 663
octopus
    Ensalada de Pulpo, 405
    Pescatora, 600
    Red Wine–Braised Octopus with
        Bulgur-Stuffed Eggplants, 200
okra
    Bamies, 406
    Glazed Okra, 423
    Short Rib & Okra Stew, 366
    Za'atar Okra & Lemons, 526
olive oil
    about, 12–13
    Fennel & Olive Oil Gimlet, 704
    Olive Oil-Poached Fluke, 166
olives
    about, 12–13
    Braised Pork with Greek Salad &
        Skordalia, 133
    Caponata, 70
    Charred Chicken with Sweet
        Potatoes & Oranges, 283
    Couscous & Shrimp Salad, 465
    Couscous Stuffed Tomatoes, 456
    Farro Salad with Olive & Whole
        Lemon Vinaigrette, 512
    Focaccia Barese, 569
    Focaccia con le Olive, 578
    Goat Cheese, Olive & Fennel
        Phyllo Triangles, 114
    Greek Salad, 451
    Honey-Glazed Tuna with Romesco
        & Warm Asparagus Salad, 162
    Lamb & Cannellini Soup, 325
    Lavash with Arugula, Eggplant &
        Olives, 535–536
    Marinated Olives, 120
    Olive Salad, 394
    Olive-leaf Infused Gin, 723
    Opening Night, 723
    Orange Chicken with Roasted
        Vegetables & Olives, 227
    Pan-Roasted Monkfish with Olive
        Relish & Braised Fennel, 222

Pissalandrea, 577
Salade Niçoise, 378
Strawberry Fields Salad, 440
Taramasalata, 37
onions
    Beef Stock, 369
    Boulettes with Chicken & Vegetable
        Soup, 362–363
    Braised Pork with Greek Salad &
        Skordalia, 133
    Bulgur with Fried Onions, 278
    Chicken B'stilla, 130
    Chicken Stock, 368
    Chicken with Turmeric Tahini,
        Chickpeas & Onions, 291
    Couscous with Seven Vegetables,
        505
    Creamy Balsamic & Mushroom
        Sauce, 789
    Cucumber, Tomato & Mango
        Relish, 469
    Fish Stock, 372
    Greek Salad, 451
    Green Zhug, 749
    Koshari, 509
    Lamb Shish Kebabs, 204
    Lamb Stew, 364
    Lentil Salad, 460
    Lobster Stock, 373
    Moroccan Cornish Hens with Pine
        Nut Couscous, 146
    Msoki de Pesaj, 350
    Mujadara, 402
    'Nduja Shakshuka, 137
    Onion Mahshi, 502
    Red Zhug, 748
    Ropa Vieja, 239
    Sfincione Palermitano, 562
    Socca, 546
    Stuffed Eggplants, 268
    Sweet Potato Börek, 34
    Turkish Coffee-Rubbed Brisket, 258
    Vegetable Stock, 371
    Vegetable Tanzia, 261
    Vegetarian Musakhan, 542
    Whitefish Poached in Pepper Sauce,
        155
    Za'atar Chicken with Garlicky
        Yogurt, 265
Opening Night, 723
orange blossom water
    Debla, 661
    Msoki de Pesaj, 350
    Sachlav, 689
    Turmeric Chicken with Toum, 260
    White Peach Sangria, 734
oranges/orange juice
    Charred Chicken with Sweet
        Potatoes & Oranges, 283
    Chilled Calamari Salad, 381
    Fig, Orange & Anise Honey Balls,
        610
    Fig & Goat Cheese Salad, 444
    Heart-Beet Salad, 428
    Honey-Glazed Carrots, 484
    Orange Chicken with Roasted
        Vegetables & Olives, 227
    Pistachio & Raisin Sauce, 762

Spiced Honey Cake with Coconut & Cream Cheese Frosting, 664
Turmeric Chicken with Toum, 260
Ottoman Empire, about former, 22
ouzo
The Escape, 724
Oxtail Ragout, Spaghetti with, 248
Oysters, Fire-Roasted, 103

paella
about, 20
Easy Paella, 126
Palmiers
Poached Pears with Candied Hazelnuts, Palmiers & Condensed Caramel, 618
recipe, 641
Pan-Roasted Monkfish with Olive Relish & Braised Fennel, 222
pancetta
Pea Broth, 138
Provençal Fish Soup, 322
Risi e Bisi, 138
Seafood & Leek Soup, 338
panko
Arancini, 60
Couscous-Stuffed Tomatoes, 456
Crispy Lemon & Chickpea Cakes, 188
Eggplant Rings, 71
Eggplant Rollatini, 226
Frutti di Mare with Penne, 217
Taramasalata, 37
Panna Cotta, Goat Cheese & Honey, 629
Panzanella, 382
Paprika Oil
Fish & Crispy Rice Cake with Saffron Crust, 150–151
recipe, 792
Parigina, 570
Parmesan cheese
Arugula Salad with Candied Walnuts, 427
Baked Orzo, 228
Cheesy Poofs, 111
Creamy Pappardelle with Crab, 235
Fire-Roasted Oysters, 103
Lavash with Arugula, Eggplant & Olives, 535–536
Panzanella, 382
Peppery Glazed Asparagus, 419
Phyllo Dough Pizza, 590
Quattro Formaggi, 597
Ratatouille with Poached Eggs, 129
Risi e Bisi, 138
Roasted Beets with Cilantro & Basil Pesto, 436
Roasted Tomato Caprese, 388
Seafood Risotto, 247
Shaved Radish Salad with Walnuts & Mint, 522
Spaghetti with Oxtail Ragout, 248
Parmigiano-Reggiano
about, 19
parsley
Albondigas, 193
Albondigas Soup, 305

Boulettes with Chicken & Vegetable Soup, 362–363
Briam, 269
Broccolini Salad, 410
Chermoula Sauce, 755
Creamy Balsamic & Mushroom Sauce, 789
Creamy Pappardelle with Crab, 235
Crispy Salmon Rice, 450
Eggplant & Chorizo Bourekas, 46
Falafel, 57
Farro Salad with Olive & Whole Lemon Vinaigrette, 512
Fava Beans with Pomegranates, 472
Fire-Roasted Oysters, 103
Frutti di Mare with Penne, 217
Ful Medames, 475
Garlic Butter, 806
Green Zhug, 749
Grilled Serrano Salsa Verde, 798
Harira, 351
Kefta with Chickpea Salad, 271
Kuku Sabzi, 141
Lahmacun Spread, 545
Lamb & Cannellini Soup, 325
Lentil Salad, 460
Marinated Lamb Heart, 171
Moussaka, 218
Msoki de Pesaj, 350
'Nduja Shakshuka, 137
Pistachio & Raisin Sauce, 762
Red Zhug, 748
Roasted & Stuffed Sardines, 75
Roasted Cauliflower, 474
Romano Beans with Mustard Vinaigrette & Walnuts, 491
Shakshuka, 172
Strawberry Fields Salad, 440
Tabbouleh, 461
Tiropitakia, 52
Turkish Eggplant Salad, 407
Vegetable Soup, 328
Whole Wheat Coques, 541
parsnips
Chamin, 321
Roasted Root Vegetables with Lemon Caper Sauce, 488
Saffron, Tomato & Fennel Soup, 355
Tunisian Butternut Squash Soup, 352
Tunisian Vegetable Soup, 354
Vegetable Soup, 328
Passion Fruit Emulsion
Crab Roulade, 179
recipe, 179
passion fruit puree
Tropical Fruit Sorbet, 715
pasta and noodles
Avgolemono, 306
Baked Orzo, 228
Bulgur with Fried Onions, 278
Creamy Pappardelle with Crab, 235
Frutti di Mare with Penne, 217
Harira, 351
Koshari, 509
Lamb Sharba, 309
Spaghetti al Tonno, 255

Spaghetti with Oxtail Ragout, 248
Toasted Pasta with Crab, 176
Pasteli, 617
pastis
Macaroni Cocktail, 694
Pea Broth
recipe, 138
Risi e Bisi, 138
Peach Sangria, White, 734
peanuts
Classic Malabi, 660
pears
Ensalada de Pulpo, 405
Poached Pears with Candied Hazelnuts, Palmiers & Condensed Caramel, 618
peas
Easy Paella, 126
Msoki de Pesaj, 350
Risi e Bisi, 138
Shaved Snap Pea Salad, 411
Split Pea Soup with Smoked Ham, 317
Stuffed Acorn Squash, 196
Vegetarian Split Pea Soup, 349
pecans
Baklava Pie, 656–657
Crunchy Pomegranate Salad, 422
Pecan Muhammara, 64
Pecan Pie Baklava, 627
Sicilian Bar Nuts, 74
Pecorino cheese
Focaccia di Carnevale Salentina, 565
Quattro Formaggi, 597
Rianata, 561
Pecorino Romano cheese
Spanakopita, 81
peppers, bell
Albondigas Soup, 305
Caponata, 70
Chilled Calamari Salad, 381
Couscous with Seven Vegetables, 505
Easy Paella, 126
Fish & Crispy Rice Cake with Saffron Crust, 150–151
Greek Salad, 451
Lahmacun Spread, 545
Lamb Shish Kebabs, 204
Lamb Stew, 364
Lavash with Arugula, Eggplant & Olives, 535–536
Mediterranean Grilled Chicken Salad, 446
Pecan Muhammara, 64
Pides, 537–538
Ratatouille with Poached Eggs, 129
Roasted Pepper Salad, 517
Romesco de Peix, 345
Romesco Sauce, 782
Ropa Vieja, 239
Sabich, 243
Salata Mechouia, 30
Seared Eggplant, 385
Shakshuka, 172
Stuffed Eggplants, 268
Stuffed Mackerel, 134

Vegetable Kebabs, 455
Whitefish Poached in Pepper Sauce, 155
peppers, chile/chili
    Broccoli & Anchovy Soup, 337
    Charred Scallion Sauce, 781
    Crab Roulade, 179
    Falafel, 57
    Fish & Crispy Rice Cake with Saffron Crust, 150–151
    Grapefruit & Fennel Salad, 389
    Green Zhug, 749
    Grilled Serrano Salsa Verde, 798
    Marinated Olives, 120
    Mediterranean-Style Hot Sauce, 800
    Meyer Lemon Marmalade, 801
    'Nduja Shakshuka, 137
    Red Zhug, 748
    Salata Mechouia, 30
    Scallop Ceviche, 95
    Short Rib & Okra Stew, 366
    Swordfish Crudo, 107
    Three-Chile Harissa Sauce, 791
peppers, roasted red
    Whole Wheat Coques, 541
Peppery Glazed Asparagus, 419
Pernod
    Bouillabaisse, 302
    Fig, Orange & Anise Honey Balls, 610
    Goat Cheese, Olive & Fennel Phyllo Triangles, 114
Pescatora, 600
Pesce All'ebraica, 275
phyllo dough
    Baklava, 606
    Baklava Pie, 656–657
    Chicken B'stilla, 130
    Goat Cheese, Olive & Fennel Phyllo Triangles, 114
    Halvah Mille-Feuilles, 649
    Pecan Pie Baklava, 627
    Phyllo Dough Pizza, 590
    Spanakopita, 81
    Sweet Potato Börek, 34
    Tiropitakia, 52
    Tuna Kibbeh Nayeh, 99
Pickled Applesauce
    recipe, 799
    Smoked Pork Belly in Pickled Applesauce, 192
Pickled Cucumber Salad, 470
Pickled Green Beans, 415
Pides, 537–538
Pignoli, 622
pine nuts
    Crispy Lemon & Chickpea Cakes, 188
    Eggplant & Pine Nut Ragout, 776
    Mansaf, 329
    Margherita, 582
    Moroccan Cornish Hens with Pine Nut Couscous, 146
    Pesce All'ebraica, 275
    Pignoli, 622
    Roasted Beets with Cilantro & Basil Pesto, 436

Stuffed Zucchini, 221
Sumac Chicken & Rice, 256
Tomato & Eggplant Soup, 346
Vegetarian Musakhan, 542
Whole Wheat Coques, 541
pineapple
    Ananda Spritz, 733
Pisco
    Faluka, 709
Pissalandrea, 577
pistachios
    Arugula Salad with Pickled Beets & Preserved Lemon Vinaigrette, 487
    Brisket with Pistachio Gremolata, 279
    Classic Malabi, 660
    Cold Roast Salmon with Smashed Green Bean Salad, 293
    Dukkah, 744
    Pistachio & Raisin Sauce, 762
    Pistachio Gremolata, 778
    Roasted Chicken Thighs with Saffron Cauliflower and Pistachio & Raisin Sauce, 231
    Sachlav, 689
    Salep, 738
    Sweet Potato & Tahini Dip with Spiced Honey, 106
Pita Bread
    Baba Ghanoush, 39
    Chicken & Tomato Stew with Caramelized Lemon, 311
    Chicken in Walnut Sauce with Vegetable Kebabs, 145
    Chicken Souvlaki, 270
    Eggplant & Zucchini Soup, 334
    Jerusalem Mixed Grill, 296
    recipe, 532
    Roasted Eggplant Pita, 187
    Sabich, 243
    Salata Mechouia, 30
    Taramasalata, 37
    White Shakshuka, 264
pizza
    Boscaiola, 594
    Caprese, 601
    Carrettiera, 596
    Diavola, 593
    forming round for, 580
    Neapolitan Pizza Dough, 581
    Pescatora, 600
    Phyllo Dough Pizza, 590
    Pizza Marinara, 586
    Quattro Formaggi, 597
    Romana, 587
Pizza Sauce
    Boscaiola, 594
    Caprese, 601
    Diavola, 593
    Margherita, 582
    Pescatora, 600
    Pizza Marinara, 586
    recipe, 582
    Romana, 587
Pizz'onta, 573
plums
    Roasted Plums with Tahini Dressing, 518

Strawberry Rosé Sangria, 735
Poached Pears with Candied Hazelnuts, Palmiers & Condensed Caramel, 618
Pomegranate Glaze
    Honey & Pomegranate Cake, 653
    recipe, 653
pomegranate juice
    Brisket with Pistachio Gremolata, 279
    Honey & Pomegranate Cake, 653
    Lamb Shanks with Pomegranate Sauce, 140
    Olive Salad, 394
    Pomegranate & Honey-Glazed Chicken, 158
    Pomegranate Prosecco Punch, 688
    Pomegranate Vinaigrette, 754
    Pomegranate-Glazed Figs & Cheese, 116
pomegranate molasses
    Crispy Salmon Rice, 450
    Fried Eggplant with Mint Vinaigrette, 113
    Onion Mahshi, 502
    Pecan Muhammara, 64
    Pomegranate & Honey-Glazed Chicken, 158
    Scallop Ceviche, 95
    Strawberry Fields Salad, 440
pomegranate seeds
    Baba Ghanoush, 39
    Crunchy Pomegranate Salad, 422
    Fava Beans with Pomegranates, 472
    Honey & Pomegranate Cake, 653
    Olive Salad, 394
Pomegranate Vinaigrette
    Heart-Beet Salad, 428
    recipe, 754
Poppy Seed Cake, Lemon, 609
pork
    Albondigas Soup, 305
    Braised Pork with Greek Salad & Skordalia, 133
    Smoked Pork Belly in Pickled Applesauce, 192
potatoes
    Bamies, 406
    Boulettes with Chicken & Vegetable Soup, 362–363
    Bourekas, 47
    Braised Pork with Greek Salad & Skordalia, 133
    Briam, 269
    Chamin, 321
    Chicken Stew with Potatoes & Radishes, 358
    Cholent, 357
    Cojada Potato Casserole, 292
    Dafina, 365
    Focaccia Barese, 569
    Grilled Romaine & Sweet Potato, 441
    Keftes de Espinaca, 43
    Lamb Belly Hash, 159
    Roasted Root Vegetables with Lemon Caper Sauce, 488
    Rosti Egg in a Hole, 210

Salade Niçoise, 378
Smoked Potato Puree, 396
Stuffed Mackerel, 134
Tunisian Vegetable Soup, 354
Turkish Coffee-Rubbed Brisket, 258
produce, about, 14–16
Project, The, 711
prosciutto/ham
   Arugula Salad with Candied
      Walnuts, 427
   Parigina, 570
   Risi e Bisi, 138
   Split Pea Soup with Smoked Ham,
      317
prosecco
   Big Trouble Spritz, 712
   Lipstick & Rouge, 708
   Pomegranate Prosecco Punch, 688
   Sgroppino Plagiato, 715
Provençal Fish Soup, 322
provolone cheese
   Quattro Formaggi, 597
prunes/prune juice
   Short Ribs with Braised Cauliflower
      & Stuffed Tomatoes, 213
   Vegetable Tanzia, 261
Puddica Salentina, 566
puff pastry
   Bourekas, 47
   Duck Breast Wellington, 182
   Eggplant & Chorizo Bourekas, 46
   Handrajo, 51
   Palmiers, 641
   Parigina, 570
pumpkin
   Honey-Roasted Vegetable Salad,
      516
pumpkin seeds
   Granola, 663

Quaglia Chinotto liqueur
   Chinotto Negroni, 727
Quattro Formaggi, 597
quinoa
   Stuffed Eggplants, 268

radicchio
   Roasted Radicchio, 384
   Roasted Squash & Feta Salad, 519
radishes
   Chicken Stew with Potatoes &
      Radishes, 358
   Cold Roast Salmon with Smashed
      Green Bean Salad, 293
   Ensalada de Pulpo, 405
   Shaved Radish Salad with Walnuts
      & Mint, 522
raisins
   Autumn Kale Salad, 498
   Eggplant & Pine Nut Ragout, 776
   Goat Cheese, Olive & Fennel
      Phyllo Triangles, 114
   Granola, 663
   Pesce All'ebraica, 275
   Pistachio & Raisin Sauce, 762
   Roasted Apricot Chicken with Mint
      & Sage Butternut Squash, 238
   Roasted Chicken Thighs with

Saffron Cauliflower and Pistachio
   & Raisin Sauce, 231
Stuffed Grape Leaves, 55
Tomato & Eggplant Soup, 346
Raphael, 692
Ras el Hanout
   Chermoula Sauce, 755
   Chicken with Mehshi Sfeeha, 282
   Cojada Potato Casserole, 292
   Couscous with Seven Vegetables,
      505
   Eggplant & Pine Nut Ragout, 776
   Fried Eggplant with Garlic & Ras el
      Hanout, 112
   Fried Eggplant with Mint
      Vinaigrette, 113
   Ful Medames, 475
   Leg of Lamb with Garlic &
      Rosemary, 147
   Moroccan Carrots, 433
   recipe, 747
   Short Ribs with Braised Cauliflower
      & Stuffed Tomatoes, 213
   Stuffed Zucchini, 221
   Tomato & Eggplant Soup, 346
raspberry jam
   Sufganiyot, 626
Ratatouille with Poached Eggs, 129
Red Cabbage, Date & Beet Salad, 445
red mullet
   Fried Fish with Agristada Sauce,
      297
Red Pepper Feta & Ricotta
   Lavash Crackers with Red Pepper
      Feta & Ricotta and Spiced
      Honey, 44
   recipe, 44
Red Wine–Braised Octopus with
   Bulgur-Stuffed Eggplants, 200
Red Zhug
   Eggplant Rings, 71
   recipe, 748
   Sabich, 243
Rianata, 561
rice
   Arancini, 60
   Avikas, 359
   Chamin, 321
   Chicken with Mehshi Sfeeha, 282
   Cornbread & Crab-Stuffed
      Branzino, 240
   Crispy Salmon Rice, 450
   Easy Paella, 126
   Fish & Crispy Rice Cake with
      Saffron Crust, 150–151
   Koshari, 509
   Lemon Rice Pudding with Roasted
      Vanilla Cherries & Lemon
      Crème, 631
   Mahshi Laban, 154
   Mansaf, 329
   Mujadara, 402
   Onion Mahshi, 502
   Risi e Bisi, 138
   Roasted Beet & Leek Risotto, 432
   Ropa Vieja, 239
   Seafood Risotto, 247
   Short Rib & Okra Stew, 366

Stuffed Acorn Squash, 196
Stuffed Grape Leaves, 55
Sumac Chicken & Rice, 256
ricotta cheese
   about, 19
   Bourekas, 47
   Eggplant Rollatini, 226
   Lavash Crackers with Red Pepper
      Feta & Ricotta and Spiced
      Honey, 44
   Pomegranate-Glazed Figs & Cheese,
      116
   Zeppole with Lemon Curd, 613
Risi e Bisi, 138
Roast Chicken with Fennel & Carrots,
   290
Roast Chicken with Harissa & Duck
   Fat, 242
Roasted & Stuffed Sardines, 75
Roasted Apricot Chicken with Mint
   & Sage Butternut Squash, 238
Roasted Beet & Leek Risotto, 432
Roasted Beets with Cilantro & Basil
   Pesto, 436
Roasted Brussels Sprouts with Warm
   Honey Glaze, 483
Roasted Cauliflower, 474
Roasted Chicken Thighs with Saffron
   Cauliflower and Pistachio &
   Raisin Sauce, 231
Roasted Eggplant Pita, 187
Roasted Grapes & Sausage, 167
Roasted Pepper Salad, 517
Roasted Plums with Tahini Dressing,
   518
Roasted Radicchio, 384
Roasted Root Vegetables with Lemon
   Caper Sauce
   recipe, 488
   Za'atar-Rubbed Spatchcock
      Chicken with Honey-Glazed
      Carrots & Roasted Root
      Vegetables, 253
Roasted Squash & Feta Salad, 519
Roasted Tomato Caprese, 388
Roasted Vanilla Cherries & Lemon
   Crème, Lemon Rice Pudding
   with, 631
Romaine & Sweet Potato, Grilled, 441
Romana, 587
Romano Beans with Mustard
   Vinaigrette & Walnuts, 491
Romesco Sauce, 782
   Honey-Glazed Tuna with Romesco
      & Warm Asparagus Salad, 162
Romesco de Peix, 345
Ropa Vieja, 239
Rosé Sangria, Strawberry, 735
rose water
   Classic Malabi, 660
   Debla, 661
   Salep, 738
   Strawberry Rosé Sangria, 735
rosemary
   Leg of Lamb with Garlic &
      Rosemary, 147
   Slow-Cooked Cherry Tomatoes
      with Coriander & Rosemary, 523

Rosti Egg in a Hole, 210
rum
    The Project, 711
    Strawberry Rosé Sangria, 735
    White Peach Sangria, 734
Rutabaga & Fig Soup, 342

Sabich, 243
Sachlav, 689
saffron
    Albondigas Soup, 305
    Bouillabaisse, 302
    Chermoula Sauce, 755
    Chickpea Salad, 397
    Fish & Crispy Rice Cake with
        Saffron Crust, 150–151
    Marinated Cauliflower &
        Chickpeas, 480
    Provençal Fish Soup, 322
    Roasted Chicken Thighs with
        Saffron Cauliflower and Pistachio
        & Raisin Sauce, 231
    Romesco de Peix, 345
    Saffron, Tomato & Fennel Soup,
        355
    Saffron & Mussel Soup, 333
    Saffron & Tomato Coulis, 805
    Saffron Water, 151
    Vegetarian Musakhan, 542
sage
    Mint & Sage Butternut Squash, 395
    Roasted Apricot Chicken with Mint
        & Sage Butternut Squash, 238
salads
    Arugula Salad with Candied
        Walnuts, 427
    Arugula Salad with Pickled Beets
        & Preserved Lemon Vinaigrette,
        487
    Autumn Kale Salad, 498
    Broccolini Salad, 410
    Celery Slaw with Seeds & Dates,
        504
    Chickpea Salad, 397
    Couscous & Shrimp Salad, 465
    Crunchy Pomegranate Salad, 422
    Cucumber, Mint & Sumac Salad,
        471
    Ensalada de Pulpo, 405
    Farro Salad with Olive & Whole
        Lemon Vinaigrette, 512
    Fig & Goat Cheese Salad, 444
    Grapefruit & Fennel Salad, 389
    Greek Salad, 451
    Heart-Beet Salad, 428
    Honey-Roasted Vegetable Salad,
        516
    Lentil Salad, 460
    Marinated Eggplant Salad, 398
    Mediterranean Grilled Chicken
        Salad, 446
    Olive Salad, 394
    Pickled Cucumber Salad, 470
    Red Cabbage, Date & Beet Salad,
        445
    Roasted Pepper Salad, 517
    Roasted Squash & Feta Salad, 519
    Salade Niçoise, 378

Shaved Radish Salad with Walnuts
    & Mint, 522
Shaved Snap Pea Salad, 411
Spinach, Fennel & Apple Salad with
    Smoked Trout, 393
Strawberry Fields Salad, 440
Turkish Eggplant Salad, 407
Warm Couscous Salad, 503
Salata Mechouia, 30
Salep, 738
salmon
    Cedar-Plank Salmon, 286
    Chilled Calamari Salad, 381
    Cold Roast Salmon with Smashed
        Green Bean Salad, 293
    Crispy Salmon Rice, 450
    Panzanella, 382
Salted Honey & Apple Upside-Down
    Cake, 642
Sardines, Roasted & Stuffed, 75
sauces and condiments
    Aioli, 214
    Agristada Sauce, 793
    Balsamic Glaze, 759
    Champagne Vinaigrette, 804
    Charred Scallion Sauce, 781
    Chermoula Sauce, 755
    Creamy Balsamic & Mushroom
        Sauce, 789
    Dijon Dressing, 788
    Eggplant & Pine Nut Ragout, 776
    Fig Vinaigrette, 752
    Garlic Butter, 806
    Green Zhug, 749
    Grilled Serrano Salsa Verde, 798
    Lemony Yogurt Sauce, 787
    Mediterranean-Style Hot Sauce,
        800
    Meyer Lemon Marmalade, 801
    Paprika Oil, 792
    Pickled Applesauce, 799
    Pistachio Gremolata, 778
    Pomegranate Vinaigrette, 754
    Red Zhug, 748
    Romesco Sauce, 782
    Saffron & Tomato Coulis, 805
    Smoked Egg Aioli, 770
    Spiced Honey, 761
    Spiced Yogurt Sauce, 803
    Spicy Honey Mayonnaise, 779
    Tahini & Yogurt Sauce, 796
    Tahini Mayonnaise, 786
    Tahini Sauce, 767
    Three-Chile Harissa Sauce, 791
    Tomato Sauce, 775
    Toum, 758
    Whipped Feta with Za'atar, 771
sausage/chorizo
    Boscaiola, 594
    Carrettiera, 596
    Easy Paella, 126
    Eggplant & Chorizo Bourekas, 46
    Focaccia di Carnevale Salentina,
        565
    Roasted Grapes & Sausage, 167
scallions
    Braised Cauliflower, 466
    Charred Scallion Sauce, 781

Crispy Salmon Rice, 450
Falafel, 57
Kuku Sabzi, 141
Mujadara, 402
Red Cabbage, Date & Beet Salad,
    445
Roasted Brussels Sprouts with
    Warm Honey Glaze, 483
Scallop Ceviche, 95
Spanakopita, 81
Swordfish Crudo, 107
Tabbouleh, 461
Turmeric & Ginger Shrimp
    Cocktail, 98
Zucchini Fritters, 288
scallops
    Frutti di Mare with Penne, 217
    Seafood Risotto, 247
Sea Bass, Chermoula, 289
Seafood Risotto, 247. see also fish and
    seafood
Seared Eggplant, 385
seasonings
    Dukkah, 744
    Za'atar, 766
sesame oil
    Modern Hummus, 31
sesame seeds
    Crab Roulade, 179
    Pasteli, 617
    Ras el Hanout, 747
Sfenj Donuts, 665
Sfincione Palermitano, 562
Sfratti, 672–673
Sgroppino Plagiato, 715
Shakshuka, 172
shallots
    Albondigas Soup, 305
    Braised Leeks, 492
    Celery Slaw with Seeds & Dates,
        504
    Crab Roulade, 179
    Dijon Dressing, 788
    Dried Fava Bean Soup with Grilled
        Halloumi Cheese, 314
    Dukkah, 744
    Farro Salad with Olive & Whole
        Lemon Vinaigrette, 512
    Fig Vinaigrette, 752
    Lamb Stew, 364
    Marinated Artichokes, 86
    Marinated Eggplant Salad, 398
    Mussels Escabeche, 94
    Passion Fruit Emulsion, 179
    Pistachio & Raisin Sauce, 762
    Risi e Bisi, 138
    Roasted Root Vegetables with
        Lemon Caper Sauce, 488
    Scallop Ceviche, 95
    Seafood Risotto, 247
    Spinach, Fennel & Apple Salad with
        Smoked Trout, 393
    Stuffed Zucchini, 221
    Tunisian Butternut Squash Soup, 352
    Turmeric & Ginger Shrimp
        Cocktail, 98
Shaved Radish Salad with Walnuts &
    Mint, 522

Shaved Snap Pea Salad, 411
Shawarma-Spiced Leg of Lamb, 250
Seafood & Leek Soup, 338
Seared Shrimp Skewers with Aioli &
    Cauliflower Cakes, 214
sherry
    Romesco de Peix, 345
short ribs
    Chickpea Poutine, 83
    Short Rib & Okra Stew, 366
    Short Ribs with Braised Cauliflower
        & Stuffed Tomatoes, 213
    Sweet & Sour Short Ribs, 209
shrimp
    Bouillabaisse, 302
    Couscous & Shrimp Salad, 465
    Easy Paella, 126
    Frutti di Mare with Penne, 217
    Pescatora, 600
    Seafood & Leek Soup, 338
    Seafood Risotto, 247
    Seared Shrimp Skewers with Aioli
        & Cauliflower Cakes, 214
    Turmeric & Ginger Shrimp
        Cocktail, 98
Sicilian Bar Nuts, 74
sides
    Bamies, 406
    Beets with Walnut Dukkah, 437
    Braised Cauliflower, 466
    Braised Leeks, 492
    Celery Slaw with Seeds & Dates,
        504
    Charred Sweet Potatoes with Toum,
        508
    Concia, 418
    Couscous-Stuffed Tomatoes, 456
    Couscous with Seven Vegetables,
        505
    Crispy Salmon Rice, 450
    Cucumber, Tomato & Mango
        Relish, 469
    Fava Beans with Pomegranates, 472
    Fried Brussels Sprouts with Tahini
        & Feta, 399
    Ful Medames, 475
    Glazed Okra, 423
    Green Beans with Za'atar & Lemon,
        513
    Grilled Romaine & Sweet Potato,
        441
    Hand-Rolled Couscous, 499
    Honey-Glazed Carrots, 484
    Kemia de Remolachas, 478
    Kemia de Zanahorias, 479
    Koshari, 509
    Marinated Cauliflower &
        Chickpeas, 480
    Mint & Sage Butternut Squash, 395
    Minty Pickled Cucumbers, 414
    Moroccan Carrots, 433
    Mujadara, 402
    Onion Mahshi, 502
    Peppery Glazed Asparagus, 419
    Pickled Green Beans, 415
    Roasted Beet & Leek Risotto, 432
    Roasted Beets with Cilantro & Basil
        Pesto, 436

Roasted Brussels Sprouts with
    Warm Honey Glaze, 483
Roasted Cauliflower, 474
Roasted Plums with Tahini
    Dressing, 518
Roasted Radicchio, 384
Roasted Root Vegetables with
    Lemon Caper Sauce, 488
Roasted Tomato Caprese, 388
Romano Beans with Mustard
    Vinaigrette & Walnuts, 491
Seared Eggplant, 385
Slow-Cooked Cherry Tomatoes
    with Coriander & Rosemary, 5
    23
Smoked Potato Puree, 396
Sumac & Apple Cauliflower, 429
Taro Ulass, 404
Vegetable Kebabs, 455
Za'atar Okra & Lemons, 526
Simple Syrup
    Ananda Spritz, 733
    Arak Sour, 739
    Drink of Laughter & Forgetting,
        697
    Fennel Syrup, 704
    Lady in Red, 716
    recipe, 739
    Strawberry Rosé Sangria, 735
    Strawberry Vinegar, 716
    White Peach Sangria, 734
Skordalia, Braised Pork with Greek
    Salad &, 133
Slow-Cooked Cherry Tomatoes with
    Coriander & Rosemary, 523
Slow-Roasted Lamb Shoulder with
    Brussels Sprouts & Crispy Kale,
    254
Smoked Egg Aioli
    recipe, 770
    Stuffed Avocados, 91
    Tuna Kibbeh Nayeh, 99
Smoked Pork Belly in Pickled
    Applesauce, 192
Smoked Potato Puree
    Cheesy Poofs, 111
    recipe, 396
Socca, 546
soups and stews
    Albondigas Soup, 305
    Artichoke à la Barigoule, 341
    Avgolemono, 306
    Avikas, 359
    Beef Stock, 369
    Bone Marrow & Matzo Ball Soup,
        324
    Bouillabaisse, 302
    Boulettes with Chicken & Vegetable
        Soup, 362–363
    Broccoli & Anchovy Soup, 337
    Chamin, 321
    Chicken & Tomato Stew with
        Caramelized Lemon, 311
    Chicken Stew with Potatoes &
        Radishes, 358
    Chicken Stock, 368
    Chilled White Tomato Soup with
        Braised Grapes, 318

Cholent, 357
Dafina, 365
Dried Fava Bean Soup with Grilled
    Halloumi Cheese, 314
Eggplant & Zucchini Soup, 334
Fish Stock, 372
Harira, 351
Lamb & Cannellini Soup, 325
Lamb Sharba, 309
Lamb Stew, 364
Lobster Stock, 373
Mansaf, 329
Moroccan Lentil Stew, 310
Msoki de Pesaj, 350
Provençal Fish Soup, 322
Romesco de Peix, 345
Rutabaga & Fig Soup, 342
Saffron, Tomato & Fennel Soup,
    355
Saffron & Mussel Soup, 333
Seafood & Leek Soup, 338
Short Rib & Okra Stew, 366
Split Pea Soup with Smoked Ham,
    317
Tomato & Eggplant Soup, 346
Tunisian Butternut Squash Soup,
    352
Tunisian Vegetable Soup, 354
Vegetable Soup, 328
Vegetable Stock, 371
Vegetarian Split Pea Soup, 349
sour cream
    Chicken Stew with Potatoes &
        Radishes, 358
    Salted Honey & Apple Upside-
        Down Cake, 642
Sous Vide Eggs
    recipe, 187
    Roasted Eggplant Pita, 187
southern Europe, about, 20
souvlaki
    about, 22
Spaghetti al Tonno, 255
Spaghetti with Oxtail Ragout, 248
Spanakopita
    about, 22
    recipe, 81
Spelt & Apple Cake, Sumac, 669
spice trade, 18
Spiced Honey
    Lavash Crackers with Red Pepper
        Feta & Ricotta and Spiced
        Honey, 44
    recipe, 761
Spiced Honey Cake with Coconut &
    Cream Cheese Frosting, 664
Spiced Honey Yogurt
    recipe, 210
    Rosti Egg in a Hole, 210
Spiced Tea Cordial
    recipe, 719
    The Top of Olympus, 719
Spiced Yogurt Sauce, 803
spices, about, 16, 18
Spicy Chickpeas
    recipe, 342
    Rutabaga & Fig Soup, 342
Spicy Chocolate Halvah, 632

Spicy Honey Mayonnaise
    Beet Chips with Spicy Honey
        Mayonnaise, 38
    recipe, 779
Spiked Lemonade, 680
spinach
    Couscous-Stuffed Tomatoes, 456
    Honey-Roasted Vegetable Salad,
        516
    Keftes de Espinaca, 43
    Lamb & Cannellini Soup, 325
    Lentil Salad, 460
    Msoki de Pesaj, 350
    Roasted Tomato Caprese, 388
    Spanakopita, 81
    Spinach, Fennel & Apple Salad with
        Smoked Trout, 393
Split Pea Soup with Smoked Ham,
    317
squash, summer
    Almodrote, 277
    Baked Orzo, 228
    Boulettes with Chicken & Vegetable
        Soup, 362–363
    Briam, 269
    Chamin, 321
    Concia, 418
    Couscous with Seven Vegetables,
        505
    Eggplant & Zucchini Soup, 334
    Lamb Shish Kebabs, 204
    Mahshi Laban, 154
    Mediterranean Grilled Chicken
        Salad, 446
    Msoki de Pesaj, 350
    Ratatouille with Poached Eggs, 129
    Stuffed Zucchini, 221
    Vegetable Kebabs, 455
    Zucchini Fritters, 288
squash, winter
    Autumn Kale Salad, 498
    Boulettes with Chicken & Vegetable
        Soup, 362–363
    Couscous with Seven Vegetables,
        505
    Roasted Apricot Chicken with Mint
        & Sage Butternut Squash,
        238
    Roasted Squash & Feta Salad, 519
    Stuffed Acorn Squash, 196
    Stuffed Avocados, 91
    Tunisian Butternut Squash Soup,
        352
    Tunisian Vegetable Soup, 354
    Vegetable Tanzia, 261
squid/calamari
    Chilled Calamari Salad, 381
    Frutti di Mare with Penne, 217
    Garlic & Lime Calamari, 272
    Pescatora, 600
    Seafood & Leek Soup, 338
    Seafood Risotto, 247
St. George Bruto Americano
    Italian Greyhound, 730
stifado
    about, 22
stracchino cheese
    Focaccia di Recco, 576

strawberries
    Black Lime & Strawberry Crostata,
        633
    Lady in Red, 716
    Strawberry Fields Salad, 440
    Strawberry Rosé Sangria, 735
strawberry jam/puree
    Raphael, 692
    Sufganiyot, 626
Strawberry Vinegar
    Lady in Red, 716
    recipe, 716
Stuffed Acorn Squash, 196
Stuffed Avocados, 91
Stuffed Eggplants, 268
Stuffed Grape Leaves, 55
Stuffed Mackerel, 134
Stuffed Zucchini, 221
Sufganiyot, 626
sumac
    Chermoula Sauce, 755
    Cucumber, Mint & Sumac Salad,
        471
    Sumac, Spelt & Apple Cake, 669
    Sumac & Apple Cauliflower, 429
    Sumac & Lime Mahimahi, 183
    Sumac Chicken & Rice, 256
    Za'atar, 766
sun-dried tomatoes
    Couscous & Shrimp Salad, 465
    Forget Domani, 726
    Sun-Dried Tomato & Olive Oil
        Grappa, 726
sunflower seeds
    Caramelized Honey Tart, 648
    Granola, 663
suze
    Forget Domani, 726
Sweet & Sour Short Ribs, 209
Sweet Potato Börek, 34
sweet potatoes
    Charred Chicken with Sweet
        Potatoes & Oranges, 283
    Grilled Romaine & Sweet Potato,
        441
    Smoked Potato Puree, 396
    Sweet Potato & Tahini Dip with
        Spiced Honey, 106
    Sweet Potato & Tahini Dip with
        Za'atar, 121
    Vegetable Tanzia, 261
Swordfish Crudo, 107

Tabbouleh
    about, 24
    recipe, 461
tagines
    about, 24
    Chicken Tagine with Warm
        Couscous Salad, 161
    Monkfish Tagine, 232
Tahini Sauce
    Falafel, 57
    Fried Brussels Sprouts with Tahini
        & Feta, 399
    recipe, 767
    Red Cabbage, Date & Beet Salad, 445
    Roasted & Stuffed Sardines, 75

Roasted Plums with Tahini
    Dressing, 518
Sabich, 243
tahini/tahini paste
    Baba Ghanoush, 39
    Black & White Halvah, 644–645
    Chicken with Turmeric Tahini,
        Chickpeas & Onions, 291
    Classic Halvah, 650
    Halvah Mille-Feuilles, 649
    Lamb Meatballs over Marinated
        Eggplant Salad, 199
    Modern Hummus, 31
    Moroccan Carrots, 433
    Spicy Chocolate Halvah, 632
    Sumac & Apple Cauliflower, 429
    Sweet Potato & Tahini Dip with
        Spiced Honey, 106
    Sweet Potato & Tahini Dip with
        Za'atar, 121
    Tahini & Yogurt Sauce, 796
    Tahini Mayonnaise, 786
    Tahini Sauce, 767
taleggio cheese
    Focaccia di Recco, 576
tamarind concentrate
    Eggplant Dolma, 259
Taramasalata, 37
Taro Ulass, 404
Tea Cordial, Spiced, 719
tequila
    Israeli Iced Tea, 683
    Triple My Worth, 696
Three-Chile Harissa Sauce
    Boulettes with Chicken & Vegetable
        Soup, 362–363
    Chilled Calamari Salad, 381
    Kemia de Zanahorias, 479
    Msoki de Pesaj, 350
    recipe, 791
    Roast Chicken with Harissa &
        Duck Fat, 242
    Tunisian Butternut Squash Soup,
        352
Tiropitakia, 52
Toasted Pasta with Crab, 176
Tomato Sauce
    Albondigas, 193
    Eggplant Dolma, 259
    Eggplant Rollatini, 226
    Koshari, 509
    Moussaka, 218
    recipe, 775
    White Shakshuka, 264
tomatoes
    Baked Orzo, 228
    Bamies, 406
    Bouillabaisse, 302
    Braised Pork with Greek Salad &
        Skordalia, 133
    Briam, 269
    Caponata, 70
    Caprese, 601
    Chamin, 321
    Chicken & Tomato Stew with
        Caramelized Lemon, 311
    Chicken Stew with Potatoes &
        Radishes, 358

Chilled White Tomato Soup with Braised Grapes, 318
Couscous & Shrimp Salad, 465
Couscous-Stuffed Tomatoes, 456
Couscous with Seven Vegetables, 505
Cucumber, Tomato & Mango Relish, 469
Dogfish Chraime, 251
Easy Paella, 126
Focaccia Barese, 569
Focaccia di Carnevale Salentina, 565
Focaccia Messinese, 572
Fried Feta, 90
Frutti di Mare with Penne, 217
Ful Medames, 475
Greek Salad, 451
Handrajo, 51
Harira, 351
Lahmacun Spread, 545
Lamb Sharba, 309
Lentil Salad, 460
Lobster Stock, 373
Marinated Eggplant Salad, 398
Moroccan Cornish Hens with Pine Nut Couscous, 146
Mustazzeddu, 558
'Nduja Shakshuka, 137
Orange Chicken with Roasted Vegetables & Olives, 227
Panzanella, 382
Parigina, 570
Phyllo Dough Pizza, 590
Pides, 537–538
Pissalandrea, 577
Puddica Salentina, 566
Rianata, 561
Roasted Apricot Chicken with Mint & Sage Butternut Squash, 238
Roasted Eggplant Pita, 187
Roasted Tomato Caprese, 388
Romesco de Peix, 345
Sabich, 243
Saffron, Tomato & Fennel Soup, 355
Saffron & Mussel Soup, 333
Saffron & Tomato Coulis, 805
Salade Niçoise, 378
Salata Mechouia, 30
Sfincione Palermitano, 562
Shakshuka, 172
Shawarma-Spiced Leg of Lamb, 250
Short Rib & Okra Stew, 366
Short Ribs with Braised Cauliflower & Stuffed Tomatoes, 213
Slow-Cooked Cherry Tomatoes with Coriander & Rosemary, 523
Spaghetti al Tonno, 255
Spaghetti with Oxtail Ragout, 248
Tabbouleh, 461
Toasted Pasta with Crab, 176
Tomato & Eggplant Soup, 346
Tomato Sauce, 775
Tomatoes Reinados, 257
Turkish Eggplant Salad, 407
Top of Olympus, The, 719

Topo Chico
    The Bitter Pomelo, 700
Top-Shelf Negroni, 701
Toum
    Charred Sweet Potatoes with Toum, 508
    recipe, 758
    Turmeric Chicken with Toum, 260
Triple My Worth, 696
Tropical Fruit Sorbet
    recipe, 715
    Sgroppino Plagiato, 715
Trout, Spinach, Fennel & Apple Salad with Smoked, 393
truffle oil
    Lamb Belly Hash, 159
tuna
    Confit Tuna, 378
    Honey-Glazed Tuna with Romesco & Warm Asparagus Salad, 162
    Salade Niçoise, 378
    Spaghetti al Tonno, 255
Tuna Kibbeh Nayeh, 99
Tunisian Butternut Squash Soup, 352
Tunisian Vegetable Soup, 354
Turkish Coffee-Rubbed Brisket, 258
Turkish Eggplant Salad, 407
Turmeric & Ginger Shrimp Cocktail, 98
Turmeric Chicken with Toum, 260
turnips
    Boulettes with Chicken & Vegetable Soup, 362–363
    Couscous with Seven Vegetables, 505
    Msoki de Pesaj, 350
    Vegetable Tanzia, 261
24-Hour Focaccia Dough
    Focaccia con le Olive, 578
    Parigina, 570
    Pissalandrea, 577
    recipe, 553
Tzatziki
    about, 22
    Chicken Souvlaki, 270
    Eggplant & Zucchini Soup, 334
    recipe, 56
    Socca, 546

Valentine's Grapefruit, 695
Vegetable Kebabs
    Chicken in Walnut Sauce with Vegetable Kebabs, 145
    recipe, 455
Vegetable Soup, 328
Vegetable Stock
    Bamies, 406
    Braised Cauliflower, 466
    Braised Leeks, 492
    Broccoli & Anchovy Soup, 337
    Couscous with Seven Vegetables, 505
    Creamy Balsamic & Mushroom Sauce, 789
    Dried Fava Bean Soup with Grilled Halloumi Cheese, 314
    Eggplant & Zucchini Soup, 334
    Modern Hummus, 31

Moroccan Lentil Stew, 310
Pomegranate & Honey-Glazed Chicken, 158
    recipe, 371
Roasted Beet & Leek Risotto, 432
Rutabaga & Fig Soup, 342
Taro Ulass, 404
Tunisian Vegetable Soup, 354
Vegetable Soup, 328
Vegetarian Split Pea Soup, 349
Vegetable Tanzia, 261
Vegetarian Musakhan, 542
Vegetarian Split Pea Soup, 349
vermouth, dry
    Artichoke à la Barigoule, 341
    Braised Grapes, 318
    The Escape, 724
    Opening Night, 723
    Provençal Fish Soup, 322
vermouth, sweet
    Chinotto Negroni, 727
    Macaroni Cocktail, 694
    Top-Shelf Negroni, 701
    Valentine's Grapefruit, 695
    Vitamin Sea, 720
vodka
    Israeli Iced Tea, 683
    Italian Greyhound, 730
    Spiked Lemonade, 680

walnuts
    Apple & Walnut Bundt Cake, 637–638
    Arugula Salad with Candied Walnuts, 427
    Baklava, 606
    Beets with Walnut Dukkah, 437
    Brisket with Pistachio Gremolata, 279
    Candied Walnuts, 427
    Chicken in Walnut Sauce with Vegetable Kebabs, 145
    Fig, Orange & Anise Honey Balls, 610
    Granola, 663
    Olive Salad, 394
    Romano Beans with Mustard Vinaigrette & Walnuts, 491
    Sfratti, 672–673
    Shaved Radish Salad with Walnuts & Mint, 522
    Shaved Snap Pea Salad, 411
    Sicilian Bar Nuts, 74
    Vegetable Tanzia, 261
Warm Couscous Salad
    Chicken Tagine with Warm Couscous Salad, 161
    recipe, 503
wheat, about, 10–11. see also bulgur wheat
Whipped Cream, Cinnamon, 684
Whipped Feta with Za'atar
    Duck Breast Wellington, 182
    recipe, 771
White Peach Sangria, 734
White Shakshuka, 264
whitefish
    Fish Stock, 372

Pesce All'ebraica, 275
Whitefish Poached in Pepper Sauce, 155
Whole Branzino, 205
Whole Wheat Coques, 541
wine
    about, 13–14
wine, red
Fig & Goat Cheese Salad, 444
Lamb Shanks with Pomegranate Sauce, 140
Lamb Stew, 364
Leg of Lamb with Garlic & Rosemary, 147
Red Wine–Braised Octopus with Bulgur-Stuffed Eggplants, 200
Short Ribs with Braised Cauliflower & Stuffed Tomatoes, 213
Spaghetti with Oxtail Ragout, 248
wine, sparkling
    Ananda Spritz, 733
    Lady in Red, 716
    Strawberry Rosé Sangria, 735
    White Peach Sangria, 734
wine, white
    Albondigas Soup, 305
    Arancini, 60
    Bamies, 406
    Braised Cauliflower, 466
    Braised Leeks, 492
    Braised Pork with Greek Salad & Skordalia, 133
    Broccoli & Anchovy Soup, 337
    Chicken in Walnut Sauce with Vegetable Kebabs, 145
    Chicken Souvlaki, 270
    Chicken Tagine with Warm Couscous Salad, 161
    Easy Paella, 126
    Frutti di Mare with Penne, 217
    Garlic & Lime Calamari, 272
    Goat Cheese, Olive & Fennel Phyllo Triangles, 114
    Lobster Stock, 373
    Moussaka, 218
    Mussels Escabeche, 94
    Poached Pears with Candied Hazelnuts, Palmiers & Condensed Caramel, 618

Provençal Fish Soup, 322
Risi e Bisi, 138
Roasted Beet & Leek Risotto, 432
Ropa Vieja, 239
Saffron, Tomato & Fennel Soup, 355
Saffron & Mussel Soup, 333
Saffron & Tomato Coulis, 805
Seafood & Leek Soup, 338
Seafood Risotto, 247
Sfratti, 672–673
Sweet Potato Börek, 34
Toasted Pasta with Crab, 176
White Peach Sangria, 734

yogurt
    Braised Pork with Greek Salad & Skordalia, 133
    Cornbread Stuffing, 240
    Honey-Roasted Vegetable Salad, 516
    Labneh, 67
    Lamb Meatballs over Marinated Eggplant Salad, 199
    Lemon Glaze, 609
    Lemon Poppy Seed Cake, 609
    Lemony Yogurt Sauce, 787
    Mansaf, 329
    Rosti Egg in a Hole, 210
    Spanakopita, 81
    Spiced Yogurt Sauce, 803
    Sweet Potato Börek, 34
    Tahini & Yogurt Sauce, 796
    Turmeric Chicken with Toum, 260
    Tzatziki, 56
    Yogurt Mousse with Blueberry Compote & Granola, 621
    Za'atar Chicken with Garlicky Yogurt, 265
yogurt powder
    The Top of Olympus, 719

Za'atar
    Chermoula Sauce, 755
    Crushed Avocado, 102
    Cucumber, Tomato & Mango Relish, 469
    Duck Breast Wellington, 182
    Fava Beans with Pomegranates, 472

Green Beans with Za'atar & Lemon, 513
Labneh, 67
Lavash Crackers with Red Pepper Feta & Ricotta and Spiced Honey, 44
Modern Hummus, 31
Pomegranate Vinaigrette, 754
    recipe, 766
Roasted Cauliflower, 474
Roasted Eggplant Pita, 187
Sweet Potato & Tahini Dip with Za'atar, 121
Whipped Feta with Za'atar, 771
Za'atar Bread, 549
Za'atar Chicken with Garlicky Yogurt, 265
Za'atar Okra & Lemons, 526
Za'atar-Crusted Ribeye, 197
Za'atar-Rubbed Spatchcock Chicken with Honey-Glazed Carrots & Roasted Root Vegetables, 253
Zamorana cheese
    Albondigas Soup, 305
Zeppole with Lemon Curd, 613
zucchini
    Almodrote, 277
    Baked Orzo, 228
    Boulettes with Chicken & Vegetable Soup, 362–363
    Briam, 269
    Chamin, 321
    Concia, 418
    Couscous with Seven Vegetables, 505
    Eggplant & Zucchini Soup, 334
    Lamb Shish Kebabs, 204
    Mahshi Laban, 154
    Mediterranean Grilled Chicken Salad, 446
    Msoki de Pesaj, 350
    Ratatouille with Poached Eggs, 129
    Stuffed Zucchini, 221
    Vegetable Kebabs, 455
    Zucchini Fritters, 288

ABOUT CIDER MILL PRESS BOOK PUBLISHERS

Good ideas ripen with time. From seed to harvest, Cider Mill Press brings fine reading, information, and entertainment together between the covers of its creatively crafted books. Our Cider Mill bears fruit twice a year, publishing a new crop of titles each spring and fall.

"Where Good Books Are Ready for Press"

Visit us online at

cidermillpress.com

or write to us at

PO Box 454
12 Spring St.
Kennebunkport, Maine 04046